Jon Nordenson is a researcher at the University of Oslo where he also completed his PhD at the Center for Islamic and Middle East Studies. His work has been published in *The Middle East Journal*, *CyberOrient* and *Babylon: Nordic Journal for the Middle East and North Africa*, for which he won the Babylon Award for best contribution by a young researcher.

'*Online Activism in the Middle East* is an excellent book! The author has a compelling argument and uses data and a multi-track methodology to explain the role of online activism in a changing Middle East.'

Deborah Wheeler, Associate Professor, Political Science Department, United States Naval Academy

'This book addresses a timely and significant topic with depth, richness and nuance. It makes a much-needed contribution to the field of media studies through unpacking the complexity of the phenomenon of online activism, exploring its political and social manifestations, and comparing its implications across two Arab countries, one of which witnessed the Arab Spring uprisings and their aftermath, and one which did not.'

Sahar Khamis, Associate Professor in the Department of Communication, University of Maryland

ONLINE ACTIVISM IN THE MIDDLE EAST

Political Power and Authoritarian Governments from Egypt to Kuwait

Jon Nordenson

I.B.TAURIS
LONDON · NEW YORK

Published in 2017 by
I.B.Tauris & Co. Ltd
London • New York
www.ibtauris.com

Library of Modern Middle East Studies 191

ISBN: 978 1 78453 778 4
eISBN: 978 1 78672 126 6
ePDF: 978 1 78673 126 5

A full CIP record for this book is available from the British Library
A full CIP record is available from the Library of Congress

Library of Congress Catalog Card Number: available

Typeset in Garamond Three by OKS Prepress Services, Chennai, India

To Helle

CONTENTS

LIST OF ILLUSTRATIONS

Figures

Tables

A NOTE ON TRANSLITERATION AND TRANSLATION

This study investigates the work of a number of activist groups located in Egypt and Kuwait. As such, the issues of both transliteration and translation are central, as a number of names, slogans, quotes and the like originally given in Arabic must be incorporated into the text in a transparent, understandable and reader-friendly manner. The book is written in English and, as a consequence, all parts of text, such as hashtags or lengthy quotes, originally written in Arabic are translated into English. However, as any translation also entails interpretation, it is often highly relevant to provide the text in question in its original language. Yet, given that all widely used word processing programs recognise Arabic text, one might question the need and even relevance of transliteration, as it would remain incomprehensible to those who do not understand the language in question, in this case Arabic, regardless of the alphabet in which it is provided. For this reason, standalone quotes and names that do not form part of the body of text are not transliterated, but are given in the original Arabic and in English translation. All text that forms part of a URL or a hashtag is naturally given in Arabic, as this is a distinct piece of text containing links to particular information that can only be given in the original alphabet. Names of articles and blogposts given in notes are also given in Arabic.

However, it is also necessary to incorporate names, for instance of individuals, newspapers or activist groups, as well as some terms, within the body of the text. In these instances, the names and words are given in transliteration. When the names of the groups studied are provided for the first time, they are given in both Arabic script and in transliteration, as well as translated into English. The transliterations are provided in accordance with the transliteration guide provided by the *International Journal of Middle East Studies* (*IJMES*).[1] This entails the following principles:

- Names of living individuals may be spelled according to their preferred English spelling. In practice, this means that the names of activists and politicians are spelled as these individuals do themselves, on their accounts on social media, their websites, etc. Most of the Egyptian activists referred to provide their own spelling, which is used accordingly. However, when I have found no preferred English spelling, which was the case for most of the Kuwaiti activists and politicians referred to, I have followed the *IJMES* guide.
- Personal names, the names of organisations, political parties, newspapers, books, and the like are spelled in accordance with the *IJMES* chart but without diacritics. 'Ayn and Hamza are preserved, with the exception of initial Hamza.
- Technical terms are written with diacritics and are italicised.
- The definite article is always written as 'al-', regardless of the following consonant.
- Arabic words that are incorporated into the English language, such as jihad,[2] are spelled accordingly. This also includes place names.
- Names of historical persons are spelled according to the *IJMES* guide (*IJMES* no longer follows 'accepted English spelling').
- When colloquial words or phrases are transliterated, an explanatory note is provided. However, the letter *jīm* is given as g when referring to Egyptian proper names or words throughout the text.
- The names of authors quoted are given as written in the source cited.
- Finally, some of the groups studied use their English name more frequently than their Arabic name. In these instances, the English name is employed, as well as a note stating the choice. In practice, this meant all the Egyptian groups, with the exception of Nazra.

ACKNOWLEDGEMENTS

It is a great pleasure to have the opportunity to thank all those who helped and supported me throughout the course of my work on this project, without whom the end result surely would not have been the same.

The book is based on my PhD thesis, and I would like to start by thanking my supervisor Albrecht Hofheinz for all his comments and suggestions, for sharing his knowledge, for his continued support and trust over many years and, not least, for awakening my interest in the field to begin with. Likewise, I wish to thank my second supervisor Bjørn Olav Utvik for great feedback, great discussions and, not least, for giving me the opportunity to work with the Middle East at the University of Oslo in the first place. I am immensely grateful for the invaluable feedback and support of my supervisors.

I am also very grateful to all my informants in Egypt and Kuwait, who took the time to talk with me despite quite challenging and stressful circumstances and without whom this work would not have been possible. Special thanks are due to Saif in Cairo and Mohammed in Kuwait for all their support and help, and for making my fieldwork very enjoyable.

Special thanks go to Kai Kverme, Nele Lenze and Eva Håland, with whom I have had the pleasure of sharing an office. They have read through various drafts and papers and have always been constructive and supportive in their feedback. Most of all, they are not only wonderful and encouraging colleagues but also great friends.

Special thanks also go to Wael Phillip Gallab, Mona Abdel-Fadil and Berit Thorbjørnsrud for reading various drafts of chapters and for always providing challenging, constructive and encouraging feedback. I would also like to thank Kjetil Selvik at CMI in Bergen for letting me use material from his fieldwork in Kuwait, for helping me with my own fieldwork in Kuwait and, not least, for constructive feedback and encouragement.

I would like to thank everyone at the Centre for Islamic and Middle East Studies at the Department of Culture Studies and Oriental Languages (IKOS) at the University of Oslo – you are the best colleagues anyone could have. Special thanks go to Gunvor Mejdell and Stephan Guth for their assistance whenever I faced a language-related challenge. Thanks also to Jacob Høigilt at Prio for great advice, both on relevant literature and on the use of Nvivo. I would also like to thank Kristina Riegert and Rasha Abdulla for their invaluable feedback, and for helping to guide this project in a very fruitful direction.

I am very grateful to the University of Oslo and IKOS for funding my work, and I would like to thank everyone at the IKOS administration for helping me and encouraging me throughout my work. I am also grateful to Morten Erlandsen and the University Center for Information Technology for developing the application used in my analysis and for continued help throughout my work. I would also like to thank Susanna J. Sturgis and Andy Platts for doing an amazing job copyediting the text. I would like to thank I.B.Tauris and, in particular, Maria Marsh, Azmina Siddique and of course Sophie Rudland – I am extremely grateful for your belief in this project and all your help and encouragement throughout my work.

I would like to give very special thanks to all my friends for their endless support and, not least, for patiently listening to innumerable monologues about Egypt, Kuwait or whatever detail of my work I was concerned with at any given time. Special thanks to Eivind Croff for helping me with the layout of the text. Many, many thanks to my parents, Anne-Britt Eggen and Svein Nordenson, and my sister, Kristine Nordenson Kallset. They are always encouraging and enthusiastic about my work, and always help me whenever I may need it.

And, of course, a very, very special thanks to my amazing wife Helle, for always being supportive and encouraging, for invaluable feedback, for reading countless drafts, for great discussions, for cheering me up whenever I needed it and, above all, for brightening every day I spent writing this book – I would never have been able to complete this work without her. Flaws and inaccuracies that have slipped through are my responsibility alone.

CHAPTER 1

INTRODUCTION

25 January – Tahrir Square
Freedom – Facebook[1]

Does the internet facilitate social and political change, or even democratisation, in the Middle East? The subject of this inquiry is the use of online platforms among activists in the Middle East, and the importance of such platforms in effecting change. The topic has received wide attention over the past few years, not least following the so-called 'Arab Spring'. The story of a generation of young, tech-savvy activists utilising Facebook, Twitter and other platforms to bring Egypt's dictator of 30 years to his knees is a powerful narrative, and one which to varying degrees has been embraced by the news media[2] and others. As illustrated in the statement above, taken from a T-shirt sold in Cairo, the part played by social media has been celebrated in Egypt as well. Yet this view also has its critics. The Egyptian revolution[3] had manifold causes, including corruption, police brutality, unemployment, low salaries and poor prospects: realities faced by all Egyptians regardless of whether or not they had a Facebook account. Moreover, as Egyptian blogger Tarek Shalaby has pointed out, 'it all comes down to taking the streets',[4] and the over 800 people killed[5] during the revolution did not die online.

The use of various online platforms was highly visible during the 18 days of the Egyptian revolution, but visibility does not equal impact. Rather, it raises several crucial questions: Did people use social media, when available, during and before the revolution? If so, what did they do online? Was it online platforms that tilted the balance in favour of the revolution? And what about the other, less dramatic but still highly influential, campaigns that activists have led in the Middle East over the past few years in which the use of online platforms was also a very visible factor: How important were blogs to the successful campaign for electoral reform in Kuwait in 2006? Could police torture have been exposed as convincingly in Egypt without YouTube? Was the Iranian uprising in 2009 a 'Twitter-revolution', or rather a revolution for Twitter? In short, what can and what cannot be attributed to the internet, and what has the internet introduced into the relationship between people and democratisation in the Middle East?

Not only are these questions intriguing in their own right, the sheer volume of online production globally makes studies of these and similar questions a necessity: every month, more than 320 million people use Twitter in more than 35 languages.[6] As for Facebook, the site had over 1 billion users daily as of December 2015, and 1.59 billion users every month.[7] YouTube has about 1 billion users, who are watching hundreds of millions of hours of video every day.[8] An enormous production takes place continuously online, the likes of which has never been seen before. Importantly, it is not mainly produced in the US, as in the early days of commercially accessible internet: for Twitter, Facebook and YouTube, usage outside the US accounts for 79 per cent, 83 per cent, and 80 per cent, respectively.[9] Of course, most of the content is not related to the subject matter of this investigation, and internet access is far from universal. Yet, the potential importance of these platforms is evident, and internet access is not static. With a growth in internet penetration of more than 3,500 per cent in the Middle East region over the past 15 years,[10] online platforms demand – and have received – scholarly attention. Questions such as those posed above have been explored and debated by researchers and others for over two decades. They will also be examined in this investigation, through a detailed, empirical study of the actual, day-to-day usage of online platforms among activists in Egypt and Kuwait. By doing so, I seek to provide a new level of detail, and on a sound, empirical basis contribute to a more comprehensive and tangible understanding of online activism.

Yet, it is not easy to articulate this subject as a question, nor is such a question, once articulated, easy to answer. Moreover, it is not obvious how we should go about answering such a question; that is, how we can best study online activism and its repercussions. We cannot simply investigate the influence of 'the internet' per se. We have to pay attention to what we mean by 'the internet', that is, which platforms are used, and for what purposes. There is a clear difference between discussing corruption in an authoritarian state and organising a revolution, though both may be important in bringing about the eventual downfall of a dictator. There certainly is a big difference between how much certain social media were used during, for instance, a revolution, and how much this usage influenced that revolution. These distinctions may be overlooked in the media and public debate, but they must be addressed from a research perspective.

Quite obviously, there are numerous relevant questions we could investigate, in many different ways, using different forms of material. However, we should not try to do so in one study. For one thing, the sheer amount of data gathered when studying online activism is usually so extensive that a clear focus is needed if one is to have manageable material to work with. Moreover, different questions demand different strategies and different material. If we are to investigate online discussion habits among, say, young Emiratis, we need to dig into the dialogues on the various platforms used. However, if we want to study the workings of a particular group or party, we might look at their work both online and offline, the strategy behind their online presence, and so on.

Furthermore, if we cast the net too wide, the ever-important task of properly contextualising our study might become difficult. In addition to the online environment, factors such as geographical location, political system and social norms, the issues discussed and the groups involved form the context within which our online material is situated, and which may add meaning and importance to various aspects of the work studied. As Shani Orgad has argued, 'It has become clear that the separation between the online and offline cannot be sustained. Researchers have consistently argued for the need to frame the online both in its own right and in relation to other contexts and realities.'[11] Orgad here underscores another important point: since we cannot separate the online from the offline, we have no reason to believe the online is less complex than the offline. That is, we can hardly expect to describe and understand online activism and politics in a single study, just as we cannot expect to explain activism and politics in general in a single study. It is better to think of it as a puzzle, where different studies build on each other to construct our understanding of various aspects of internet usage and its implications in the Middle East, and elsewhere for that matter. In putting together this puzzle, we need to identify the pieces that are missing and, clearly, we do not start from scratch.

Overview of the Field

First of all, defining the field within which this study should be seen is in itself problematic. As pointed out by Lynch, '[t]he spread and potential impact of these new social media is relevant to broader debates in political science, sociology, and media theory',[12] and to debates in other fields as well. In addition, the questions that one decides to explore will influence which fields might be relevant, and these in turn may dictate particular methodological choices. For instance, quantitative analysis of big data is quite different from a close study of one or more bloggers, perhaps both online and offline. Yet, even though there are different methodological and theoretical approaches, they have something in common: in studies concerned with the internet, the material used is often obtained online, or at least concerned with activities taking place online. As such, there are many common challenges and problems to be dealt with, and much has been written on what is often referred to as internet studies, or internet research.[13] Such methodological considerations will be dealt with extensively in Chapter 3. The aim of this study is to gain further knowledge on the use and effect of online platforms as employed by activists in the Middle East. This inevitably involves engaging with challenging concepts, such as political and social change, democracy and democratisation, and the relevant literature is not restricted either to internet studies or to any particular geographical area. Accordingly, in discussing methodology, theoretical debates within the field and, later, my own findings and analysis, a variety of sources from different fields will be used. Still, the focus throughout is on the use and effect of online platforms.

In her 2006 study of internet usage in Kuwait, Wheeler writes that '[s]everal scholars of contemporary Middle Eastern studies have probed the relationship between the Internet and democratization in the Islamic world. Their findings are mixed.'[14] Most would find it hard to argue with this statement. There is little consensus within the field, but rather a lively debate as to what we actually can observe, and how to interpret it. Wheeler, for her part, argues for the need to see the internet and its use within its proper context, avoiding western-centrism in order to understand its meaning within the local setting, both online and offline. Looking at the habits of Kuwaiti users, she finds that the internet might offer new opportunities and more freedom to both young people and women, but that political views were not necessarily expressed widely online.[15] At the same time, she also showed that the internet provides an arena for bypassing traditional barriers separating men and women, and even to protest against formal barriers created for that very reason.[16]

Online habits are also the subject of Hofheinz's 2005 study of internet use in the wider Arab world. Based on an analysis of extensive online material, he identifies two characteristics of internet use in the region: 'First, religion has a greater weight than anywhere else in the world, and secondly, Arab users are particularly eager to engage in discussion – not least of politics, religion, and sex.'[17] This observation is further supported by a 2012 survey by the Pew Global Attitudes Project, which found that '[e]xpressing opinions about politics, community issues and religion is particularly common in the Arab world'.[18] The study shows that almost twice as many users are likely to discuss politics in the Arab countries included in the survey compared to the median of all countries surveyed.[19] The mere fact that people are discussing sensitive topics online does not, in itself, necessarily lead to political change, but it may create important expectations and, no less important, practices, as argued by Zayani.[20] This point is further developed by Dahlgren and Olsson, although their argument is based on a study of online habits among young internet users in Sweden.[21] In their view:

> it can be argued that as the young, active citizens use the internet, they inevitably become involved in discussions and debates; even if this takes place largely on sites where they encounter like-minded participants, this tends to cultivate a loyalty towards democratic values and procedures.[22]

Clearly, Sweden is a well-established democracy, and there are many factors that would predispose these users to favour 'democratic values and procedures'. Nevertheless, the effect of speaking one's opinion and participating in discussions within authoritarian states can, as we shall see, hardly be disregarded although it is hard to assess.

In line with the studies mentioned above, the 2009 Mapping the Arabic Blogosphere project also found politics and religion to be important subjects.[23] The comprehensive study identified a base of 35,000 blogs in the region, created a network map of 6,000 of them and hand-coded 4,000. On this firm empirical basis, the study observed that the Arabic blogosphere is predominantly organised around countries, with the Egyptian and Kuwaiti blogospheres being two of the largest.[24] Within these country-specific spheres, they identify several sub-groups, which in Egypt are partly related to ideological orientation. They further argue that these countries contain two of the most politically engaged blogospheres, with Kuwaiti bloggers engaged in electoral politics and their Egyptian counterparts playing 'key roles in movement politics'.[25] Of the two, the Egyptian blogosphere is by far the largest, comprising almost one-third of the blogs included in the study.[26] Thus, it may not be surprising that there exists a – comparatively – extensive literature on bloggers and online activism in Egypt. For instance, a 2008 article by Radsch traces the development of the Egyptian blogosphere, arguing that, by the time of her writing, it had been through three distinct phases: an early experimentation phase, an activist phase during the period 2005–6, followed by a phase of diversification and fragmentation from then on.[27] She ties the rise of the Egyptian blogosphere closely to the beginning of the secular pro-democracy movement in the mid-2000s, part of which is known as Kifaya, and the diversification phase with the demise of this movement, along with the entry of new groups online, including young members of the Muslim Brotherhood.[28]

This chronology, as well as the centrality of the bloggers to the early pro-democracy movement and the importance of the discussions conducted online by young Brothers, is largely reiterated in other articles.[29] Several important events have been attributed to bloggers, particularly connected to exposing malpractice or indifference on the part of the regime. Online debates have also been given great significance in and of themselves,[30] although, as Eaton points out, it is not always clear why this is done: 'many political scientists have heralded the importance of freedom of expression through the internet in the Middle East, though few tackle the specifics of how this may actually effect political change'.[31] This problem is also raised by Salvatore, who argues that the promises of the public sphere seem to be 'fulfilled in unexpected ways' by the internet's ability to 'transform passive connectivity into active mobilization' as seen in the so-called Arab Spring.[32]

Not surprisingly, the 2010/11 uprisings, and in particular the Egyptian revolution, and the role of online platforms in them have provoked much debate, as well as academic attention. Using an extensive data set covering several countries, Howard and Hussain argue that '[d]igital media had a causal role in the Arab Spring in that they provided the fundamental infrastructure for social movements and collective action'.[33] Rane and Salem, also looking at several countries, argue that social media played an important part in diffusing ideas across national boundaries and in facilitating communication among activists, but point out that success or failure largely depended on other factors.[34] Similarly, in their study of the Egyptian uprising, Eltantawy and Wiest make use of resource mobilisation theory, arguing that '[s]ocial media introduced a novel resource that provided swiftness in receiving and disseminating information; helped to build and strengthen ties among activists, and increased interaction among protesters and between protesters and the rest of the world'.[35] In another case study of the Egyptian revolution, Khamis and Vaughn argue that cyberactivism played a crucial role in providing forums for 'free speech and political networking opportunities'.[36] In their view, 'these aggregate efforts resulted in tilting the political and communication balance in Egypt in favor of freedom-fighters and political activists', although they do caution that 'new media were nothing more than powerful tools'.[37]

Also concerned with Egypt, Tufekci and Wilson have investigated the role of social media in the decision to partake in protests, and argue that there was a positive connection between respondents' social media use and whether or not they attended the first day of protests.[38] The study is based on what the authors refer to as the 'Tahrir Data Sets', which include survey data from protesters, interviews with selected 'power users' and a sample gathered from Twitter based on the most used hashtag during the uprising. As such, it demonstrates both the possibilities inherent in combining quantitative and qualitative material, and the value of larger samples of material, as is also the case in some of the studies mentioned above.[39] In a different study based on the same material, Wilson and Dunn come to a rather more ambivalent conclusion.[40] They found that digital media was not 'dominant in

Egyptian protest activity', although it was an 'integral and driving component in the media landscape'.[41] Moreover, they argue that Twitter was used successfully to gain international attention, primarily due to a limited number of 'power users' – influential activists online.[42] The centrality of power users is reiterated by Faris, who conducted extensive fieldwork in Egypt both before and during the 2011 revolution. He argues that social media is key to gaining wider attention for any specific issue through links between power users and journalists.[43]

Yet, while several studies agree that online platforms did play an important part during the uprisings, particularly due to their ability to connect people, to enable mobilisation and to document the situation and connect with the outside world, the conclusions drawn so far are relatively modest and somewhat tentative. For instance, in his study of the Egyptian revolution, Eaton also argues that the:

> significance of internet-based information and communication technologies (ICT) [. . .] was twofold: first, in their utility as a tool for activists to mobilize, organize and inspire Egyptians [. . .] and, second, in their use as a medium to document events in Egypt beyond the reach of the authorities.[44]

However, he further argues that 'while it may appear logical, even obvious, to suggest that WAAKS [We are all Khalid Said][45] increased the likelihood of its members participating in the demonstrations, there remains a lack of concrete evidence'.[46]

Even so, it is well-established that there is a wide array of online political discussion taking place in the Arab world, more than in other regions. The Egyptian blogosphere is both dominant and, to a substantial degree, political; from the beginning it has been closely connected to activism. Yet, the precise effects of these online deliberations have been more difficult to establish. Furthermore, the studies discussed demonstrate clear differences in their methodological choices: whereas some studies are based on analysis of online material and/or other sources, others provide a broader overview using detached examples from various sources. Moreover, the case or field covered in each study varies greatly, as some seek to cover the Egyptian revolution as such, whereas others focus on particular sites or samples. Naturally, this has clear implications for the level of detail that can be provided.

In terms of theoretical approaches to the material, different sources are drawn upon, including social movements theory,[47] diffusion theory[48] and resource mobilisation theory.[49] By far the dominant framework, however, is that of the public sphere.

To some extent, this debate has produced two lines of inquiry. Some studies look at particular sites, places, campaigns, and so on, and discuss their findings within the framework of the public sphere.[50] Other studies are more purely theoretically constructed and are often concerned with the structural features of the internet itself, particularly with the advent of Web 2.0, and with whether or not the conditions provided encourage and/or have established one or more public spheres in a more or less Habermasian sense.[51] Yet, as Richard Butsch points out, '[t]he debates have produced fewer answers and no consensus on what is a public sphere, or whether or in what form it exists. It has generated relative less empirical investigation into actually existing public spheres.'[52] Being a debate on internet use as well as on internet structure, it is concerned not only with how we are to understand internet use, but also with its potential. As such, Papacharissi claims that '[r]esearch on the political potential of the internet is frequently rapt in the dualities of determinism, utopian and dystopian'.[53] A similar view is presented by Hofheinz, who argues that:

> [i]n other words, we haven't come past the stage of hypothesis building. In the absence of more systematic research, cyber-utopians and cyber-skeptics will continue to throw anecdotes at one another to demonstrate how effective or not social media is in bringing about revolutions.[54]

For his part, Lynch argues that the recent events in the region and social media's role in them should 'push debates about the effects of new media away from stylized arguments between optimists and sceptics and towards more careful empirical testing of specific mechanisms and claims'.[55] This, in his view, would entail using new tools of analysis, and empirically investigating more specific questions 'lurking behind sweeping arguments'.[56] This view is echoed by Gerbaudo, who argues that we must abandon pessimistic or optimistic outlooks in favour of a more balanced view, 'considering how these forms of communication are adopted within specific social movements, rather than assessing their properties in the abstract'.[57]

In a similar vein, Ben Moussa argues that '[e]xisting literature, however, is marked by numerous lacunas, chief among them an insufficient number of studies in the field, their overtly descriptive nature, and the excessive focus on religion-oriented political groups and discourses'.[58] Here, he points to a crucial factor: namely, that the lack of empirical studies is connected to the vagueness both of the findings and of the theoretical debate. As argued by Couldry et al.: 'The decades-long debate on media and the public sphere has primarily been normative, rather than empirical, in character.'[59] Theory is meant to help us understand what we observe. If it is too abstract or too normative, it does not necessarily describe what we observe. Through theory, we may identify and explain the crucial features of what we observe and the mechanisms through which what we observe works. Without this understanding we may overlook crucial parts and end up with vague and descriptive findings. Clearly, many studies conducted to date have provided extremely valuable insights but, in order to move on, we need to develop our theoretical understanding on the basis of empirical studies. Moreover, I argue that we need to do so on the basis of *new* cases and *new* material: much of the focus so far has been either on well-known examples of successful activism in Egypt in the 2000s[60] or on the Egyptian uprising in 2011.[61] Clearly, such events demand and deserve academic attention. Still, we also need to study the use of online platforms beyond the established successful cases or extreme situations. If such instances are the only examples we can find of successful online activism, one might ask if we are, in fact, studying the benefits brought forth by online platforms, or rather cases of activism in which online platforms were used. Thus, I argue, we need to examine practice on a day-to-day basis.

Clearly, one could argue that some of the studies referred to above are concerned with everyday usage in the sense that they investigate, for instance, the Egyptian blogosphere in general. However, this inevitably involves enormous amounts of material, and thus often ends up focusing on well-known examples. Similarly, while the studies mapping habits across the region are extremely valuable, the sheer amount of material involved prohibits highly detailed analysis. The devil may very well be in the details, and I argue that a detailed investigation into the day-to-day use of online platforms by groups and activists working in the region, and the contributions this usage provides, would produce new insights. By restricting the scope, and thus the amount of material, examples can be replaced by a comprehensive description and analysis of internet use and its benefits. This, in turn, can be used to identify *how* online platforms contribute, and thus help to generate a more comprehensive theoretical understanding of their importance. This study aims to provide such an investigation, which has clear implications for the research design, regarding both what to study and how to study it. I believe a qualitative, properly contextualised case study of a limited number of sites/groups offers the best approach to make possible the required level of detail. Importantly, as Stake points out, '[f]or a qualitative research community, case study concentrates on experiential knowledge of the case and close attention to the influence of its social, political and other contexts',[62] and in what follows great attention will be paid to the relevant context(s).

Inherent in this focus on contextualisation is an expectation that the specific possibilities, needs and limitations that a particular context provides influence the online behaviour of the actors involved. That is not to say that online behaviour depends on offline context alone: the online is also a context, and the technical possibilities which different platforms provide are common to all. Yet, as Zayani argues, there exists a 'pervasive tendency to homogenize the Arab digital experience', which should be avoided.[63] This, in turn, raises the issue of what is context-specific, and what is more general, when it comes to internet use among activists in the Middle East. This study includes two cases, one from Kuwait and one from Egypt, and a comparison of the two will be included, in order to shed light on this issue.

Case Selection

I have established the phenomenon I wish to investigate: the actual, day-to-day use of online platforms by groups and activists working for a cause in the Middle East, and the benefits achieved through this usage. As case studies are 'opportunities to study the phenomena',[64] the task is to identify a suitable instance of the phenomenon. While it is important to avoid 'selection bias', case selection for very small samples 'must employ purposive (nonrandom) selection procedures'.[65] I need to know that the cases are instances of the phenomenon, and I need to know that I can expect to find the material I need, and that it will be manageable.

I also argue that it would strengthen the study to follow cases that are contemporary. Though the permalink makes it possible to access old data, which I have also done in this study and which always will be necessary in order to provide the proper context, one can of course also delete data online.[66] Tweets, blog posts, anything on an organisation's website – it can all be deleted should the author wish to do so. Crucially, such a deletion might in itself be of interest to the study. One should bear in mind, however, that publishing and deleting something online might take only a few seconds, and thus we can never claim to have collected *all* the material for one case. Rather, the idea is that, in the tradeoff between the desirable and the possible, we should try to get as good a grip as possible on the material involved.

The study consists of two cases. One covers the work of various groups and organisations currently working against sexual harassment and sexual violence in Egypt, predominantly in Cairo; the other covers Kuwaiti oppositional youth groups who worked for a constitutional, democratic monarchy in the emirate. While the Egyptian groups are still active, the Kuwaiti groups are, by and large, not. However, I have set clear time frames for both cases and, as such, their inactivity following this time frame should not be a problem, although it certainly is an important element in my discussions.

There are several reasons why I chose to study cases in these two countries in particular. Importantly, both countries are prominent in terms of online activism, with Egypt perhaps being *the* country in the Middle East in this regard. Since the early 2000s, Egyptian activists online have documented police brutality, instigated strikes and movements, such as the famous April 6 Movement, and created a space where bloggers have proved to be 'politically influential'.[67] Although internet access is far from universal, it has increased substantially over the past few years. No less crucially, Egypt is generally seen as the leading Arab country, in addition to being the most populous. As for Kuwait, youth organisations in the country demonstrated their abilities in 2006, when they successfully campaigned for electoral reform. Though it may seem trivial, the change in electoral districts took place much to the dismay of the ruling Al-Sabah family, and both the campaign and its results were unprecedented. Since then, online activism has become an important part of Kuwaiti politics, to the extent that Kuwaiti TV now has a show dedicated to the country's Twitter-sphere. While Kuwait is hardly the centre of the Arab world, its relatively open political system is followed closely, and with substantial scepticism, by others, especially fellow Gulf Cooperation Council (GCC) countries. As argued above, I need to know that the cases are instances of the phenomenon I seek to study and that I will find the material I need, and in Egypt and Kuwait online activism is well established.

Similarly, I also need to know that I will be able to conduct my study and gather the relevant material, both online and offline. At the time, this was possible in Egypt and Kuwait. It might have proven difficult, however, in other countries that might otherwise have constituted interesting cases, such as Bahrain. The effects of the popular revolts of 2010/11 must clearly be taken into account when selecting cases and, while I argue that both countries were affected by the events usually termed 'the Arab Spring', I believe it is a strength that I have included one country that saw its leader step down due to popular pressure, and one which did not. The ever-changing situation in Egypt following 2011, while perhaps complicating the issue of contextualisation, is also quite intriguing from the perspective of online activism. Moreover, while I do not claim that the cases are representative of all of the Middle East and North Africa, it is important that they reflect some of the social, economic and political differences between the countries of the region, as these are likely to be relevant to the way in which online platforms are utilised by activists. For instance, the differences between the countries in terms of gross domestic product (GDP) per capita and internet access are factors that must be accounted for in my analysis, but also differences which may contribute to understanding patterns of internet usage among activists in different parts of the region. The similarities and differences between the cases are discussed further in Chapter 3, and in detail throughout Chapter 6 as I present the comparative analysis.

There are clear political differences between the two countries, but also important similarities. While both Kuwait and Egypt during the period studied had elected, representative assemblies, neither country is usually termed a democracy, and activists in both countries face severe repression. As is almost inevitable when studying the Middle East, this is a study of online activism in authoritarian contexts. For one thing, this illustrates how the question of effecting social and political change in a very concrete way is also a question of democratisation. Moreover, it further strengthens the need for a detailed study of the mechanisms at play, as argued by Eaton:

> While the link between online communities and participation has been identified, work in this area has thus far focused on case studies conducted in the west [. . .] The need for a detailed study of events in an authoritarian context is acute and would be extremely valuable to scholarship in this area.[68]

This view is also expressed by Boas and Kalathil, who argue that the answer lies partly in proper contextualisation:

> Proponents see the Internet as leading to the downfall of authoritarian regimes, but the mechanisms through which this might occur are rarely specified. Instead, popular assumptions often rest on anecdotal evidence, drawing primarily on isolated examples of Internet-facilitated political protest. Subsequent assertions about the technology's political effects are usually made without consideration of the full national context in which the Internet operates in any given country.[69]

Moreover, the authoritarian context also has implications for our theoretical understanding of online platform usage and democratisation, as argued by Zayani: 'attempts to conceptualize the political implications of media in an undemocratic Arab context are fraught with theoretical difficulties, not least because they are embedded in normative claims about democratic politics and mass media workings'.[70] This will be discussed in detail in Chapters 2 and 8. Suffice it to say for now, the particular context of each case is of great importance in terms of the challenges and possibilities faced by activists, and in terms of what constitutes change and/or democratisation. Clearly, it is a factor that must be included in my analysis. While Kuwait and Egypt share many similarities, they constitute two different contexts, and will be treated as such.

Egypt

The issue of sexual harassment and sexual violence is, sadly, all too well known to most, if not all, Egyptians. In fact, a recent study by the United Nations Entity for Gender Equality and the Empowerment of Women (UN Women) and others report that 99.3 per cent of female respondents 'replied that they have been subjected to one form or another of harassment'.[71] Moreover, a clear majority replied that all women are subjected to harassment, regardless of class, attire and so on.[72] These findings are further confirmed by various groups and activists working against harassment, who have described the problem as 'endemic'.[73] In other words, sexual harassment and sexual violence are problems faced by all Egyptian women.

Yet, for many years, the issue was seldom raised in public.[74] Although bloggers and journalists drew attention to the issue in 2006, most women did not talk about their experiences because it might be considered shameful and their families might react negatively.[75] This is closely connected to the widespread view that women themselves are to blame and that, if they are harassed, they must have done something wrong. This, in turn, connects to a widespread acceptance of harassers in Egypt: they're not doing anything wrong, they simply react to women who, for some reason or another, are 'asking for it', a view echoed in all parts of the society. During a debate in Egypt's since-dissolved Shura Council (upper house of Parliament) on the horrific sexual attacks on female protesters, many MPs blamed the women, with one parliamentarian even claiming that women themselves bear '100 per cent responsibility' for the attacks.[76] In this light, it is perhaps not surprising that the Egyptian police seldom follow up on cases of harassment, or even interfere should they witness one.

Two issues face those working against sexual harassment and sexual violence in Egypt, and they are closely connected. On the one hand, is the harassment that Egyptian women face every day, in the streets, in the workplace, at schools and hospitals, on public transport, and so on. On the other, are the organised attacks on female protesters involving rape and an extreme level of violence, particularly following the first anniversary of the 2011 revolution. They are connected in the sense that these attacks took place at crowded demonstrations, and could not have happened if not for the widespread acceptance mentioned above.

Sexual harassment and violence has triggered a forceful response from several groups and organisations, some of which have worked on this and other issues for years, and others that were established following the 2011 revolution. Both well-established organisations and ad hoc groups, some of which are becoming more professional and permanent, have managed to raise awareness of the issue among the Egyptian public. Following these groups' numerous appearances on various TV-shows, including Bassem Youssef's highly popular *al-Barnamig* ('The Show'/ 'The Program'), as well as articles in newspapers and magazines, sexual harassment is no longer hushed up or ignored in public debate. Moreover, through testimonies on their websites, platforms for registering attacks, and discussions on Twitter, these groups have managed to break the silence and have provided a framework where women can talk about their experiences, and where first-hand accounts make it all the more difficult to deny the problem. All groups have made extensive use of social media, and some have their own websites. Importantly, they also work offline, through demonstrations, patrolling, awareness campaigns, or rescue teams in Tahrir Square. The time frame set for this case extends from 1 June 2012 to 1 August 2013.

Kuwait

The Kuwaiti political system was, and to a certain extent still is, viewed as one of the most open among the Arab states. After gaining independence from Britain in 1961, the 'fairly democratic constitution' instituted a parliament, elected by the people.[77] However, the government is appointed by the emir, and the post of prime minister, as well as other key portfolios, is reserved for members of the ruling Al-Sabah family. While competition in the elections certainly is real, they have also been tainted by accusations of vote buying and gerrymandering,[78] as well as biased coverage in the media.[79] The powers of the parliament are limited, and if the MPs go out of bounds, the emir may dissolve it, as happened between 1976 and 1981, and again between 1986 and 1992.[80] The powers that parliament does have are 'largely negative'[81] and, in particular, MPs' right to direct interpellations against cabinet members has resulted in the resignation of many governments and in calls for early elections. Because these can be followed by votes of no confidence, Al-Sabah ministers usually prefer resignation, often of the entire government, to avoid a humiliating defeat in parliament. As Michael Herb points out, 'the structure of the Kuwaiti political system tends to encourage political dead-lock'.[82]

Deadlock has also been the name of the game in Kuwait, especially since 2006. This was the year in which the highly unpopular Sheikh Nasir Muhammad al-Ahmad al-Jabir al-Mubarak Al-Sabah was appointed prime minister and, as a result of constant battles with opposition MPs, he headed no fewer than eight governments and saw three elections before he was forced to resign in November 2011. It was also the year of the aforementioned successful youth-led campaign for electoral reform, known as 'We Want Five', or the 'Orange Movement'.[83] Perhaps empowered by their success, many of the same activists turned their attention to the unpopular PM in the autumn of 2009 and launched the 'Nastahiqq al-Afdal' ('We Deserve Better') campaign. The initiative grew and, following a heavy-handed police intervention at a gathering of opposition MPs in December 2010, a number of new youth-led groups came into being, all calling for democratisation. All groups made extensive use of online platforms, but also worked offline.

From the beginning, their demands centred on a new PM, the fight against corruption and a 'new approach' – a term that soon came to mean a full parliamentary system. The various groups worked together and managed to include Islamists, tribal activists and liberals in a joint campaign. They also gained the support of most opposition MPs, and on several occasions demands made by the activists were later endorsed by the politicians. After a dramatic demonstration in late 2011, ending with protesters storming the parliament building, Sheikh Nasir was forced to resign.[84] This did not, however, mean the end of the youth-led campaign, and in the course of 2012 the demand for a full parliamentary system articulated by the youth groups was adopted by prominent politicians. This clearly posed a threat to the ruling family, and the police took a more confrontational approach to the almost weekly demonstrations, one of which was the biggest in Kuwait's history.[85] Seeking to limit the influence of the opposition, the regime dissolved the parliament elected in February 2012, in which the opposition held a majority. Disagreements over whether or not to boycott the resulting, controversial December 2012 elections took their toll on cooperation between the groups, and the boycott itself left the opposition almost unrepresented in the new assembly. Although the groups held large demonstrations both before and after the elections, the heavy-handed police response led these to die out in January 2013. Thus, by the time the opposition declared the formation of a unified 'opposition alliance' in March 2013, their momentum seemed to be gone.

That is not to say that the opposition in Kuwait was gone, or that the desire for democratic reforms had died, but that at that time the opposition seemed to be at an impasse. This also marks a natural end for the time span of my case; I will be concerned with the work of the youth groups from the launch of the campaign against the prime minister on 27 October 2009, until the launch of the alliance on 3 March 2013. As is evident, this time frame is substantially longer than that of the Egyptian case. I have chosen to do this for two main reasons. For one thing, the Kuwaiti groups published much less online than their Egyptian counterparts and it was therefore possible to consider a longer period while still maintaining a manageable amount of material. In the trade-off between the desirable and the possible, pragmatic choices must be made to ensure both a manageable and, not least, a sufficient amount of material. This, in turn, brings us to the second, and most important, point: the two time frames provide natural beginnings and ends for both campaigns. Most of the Egyptian groups were formed following 1 June 2012, and their campaign reached its peak in the spring of 2013. Following 1 August 2013, there have hardly been any large demonstrations in Egypt attended by the groups studied, and thus a substantial part of their work can be said to have ended. Similarly, the events of the Kuwaiti campaign began in 2009, and it had been crushed by the regime by March 2013. Thus, I believe the different time frames are necessary to study the two cases from a logical beginning to a logical end, while maintaining a manageable amount of material.

Research Question and Guiding Hypothesis

I have chosen these cases for my study for a number of reasons. First, the issues involved are of concern to many people. If we are to establish the benefits of using online platforms, it is hardly useful to study a campaign for an obscure or extremely unpopular issue, because such campaigns are likely to fail regardless of their strategies. Second, all the groups and organisations involved use online platforms extensively. Third, both cases presented an opportunity to follow them as they unfolded, thus reducing the risk of missing important material. Although the material gathered is substantial, which admittedly has caused some problems that will be discussed later, it has proven to be manageable. Fourth, and most important, they are suitable cases to address the lacuna(s) in the literature discussed above.

The main research question applied to the cases is as follows:

- How are various online platforms utilised by the groups and organisations working in Egypt and Kuwait, and are online platforms beneficial for the groups in terms of realising their goals and, if so, how?

The following sub-questions will further guide my investigations:

- Which platforms are used, for what purposes, and what is the intended audience?
- What has been made possible that would otherwise have been impossible, and what has been made significantly easier through the use of the internet?
- Can any factors for success be identified?

My guiding hypothesis is as follows: the internet's biggest and most important contribution lies in the space it creates and the publicness it provides. It is relatively open and beyond the reach of the traditional gatekeepers, making it ideal for excluded and marginalised groups. Through such counterpublicness, new voices make themselves heard in public and may set the agenda for public debate. It is suitable for everything from discussions to citizen journalism to mobilisation, and more. The biggest challenge in terms of effecting social and political change is to transform online engagement into offline engagement, which in turn is dependent both on activists' ability to implement a meaningful strategy online and on factors that are not controllable online. Thus, online platforms alone will never be sufficient to ensure successful activism, but they might be an important, necessary or even decisive factor.

The issue of sexual harassment and violence could, and indeed should, be studied from various angles. The response from groups involved, from the state as well as from individuals, and not least the consequences of the problem for Egyptian women and for Egyptian society as a whole are of obvious importance and need to be investigated. The same goes for the Kuwaiti case: the prospect of democratic transition in a GCC country could be, should be and indeed *is* studied from a variety of angles. The present study, however, is primarily concerned with the use of online platforms and, by extension, its relation to online and offline activism in Egypt and

Kuwait. The material used consists of all the material published online by the groups studied, in addition to semi-structured interviews with representatives from various groups, and a range of secondary sources, such as newspaper articles and TV shows. How the material has been gathered, used and analysed – in short, the methodological choices I have made to answer the questions posed above – will be discussed in Chapter 3. In order to draw conclusions regarding whether or not online platforms helped the groups to realise their goals, I will also need to discuss and assess the effectiveness of using such platforms. Thus, I will discuss the issue of *measuring* or *assessing* the impact of online activism and of the campaigns, and a framework with which to do so is suggested and applied. Hopefully, both this framework and the general design of this study will be of use to others conducting concrete, empirically based investigations into online activism in the Middle East.

Finally, there is the question of how we are to understand the findings presented here, and situate the study within current theoretical debates. Case studies can be of value in refining and testing theory, as well as in generating theory.[86] Yet, as described above, the current debates within the field have neither reached any consensus nor articulated any theory with an expected outcome that can easily be tested. The framework of 'the public sphere', or more recently 'publicness', has been widely used, but predicts no certain outcomes, as will be discussed in detail below. This is not to say that this approach is not useful, but rather to point out that, at the current stage, its implications for online activism in the Middle East remain vague. As argued above, this study aims to address this theoretical vagueness. Based on the material presented, I suggest a departure from the deliberative focus of Habermas and many of his critics, towards the less normative, agonistic view of democracy and of the public as championed by Chantal Mouffe. Such a view allows us to identify the mechanisms through which the publicness provided by online platforms effects change and democratisation.

Thus, I will answer the research questions posed above through an empirical investigation into actual usage of online platforms among activists in Egypt and Kuwait. Having established how, why and for which purposes online platforms are employed, I seek to identify the benefits that this usage offers in terms of realising the aims of the activists. By comparing the two cases, I seek to identify the general features of usage, as opposed to the more context-specific features.

From there, I seek to further develop the answer concerning the benefits of using online platforms by assessing the impact of the campaigns studied. Finally, using the theoretical framework described in the next chapter, I seek to identify how and through which mechanisms online platforms may help to effect social and political change within the contexts studied, hopefully contributing to a more comprehensive and less vague understanding of online activism.

Outline of the Book

Chapter 2 presents a discussion of the theoretical approach employed in this study. I begin with a brief discussion of social movement theory and other possible approaches, arguing that publicness holds the greatest promise for this investigation. From there, I engage with the concepts of publicness and the public sphere in light of Habermas and his critics, and how these have been applied in studies of online activism in the Middle East. I then turn to Chantal Mouffe, and argue that her concept of agonistic pluralism is better suited to explain and understand the use of online platforms. Central to this discussion are concepts such as power, hegemony, democracy and democratisation. I end by providing my understanding of counterpublicness as *the* central concept employed in this study, and as a fruitful avenue away from the vagueness discussed above. This understanding is further developed in Chapter 8 as I engage with the findings from my empirical investigation.

Chapter 3 presents the design of this study. Following a short presentation of the selected cases, the process of identifying, gathering and sampling the material used is detailed. From there, I turn to contextualising the material and the cases, before the analysis of the material itself, as well as the tools employed in this process, is presented. These tools include coding of the entire Twitter accounts of all groups studied within the time frames, in order to answer the question of *how* they made use of the platform. Finally, I present my framework for assessing the impact of campaigns such as those studied here, before I sum up what I have studied, how I studied it and how I intend to interpret my findings.

Chapters 4 and 5 constitute the main part of the study and present both cases in detail: the contexts, the material gathered and the analysis of this material. In line with the discussion presented above, the presentation given in these chapters is both comprehensive and extensive. Both chapters begin with a discussion of the relevant contexts. While the focus is naturally on the past few years, I also go further back in time in order to establish the origins of laws, conflicts, practices and the like, which I argue are still relevant. For instance, the question of power sharing between the royal family and the people of Kuwait has a long history, which in my view had clear implications for how the groups studied here worked, and which adds meaning and importance to the work they conducted. Similarly, the current laws regulating non-governmental organisations in Egypt dates back to al-Nasir's regime, and the desire of this and subsequent Egyptian regimes to control civil society is highly relevant to the present case. I then turn to the particular issues at hand for the groups studied and their campaigns. From there, I move on to present the collected material through a thematically organised and extensively exemplified analysis, discussing the similarities and differences between the groups in each case, the influence of the relevant contexts, and any offline results traceable to the groups studied.

Chapter 6 provides a comparison of the two cases, with the goal of separating contextually dictated features from more general features of internet usage among activists in the region. I begin by comparing the two contexts, the issues involved in each country and how the groups organised their work. From there, I move on to the question of internet usage, and compare both the platforms used in each case and how they were used. A comparison of the results from the coding of the Twitter material is also provided.

The suggested framework to assess the impact of the campaigns studied is put into practice in Chapter 7. In Chapter 8, I pick up the discussion introduced in Chapter 2, and demonstrate how the concept of counterpublicness helps us to interpret and identify the crucial features of the empirical material, and the mechanisms through which the groups studied had an impact.

Finally, in Chapter 9, the conclusions drawn from the study are presented. I begin by – quite literally – answering the research questions asked in the present chapter, before I conclude by summing up my findings and my interpretations, hopefully contributing to our knowledge and understanding of activism and internet usage in Egypt, Kuwait and beyond.

CHAPTER 2

HOW SHOULD WE UNDERSTAND ONLINE ACTIVISM?

In the following, I continue the discussion begun in Chapter 1 on how we are to understand online activism or, more specifically, the findings presented in this study of online activism. I argue that the concept of the public sphere provides the most promising approach for interpreting our material and identifying the central features of the use of online platforms by activists that may help to create social and political change. The term *public sphere* is perhaps most closely associated with Habermas, and is concerned with how citizens take part in public deliberation to form public opinions, and to affect and legitimise political decisions. More recently, the term *publicness* has been suggested instead, as will be discussed in detail below.

However, this is certainly not the only possible approach for this study. Given that this is a study of the work of several rather informally organised groups working on social and political issues, social movement theory (SMT) may also have a lot to offer. The study of social movements is concerned with how 'ideas, individuals, events, and organizations are linked to each other in broader processes of collective action'.[1] Della Porta and Diani introduce four crucial questions for social movement analysis: Is social change creating conditions for the emergence of new movements? How do we define issues as worthy objects and actors as worthy subjects of collective action? How is collective action possible? What determines the forms and intensity of collective action?[2] All these questions are potentially relevant for a study such as this one, and a discussion of the two approaches is in order.

Movements vs. Mechanisms

In an article on the role of social media in the Arab Spring, Ben Moussa argues that a theoretical shift is needed, and that we should move away from the widely used framework of the public sphere and publicness towards SMT.[3] In doing so, he eloquently raises a number of issues that he perceives, correctly in my view, as problematic in talking of the public sphere when studying activism and the use of online platforms in the Middle East. As a very concrete articulation of some of the important questions in the current theoretical debate within the field, his critique constitutes a fruitful starting point for my discussion. For one thing, he argues that 'the public sphere' has been tainted by orientalist notions of 'the Arab street' in which the Arab Spring is 'less about groups and people militating for freedom and justice than about hordes and unruly mobs'.[4] He further holds that SMT is better suited to incorporating the importance of context and identity politics into the analysis, and that the disappointing results of the Arab Spring show that effective use of social media, on its own, is far from sufficient to effect lasting change. More fundamentally, he argues that the notion of the public sphere 'does not allow us [. . .] to explain the link between mediated political discourse, on the one hand, and direct forms of contention and political transformation, on the other'.[5] While these are all crucial issues that need to be addressed in order to enhance our understanding, I will argue that we can do so more persuasively by revising our conception of the public sphere rather than by switching our focus to social movements.

To begin with the problem of 'the Arab street': prejudice and orientalism in a negative sense are obvious problems for any scientific (and non-scientific) endeavour, and have no place in an analysis. While it may be tempting to point out that such prejudice is no longer relevant, given the many studies of public spheres in the Middle East that are not tainted by it,[6] continued references in public debate to culturalist explanations in line with Huntington[7] show that it is still relevant. Yet, the prejudice of some observers is hardly an argument against the importance of the public sphere; it is more a methodological issue than a theoretical one. It does, however, point to one key problem with wider relevance: the treatment of the public sphere as *one* sphere. For instance, in a similar though not necessarily orientalist manner, Eickelman and Anderson as well as Siapera talk of 'the Muslim blogosphere as if it were a single entity,[8] even though talk of a distinct Muslim blogosphere in itself implies the existence of others. Seemingly, we face a fundamental problem: if there is *one* public, it can hardly be inclusive; if there are several publics, how can decisions be made and unified public opinions be formed? This is an important question, which will be discussed further below, as a problem regarding our understanding of the public sphere and of public debates and decision making. As such, it is a powerful argument for revising our understanding of the public sphere, or public spheres, rather than abandoning the concept in favour of SMT.

Similarly, there is no reason why the public sphere as a framework should hinder proper contextualisation. If our understanding of the public is such that it prohibits us from studying online activism within its context, then it will hardly enhance our knowledge. As argued in the previous chapter, contextualisation is of great importance in terms of the challenges and possibilities faced by the groups studied, and in understanding their work and its effects. However, in spite of such contextual differences, the mechanisms at play may be similar. This, in turn, suggests an important point regarding our theoretical approach: while it is imperative that it allows for proper contextualisation of the material and our findings, it should at the same time help us recognise mechanisms and features of a more general nature. Proper contextualisation is an important methodological task that must inform our analysis, but it does not exclude a focus on publicness. Neither does the importance of identity. In fact, as we shall see below, various publics may be of great importance in articulating the problems faced by marginalised groups, and the public aspect is crucial in enabling these publics to come together, based on shared experiences. Thus, while the problems discussed so far have clear implications for our understanding of the public, they do not dictate a shift toward SMT.

Ben Moussa's main critique pertains to the inadequacy of the concept of the public sphere in explaining the link between discourse and contention and political transformation. As we saw in the previous chapter, it has been challenging for the literature to explain *why* and *how* the increase in online discussion has been so important. This problem, I will argue, is also one faced by proponents of SMT when they are asked how social movements effect change. As Della Porta and Diani point out, social movements are seldom the only forces concerned with an issue, and thus it is 'difficult [...] to identify which of the many actors involved in a given policy area are responsible for one reaction or another'.[9] Furthermore, they argue that '[w]hile the capacity of social movements for the realization of their general aims has been considered low, they are seen as more effective in the importation of new issues into public debate, or thematization'.[10] This may be done through mobilisation, the media, 'referendum campaigns', participation on ad hoc commissions, and so on.[11] In doing so, social movements may alter norms and practices, or the understanding of issues that are of public interest. As such, they may enhance democratic practices in established, representative democracies, and they may contribute to democratisation in authoritarian contexts, although mobilisation may also cause increased repression.[12] Thus, the mechanisms through which social movements are seen to effect change are the mechanisms of the public sphere, or of publicness, and so the problems pointed out by Ben Moussa are also problems of SMT.

That is not to say that SMT only provides insights inasmuch as publicness provides insights – there is a difference in focus between the two approaches. SMT helps us to understand how social movements work, why people take part, and so on. It provides a focus on organisation that is not necessarily present if we are concerned solely with publicness. However, publicness, in turn, gives attention to features that may be overlooked when one focuses on movements. For instance, Gerbaudo argues that 'only a section of the "mobilization potential" of a social movement is transformed into "actual mobilization"', and this depends on a number of factors.[13] Moreover, the availability of information and mediated connections online may give rise to 'spectatorship' and even hinder mobilisation – an obvious problem for a social movement aimed at mobilisation.[14] Yet, if the ability to raise issues in public is a central feature of social movements, then the availability of information and opinions online may be of great importance in realising their goals. Although several observers have rightly questioned the value ascribed to online discussions in and of themselves, we should hardly assume that they are insignificant. Online debate may be important at both an individual and a group level in terms of empowerment and awareness, and may contribute to changes in the public debate and in the norms of society.

Yet, if we focus on the organisations and their activities, these features may be overlooked. Similarly, Warner argues that when 'alternative publics are cast as social movements – they acquire agency in relation to the state [. . .] For many counter-publics, to do so is to cede the original hope of transforming, not just policy, but the space of public life itself.'[15]

While social movements clearly are actors in public debate, the value of public debate and public participation goes beyond the abilities of social movements to mobilise around their particular issues.

Therefore, I agree with the description of the problem provided by Ben Moussa: our conception of the public sphere and how it works is vague. However, I do not agree with his conclusion, that this necessitates a shift towards SMT. For one thing, this shift is also a shift in focus from the mechanisms of the public sphere towards the workings of movements and organisations inherent in SMT. While my cases consist of groups and movements, my main aim is to identify the benefits brought forth by the use of online platforms, and I have hypothesised that the main contribution of such platforms is the publicness they provide. The focus of my inquiry is on mechanisms rather than movements and, as such, it favours publicness rather than SMT. Moreover, I believe the problems identified by Ben Moussa also are valid for SMT as well as for other similar approaches, as participation in the public sphere is given as the central mechanism through which change is effected. For instance, we saw in the previous chapter that Eltantawy and Wiest, using resource mobilisation theory, found that social media facilitated communication between activists and between protesters and the rest of the world.[16] Rane and Salem, using diffusion theory, found that social media were important in spreading ideas between activists, and in disseminating information.[17] Hamdy and Gomaa, in examining the framing of Egypt's 2011 revolution, found that social media play a part in shaping public opinion and have wide appeal in times of political crisis.[18] The point, of course, is that the ability to affect the public and communicate in public is central to all these approaches, and along with it the problems identified by Ben Moussa. This is in no way meant as an argument against such approaches, and differences in focus will shed light on various aspects, all of which are important to our understanding. Rather, it is an argument for the centrality of the public aspect of the use of online platforms among activists, and the need to further develop this concept in order to provide a more concrete and tangible understanding of the importance of such platforms. Thus, we need to revise our understanding of the public sphere, publicness and its relation to online platforms.

Habermas and the Public Sphere

Jürgen Habermas's *Structural Transformation of the Public Sphere* is, of course, the natural starting point for any discussion of the public sphere and deliberative democracy, and it has informed many studies on the use of online platforms in the Middle East and elsewhere. By the term 'the public sphere', according to Habermas, we 'mean first of all the realm of our social life in which something approaching public opinion can be formed'.[19] It is a space in which citizens can raise problems, discuss them and form an opinion and, ideally, these opinions and decisions will be acted upon. Such participatory and deliberative practices, argued Habermas, are important both for a well-functioning democracy and for the legitimacy of political decisions. In the bourgeois public sphere, Habermas identified a normative ideal that was later lost in the representative democracies of the modern welfare state. He identified certain features of this public sphere which he saw as crucial for it to function in an ideal, democratic manner, on which he based his model. According to this model, the public sphere should be inclusive, and decision making should be based on rational-critical discourse and strive for consensus. The force of the argument should guide the protagonists' striving for consensus and, in order for this to be possible, one should disregard the status of the various participants.[20] As a normative model which identifies crucial democratic features, it can be used to analyse and discuss the actual democratic practices we can observe.

Although his concept has been widely criticised, as will be discussed below, there is wide agreement that there are public spaces in which debate takes place that may have an impact on political decisions made, and that this is important for democratic practice. Moreover, Habermas's concept has been widely used to explore and explain the possibilities inherent in the internet. As stated in the previous chapter, this debate has in part been related to the architecture and structure of the internet itself, not least following the advent of what is commonly referred to as 'Web 2.0'. At the core of Web 2.0, a term popularised by Tim O'Reilly, we find the writeable web, which facilitates user-generated content.[21]

The web is a platform, inviting people to take part, and so service providers should act as 'intelligent brokers'.[22] Users can take part directly in developing open-source projects; provide content, as is the case with, for instance, YouTube and WordPress; or do a bit of both. Another important feature is the 'harnessing of collective intelligence', which acts as a kind of filter, improving services and content. People can not only read a blog post, they can link to it and recommend it, collectively sorting out the 'best' material. Thus, it is not just that you can write online (on a given platform), or that you can link to and share particular content; it is the combination of all these features which enables rapid production, sharing and filtering of content and continuous development of platforms and services. Moreover, to an ever-increasing degree, you can do so seamlessly on various devices and platforms. In short, this is the technology that facilitates platforms like Twitter, Facebook, YouTube and blogs and, crucially, that facilitates the way we use these platforms today. As Manovich points out, 'if in the 1990s the web was mostly a publishing medium, in the 2000s it has increasingly become a communication medium'.[23]

In theory, the architecture of Web 2.0 facilitates the features of Habermas's public sphere, perhaps better than previous technological advancements and communication platforms. Whereas Horkheimer and Adorno complained about the lack of any 'comment feature' on the radio, as well as the excluding nature of its economic structure,[24] the internet now offers a potentially global arena for reciprocal communication at a cost that is relatively low compared to the alternatives. Moreover, the dangers of passive consumers pointed out by Habermas, as well as by Horkheimer and Adorno,[25] can now be countered with the massive amounts of user-generated content being published online. Accordingly, Habermas's concept has been applied to study not only the structural features of the internet, but also actual usage of various platforms. Many studies have argued that online platforms have facilitated new (emerging) public spheres,[26] or even a re-emergence of the public sphere in a Habermasian sense,[27] and, not least, made it possible for new voices and opinions to make themselves heard.[28] However, his concept has also generated much criticism, both in and of itself and in its application to online platforms. Though the technology of Web 2.0 may facilitate many of the features of the public sphere, there are also clear problems pertaining to technology, practice and access. In the following, I discuss this criticism, beginning with the more technical issues, then moving on to problems inherent in the concept itself.

The issue of access, in a technical sense, is perhaps the most obvious problem. In spite of the dramatic increase in internet access over the past 15 years, it is still far from universal, and any public sphere online is obviously not all-inclusive. Moreover, a socio-economic factor is in play and, in a sense, the internet is both revolutionarily cheap and inaccessibly expensive at the same time. Compared to alternative means of disseminating and accessing information, it is extremely cheap; in fact, there is no real alternative that can deliver the same possibilities at the same speed. The internet offers the potential to communicate and express one's views on a scale hitherto inaccessible for all but those with access to vast resources, including newspapers and TV stations. On the other hand, it is still miles away for those struggling to make ends meet, and certainly not a necessity when decisions on priorities are made. There is also a gender bias involved, with more men than women being online globally.[29] In addition, there is the issue of illiteracy: in the Middle East and North Africa, about 23 per cent of the adult population is illiterate.[30] Finally, the question of technological competence clearly comes into play. Thus, there are important restrictions on the inclusiveness deemed so important by Habermas due to issues of access related to technology, poverty and competence.

Access is not the only technological issue problematic in terms of accommodating Habermas's ideal. Another important point is what Yochai Benkler refers to as the 'Babel objection': 'when everyone can speak, no one can be heard, and we devolve either to a cacophony or to the reemergence of money as the distinguishing factor between statements that are heard and those that wallow in obscurity.'[31] Yet, O'Reilly argues that this is not necessarily what happens:

> If it were merely an amplifier, blogging would be uninteresting. But like Wikipedia, blogging harnesses collective intelligence as a kind of filter. What James Suriowecki calls '[t]he wisdom of the crowds' comes into play, [. . .] the collective attention of the blogosphere selects for value.[32]

Filtering based on content takes place, and we have all experienced how, for instance, a well-written blog piece by an unknown author might spread among a group of friends or even 'go viral'.

Yet, while this may seem close to Habermas's force of the argument ideal, the process of filtering can be manipulated in several ways, related to power, resources and status. For one thing, the concept of buying likes, clicks and followers has become big business over the past few years. According to a piece by the Associated Press, users can buy 1,000 Twitter followers for as little as \$10, generated through so-called 'click factories', which are often located in low-income countries. These services appear to be bought by all kinds of users, including the US State Department, which spent US\$630,000 to 'boost the numbers'.[33] Social media favour popular content and popular users through mechanisms such as Twitter's 'Top Tweets', meaning such manipulation may help to influence which content is spread and discussed most widely. There is also a more open and legitimate way to buy influence and attention, namely advertising. As private corporations, platforms such as Twitter, Facebook and YouTube need to make money, and advertising is an obvious choice. On Facebook, ads are placed both next to the user's timeline and within it, and are sometimes specifically designed to appeal to the user based on his or her online habits.[34] Finally, there is the obvious point that people who are famous in one way or another, such as football players or popular musicians, tend to gain a substantial following online as well.[35] As such, they can set the agenda or dominate debates based on their status.

Another manner in which publishing and dissemination of content is manipulated, and one sadly relevant for the Middle Eastern context, is through regime intervention. Many governments conduct surveillance and censorship online, and some even arrest citizens for making critical statements on the internet.[36] *The Atlantic* has documented how the Tunisian state sought to retrieve Facebook passwords during the uprising in that country, potentially compromising the identity of thousands of activists and protesters that the regime hardly looked kindly upon[37] and making the perceived free arena of the internet a vehicle for oppression. Though such incidents might, to a certain degree, be avoided using tools such as Tor, this demands a level of technological knowledge that in itself excludes most people. Moreover, the platforms that host these publics, such as Twitter, Facebook and Blogger, are privately owned companies with commercial interests. Though they claim to adhere to the principle of free speech, they are, of course, free to set their own policies. In the above-mentioned episode from the Tunisian uprising, Facebook actively met the threat from the Tunisian regime with countermeasures. While one might argue that this meant actively supporting the revolt, the attempt to obtain users' personal information also clearly constituted a breach in security for the platform. In a similar manner, when Facebook closed down a group calling for a third Palestinian intifada, the reason given was that it violated the platform's guidelines by calling for violence, although this was doubtlessly seen as a political move by some.[38] The crucial point, of course, is that what Habermas sees as given, universal features of public debate and well-functioning democracy are, at least to some extent, business decisions for these companies.

Thus, there are several issues pertaining to technology and practice that make the realisation of Habermas's ideal online difficult. Moreover, to the extent that the technology enables such a realisation, this does not mean that it will happen. As Benkler argues: 'technological determinism in the strict sense – if you have technology "t," you should expect social structure or relation "s" to emerge – is false'.[39] We can only counter this argument with sound empirical research into the actual usage of various platforms, which is what this study intends to do. However, issues of technology and practice are not the only problems, and Habermas's normative model has also been the subject of more fundamental criticism.

One central element in this critique is the inclusiveness that Habermas ascribes to the bourgeois model, in terms of both participants and subjects of discussion. Although 'inclusiveness' and 'issues of public interest' are implied as something given and universal, the bourgeois public to which he refers was located in a particular context, and this had clear repercussions in terms of participants and the issues discussed. Nancy Fraser, among his most influential critics, argues that the bourgeois public was never particularly inclusive, and that it was never *the* public.[40] She introduces the concept of *subaltern counterpublics* where excluded groups interpret and formulate their identities and interests, and develop language and terms to discuss these interests. These counterpublics are also arenas to contest what is discussed in public, or what is of public interest, and how it is discussed:[41]

> In this public sphere [late twentieth-century US feminist subaltern counterpublic], feminist women have invented new terms for describing social reality, including 'sexism,' 'the double shift,' 'sexual harassment,' and 'marital, date, and acquaintance rape.' Armed with such language, we have recast our needs and identities, thereby reducing, although not eliminating, the extent of our disadvantage in official public spheres.[42]

As Fraser demonstrates, who is included has changed over time, and which issues are considered private and which are considered to be of public interest have also changed over time. As such, it is hardly universal, and it is hardly given a priori. As Warner argues:

> Dominant publics are by definition those that can take their discourse pragmatics and their lifeworlds for granted, misrecognizing the indefinite scope of their expansive address as universality or normalcy. Counterpublics are spaces of circulation in which it is hoped that the poesis of scene making will be transformative, not replicative merely.[43]

Dominant forces in society are able to articulate the boundaries of inclusiveness in the public, in terms of both issues and participants. As argued by Laclau and Mouffe: 'The distinctions public/private, civil society/political society are only the result of a certain type of hegemonic articulation, and their limits vary in accordance with the existing relations of forces at a given moment.'[44]

These observations have important repercussions for Habermas's concept. For one thing, participation and subjects of discussion are not universally given, but contested, and they change over time. While there may be a dominant public, there are several other publics as well, not only from a theoretical perspective, but in a very literal sense, as argued by Dahlgren: 'The term "public sphere" is most often used in the singular form, but sociological realism points to the plural.'[45] The dominant public is a hegemonic public reflecting power relations in society, in contrast to Habermas's argument that power and status should be overlooked. This hegemony may be challenged by subaltern groups who organise in counterpublics. As they challenge the very boundaries of the dominant public, consensus based on rational-critical discourse as prescribed by Habermas would hardly be in their interest, as such consensus would have to happen within the very framework they seek to change. Consequently, as argued by Eley, 'the public sphere makes more sense as the structured setting where cultural and ideological contest or negotiation among a variety of publics takes place'.[46] Again, this is not only a theoretical point, but an empirical observation: 'In the advocacy/activist sector of the online public sphere [...] the thrust of their political address [...] is not to attain consensus, but rather to affect policy.'[47]

In his response to this criticism, Habermas acknowledges that throughout history more than one public sphere has existed, in parallel to a 'hegemonic' one.[48] He warns, however, of too much fragmentation, with reference to the internet:

> The Internet has certainly reactivated the grassroots of an egalitarian public of writers and readers. However, computer-mediated communication in the web can claim unequivocal democratic merits only for a special context: It can undermine the censorship of authoritarian regimes that try to control and repress public opinion. In the context of liberal regimes, the rise of millions of fragmented chat rooms across the world tend instead to lead to the fragmentation of large but politically focused mass audiences into a huge number of isolated issue publics. Within established national public spheres, the online debates of web users only promote political communication when news groups crystallize around the focal points of the quality press, for example, national newspapers and political magazines.[49]

Moreover, he recognises the existence of power relations and the possibility of exclusion or lack of participation based on one's background, although he argues that such problems may be countered.[50] Perhaps most importantly, he argues for the continued use of a normative model of deliberative democracy:

> In the final analysis, we are nevertheless confronted with the prima facie evidence that the kind of political communication we know from our so-called media society goes against the grain of the normative requirements of deliberative politics. However,

> the suggested empirical use of the deliberative model has a critical thrust: It enables us to read the contradicting data as indicators of contingent constraints that deserve serious inquiry.[51]

This is a central point for our discussion. Habermas's concept is a normative ideal against which reality might be measured,[52] and is not intended as a description of what we observe. Thus, even though internet access is an issue, online publics may, of course, be of value. Even though debates are not guided by rational-critical discourse, they may still be important. In order to show the value of online debates and online activism, we need not look for public spheres in line with Habermas's ideal. Rather, we should use his conception as a tool to analyse and understand what we observe. As shown above, criticism of this model has produced extremely valuable insights. However, we still face the difficulties of providing a more comprehensive and less vague theoretical understanding of online activism discussed in Chapter 1. This, I will argue, is because the problems raised in the criticism above are of a fundamental nature in that they demonstrate that his concept is problematic also as a model with which to understand what we observe: it misdirects us in the search for the mechanisms by which online activism affects social and political change.

For instance, Siapera argues that 'the political function of the public sphere as the space/means by which public opinion is formed, subsequently legitimizing political decisions, cannot be guaranteed at least insofar as dialogue and deliberation do not take place'.[53] We do not observe what was expected to be an important explanatory feature. As we have seen above, several observers argue that the rational-critical striving for consensus referred to by Habermas does not take place and, instead, various groups seek to gain acceptance for their views in a constant struggle. How can we expect to understand the mechanisms in play in such a situation if we are concerned with the degree to which discussions match our normative ideal? Similarly, if we are concerned with whether or not publics are inclusive, do we not risk focusing on acceptance for the current hegemonic understanding of the term rather than discovering how subaltern groups challenge this notion and make themselves heard? If we investigate whether or not the force of the argument is decisive, do we not miss how other factors, including wealth and status, play a role?

And perhaps most importantly, if the public reflects existing power relations, and if its boundaries and agenda are determined by them, should we not investigate how these work and how they may be challenged rather than the degree to which they may be overlooked? Obviously, Habermas's concept has been of immense value in understanding democracy, participation, how decisions are made and legitimised, and so on. But in order to move on, I argue that we must depart from his deliberative model in favour of a less normative framework.

Deliberative Democracy vs. Agonistic Pluralism

In her critique of Habermas's notion of the public sphere and of deliberative democracy, Chantal Mouffe argues that some of the normative ideals raised by Habermas are, in fact, counterproductive or even harmful to democracy. As we have seen, she also argues against operating with ideal or universal categories of inclusiveness and issues of interest:

> What is at a given moment accepted as the 'natural order', jointly with the common sense that accompanies it, is the result of sedimented hegemonic practices; it is never the manifestation of a deeper objectivity exterior to the practices that bring it into being.[54]

Consequently, '[t]hings could always have been otherwise and every order is predicated on the exclusion of other possibilities'.[55] The framework for public deliberation is not universal, it is the articulation of power relations that could and should be challenged. It follows that she also argues against Habermas's normative focus on consensus. In this critique, she is not alone. For instance, Dryzek and Niemeyer argue that the consensus ideal can be oppressive, as 'deliberation so oriented all too easily equates the common good with the interests of the more powerful, thus sidelining legitimate concerns of the marginalized'.[56] Yet, for Mouffe, this problem is far more fundamental.

Mouffe recognises that Habermas and proponents of deliberative democracy advocate an ideal which is not necessarily realised today and, as such, cannot be dismissed simply because we do not observe it.

For consensus based on rational-critical debate to make sense, other criteria must also be met to create an ideal speech situation. As she points out, 'Habermas and his followers do not deny that there will be obstacles to the realization of the ideal discourse', yet 'these obstacles are conceived as empirical ones'.[57] In her view, however, 'far from being merely empirical, or epistemological, the obstacles to the realization of the ideal speech situation are ontological'.[58] This is because the deliberative model seeks to eliminate power and contestation, whereas in fact these are central elements of democracy itself. Thus, when one attempts to eradicate these features through procedures, through normative ideals in which one thing is more right than other things, this will be damaging for democracy: 'This theoretical trend that conflates politics with morality, understood in rationalistic and universalistic terms, has very negative consequences for democratic politics because it erases the dimension of antagonism I take to be ineradicable in politics.'[59]

As a consequence, she argues, consensus is killing politics. Speaking of European democracies in the 2000s, she argues that politics is increasingly moralised or juridified – that is, made into questions of morals and law. Yet, although consensus is imposed in politics, this does not mean that antagonisms disappear. Instead, they are moved from political identities to other identifications of a 'ethnic, religious, or nationalist' nature.[60] Old differences of a political 'us' and 'them' are recast as a moral 'us the good' and 'them the evil ones'.[61] Thus, one cannot present political challenges *to* the hegemonic consensus, as everything must take place *within* it. In her view, the 'main consequence of visualizing our societies in such a "post-political" manner is to impede the articulation of any possible alternative to the current hegemonic order'.[62]

Thus, we must accept that 'every consensus exists as a temporary result of a provisional hegemony, as a stabilization of power and that always entails some form of exclusion', and when we do so we can 'begin to envisage the nature of a democratic public sphere in a different way'.[63] Power is integral to politics and to democracy, and so is conflict. Rational-critical consensus is not possible because it must take place within the hegemonic framework, yet a crucial democratic feature is for excluded groups to challenge this very framework. Conflicting views must be allowed to be articulated as political demands, lest they take on another form, to ensure what Mouffe refers to as 'agonism' between opposing views rather than the more destructive 'antagonism'. 'Agonism' makes possible a confrontation between adversaries, which should be played out under conditions 'regulated by a set of democratic procedures accepted by the adversaries'.[64] While the rather vague reference to these procedures and how they are agreed upon is problematic, her main point on the importance of conflict, power and challenging the existing hegemony remains valid. In my view, this is also extremely relevant to the study of online activism in the Middle East and, for that matter, elsewhere.

For one thing, this approach allows us to operate with several publics, with various counterpublics of excluded groups oriented towards one hegemonic public, similar to what is often referred to as 'the public at large'. This also helps to solve the more technical issue of access and usage, as each counterpublic does not need to be inclusive to any given degree in order to operate or even have an impact: the important part is that those concerned with an issue come together and are able to articulate and raise their demands. A convincing example in this regard is that given by Fraser, mentioned above, namely the American feminist movement. This does not mean that access is not important, and it may clearly have repercussions in terms of the ability to effect change, how representative a claim is, and so on. Moreover, it shows how the online public can be of importance even though there is little debate or rational-critical deliberation taking place: the boundaries of public debate are hegemonic, and the various counterpublics seek to challenge this very framework. They would have no interest in seeking consensus on the basis of what they contest, but would seek instead to gain acceptance for their view, in line with the observations made by Dahlgren. Here we touch upon Mouffe's perhaps greatest contribution: her framework allows us not only to incorporate relations of power into our analysis, but to understand their centrality. Habermas's normative ideal inhibits our understanding because relations of power are the very thing most groups are fighting, the thing that is holding them back and making them subaltern, and that is providing the hegemonic framework for debate that the groups seek to challenge. From this follows the centrality of 'counter' or 'subaltern' in studying such publics: they are in opposition to a hegemonic one; they are excluded. This is also informative in terms of who will be active in forming counterpublics:

if one is content with the current hegemony, one has no reason to invest time and effort in challenging it. Likewise, those who challenge it will not necessarily do so with a normative 'better' aim. A challenge may also come from groups who do not seek democracy, or who advocate the exclusion of others. Determining the order in the public at large is a constant battle, and it is defined not by given values or criteria but rather by those who participate. For instance, we have seen online that terrorist organisations such as the so-called Islamic State are extremely active, and quite obviously challenge the order of many different publics. Yet, in authoritarian contexts, we have also seen that pro-democracy activists are highly active, and challenge the repressive order of the regime.

This, in turn, brings us to a crucial point: whereas both Habermas and Mouffe speak of the democracies of Europe, this study is concerned with two authoritarian countries. As Kapoor points out, we should, for several reasons, be cautious in applying these theories in very different contexts.[65] Nevertheless, I argue that Mouffe's framework has great promise for our investigation. For one thing, her observation that a lack of political articulation of conflicts will be replaced by other conflicts is identifiable in the authoritarian context of the Middle East: there are numerous examples in which political differences are played out as sectarian issues, for instance in Bahrain. This is no accident, but a widely used strategy by authoritarian regimes: the Bahraini authorities were quick to point to Iran and the Shi'a/Sunni[66] divide once protests began. Similarly, the Egyptian regime prior to 2011 routinely sought to hinder the articulation of domestic problems as political issues by instead pointing to Israel, the West or some other party or reason that did not challenge their hegemonic discourse. This is in line with the defence Mouffe shows that we should expect from hegemonic forces: political problems are cast as something else, such as a moral issue. This also holds true of authoritarian regimes, which share the goal of hindering the articulation of any possible alternative to the current hegemonic order. Thus, what Mouffe views as democracy-enhancing practices in Europe may be democratising factors in authoritarian contexts. However, authoritarian regimes often also have the possibility of fighting off challenges through outright repression and violence. This step, however, comes at a price, in terms of the regime's standing internationally, its legitimacy with its own population, and so on. As such, it is perhaps more of a last resort, and it will not necessarily be possible to use it, as we have arguably seen in Tunisia. Nevertheless, it is an additional factor which may interfere with the mechanisms described by Mouffe, and it will be included in our analysis. Once again, this points to the centrality of proper contextualisation, and of recognising that, as the context changes, the possibilities for online activism change with it. That being said, I believe the move from Habermas's ideal towards Mouffe's agonistic pluralism enables us to provide a more concrete and comprehensive understanding of online activism.

Counterpublicness, Authoritarianism and Democratisation

The importance of online platforms is more easily identifiable when we apply a less normative framework. Although access is an issue, online platforms constitute relatively cheap vehicles for public communication. The crucial aspect for those concerned with any given issue is not necessarily to reach everyone or to be as inclusive as possible, but to reach and be accessible to others concerned with the same issue. They do not need to discuss the issue according to any criteria, but will rather argue for their cause and seek to convince the public at large. They enter the dominant public from a subaltern position, in an anti-hegemonic struggle. In this sense, the existence of several publics online, or fragmentation as Habermas calls it, is not a threat to democracy, but rather a precondition of it. The architecture of the internet may be an asset for pro-democracy forces, but not as a realisation of Habermas's normative ideal. Similarly, Dahlgren and Olsson are right when they argue that online users gain important experience in terms of democratic practice and democratisation,[67] but wrong in assuming that this must be in line with the Habermasian ideal. Rather, this is correct in an agonistic way, in that they gain experience in articulating their demands in public and fighting for them in public as a means of affecting policy and their own lives.

That a crucial feature of counterpublics is to challenge the existing hegemony has been observed by many, also with reference to the Middle East.[68] However, armed with Mouffe's framework, we can gain a more concrete understanding of how this works and how it is democratising. For one thing, as pointed out by Ives, a central feature of subaltern, or non-dominant, social groups as described by Gramsci is that 'they lack a coherent philosophy or world-view from which to understand and interpret the world. One could say, they lack their own language', and instead work with a 'common sense' originating from traditional intellectuals from other parts of society.[69] For instance, with reference to the 2005 Arab Human Development Report, Abu-Lughod shows that the use of a particular hegemonic language has consequences for how a problem is framed and how it is proposed to be solved.[70] This is in line with the argument presented by Fraser: excluded groups need to articulate their own experience of the world and their problems, and make these issues of public concern. Online platforms may be crucial in this transition: they allow people to come together over an issue and to discuss it and articulate it, and not least to make the crucial leap from private problem to public concern. This act alone challenges the hegemony: it alters the content of public debate, it alters the participants' perception of themselves and the problems they face, and the debate itself may have a normative effect on society. It is democratising in that it increases participation in terms of both actors and issues. We should then expect the hegemonic power to fight back by seeking to portray the issue at hand as something other than a political question, and the ability of activists to withstand such attacks will clearly be important to their success.

This work may be democratising in other ways as well, given that the issue is raised in public. Those involved may gain wide support for their views, and thus force a regime, even an authoritarian one, to act – be it due to fear of unpopularity, having been convinced, or other factors. If the issue had been raised in private with the regime, the regime could later have claimed to have acted on its own initiative. Yet, when the challenge has been presented in public, it is evident that the regime was forced to act by the demands put forth, and power is very visibly taken from the regime. As noted by Siapera, this would be democratising also in line with Habermas's ideal.[71] However, even though power may be taken from the regime, it does not necessarily mean the beginning of a process ending with something which may meaningfully be termed democracy. Yet, this does not mean that democratisation does not take place. As Bollen argues, it would serve us well to recognise the continuous nature of political democracy, rather than seeing it as a dichotomous phenomenon.[72] Thus, democratisation here is understood in line with the debate so far; as a change in participation, in practices, and perhaps even in social relations and power relations, but not necessarily as a process that culminates in a democratic state similar to those of western Europe.

Exactly how activists online and offline engage in such struggles is, of course, a matter for empirical investigation, which this study seeks to provide. For instance, whether the dominant public is addressed directly online, or, as suggested by Faris, through traditional media, will be one of many questions raised in the analysis. Moreover, discussion and argumentation is not the only way in which hegemony may be challenged. Whereas Habermas's ideal has a certain passivity to it, in that decisions made 'should be implemented', Mouffe's framework makes clear that it is an active struggle. We should not forget that we study activism and, as argued by Salvatore, one crucial feature of online publics may be to facilitate mobilisation.[73] This, in turn, has repercussions for the terms we use in our analysis. The passivity referred to above is quite evident in the term 'the public sphere', as a place where deliberation occurs, and stands in contrast to the notion of subaltern groups actively challenging the hegemonic order. Haugbølle and Salvatore have suggested replacing the 'public sphere' with 'publicness' as a translation of Habermas's *Öffentlichkeit*. This is meant not just as a translation, but as a conceptual shift towards 'concrete ways of going and being public'.[74] This term is further developed by Jurkiewicz in her study of blogging in Beirut. Combining Haugbølle and Salvatore's work with the critiques of Fraser and others, she also uses the term 'counter-publicness', which is to be understood as 'ways of going and being public with an emphasis on "counter" [. . .] from a position that is understood as marginal and oppositional'.[75] As is evident from the discussion above, I agree with this conceptual change.

In summary, I argue that *counterpublicness* is a term well-suited for the framework described here, and for developing our understanding of online activism. We should depart from Habermas's deliberative public in favour of Mouffe's less normative agonistic pluralism. From this perspective, online platforms are crucial in that they facilitate publicness on the part of excluded groups, who may come together and articulate their issues of concern. By raising their interests in the dominant public, they challenge the existing hegemonic order. This is democratising in itself, and the public aspect may be even more crucial should they succeed in forcing the current hegemonic forces to act. It is an active endeavour, and activities in the public are not limited to discussion and argumentation. We should expect hegemonic forces to fight back by seeking to de-politicise their struggle, and their ability to meet this challenge will be crucial for their success. Finally, the ability of the subaltern groups to raise challenges is dependent on the context, which must be an integral part of our analysis.

CHAPTER 3

HOW SHOULD WE STUDY ONLINE ACTIVISM?

I have argued that a detailed, empirical study of activists' use of online platforms on a day-to-day basis is the best option to answer the questions raised in this investigation. With reference to language use online, Ramsay has argued that 'establishing valid theories and efficient methods for studying the Arabic blogosphere with respect to linguistic code is a substantial task yet to be carried out'.[1] Similarly, while many brilliant and solid studies of online activism have been conducted, no clear methodological precedent has been set, and there are several challenges that remain problematic. This is not to say that all studies should use the same methodology – clearly, methodological choices are dependent on the questions asked, the material used, and so on. Rather, my point is that a study such as this one requires close consideration of how we can best study the use of online platforms among activists. In what follows, I will discuss the methodological choices made in this investigation, and detail the design chosen. It is the ambition of this study to contribute to the methodological development within the field, and it is hoped that the design chosen for this analysis will prove valuable to others concerned with similar questions.

What I Studied

The two cases studied here were chosen as examples of the phenomenon I seek to investigate, namely online activism. The Egyptian case consists of six groups and organisations working against sexual harassment and sexual violence, and the Kuwaiti case consists of eight oppositional groups working for democratic reform. While the groups and their issues of concern are far from irrelevant, as discussed in Chapter 1, my main concern is their use of online platforms. The following groups were included in the Egyptian case:

حركة بصمة (Harakat Basma) (Imprint movement)
شفت تحرش (Shuft Taharrush) (I Saw Harassment)
خريطة التحرش الجنسي (Kharitat al-Taharrush al-Ginsi) (HarassMap)
نظرة للدراسات النسوية (Nazra lil-Dirasat al-Niswiyya) (Nazra for Feminist Studies)
قوة ضد التحرش/الإعتداء الجنسي الجماعي (Quwwa didd al-Taharrush / al-Iʿtida' al-Ginsi al-Gamaʿi) (Op Anti-Sexual Harassment / Assault [*sic*] [OpAntiSH])
حماية التحرير (Himayat al-Tahrir) (Tahrir Bodyguard).[2]

These groups were not selected randomly. After an initial phase of reading articles on the issue, following links to blogs, Facebook groups and Twitter streams, as well as Google searches, these movements soon crystallised as central groups. They also represented the breadth of those working on the issue, from well-established centres to more ad hoc groups created as a reaction to recent events. The centrality of the groups studied was confirmed during my interviews. It should be noted that there is substantial interplay between the groups, both in terms of cooperation between organisations and in terms of individuals working with more than one initiative.

The following groups were included in the Kuwaiti case:

السور الخامس (al-Sur al-Khamis) (translation: The Fifth Fence, a reference to Kuwait City's old city wall)
كافي (Kafi) (Enough)
العدالة الدستورية (al-ʿAdala al-Dusturiyya) (Constitutional Justice)
الحركة الديمقراطية المدنية (حدم) (al-Haraka al-Dimuqratiyya al-Madaniyya, Hadam) (The Civil Democratic Movement)
حركة شباب الحرية (Harakat Shabab al-Hurriyya) (Youth of Freedom Movement)[3]
كرامة وطن (Karamat Watan) (Dignity of a Nation)

شباب التغيير و التطوير (Shabab al-Taghyir wa-l-Tatwir) (Youth of Change and Development)
مقاطعون (Muqatiʿun) ([We Are] Boycotting/'Boycotters').[4]

In identifying and selecting the groups included, my previous research experience was of great value. I had studied the 'Orange Movement' earlier,[5] and thus knew of many of the activists beforehand. Following links, hashtags and the like from their sites, as well as looking into their followers and who they themselves follow on Twitter, led me to many of the other sites used. I have also used Google searches. It should be noted that these groups do not cover *every* oppositional initiative that has taken place over the past few years in Kuwait. However, the selection made here covers the spectrum of the opposition, and includes the most central actors. This has been confirmed to me during fieldwork in Kuwait. I have also made use of material from several individual activists of different ideological persuasions, all of whom were engaged in the issues at hand, and often in one or more groups as well. Some of these activists have widely read blogs which, together with some blogs by unknown authors, were used to further contextualise the study and to trace the beginnings of the campaign studied and how it spread, as well as to shed light on the impact of the various groups. The groups included from both Egypt and Kuwait will be presented in more detail in Chapters 4 and 5.

The material from both cases consists of the online content published by the groups within the time frames,[6] interviews with key persons in these groups and numerous secondary sources, including extensive media coverage of the issues, the groups and their offline activities. The online material includes social media platforms, such as Facebook, Twitter and YouTube, as well as websites and blogs operated by the groups. It also includes debates on Twitter following particular hashtags introduced by the groups or by others, as well as some relevant material from other blogs, Facebook pages, and so on. All the online material has been collected from open sites; that is, it is public and accessible to all. Though substantial, the material proved to be manageable.

Sampling and Material

Online material provides intriguing opportunities for researchers, but it also presents certain challenges. Even though I closely followed the events studied online as they unfolded, I cannot be certain that I have caught everything that took place. Posts, tweets and similar material may be removed quickly, and for practical reasons, I did not follow all sites studied around the clock. I discovered some additional sites and debates beyond the main sites that I was following, but only some time after they were published, at which point the risk that they had been altered was greater. Moreover, when following a debate on Twitter, participants may misspell the hashtag, and thus not be part of the stream in question. Technical hiccups of various sorts can play a part, as well as mistakes made by me. In addition, the various platforms may have their own limitations in terms of harvesting material published through them. During my investigations, this became a problem with Twitter. The site apparently limits the number of tweets it is possible to download from each particular user to 3,200; this caused some problems for my study. While most samples are complete, some are not, which raises a number of concerns.

First of all, I have collected the material in three different ways, to be used for different methods of analysis. From the beginning, I have followed the groups online and continuously downloaded and archived their online production. All these samples are complete, with the exception of two Twitter samples, those of Harakat Shabab al-Hurriyya and Hadam in Kuwait.[7] This problematic aspect should, of course, be taken into consideration when reading this study. Luckily, the manner in which the groups whose samples are incomplete have operated online is quite consistent, and I have no reason to believe that they behaved differently within the time spans not covered. Moreover, the overwhelming majority of the online activities of *all* groups within the time frames *is* included. Thus, I argue that the material I have collected reflects the online work of the groups included in the cases. I have not interfered in the online deliberations in any way. Through my interviews I made it known to the activists that I was following their sites online, but I have no reason to believe that this altered their behaviour in any way.

I have also gathered parts of the same material through two additional means. This is related to how I have conducted my analysis, as will be described in detail below. Suffice it to say for now, I have coded parts of the material in order to establish what the groups did online, using the program Nvivo. This program allows the user to import Twitter profiles and timelines directly, and then to aggregate data automatically. By the time I did this, however, some of the groups had written so extensively online that the 3,200-tweet limit imposed by Twitter prohibited me from importing complete timelines of all groups, and thus these samples are partial. These data have been used only to establish when the groups were most active within the time span actually covered by the sample.

Finally, at a late stage in my research, the University of Oslo's Center for Information Technology made new tools available to me.[8] These allowed me to harvest material from both Twitter and Facebook, based on a variety of criteria, such as location, hashtags, users and words mentioned. I limited myself to downloading the timelines of the groups I follow on Facebook and Twitter, for the sake of maintaining a manageable amount of material. The material can then easily be used to establish which posts on Facebook gained the most likes and the most comments, which tweets were most retweeted, and so on. Once again, however, Twitter's 3,200-tweet limit came into play. As a consequence, all the Facebook samples are complete, but some of the Twitter samples are not.[9] Even so, in my view, the benefits of using this material clearly outweigh these drawbacks, and I have only made use of the parts of this material that are complete, as detailed below. In all, I have three separate archives. The first sample, downloaded manually, is the basis for my analysis. The other two archives have been used only to supplement the findings from the first sample, in the manner described below. I have obtained the material necessary to answer the questions posted in this study, and I argue that it accurately reflects the work of the groups studied.[10]

Material and Contextualisation

Identifying, downloading and organising the required samples are not the only challenges one encounters when working with online material. Another potential challenge pertains to the anonymity, or even the use of false personas, enabled by various platforms. While valuable for many reasons, it also makes it difficult to determine the age, gender, socio-economic background and other factors for the people participating online, and it makes it difficult to determine how many *different* people are actually participating. Moreover, the motives and views of the people participating are not necessarily easy to read from their online activities, and any analysis of such material must be sensitive to these challenges.

A key concept in this regard is contextualisation. The separation of online and offline is not sustainable, as actions online are part of a larger context. Thus, familiarity with the activist sphere in Egypt and Kuwait makes it easier to know the people participating, who they are, what their background is, whether they are influential or not, and so on. This can be extended to society at large, where it might include, among other things, influential politicians, their background, and whether they are likely to support a cause. Similarly, solid knowledge of society, politics and culture is crucial for my analysis, and for recognising the importance and significance of various actions. Contextualisation is also relevant in understanding the strategies chosen by a particular group, and the limitations and possibilities inherent in their offline situations are likely to affect what they need from their use of online platforms. A discussion of the Egyptian and Kuwaiti contexts and the issues at hand will be provided in Chapters 4 and 5 and, whenever context is relevant in the analysis, it will be given.

Good knowledge of the context in itself does not guarantee a proper understanding, however, and information from the protagonists themselves is, of course, of great value. Thus, in addition to the online material, I have conducted interviews with key figures in the groups studied. These interviews give insight into the strategies and choices made by the activists about internet usage, how they perceive its effects, their struggle and the issue in its context. They have helped to identify information I might otherwise have missed, as well as providing further context for my understanding of the material. This goes both ways, and good knowledge of the context has also helped me to understand and interpret the interviews. The interviews were conducted during fieldwork in Egypt and Kuwait, which also gave me the opportunity to follow the various groups closely.[11]

I have spoken to representatives of all the groups studied in Egypt, and the groups themselves picked the representatives. In Kuwait, however, I encountered severe challenges in making contact with potential informants, and I have spoken to representatives of only a few groups. This was mainly due to difficulties in reaching representatives of the groups: by the time I arrived in Kuwait, the government had started arresting well-known activists, and others had fled the country, including some of my contacts from earlier visits. While some were reached online at a later stage, the limited interaction with protagonists in Kuwait remains problematic. Importantly, the interviews were primarily intended and used as a supplement to the main empirical material of this study. The names of the interviewees are not given. This should not be taken as an indication of the content of the interviews, but purely as a reflection of the current political situation in the countries studied. All details concerning the interviews are given in the 'Interviews Conducted' section, following the list of references.

Analysis

The case is a historical incident of the phenomenon studied – in this case, online activism – and the first order of business is to obtain a good understanding of the incident. Thus, in addition to a thorough discussion of the relevant contexts, I will also elaborate on the issues of concern for both cases, and how these issues have evolved over time within their contexts. As for the analysis of the empirical material at hand, my rather open-ended questions must guide my work. Yet, there is no easy answer to exactly how I should do this, nor is there a clear precedent from the current literature to rely on. To further complicate matters, there are differences between the two countries in the use of online platforms, which complicate both my methodological choices and the task of comparison. Although blogs are a crucial part of the online opposition studied in Kuwait, they are not so prominent for the groups working against sexual harassment in Egypt. Likewise, while Facebook is a main platform for my Egyptian case, it is hardly used at all in Kuwait. Some of the groups in both countries have their own websites, others do not. The same goes for YouTube: some use it, some do not. In fact, Twitter was the sole platform used by all groups in both cases. These differences in usage are a crucial part of the comparison, and may in themselves tell us much about what is general and what is context specific. At the same time, Twitter is the platform that allows for the most direct comparison of similar usage. I have met these challenges by presenting various layers of analysis of the material, aiming to provide a comprehensive description and analysis of the groups' online activities, making use of the separate archives I have gathered, and supplementing them with the interviews and various secondary sources.

The material harvested through the applications made available by the University of Oslo's Center for Information Technology as well as directly in Nvivo has allowed me to generate some quantitative data on online practice. For the Facebook samples, which are complete, this provides data on the number of posts, number of comments, number of likes, when they were most active, and so on. This tells me about their patterns of work, if online activity can be connected with any offline activities, what content is most popular and most frequently discussed, and so on. The same data are easily generated for the Twitter samples but, as discussed above, the samples for some of the Egyptian groups are incomplete due to the 3,200-tweet limit. However, I have complete samples for all Egyptian groups from the middle of January 2013 onwards, which allows me to generate the abovementioned data for two of these groups' most active periods: in connection with the second anniversary of the 2011 revolution, and in connection with the June 30 demonstrations that resulted in the ousting of President Mursi. Regarding the Kuwaiti groups, all samples are complete, covering all Twitter usage within the time frame, with the exception of those for Harakat Shabab al-Hurriyya.[12]

In answering my research questions, however, statistics will only take me so far. In order to establish *how* and *for what purposes* online platforms are utilised, I need to look at the content of the groups' online work. This requires a close reading of all content, which will result in a detailed description of it and an interpretation of the intention behind it: do they seek to present their cause, to appeal to potential volunteers, to provide documentation of their offline work, to disseminate evidence of media attention to their work, to mobilise for an online or offline event, to engage their followers, and so on. This work is based on the main sample described above. In order to keep the material manageable, I have not included all comments for the Facebook samples. Some references to the comments posted will be provided, but without an all-inclusive analysis. Likewise, I have not included all comments in the content gathered from YouTube, blogs and the websites of the groups.

The material from Twitter, however, proved somewhat more challenging. As this was the one platform used by all groups, it provided the best opportunity for assessing the groups' use of an online platform, and for comparing usage both within each case and between the cases. This was also the most extensive sample, consisting of approximately

17,000 tweets. Clearly, to aptly describe and analyse such a vast quantity of material in a transparent, replicable and accessible manner is challenging. My solution was to code the material according to given criteria concerning content, thus allowing for a manageable display of actual usage among the groups and facilitating comparison between them.

The method usually chosen to conduct such an analysis is referred to as content analysis.[13] In its most basic form, such analysis may register, for instance, the occurrence of particular words in a given text. However, as I seek to investigate *how* and *for what purposes* the groups studied use Twitter, the occurrence of particular words in itself will hardly provide satisfying answers, as I am more concerned with the meaning, intention and function of the material studied. In this regard, what is referred to as *qualitative content analysis* is relevant: 'One of the key features of qualitative content analysis in contrast to classical quantitative content analysis is that the context is also central to the interpretation and analysis of the material.'[14] It is crucial for my investigation to also incorporate contextual information and qualitative interpretation of the material at hand, and I have drawn heavily on qualitative content analysis in my design. However, for reasons of both methodology and resources, I have conducted an analysis which is different from the common, given form of content analysis, as will be discussed in what follows.

In their 2010 study of online political discussions in four Arab countries, Al Nashmi et al. employed 'each discussion posted' on online forums as the unit of analysis.[15] Hamdy and Gomaa, for their part, employed 'posts' as the unit of analysis for social media in their study of the framing of the Egyptian uprising in 2011.[16] I have also employed posts, or more precisely tweets, as my unit of analysis. This is because my main concern is the meaning conveyed through each tweet: whether it is an argument presented for a group's cause, a message to a group's volunteers, a call for people to participate in a demonstration or something else. Analysis of the use of single words would hardly be useful in answering my research questions. I have coded all the material myself. This is a consequence of the resources available to me: I have not had the opportunity to engage others to take part in this work.[17] However, as will be discussed below, validation of my findings through triangulation will be of great importance for this study. Moreover, it is important in this regard to note that I do not make statistical inferences from my analysis. Rather, it is a visualisation of my own interpretation, and an attempt to make the analysis of a vast quantity of material more transparent, organised and manageable.

The categories used were based on observations made during a first reading of the material, the interviews conducted and my own expectations of what I might find. Perhaps not surprisingly, a few adjustments had to be made during the initial stages of the process. The provisional categories were 'checked, corrected, and modified on the basis of the textual material, until the text {could} be adequately recorded with them',[18] which is what I did. The categories used cover the various aspects of the groups' online workings and are well suited to describe their work. Not all categories are mutually exclusive. Understandably, this is seen as a critical feature of quantitative content analysis. For instance, if we wish to investigate whether newspapers in a given country provide more negative or more positive coverage of a politician, we need to clearly distinguish between one thing and the other, not least if we are to infer whether there are any significant differences to be identified between newspapers. If a news item contains both positive and negative coverage, the solution would be to make the unit of analysis smaller. However, as argued above, I believe a tweet is the only workable unit of analysis given my research question. Moreover, my aim is not to identify whether an item is one thing or the other, it is to depict and analyse the groups' usage of online platforms within its context. If a single tweet is used to mobilise for an event *and* to partake in a debate and perhaps even to respond to a particular user as well, it is crucial for me to reflect these multiple purposes in my coding. If I were to separate between one thing *or* the other, this would not reflect the actual usage of the platform, and would not enable me to answer my research questions. As noted by Stemler, 'methodology is always employed in the service of a research question'.[19] Naturally, this must be reflected in my categories and in the way in which they are employed.

As follows, each tweet may be coded in more than one category. For instance, a tweet written by the group itself, asking people to volunteer, containing information on how to do so and marked with a frequently used hashtag will be marked as 'Own tweet', 'Appeals to volunteers', 'Practical on volunteering' and 'Taking part in a discussion'. Thus, it will provide answers as to *how* and *for what purpose* the groups make use of

Table 3.1 Categories Employed in Coding

Main category	Subcategory
Mobilisation	– Offline events
	◦ Information about event/Invitation
	◦ 'Please come'
	– Online events
	◦ Information about event/Invitation
	◦ 'Please come'
	– Encouragement in general
	– Part of online event
	– Linking/spreading own sites
	– Asking for material support
Discussion	– Polls
	– Questions for discussion
	– Agitation
	– Statements
	– Other posts that generate discussion
	– Taking part in a discussion
	– Responding/Communicating with others
	– News
Media	– On themselves
	– On other groups
	– On the issue
	– Press releases
	– Communication with media/journalists
	– Response to others
Documentation	– Pictures/text/video from event
	– Testimonies
	– Reports
	– Pictures/videos/text on the issue
	– Live reporting from event
	– Warning, call for help, communicating
	– Asking for information, etc.
Information	– Papers, etc.
	– Guides, instructions
Recruitment	– Appeals to volunteers
	– Practical information on volunteering (forms, applications)
Other groups	– Reposting/linking to others' content
	– Communicating with others
	– Cooperating with others
Other	
Tweets	– Own tweet
	– Retweet

Twitter, but it will not provide a definitive answer as to how much time/space is devoted to the various activities described. Rather, it provides information on the proportional relationship among them. One main category, such as 'Discussion', may cover more than 100 per cent of the tweets of a group, as the relevant subcategories are employed frequently and often simultaneously. The categories I have used are shown in Table 3.1.[20]

The first category is meant to cover what can be interpreted as mobilisation, in a wider sense than just asking people to attend an event. This is, naturally, also included but, in addition, I have added subcategories pertaining to bolstering morale and resources, promoting their own sites through links and mobilising their followers – and others – online. Tweets that were published as part of an online event are also included in this category. The second category is concerned with discussions and deliberations online, as well as agitation and argumentation for a cause, and most of the subcategories are quite straightforward. The subcategory 'Taking part in a discussion' is meant to be interpreted in a literal sense, but establishing whether or not someone is taking part in a discussion on Twitter is more difficult. When the groups studied discuss a particular issue, they often introduce specific hashtags. When they argue in general, or disseminate practical information for that matter, they often use recurring hashtags as well. Thus, when a well-known hashtag is used, this potentially means taking part in a discussion in the sense that the protagonists direct their statement in such a manner that others might find it and respond, should they wish to do so. However, there is no guarantee that this actually happens. It is impossible to know whether or not they are read, or if someone responds or not. Yet, because using hashtags in this manner is a deliberate attempt to reach more people and/or to attach the tweet to a subject or debate, I have coded all tweets that include the use of such hashtags within this subcategory. I have not, however, included all tweets that randomly mark words in the tweet as hashtags, of which I have found several examples. In addition, I have included tweets that are clearly part of a discussion, even though no hashtag is employed.

The subcategory 'Responding/Communicating with others' refers to the groups, or other users, responding directly to another user, often answering questions of a practical nature. The third category mainly refers to the groups' dissemination of media items relating to themselves, to other groups or to the issue, which they spread frequently. Moreover, this category includes their contact with journalists, their press releases, and their reactions to the media appearances of third parties ('Response to others'). The fourth category covers their efforts to document their own work, or events and incidents relevant to their issue of concern. The subcategory 'Warning, call for help, communicating' mainly covers information on what is going on during offline events, as well as warnings about and documentation of harassment and harassers in the Egyptian case. In the following category, 'Information', the subcategory 'Guides, instructions' refers primarily to instructions given out before offline events, such as where to meet, what to wear and how the event will be organised. In addition, it includes some general instructions and hints, such as how to deal with tear gas fired during demonstrations. The following two categories should be self-explanatory, but the last two warrant a few comments. The category 'Other' is for those tweets that did not fit into any of the other categories, usually content not related to the group's work. The last category is simply used to distinguish between a group's own tweets and its retweets. Multiple examples of different categories will be provided throughout the analysis.

This approach allowed me to transform a vast amount of material into something more manageable, both for the discussion of each case and for the comparison. Moreover, it ensures a thorough reading of all the material, as it is readily apparent whether or not one has looked into each specific tweet, and one's findings can be quickly summarised. Taken together with the statistical material described above, it will provide information on the relationship between time spent online on a given category (or, if you will, activity), and those tweets that are most popular, as indicated by the number of retweets/favourites. Combined with information on offline events and results, it will shed light on the relationship between work done online and its offline ramifications. In summary, while I did encounter some problems, I believe this approach to be valuable both in order to provide an apt description and analysis of the material at hand, and to answer the questions posed in this study.

Clearly, we must always be attentive to the fact that qualitative analysis and interpretation, as in the coding and close reading of the material, is based on our own subjective reading of the content. We all have our own expectations and experiences that may affect our understanding, and sensitivity towards this aspect is crucial. Furthermore, the use of multiple sources is key in this regard. Using multiple sources together is usually referred to as triangulation, which in a qualitative context has generally been 'considered a process of using multiple perceptions to clarify meaning, verifying the repeatability of an observation or interpretation'.[21] While central to minimising the risk of misinterpretation, triangulation is also important in answering the other questions I have asked of the cases, concerning the benefits of internet usage both online and offline, and whether or not any potential factors for success can be determined. The analysis described above might answer how the internet is used, for what purposes and with what online benefits, but assessing the wider ramifications of this usage demands additional sources. This means piecing together the information from the online material with the interviews, as well as with secondary sources, such as newspaper reports and statements from politicians and other organisations and groups. As George and Bennett point out, '[t]racing the processes that may have led to an outcome helps narrow the list of potential causes',[22] which, in essence, is what I will be doing in order to establish online and offline benefits. This procedure is at the heart of the dimensions I suggest below as a structured framework for assessing the impact of the campaigns studied. First, however, we turn to the question of comparing the two cases.

Comparing the Cases

The main aim in comparing the cases is to identify which features can be said to be general, and which are the result of the specific needs and possibilities each context provides. Yet, this is hardly a 'controlled comparison', as the cases do not 'resemble each other in every respect but one'.[23] While the Kuwaiti and Egyptian contexts share many similarities, there are clear differences in terms of both offline and online contexts and the issues at hand. Thus, one may ask if the cases are indeed suitable for comparison, or if it would have been better to look at more similar groups concerned with more similar issues. Yet, I will argue that this would have been both difficult and counterproductive. For one thing, context is of great importance not only in understanding the work of the groups, but also in understanding their issues of concern.

What constitutes, say, a struggle for democratic reform will depend on the context. The point, of course, is that in studying what appear to be similar issues, we may perhaps interpret the campaigns in question as more alike than they really are.

Far more importantly, however, is my aim to distinguish between context-dependent features and more general features of online activism. If certain features are indeed general, they should be present both among Egyptian groups fighting sexual harassment and Kuwaiti groups demanding constitutional change, given that online platforms are the vehicles for change in both instances. The same holds true for the theoretical approach employed. My aim is to provide less vague findings by identifying and theorising how and through which mechanisms online platforms help activists to effect change. If such mechanisms only hold true for one particular case or issue, they hardly provide more clarity. They must be of a more general nature, and therefore it is a strength that the applicability and explanatory abilities of my theoretical approach as well as my framework for assessing the impact of campaigns is tested in two different cases in two different settings. Clearly, this dictates close attention to context, including the issues at hand, and this will be discussed in detail in the comparison in Chapter 6.

Assessing the Impact

The research questions ask how activists make use of online platforms, and if and how this usage helps them to realise their goals. In assessing goal-realisation, and not least to understand the importance of such work and, by extension, the use of online platforms in it, we must also assess the effectiveness, or impact, of the campaigns on the contexts they seek to affect. Such assessments, however, have proven difficult to conduct, and any attempt to measure the impact of online activism has to begin with two very difficult questions: what should we measure, and how should we measure it? Ideally, if we can identify some quantifiable factor to which we can assign a value, we could conduct larger quantitative studies and single out the crucial factor(s) for success and also the crucial levels of those factors, and perhaps even predict the outcome of new initiatives.

One obvious measurable dimension is access to online platforms – that is, to the internet. However, even though it is clearly important for our purpose, it does not tell us much about the work of different initiatives, but rather about their shared potential. In terms of offline results, these numbers are ambiguous at best. The four countries which saw an authoritarian leader fall from power during the so-called 'Arab Spring' – Egypt, Libya, Tunisia and Yemen – all have internet penetration rates (IPRs) below the Middle East average.[24] This is also the case with Syria. Yet, Bahrain, which has also witnessed, and indeed is still seeing, massive unrest and rebellion, has the highest IPR in the region, together with Kuwait, which has also experienced demonstrations on a large scale. Countries with both low access and high access have seen rebellions, and countries with both low access and high access have *not* seen rebellions. In short, while access is, of course, important, it does not, on its own, provide clear answers to the questions asked in this paper.

There are, however, other numbers to look at, such as likes and followers. Looking at the Egyptian revolution of 2011, these numbers are quite impressive. By the time the demonstrations began, the main Facebook group, Kulluna Khalid Saʿid[25] ('We are all Khalid Saʿid'), had some 350,000 likes.[26] The most used hashtag on Twitter in 2011 was #egypt, and the eighth most used was #jan25. The most referenced cities and countries were Cairo and Egypt, respectively. And the most discussed news story was former Egyptian president Husni Mubarak's resignation.[27] This, however, could tell us just as much about the impact of the 2011 revolution on Twitter as about the impact of Twitter on the 2011 revolution. That is not to say that these numbers aren't important: a Facebook group with only ten likes will hardly make an impact. Then again, as pointed out by Eaton, some argue that engagement online leads to passivity offline, and as such may even be harmful to a cause.[28] While I find little support for such a view in my material, it is a valid argument against judging campaigns by likes and shares alone. Such figures only reveal part of the picture, which, in all likelihood, is quite complex. Other factors, such as the people involved, the issue involved, their offline actions and their relationship with traditional media, are also important. Again, we should not draw a clear distinction between online and offline, and various factors must be included in our assessment.

Therefore, I suggest instead a different approach, inspired by Dahlgren's concept of using three dimensions to identify and examine 'the public sphere of any given society or analyzing the contribution of any given communication technology'.[29] Given the complexity of the process at work, I suggest a set of core features, or dimensions if you like, around which to develop a discussion on the impact of an initiative. These are not intended to cover just the online part of the campaign. Rather, an essential element is the connection between online and offline, which I suggest is a crucial point for gaining influence. This also entails an assessment of the groups' ability to realise their goals, which is inevitably problematic: among the many possible factors that may have affected an outcome, how can we establish what has been caused by the campaigns studied? My answer is twofold. First, context is once again of great importance. Detailed knowledge of society and the actors involved is key to assessing who might have caused a result and to tracing the process that led to a given outcome. Second, I assess the campaigns in broader terms than simply goal realisation. By looking at factors such as their ability to recruit, to gain media coverage and to provoke reactions and adjustments from others, we can establish as probable their ability to have an impact and further substantiate our assessment. The framework is an attempt to move forward in the difficult debate on the impact of online activism. As follows from my hypothesis, I suggest that the key feature of 'the internet' in this regard is the publicness it provides, which I take as a precondition for the practices inherent in the dimensions suggested below. I suggest the following dimensions as crucial in assessing the impact of online campaigns:

1. **Evolution of the campaign** This dimension covers the development of the campaign in question and deals with issues such as the following: Did the campaign grow? Did the content and actions evolve and develop during its course, or did it stagnate after the initial phase? Did the campaign attract new followers, and was it spread through mentions, links, and so on, to sites other than the one it started from? Did it receive attention from the traditional media? These questions should be seen in connection with the campaign's stated goals: whether these are realised partially or completely, temporarily or permanently could affect any further development of a campaign.
2. **Intra-campaign build-up and evolution** This dimension deals with the internal workings of the campaign, how the campaign responded to various incidents, if it provided training for its

members, if it changed its methods, the way it recruited, and so on. Important questions in this area include what the needs of a campaign were and whether these were met, if the campaign became more professional and if online platforms were used strategically to achieve something, or if the campaign merely had an online presence.

3. **Reactions and adjustments** This dimension covers both reactions and adjustments made by a campaign and others and those sparked by the campaign. Did the campaign provoke any reactions from the government? From opponents? Did other forces adjust their view because of the campaign, either to accommodate it or to stand as a clear alternative to it?
4. **Offline–online relations** This dimension covers the crucial question of whether a campaign managed to work both online and offline. Did the campaign manage to be visible offline? Were there any connections between suggestions and decisions reached online and actions offline? Did they document their offline actions online? Did online growth materialise offline? Can links between offline events, achievements and the like be traced to activity online?
5. **Goal realisation (in degrees)** This dimension deals with the outcome of the campaign. Was the campaign's goal realised? Was it partially realised? Did others move their position towards that of the campaign? Were the topics raised by the campaign discussed among the public at large, in the traditional media, in certain groups, and so on? Can any direct links be identified between goal realisation and one or more of the other dimensions? Was the campaign's goal realisation acknowledged by others? Did participants change their view on the issue, or was their view strengthened through the campaign and its aftermath (and was this affected by their goal realisation)?
6. **Experience and expectations (changes in social relations)** This dimension covers the effects of the campaign, or perhaps rather of the activism, on the participants and the followers, and on the issues that were raised. Were new groups mobilised and/or heard? Were the subjects of discussion changed or expanded? Did the protagonists change their methods and/or their expectations? Did new groups or individuals gain new experience in democratic practices or democratising practices? How did they perceive their own influence and impact? Did other social groups have to adjust or respond to

groups to which they would not otherwise have paid attention? Were the social relations between one or more groups towards other groups or society at large changed?

7. **Copying/follow-ups** The final dimension covers the issue of continuity and the lasting effects of the campaign/activism in question. Did others copy the campaign? Were there any follow-ups on the same subject or from the same groups? Did it evolve into something lasting and/or bigger? Was the issue picked up by other groups in society?

I argue that these dimensions provide a fruitful framework for the discussion, and may hopefully be employed and further developed in other studies. Ideally, if different studies make use of this or similar frameworks, it could provide us with comparable results on a larger scale and make the tasks of identifying crucial factors for success and of developing theory easier. Here, the framework is intended to help us assess the impact of the campaigns, whereas the theoretical approach discussed in Chapter 2 will help us to understand this impact, and how it effects social and political change.

Summary: What I Studied, How I Studied It and How to Make Sense of It

What I have set out to do is to provide an empirically based study of actual internet usage and its benefits for groups and activists working in the Middle East, or more precisely, in Egypt and Kuwait. Through a study of two cases involving groups working in the two countries, I aim to provide an accurate description and analysis of their online and offline work, the connections between the two and how they benefit from using online platforms and, if possible, to identify any factors for success in this regard. Through a comparison of the cases, I seek to establish what can be considered general features of online activist work in the region, and what can be identified as a result of the particular context within which they work. The material consists of online writings, interviews and secondary sources, and has been analysed as described above. I have provided a framework for assessing the impact of the online parts of the campaigns, I have situated my study within the current theoretical debates in the field and I have presented my understanding of counterpublicness and agonistic pluralism as a framework within which to identify and understand the central mechanisms through which online platforms help and/or enable activists to effect social and political change. The goal is to present a concrete, empirically sound study that will provide new insights in an area often dominated by more abstract debates, and in so doing to contribute to a more comprehensive theoretical understanding of online activism. Hopefully, the approach presented here will inspire further work along similar lines, which in my view is sorely needed.

CHAPTER 4

THE EGYPTIAN CASE: THE CONTEXT, THE ISSUE, AND MY FINDINGS

On Thursday 14 March 2013, at 10:00 in the morning, those administering the Facebook page of Tahrir Bodyguard (TBG) published a picture of some of their volunteers along with the text 'Can any one [*sic*] guess outside which TV show studio was this picture of the Tahrir Bodyguards Team taken?'. It was the latest in a series of messages on both Facebook and Twitter providing teasers for the group's upcoming participation in an as-yet undisclosed popular TV show. When the show aired the next day, it was revealed: both TBG and OpAntiSH took part as comedian Bassem Youssef dedicated an entire episode of his extremely popular satirical show *al-Barnamig* to the issue of sexual harassment and sexual assault.[1] In a familiar manner, the show combined skits making fun of harassers and their excuses with serious interviews with the activists. And, as always, up-and-coming local musicians were given the stage to conclude the show – this time a band called 'Abo Wel Shabab', singing critical songs against the elected president. Participation on the show gained the groups many new volunteers and thousands of new followers online, and in many ways it represented the zenith of the public fight against sexual harassment and sexual violence. In hindsight, it also represented the zenith of free public debate, of political satire and of political cultural expressions in post-revolution Egypt. Within months, the programme would be cancelled as the new military regime tightened its grip on society. The number of attacks on female protesters decreased dramatically, but only because the new regime prohibited the very protests that the groups had worked so hard to make safe for female participants. Thousands of protesters would be arrested, along with scholars, journalists and non-governmental organisation (NGO) workers. And while the new regime did promise to fight harassment and assaults, they turned the political issue of women's rights and female participation that the groups had raised into a simple question of increased security. The groups were allowed to continue their work, but they, like everyone else, were expected to do so within the boundaries set by the new regime.

In the following, I present the Egyptian case studied: the groups, their issue of concern, the context within which they worked and, of course, my material, my analysis and my initial findings. I will argue that the groups were able to raise a previously private issue in public and were able to claim it as a political matter of public concern rather than the moral or security issue that the authorities thought it ought to be. In doing so, I believe the particular context of post-revolution and pre-coup Egypt was important, as were the experiences which many of those involved had gained from the pro-democracy movement of the 2000s, when activism came to the fore in Egypt. Thus, in order to properly contextualise the work studied, I begin with a discussion of civil society, government restrictions and the advent of (online) activism in Egypt, as well as the 2011 revolution and its aftermath. From there, I move on to the issue at hand, before I turn to a detailed description of the campaign studied. This, in turn, leads to the analysis and the initial findings.

The Egyptian Context: Why Activism?

Until 30 June 2012, Egypt had not had an elected, civilian president. The successive authoritarian regimes of al-Nasir, al-Sadat and Mubarak all came to power without competing in elections, and they never allowed for the possibility that their power would be challenged through democratic means. This necessitates a strong degree of control over both citizens and society, which in turn has major implications for activism and civil society. In his magnificently detailed study, Kienle shows how a combination of legal measures, co-optation and coercion was used to prevent serious challenges to the regime, whether from political parties, trade unions, professional syndicates, independent media, NGOs or even popular personalities within the regime.[2]

These legal measures included various laws designed to ensure state control. For instance, political parties were regulated through Law 40 of 1977, which stipulates several, often vaguely defined conditions for gaining state recognition as a legal political party.[3] To 'further ensure state control',[4] this licensing was administered by the Committee for the Affairs of Political Parties (PCC), which also surveilled and, if deemed necessary, could freeze the activities of those parties that obtained legal status. As a result, almost no parties were recognised, although some gained legal status following lengthy and costly court battles.[5] In all, political parties were so weak, Langohr argued in 2004, that NGOs 'have become the most vocal secular opposition in several Arab countries', including Egypt.[6] However, through Law 32 of 1964, then the short-lived Law 153 of 1999 and finally through Law 84 of 2002, the actions of civil associations in Egypt have been severely restricted as well. While there are differences between the three laws, the general principle is the same as that governing the political parties: to ensure control through strict conditions, bureaucratic hindrances and direct intervention. For instance, such organisations were prohibited from conducting 'political work' and, if deemed necessary, the state could interfere in the selection of an organisation's board.[7] As a result, Kassem argues, 'associations found themselves incorporated into the formal state structure, dissolved, or rendered obsolete'.[8]

Other civil society organisations, namely the trade unions and professional syndicates, experienced similar obstacles. Trade unions faced both state co-optation and tight regulation, and the law regulating these unions was amended in the early 1990s to further strengthen regime control.[9] While the professional syndicates were allowed a certain degree of freedom in the 1980s, new obstructions were imposed on their operations in 1993, following the success of the Muslim Brotherhood in the elections for several of their boards from the mid-1980s onwards.[10] Moreover, the particular laws concerning civil society were by no means the only legal measures employed by the regime to ensure control. Perhaps even more important was the state of emergency, which was in effect from when Mubarak took office following al-Sadat's assassination until 31 May 2012.[11] It allowed for censorship of political activity, the arrest of political activists and people demonstrating without permission, and 'any measures "required by the circumstances"'.[12] It also allowed the president to refer any crime to the military judiciary, that is, to try any civilian in a military court.[13] Moreover, the Mubarak regime repeatedly chose to overlook the judicial system, both military and civilian, altogether, by resorting to 'administrative detention', which sometimes lasted several years.[14] Finally, the Mubarak regime also used extra-legal measures and outright bullying to hinder opposition forces, frequently by employing the infamous *balṭagiyya*.[15]

In spite of all this, opposition political parties existed throughout Mubarak's 30-year reign, and civil society, including professional syndicates and trade unions, was at least a contested arena. Moreover, the regime at times appeared to liberalise its policies, for instance allowing for opposition gains in the 1987 parliamentary elections.[16] However, according to Kienle and Kassem, this apparent liberalisation in fact constituted adjustments designed to ensure continued authoritarian control.[17] Or, as argued by Brynen et al., they were part of a wider 'authoritarian upgrading' in the region, which 'was intended as a substitute for, rather than a step toward, fuller democratization'.[18] Moreover, if the regime did indeed open up the political sphere in the 1980s, there is wide agreement that any opening was closed again in the 1990s.[19] El-Mahdi even argues that 'the Mubarak regime closed the political system in the early 1990s'.[20] Although the regime's battle with militant Islamists during the 1980s and 1990s often was put forth as the reason behind the tightened control on civil society, al-Sayyid points to Egypt's 1991 deal with the International Monetary Fund (IMF) and its painful repercussions for the Egyptian working class as equally important,[21] a view echoed by Kienle.[22] In either case, by the late 1990s, 'official' civil society was firmly controlled by the government, and those eager to voice their opposition would have to look for alternative arenas of protest. Starting in the early 2000s, a turbulent period of both economic hardship and unprecedented activism, mobilisation and labour actions took place in Egypt, referred to by many as the origin of, and the process that led to, the fall of President Husni Mubarak in 2011.[23]

The Protest Movements of the 2000s

Shaped by the system described above, the protests of the 2000s may be said to have started in 1998 precisely with mobilisation against the regime's repressive judicial measures, namely the introduction of the new law on civil society.[24] Although unsuccessful, this work brought NGOs from various fields together in an organised manner.[25] Cooperation continued two years later, when the second Palestinian intifada brought Egyptians into the streets. According to Filiu, the importance of the second intifada must be seen in connection with the advent of new media in the Middle East.[26] Authoritarian regimes had long enjoyed an almost complete control over the media, but this changed when Al-Jazeera entered the scene in the late 1990s.[27] Suddenly, young Egyptians could watch the events unfolding in Palestine live on TV, just as they could witness the resounding inaction of the Arab world. The perceived injustice resulted in public protests, in which students took the lead and renounced their 'decade-long political apathy and stage[d] demonstrations across the country despite the 19-year-old Emergency Law which strictly prohibits street demonstrations'.[28] According to el-Mahdi, these demonstrations would be the 'turning point for contentious politics in Egypt'.[29] Then, following an anti-war conference in Cairo in December 2002, demonstrations against the coming American attack on Iraq spread across the country.[30] These culminated on 20 March, the day after the hostilities began, as the city witnessed 'two days of protests like nothing seen since the 1970s', in which activists occupied Tahrir Square.[31]

The emerging protest movement soon turned its attention to domestic issues. Already, on 5 March, 150 people gathered outside the Parliament to protest against the renewal of the Emergency Law. The 20 March Popular Campaign for Change was formed in July 2003;[32] a few months later it became the Popular Movement for Change. At around the same time, the Egyptian Movement for Change, popularly known by the slogan 'Kifaya', announced its establishment.[33] These movements built on the momentum created by the recent demonstrations and, according to Lim, Kifaya activists were able to turn the anger against Israeli oppression and US aggression 'to an oppositional movement calling for the [*sic*] political reforms and the end to President Mubarak's rule'.[34] In addition, many were concerned with the presidential and parliamentary elections to be held in 2005. Fearing a Syrian scenario, they wanted to make sure that President Mubarak was not succeeded by his son, Gamal Mubarak, when his fourth term ended.[35] Having risen through the ranks of the ruling National Democratic Party (NDP) in the early 2000s, Gamal Mubarak was closely associated with the neoliberal economic agenda of increased privatisation, which for many resulted in lower standards of living.[36] According to el-Mahdi, this agenda is key to understanding why this movement came to the fore in 2004–5, as it represented a breach in the traditional 'democratic bargain', in which citizens forgo democratic rights in exchange for socio-economic ones.[37] In a situation of increased economic hardship, the middle class saw 'no reason why political participation should be further postponed', and Kifaya was indeed a middle class based movement.[38]

On 12 December 2004, Kifaya held its first public demonstration to demand President Mubarak's resignation and free, competitive elections.[39] This initial demonstration was followed by several others until the movement fizzled out by late-2006. The mobilising capabilities of Kifaya and other groups turned out to be quite limited, and the number of protesters never exceeded 2,500.[40] Even so, popular mobilisation in Egypt was revived in a manner not seen in decades.[41] Moreover, it appeared that tangible results were achieved. On 26 February 2005, President Mubarak asked Parliament to amend article 76 of the constitution to allow for multi-candidate elections.[42] However, the protest movement saw the changes as little more than the kind of cosmetic changes that, in reality, further strengthened autocratic rule.[43] Thus, Kifaya held a demonstration in downtown Cairo on 25 May 2005, a day later known as 'Black Wednesday'. While the pro-democracy demonstrations were routinely met with a heavy police presence, on this day they also faced the infamous *balṭagiyya*, who attacked the protesters already contained by the police. The *balṭagiyya* attacked women in particular, sexually harassing female protesters in public.[44] This attack is seen as an important event in the chronology of Egyptian women's movements, and later of the anti-harassment movement, and it also shows the interconnectedness of the Egyptian activist scene, including the anti-harassment groups. Unsurprisingly, Mubarak won the presidential elections, and his NDP the parliamentary elections. Although the outlawed Muslim Brotherhood made unprecedented gains as independents, neither election brought lasting democratic gains. Still, the pro-democracy movement succeeded in challenging the status quo openly and thus providing an alternative to the ineffective and more or less co-opted 'official' opposition.[45] Perhaps equally importantly, it brought with it the breakthrough of online activism in Egypt.

The Advent of Online Activism

There is widespread agreement among observers and scholars about the importance of Kifaya for online activism, as well as that of online activism for Kifaya.[46] According to Isherwood, the origins of the Egyptian blogosphere can be traced to Usenet groups and email list servers in the late 1990s, run by, among others, the later renowned blogger Wael Abbas.[47] The blogosphere itself came into being between 2003 and 2005, the period which Radsch termed the 'experimentation phase'.[48] At this time, the number of internet users in the country was increasing rapidly, due to ambitious government efforts.[49] Whereas only 0.64 per cent of the population used the internet in 2000, this figure had risen to 12.75 per cent in 2005.[50] Similarly, the blogosphere grew from fewer than 40 bloggers prior to 2005, to more than 1,800 by September 2006,[51] reflecting both the popularity of and the importance quickly ascribed to the platform. The blogosphere was closely tied to the pro-democracy movement and Kifaya in particular. Lim argues that it expanded the 'repertoire of contention' available to the group, as blogs were used to mobilise, to document offline events and to counter reports in state-controlled media.[52] The blogs also provided a space for free discussion and deliberation among activists and others, crucial for an organisation that, as Lim notes, 'had neither physical headquarters nor [a] permanent meeting place'.[53] This might not be particularly surprising given the strategies of the regime discussed above; a loose, informal structure based online makes sense in the context of tight regime control over civil society. Importantly, those involved in the pro-democracy movement and the early stages of the blogosphere did not limit their activities to those directly related to Kifaya.

In February 2005, Wael Abbas started the blog Al-Wa'i al-Masri on misrdigital.com, a site also used by Kifaya, according to Lim.[54] On the blog, he posted pictures from political protests that 'conventional newspapers would often refuse to print, or simply did not have space for on a particular day'.[55] This highlights an important feature of the Egyptian blogosphere from early on, namely that of providing uncensored news and information, often referred to as 'citizen journalism'.[56] Wael Abbas would become perhaps the most prominent blogger in this regard, but many others would take part as well, exposing police abuse, torture and other wrongdoings on the part of the government. Moreover, on more than one occasion, they proved able to tangibly affect offline outcomes. One often-cited example is that of ʿImad al-Kabir, a microbus driver arrested and tortured by the Egyptian police on 18 January 2006.[57] The police officers beat al-Kabir, raped him with a stick and filmed what they did with a mobile phone in order to further humiliate him by showing it to other drivers.[58] However, in November 2006, the video reached the blogosphere, being posted on Wael Abbas's blog, among others.[59] From there, it was picked up by the conventional media, including the newspaper *Al-Masri al-Yawm*, and al-Kabir was persuaded to pursue the case through the legal system. As the evidence was rather clear-cut, in November 2007 the officers involved were sentenced to three years in prison,[60] making it the first conviction for police brutality in Egypt's history.[61]

At around the same time, a different scandal was brought to the attention of the Egyptian public by bloggers. On the night of 24/25 October 2006, as most Egyptians celebrated the holidays, women were attacked and sexually harassed by 'hundreds of young men' outside the Cinema Metro in downtown Cairo.[62] Policemen on the scene refused to intervene and the incident was ignored by the conventional media. However, Wael Abbas and his blogger colleagues Malek Mustafa and Muhammad al-Sharqawi were present at the scene, and documented the incident in pictures and words. Three days later, activist Nawara Negm raised the issue while participating on a TV show, prompting an investigation by the show's hostess. From there, the issue was picked up by a number of established news outlets,[63] and coverage of the problem in general increased dramatically.[64] Clearly, the incident was picked up after it was raised on a traditional medium – TV. Nevertheless, one of the bloggers mentioned above was among those interviewed for the piece later broadcasted, and the incident is often cited as an example on the impact of online activism in Egypt.[65] Moreover, at around this time, Egyptian newspapers started to use blogs as a source on a more regular basis, not just in specific, highly visible cases.[66] In addition, online platforms remained crucial for offline mobilisation and, according to Lim, 54 out of 70 recorded street protests between 2004 and 2011 'substantially involved' online activism.[67] Soon, the emerging online activist sphere would connect with another group challenging the regime outside the 'official' channels, namely the workers.

According to Beinin, '[w]orkers were by far the largest component of the burgeoning culture of protest in the 2000s that undermined the legitimacy of the Mubarak regime'.[68] Between 1998 and 2010, 'well over 2 million and perhaps as many as 4 million Egyptian workers participated in some 3,400 to 4,000 strikes and other collective actions'.[69] The number of such actions increased markedly after 2004,[70] as the government intensified their privatisation efforts.[71] These efforts also hit those seeking employment hard, and unemployment rose among Egypt's increasingly well-educated youth.[72] Thus, the changing economic conditions that led to revived labour protests also played an important part in mobilising the youth, as noted by Filiu and others.[73] In 2008, they joined forces, as young activists organising online supported a workers' protest planned for 6 April demanding a monthly minimum wage.[74] The activists, some of whom had experience from Kifaya, took the name the April 6 Youth Movement. Introducing Facebook as a tool for political organisation in Egypt, they called for a general strike to coincide with the planned protest.[75] Later, of course, the group would become one of the most central activist groups in Egypt, both during the revolution of 2011 and in the time that followed.

Another group that challenged the regime was the Islamists, first and foremost the Muslim Brotherhood, who did so through the 'official' channels. While they did make some gains, such as in the 2005 parliamentary elections, they also faced severe repression, including mass arrests. This, in part, led to the entry into the blogosphere in 2006 of young members and sympathisers, and an important feature of this online engagement was campaigns to gain the release of imprisoned members.[76] By this time, the Egyptian blogosphere had evolved from what Radsch termed an 'activist stage', lasting from 2005 until 2006, to a period of 'diversification and fragmentation'.[77] Whereas the blogosphere was rather homogeneous during the initial activist phase, this changed as it expanded and evolved, producing a blogosphere with various enclaves of 'different types of people', with 'some' contact between the enclaves. These included 'citizen journalists, non-denominational activists, leftists, Muslim Brotherhood and Islamists, culture and arts enthusiasts', and others.[78] In addition to campaigning for the release of their fellow brethren, the newly established MB bloggers contributed to presenting the organisation, and themselves as its representatives, to a wider audience. For a group vilified in the media, and perceived as secretive by many, this was an important feature, according to Lynch.[79] But perhaps the most prominent feature of MB bloggers was their willingness to challenge the strict discipline of the organisation by discussing the group's policies online, in public. In September 2007, a debate about the political platform of the brotherhood broke out on several blogs, which led to sharp criticism from parts of the leadership who argued that such a debate should not be made public.[80] Similarly, young people took the lead in the secular pro-democracy movement, although well-known older opposition figures held positions in the leadership. As such, the young activists challenged not only the regime online and offline, but also the patriarchal nature of their organisations and of society as a whole.

The crackdown on the Muslim Brotherhood in 2006 and 2007 also hit the pro-democracy movement both online and offline, according to Radsch.[81] Yet, while it is clear that many activists and bloggers were targeted by the authorities, the arrests themselves were usually linked to offline activities: '[m]any more bloggers have been arrested for their offline activities than for what they actually wrote online'.[82] In fact, Freedom House argues that 'until 2008, authorities [in Egypt] showed a relaxed attitude toward internet use and did not censor websites or use high-end technologies to monitor discussions',[83] and there were few clear-cut cases in which bloggers were arrested for what they said online. One infamous example, however, was that of Kareem Amer, who served four years in prison for insulting Islam and the president.[84] Even so, the use of various online platforms was an integral part of activism in Egypt, as was challenging the regime outside the 'official' channels. Thus, when in June 2010 the perhaps most famous online group of them all, Kulluna Khalid Saʿid (We Are All Khalid Saʿid), was formed following the brutal murder of a young man at the hands of the police,[85] it built on the experiences, networks and online arenas established over the past few years.

The 2011 Revolution and the Post-Revolution Context

In hindsight, the year 2010 might seem to be a crucial one in explaining the revolt that broke out only weeks into 2011: the return of Mohamed ElBaradei, a man in whom some activists saw a potentially successful challenge to the regime;[86] the parliamentary elections in which the regime 'lost all inhibitions in terms of electoral fraud';[87] the brutal killing of Khalid Saʿid and the rise of the Facebook group to protest against it; and, of course, the beginning of the successful Tunisian uprising. This last event might have been particularly important, as it showed that instigating actual change was indeed possible. Yet, with the exception of the Tunisian example, there was nothing new about the events of that year; police violence and election fraud were the norm. Egypt by 2010 was a 'a semi-failed state [that] had produced a failed society';[88] it was a country 'ripe for revolution'.[89] Moreover, internet access had increased markedly over the past few years, reaching 25.6 per cent by 2011.[90]

Then, as we now know, the revolution did take place, and in just 18 days Egypt's longest-serving ruler since Muhammad ʿAli was forced to step down. The lessons learned during the 2000s were put to good use: protesters were mobilised online and offline, citizen journalists brought the events to a wider audience, Islamists and secularists cooperated on the ground[91] and workers' strikes brought the regime to its knees. Not surprisingly, the revolution has already been the subject of several books and journal articles, both from an academic standpoint[92] and from a participant's perspective.[93] Undoubtedly, it will also be the subject of many works yet to come. Three issues that have already been the subject of much debate are of particular importance for the context of this investigation: why the revolution happened, the importance of online platforms for the revolution and whether or not this revolution really brought about tangible change. I have discussed the reasons behind the revolution only briefly, but the main point here is to show that it happened in the context of a long period of growing discontent with the government, and a long period of oppositional activism. The development of activism online and offline during the 2000s gave many young Egyptians valuable experience, but it also raised their expectations. Following the revolution, these activists took it upon themselves to create a new and better Egypt, using the tools and strategies they knew – but also inventing new ones. Various groups raised their issues in public with new confidence, including the demand for a minimum wage, the demand to end torture and, of course, the demand for an end to sexual harassment and sexual violence.

The question of the importance, or impact, of online platforms during the revolution is both crucial and difficult to answer. The regime obviously deemed online platforms dangerous, and even shut down internet access in the country,[94] although, as noted by Gerbaudo, this did not have the desired effect.[95] Khamis and Vaughn argue that online tools 'tilted the balance' in favour of the 'freedom-fighters and political activists', particularly in terms of dissemination of news and information, but stress that they were nothing more than 'powerful tools and effective catalysts'.[96] In a similar vein, Eltantawy and Wiest argue that they played a 'significant role',[97] whereas Lim argues that they expanded the 'sphere of participation'.[98] Faris, for his part, points to the ability to create 'informational cascades' that may alter individuals' behaviour and risk-assessment in authoritarian regimes.[99] Similarly, Tufekci and Wilson have found a positive connection between social media use and participation in the first day of protests.[100] Wilson and Dunn found that Twitter was used successfully to gain international attention, and that a limited number of 'power users' in particular – influential activists online – managed to attract international notice and support.[101] This last finding points to a central concern for all those cited above: how to reconcile the apparent importance of online platforms with low usage figures. The distinction between access and usage is crucial: while Internet World Stats put the number of people with internet *access* at approximately 50 per cent in 2013,[102] the International Telecommunications Union estimated that, in 2011, 25 per cent of the Egyptian population made *use* of the internet.[103] A 2012 survey conducted by Pew found that about 37 per cent of the population in Egypt made use of the internet,[104] whereas a 2013 survey of the greater Cairo area found that 69 per cent *never* read news websites, and 77 per cent *never* read 'blogs and other websites'.[105] The number of people reading news websites and 'blogs and other websites' was markedly higher among those identified in the survey as the 'rich third', and among those with university level education or higher. Such figures do not contradict the importance of online platforms, but they are an important part of the context of the revolution, as well as of the campaign studied here. Moreover, usage is a factor to account for in any analysis, and at the heart of the central questions raised in this study: can we *measure* the impact of online activism, and, of course, *how* can online activism have an impact.

Then there is the matter of change, or whether or not a revolution actually took place. In a January 2012 press release from Human Rights Watch, its Middle East director, Sarah Leah Whitson, pointed out that 'changing leadership without changing laws will not ensure freedom'.[106] Following the 2011 uprising, the judicial tools used to keep the population in check remained in place, as did the laws of the Mubarak era. Moreover, the four regimes that have since followed – that is, the SCAF, the presidency of Muhammad Mursi, the transitional regime of President ʿAdli Mansur and the presidency of ʿAbd al-Fattah al-Sisi – have all made good use of these tools, albeit to varying degrees. However, this is not to say that no change has taken place. The old constitution was suspended after the revolution, and has been replaced twice. The media scene was opened up, as was the political arena, and a range of new parties were formed. Indeed, the Muslim Brotherhood won every election until the summer of 2013 – quite a contrast from being banned during the Mubarak years. Perhaps most importantly, countless new activist groups and initiatives have been formed, although many of those involved have paid a high price for their engagement.

Following President Mubarak's resignation, the Supreme Council of the Armed Forces (SCAF) took power. They disbanded the Parliament, suspended the constitution and promised a swift transition to civilian rule. This transition, however, lasted until 30 June 2012, when Mursi was sworn in as president. Moreover, the much-hated state of emergency, the removal of which was a key demand of the protesters, was kept in place until 31 May 2012. In general, this period was, predictably, characterised by chaos and a messy attempt at a democratic transition, but also by extreme government repression, in many aspects worse than it had been during the Mubarak years. For one thing, the SCAF continued the practice of trying civilians in military courts, to a far greater extent than the previous regime had: in 2011, more civilians faced such trials than during Mubarak's 30-year rule.[107] Moreover, they continued Mubarak's policy of seeking tight control over civil society, including trade unions and NGOs. Strikes and demonstrations that 'obstruct public works' were criminalised through Law 34,[108] and on 29 December 2011, 'security forces raided the offices of 17 domestic and international civil society groups, confiscating equipment and temporarily detaining some staff'.[109] The raid was justified by reference to the abovementioned Law 84 of 2002. While freedom of the press visibly improved following the ousting of Mubarak, in terms of new independent TV stations and newspapers, journalists continued to be harassed and restrictive laws on defamation were kept in place.[110] Sexual harassment and sexual violence were employed by the regime against protesters, as was torture.[111]

Elections were held for the two chambers of Parliament in the winter of 2011/12. Islamists, with a particular strong showing from the Muslim Brotherhood, won sweeping victories in both.[112] In May and June, presidential elections took place, with MB candidate Muhammad Mursi achieving 51.7 per cent in the second round, beating former Mubarak-era prime minister Ahmad Shafiq. However, the day before the elections, on 15 June the military dissolved the lower house of Parliament on the basis of a ruling from the Supreme Constitutional Court, and granted itself sweeping powers, including legislative powers.[113] Nevertheless, the first civilian president in Egyptian history was sworn in two weeks later. However, the coercive tactics described above, although employed to a lesser extent, also marred Mursi's one year in power. The practice of military trials for civilians continued, although to a much lesser extent than was the practice of the SCAF.[114] A new constitution, approved in a referendum in December 2012, made possible the continued use of such trials. This constitution, and not least the process leading up to its adoption, was in itself extremely controversial. In August of 2012, Mursi assumed the legislative authority previously bestowed by the SCAF upon themselves. Fearful of judicial interference in the political process, he granted himself sweeping powers through a presidential decree on 22 November, which included giving the president's decrees and laws immunity from judicial oversight.[115] Moreover, in order to ensure that the referendum on the controversial constitution went through, the military was granted the right to arrest civilians and refer them to military trial until the result of the vote was announced.[116] Taken together, these measures augment the legal grounds for unrestricted authority on the part of the presidency, in an even more straightforward manner than was seen during the Mubarak era. That is not to say that they were used in the same manner, but they certainly followed the pattern of the two previous regimes.

Not surprisingly, these moves sparked massive protests, and were eventually retracted on 8 December. Legislative powers were transferred to the upper house of Parliament until a new lower house was elected, but this did not stifle the demonstrations. At the height of the protests against the presidential decree, clashes broke out outside the Presidential Palace between anti-government protesters and the police, who were later joined by pro-government protesters; at least ten people were killed and more than 700 injured.[117] In general, the police responded harshly to most protests during the autumn of 2012 and the spring of 2013, and there were several clashes between pro- and anti-government demonstrators. Finally, the massive demonstrations of November and December 2012 saw an unprecedented rise in the number of sexual assaults and rapes of female protesters, as will be discussed further below.

Reporters Without Borders (RSF) claims that the Mursi administration also sought control over the media in ways similar to those employed by Mubarak. These included installing their own preferred candidates in key positions in state media, and legal complaints filed against journalists for 'insulting the President'.[118] Furthermore, the Mursi administration sought to crack down on criticism online, although, again, not to the same extent as its predecessors. During the rule of the SCAF, 'bloggers and netizens critical of the army' were 'harassed, threatened, and sometimes arrested'.[119] During Mursi's reign (that is, the period most relevant to this study), Freedom House characterised the internet in Egypt as 'partly free', and reported a number of disturbing incidents. These included the arrest of an 'unprecedented number' of liberal bloggers and online activists, on charges of insulting the president or of blasphemy. Moreover, administrators of anti-government and anti-Muslim Brotherhood sites were victims of extralegal killings and abductions, websites were blocked by court orders, and mobile services and internet services were repeatedly throttled in areas of protest.[120] As for the NGOs, Mursi did launch an initiative to replace the much-hated Law 84 with a new one, although this was never completed. Moreover, Human Rights Watch argues that the proposed law would have 'allow[ed] the Government and its security agencies to arbitrarily restrict the funding and operation of independent groups'.[121] The widespread judicial reform that was so badly needed never took place during the reign of Muhammad Mursi, and neither did any meaningful reform of the more practical means of oppression, that is, the police, the army and the security services. However, one can argue that Mursi would not have been able to do so even if he had wanted to, as he clearly did not control the army.

The military seized power in a coup on 3 July 2013,[122] following massive demonstrations against the president organised by a group called Tamarrud (Rebellion). While clearly reflecting widespread frustration with the president, the campaign has also been accused of nurturing very close ties to the army.[123] Following the military coup, a formally civilian government was put in place with former judge and head of the supreme constitutional court 'Adli Mansur as president and Hazim al-Biblawi of the Egyptian Social Democratic Party as prime minister. The coup was followed by the swift closure of several TV stations and newspapers presumably critical of the move and the reintroduction of the state of emergency. Supporters of the ousted president organised sit-ins at two locations in Cairo, which were brutally broken up in August, with more than 700 people killed in one single day.[124] Since then, al-Sisi has been elected president, and it is quite clear that Egypt will not become a democracy anytime soon. This development, however, lies beyond the scope of this study.

After a decade of activism online and offline, the 2011 revolution brought with it a substantial expansion of the political space in Egypt. Many new groups, initiatives and parties were formed, and political opinions were expressed publicly in an unprecedented manner. This often happened at great personal cost to those involved, however, and always under the threat of potential persecution, which was rather arbitrarily enforced. The laws and regulations of the Mubarak era remained in place, as did the unreformed institutions of regime power. While people's willingness to express their views clearly increased, the ability and the willingness of the state to hinder them did not decrease in equal measure. In hindsight, it is tempting to argue that no revolution actually took place, but this question is outside the scope of this investigation. Rather, I will argue that the possibilities for and limits on activism during the Mubarak era remained relevant after the 2011 revolt. More importantly, the experience gained in that era formed the backdrop for activism after 2011, and for those involved in the campaigns studied here. Activists had come to prefer loose organisational structures, as the limitations on formal organisation were profound. The use of online platforms was an integral part of the work, and any potential activist with internet access knew to go online in order to take part. The issue of sexual harassment and sexual violence had been raised by activists in the mid-2000s, and following the revolution, they would once again bring it to the attention of the Egyptian public.

The Issue: Sexual Harassment and Sexual Violence in Egypt

The issue of sexual harassment and sexual violence in Egypt has made international headlines over the past few years, following horrific and extremely violent attacks on female protesters, particularly in Tahrir Square and the surrounding area. As we have seen, the issue is far from new in Egypt, and it involves two closely related subjects. The organisations studied here are concerned both with the sexual harassment that all Egyptian women face on a daily basis – on public transportation, in the streets, in the workplace, at home, and so on – and with the apparently organised attacks on female protesters in demonstrations. The latter would not be possible without widespread acceptance, however, as they usually took place in the midst of large crowds. As was pointed out by all the groups studied: if the attacks are indeed organised, 'ordinary' people also take part, or at least do not intervene. This acceptance, in turn, is manifested in the harassment that all Egyptian women face on a regular basis. Accordingly, the groups involved use two terms when describing the phenomena they fight: *taḥarrush ginsī*, meaning sexual harassment, and *iʿtidāʾ ginsī*, meaning sexual assault or violence. While the groups may differ slightly in their strategies and views on how to combat the problems, they all agree that a change in the culture of acceptance is needed in order to eradicate both sexual harassment and sexual violence. In the following, I discuss first the issue of sexual harassment, then that of sexual violence, and then show how they are connected.

Sexual Harassment

A common sentiment expressed by some of the groups studied, and in popular culture as well, is that Egypt used to be a more progressive and equal society, and that sexual harassment has become a problem more recently, along with the rise of Islamism. Old black-and-white pictures of women in short skirts or at the beach are often published in social media, as a contrast to the contemporary situation. In an op-ed in the *New York Times*, the Egyptian writer Alaa al-Aswany points to the seemingly paradoxical situation of increased harassment in a more modest society: 'Why is it that men did not harass Egyptian women when they wore short skirts but that sexual harassment has increased against women in head scarves?'[125] Yet, while such references are common online, the groups studied first and foremost engaged with the current situation, and often refer to the mid-2000s as the beginning of the ongoing struggle.

As we have seen, the now infamous downtown sexual harassment during ʿId al-Fitr in 2006 brought the issue to the attention of the Egyptian public. The first incidents took place on the evening of 24 October 2006, and were described as follows by renowned blogger Sandmonkey:

> Mobs of males gathered trying to get in [to a cinema], but when the show was sold out, they decided they will destroy the box office. After accomplishing that, they went on what can only be described as a sexual frenxy [*sic*]: They ran around grabbing any and every girl in sight, whether a niqabi, a Hijabi or uncover[e]d. Whether egyptian or foreigner. Even pregnant ones. They grabbed them, molested them, tried to rip their cloth[e]s off and rape them, all in front of the police, who didn't do shit. The good people of downtown tried their best to protect the girls. Shop owners would let the girls in and lock the doors, while the mobs tried to break in. Taxi drivers put the girls in the cars while the mobs were trying to break the glass and grab the girls out. It was a disgusting pandemonium of sexual assaults that lasted for 5 hours from 7:30 PM to 12:30 am, and it turns my stomach just to think about it.[126]

The incident was first reported by blogger Malek Mustafa in a post entitled 'The Sexual Rabies of Downtown'.[127] Videos of what took place were published on YouTube, and one can clearly see how an ever-growing group of men chase women down the street.[128] Yet, as we have seen, the scandal did not break publicly until activist and blogger Nawara Negm raised the issue while participating in a popular evening talk show. The events also sparked a response by activists, and a demonstration against sexual harassment was held in front of the journalists' syndicate on 9 November. According to the abovementioned blogger Sandmonkey, the demonstration was initiated on the blog Nermeena,[129] following a debate on the comments field of a post asking what should be done about the issue. This same blogger earlier published testimonies of harassment collected by the Egyptian Center for Women's Rights (ECWR). In December of the same year, the American University in Cairo organised a debate on the topic, and among the speakers was a representative of ECWR, later engaged in the establishment of HarassMap.[130] The ECWR had started a campaign against harassment in October 2005, called 'Making Our Streets Safer [. . .] For Everyone', in response to 'many complaints' from women.[131] In their own words, the group was the first organisation to raise the issue in Egypt,[132] and a central focus was to create awareness of the problem. In order to do so, the group stressed the need to work together with other NGOs concerned with the issue, such as the El-Nadeem Center for Rehabilitation of Victims of Violence and Egyptian Initiative for Personal Rights (EIPR), as well as with the media.

In many ways, this focus is revealing of how the issue was treated in Egypt at the time: it was mostly not spoken of. In the interviews with the representatives of the groups studied, this was one of their main concerns. It was, and still is, seen as shameful to 'admit' to having been harassed:

> Usually, women are discouraged from filing complaints with the police by both people in the street and police officers. Women often find themselves in a weak position when they try to act against their harassers since they do not receive any moral support from the people around them. Some even have to go against their families to file complaints against sexual harassers.[133]

Accordingly, if no one was speaking of the issue, it certainly would not be solved. Thus, a key component of the campaigners work is to raise the issue in public, and to combat prejudice and misconceptions surrounding the problem. One such view that the groups seek to combat is that the problem in reality is a question of modesty, a position frequently promoted by Islamist politicians. In 2008, campaigns were initiated by Salafis and parts of the Muslim Brotherhood stressing the importance of 'proper attire' to avoid harassment,[134] including the infamous 'veil your lollipop' campaign circulated on email.[135]

However, a report released in 2008 by ECWR as part of the abovementioned campaign proved this position wrong. The study found that 83 per cent of Egyptian women and 98 per cent of foreign women had experienced sexual harassment, that harassment was not class-based and that the attire of women did not necessarily make any difference.[136] These findings were confirmed in a 2013 UN Women study which found that 99.3 per cent of women in Egypt were subjected to harassment, and that all women were targeted, regardless of attire.[137] A 2013 Thomson Reuters Foundation poll found that Egypt was ranked as the worst Arab state for women, among other things due to the extreme levels of sexual harassment.[138] The problem was – and still is – an all-encompassing feature of Egyptian society, which affects *all* women. Accordingly, awareness and education are important topics for activists working on the issue. HarassMap, launched in December 2010, specifically aimed to document harassment and raise awareness, and to provide help and assistance. The state, however, failed to provide any response. At best, with sexual harassment, it preferred to downplay the problem. At worst, with sexual violence, it was a perpetrator causing the problem to begin with. The two were closely connected, and the latter could not have taken place without the acceptance of the former – an acceptance built on the abovementioned pervasive climate of silence, shame and moralism.

Sexual Violence

The World Health Organization (WHO) defines sexual violence as follows:

> [A]ny sexual act, attempt to obtain a sexual act, unwanted sexual comments or advances, or acts to traffic, or otherwise directed, against a person's sexuality using coercion, by any person regardless of their relationship to the victim, in any setting, including but not limited to home and work.[139]

The WHO further makes it clear that sexual violence may be used during conflicts, and that it may be used to punish women who for some reason are perceived to deserve it, for instance by wearing 'indecent' clothing,[140] sentiments that are echoed in Egyptian society. In Egypt, sexual violence against female activists was introduced by the state, as a weapon to hinder and subdue political participation. While the 25 May 2005 attack on female protesters in Cairo is often referred to as the beginning of the problem in its current form, Kassem shows that the roots go back to the government's fight against Islamists in the 1980s: 'In an unprecedented move beginning in late 1986, roundups of female family members [of those wanted by the regime] became common'.[141] This provoked a violent response from male Islamists, as it was seen as degrading the women and an attack on their honour.[142] Kassem also reports attacks on women during the 2000 legislative elections, in which plainclothes state security 'pulled women to the ground by their hair' at a polling station.[143] Similarly, in a 2005 article, Osama claims that the events of 25 May did not represent a new departure on the part of the security services: 'I have argued that targeting women violently is a common tool in the hands of the security forces in Egypt'.[144] This violence could take the form either of police and/or hired thugs assaulting female protesters, or of harassment, abuse or rape of female detainees or inmates.[145] An article by *MadaMasr* also refers to routine use of sexual violence and assault against detainees.[146] The question, then, is why the regime chose to target women in this manner.

According to Amar, the waves of protest in the early 2000s posed a problem for the regime. In order to delegitimise and vilify the protesters, hired thugs were inserted into their midst, wreaking havoc and shouting extremist slogans. This made it possible for the regime to portray the demonstrators as terrorists, villains or worse. However, when respectable middle-class women also took part, this portrayal became less convincing, and the government changed its tactics:

> The state responded by shifting its aims from using demonized masculinity in order to delegitimize political opposition to using state-imposed sexual aggression in order to undermine class respectability. Women who protested were sexualized and had their respectability wiped out: not just by innuendo and accusation, but literally, by sexually assaulting them in public and by arresting them as prostitutes, registering them in court records and press accounts as sex criminals and then raping and sexually torturing them in jail [...] The aim was to render impossible the figure of the respectable, pious woman who is a legitimate protester against the police rather than a victim protected or rescued by the police.[147]

Again, this illustrates the interconnectedness of the activism of the 2000s and the issue at hand: sexual violence was employed by the state as a weapon to fight the very activism on which the current movements are based. Clearly, the fight against sexual violence is, in a very literal sense, a fight for participation.

As is evident, the events of 25 May 2005 were part of a wider pattern of regime violence. However, they were the most public occurrence of this practice up to that time[148] and, as such, it is not surprising that great importance is ascribed to this particular attack. The demonstration was attacked by both police and hired thugs, the *balṭagiyya*, and women in particular were targeted and both beaten and abused. The police did nothing to prevent this:

> Witnesses said that groups of men arrived in buses and were allowed, with the police standing by, to attack and beat the protesters. Witnesses said that in some instances the police kept protesters trapped and unable to flee while the men from the buses beat them.[149]

Although the ruling National Democratic Party condemned the attack, as of February 2013, no one had been held responsible.[150] However, the Egyptian Initiative for Personal Rights, an independent rights organisation founded in 2002, left no doubt as to who was responsible, arguing that this could not have happened without the knowledge, or even under the direction, of then-minister of interior Habib al-ʿAdli.[151] The attack prompted other reactions as well, as the El-Nadeem Center, together with 'a few other bold groups', began filing lawsuits against police and 'other individuals for having committed [. . .] sexual harassment'.[152]

Yet, the state was not about to accept any form of responsibility, and the abovementioned interior minister claimed that there was no such thing as sexual harassment[153] – that is, until they realised that this could be used to their own advantage. According to Amar, several NGOs failed to lay the blame on the security establishment and pointed instead to vilified young men. The state saw their chance, and promptly moved to arrest hundreds of young men, serving as the protector once again. In Amar's view:

> [t]he sexual harassment controversy that had begun as a thorough critique of repressive policing and the torture of dissident women and youth had been appropriated by the security state and NGO establishment as justification for extending police brutality, mass arrests, social cleansing of the city and the necessity of the emergency decree.[154]

This is important to bear in mind when assessing the work of groups currently concerned with the issue: they have no incentive to trust the state, and they have every reason to be sceptical of NGOs close to the state. Moreover, it illustrates the importance of the groups' efforts to discuss and frame the issue in their own terms, in opposition to the narrative presented by the state.

Targeted attacks on female protesters again came to the fore following the 2011 revolution. The groups often portray the 18 days of the revolution itself as a model of how things should be: men and women protested together without instances of sexual harassment. However, on the last night of the protests, as Husni Mubarak stepped down, CBS reporter Lara Logan was attacked by several men in the middle of Tahrir Square. This was not the first attack on reporters during the uprising, but it was the first sexual assault. A mob of more than two hundred people attacked her in an extremely brutal manner, and it lasted more than 25 minutes before soldiers were able to get her out.[155]

Following the revolution, the SCAF soon took an implacable stance towards protesters, violently dispersing sit-ins and demonstrations, and detaining and arresting thousands of activists. They also targeted female activists specifically. In March 2011, the SCAF subjected female detainees to so-called 'virginity tests', explicitly mentioned by the WHO as acts of sexual violence.[156] During the summer of 2011, several female activists were beaten by police and soldiers during clashes, but Nazra for Feminist Studies, one of the groups studied here, points out that women were not targeted explicitly.[157] While concerned with a variety of issues, Nazra have been particularly important in terms of documenting harassment and violence, and are frequently referred to by domestic and international media.[158] In their report, however, they argue that this changed in the autumn of that year. During the now infamous 'Muhammad Mahmud clashes' of November 2011, the testimonies collected tell of organised harassment and assault on female protesters carried out by hired thugs and the Central Security Forces (CSF). Soldiers of the Egyptian Army are also implicated, and it is said to have been organised to the extent that code words were used by senior officers signalling that female detainees should be harassed and assaulted.[159] On 17 December 2011, a woman was attacked by the CSF during the brutal dispersal of a sit-in at Tahrir; her *ʿabbāya* was pulled up so that her blue bra became visible as CSF personnel beat her with sticks and stamped on her chest. The incident was caught on camera and sparked outrage in Egypt, which resulted in what 'observers' deemed 'the largest demonstration of women in Egypt in decades'.[160] Then, as Egypt celebrated the first anniversary of the revolution on 25 January 2012, a testimony published by Nazra and others tells of an attack similar to those that, unfortunately, would become all too common later that year: female protesters were separated from their friends, encircled by men, and harassed until they managed to escape.[161]

The Campaign Studied: Fighting Harassment in the New Egypt

On 2 June 2012, former president Husni Mubarak received his sentence on charges of killing unarmed protesters. Even though he was sentenced to life in prison, the verdict was seen as too soft, and as one that could soon be overturned. Many others facing similar charges were acquitted. Thus, in the evening, thousands of demonstrators congregated in Tahrir Square to protest against the verdict.[162] Several female protesters were attacked in a similar manner as on 25 January, with dozens of men isolating, encircling and then assaulting them. One protester was assaulted and raped over a prolonged period of time.[163] One of the activists attacked wrote publicly about what had happened, and, together with others, initiated a protest on 8 June against targeted attacks on female protesters.[164] A friend of this activist also initiated the first group to actively fight these kinds of attacks during protests.[165] Some weeks later, activists involved in these initiatives started one of the groups studied here, Imprint, to combat sexual harassment and other problems in Egyptian society.[166] Yet, the 8 June demonstration was also attacked. In the abovementioned report, the groups leave no doubt as to why this happened: 'The attacks on women was [*sic*] calculated and organized so as to scare women away from the public sphere, to punish women for their participation.'[167] In a testimony published by Nazra and others discussing the reasons for the protest, it is said that the attacks on female protesters started in July 2011.[168] This is, however, not confirmed in other reports. Nevertheless, by the summer of 2012, it seems clear that female protesters risked being attacked and assaulted when protesting in Tahrir.

In August 2012, the newly formed Imprint movement launched patrols on Cairo's metro, with the aim of keeping men out of the cars reserved for women. The campaign was run in cooperation with the Metro Company, a private security firm, as well as the police – a somewhat controversial collaboration in the view of other activists. The campaign was timed to coincide with the celebration of ʿId al-Fitr.[169] As in 2006, downtown Cairo continued to be unsafe during public holidays, and *Egypt Independent* reported on a 'wave' of sexual harassment.[170] Before the ʿId al-Adha celebrations in October, the group I Saw Harassment (ISH) was formed, launching a campaign to monitor and intervene in situations in downtown Cairo that gained wide media attention. Similarly, the Imprint movement, together with a newly formed initiative called Anti-Harassment, launched a campaign to keep the Talaʿat Harb square in downtown Cairo a harassment-free zone. Some 735 cases of sexual harassment were reported to the police during the holidays, prompting the president to acknowledge the problem and the need to fight it.[171]

In late November and early December 2012, Egypt witnessed several violent protests against the aforementioned emergency decree issued by President Mursi. Again, female protesters were targeted. While groups documenting the attacks do not state how many took place, they provide several testimonies telling of attacks that followed the same pattern as before, and with the same extreme level of violence.[172] An article in the *Daily Mail* cites activist sources saying that 20 attacks took place over ten days leading up to 1 December.[173] The article also cites an activist claiming that the Muslim Brotherhood, in power at the time, paid thugs to carry out the attacks. An episode of UK Channel 4's *Unreported World*, aired on 7 December 2012, seeks to clarify this question. The programme includes an anonymised interview with a man claiming to have been paid to participate in the assaults on female protesters, but he does not disclose the source of the money.[174] During the interviews conducted in Cairo, all representatives of the groups expressed the view that the attacks were organised, but they did not identify who was behind them. In any case, the situation was becoming unbearable, and something needed to be done. Thus, in late November 2012, two of the groups studied here – OpAntiSH and Tahrir Bodyguard – were formed, with the aim of safeguarding female protesters and combating the attacks. Both groups were launched online, but with several clear differences. Whereas the former was organised by well-connected and experienced activists, the latter was the spontaneous result of one person's activity on Twitter. The issue also started to receive international media attention but, according to Nazra, it was not until the second anniversary of the 2011 revolution that the problem received broad attention in the Egyptian public.[175]

In the days leading up to the second anniversary of the revolution, the newly formed OpAntiSH organised 'two days of blogging and tweeting for the sake of Dignity', an online event discussing the issue of harassment on Twitter using the hashtags #EndSH and #مصر_من_غير_تحرش (Egypt Without Harassment). A number of groups were listed as participants, including Nazra, HarassMap, ISH and Anti-Harassment,[176] but participation was quite limited.[177] During the protests of 25 January 2013, violence against female protestors would reach unprecedented levels. OpAntiSH documented 19 attacks and assaults on female protesters, many of which included rape, and volunteers from the group ISH documented another five cases.[178] Again, the attacks followed the same pattern, as pointed out by Amnesty International:

> A clear pattern of attacks emerged through accounts given by survivors as well as activists, lawyers and doctors involved in rescue operations and follow-up support. The targeted women were either approached alone or separated from their friends and colleagues by a group of men, mostly in their twenties or thirties, which gradually grew in number. They were encircled by the mob and then countless hands groped their bodies, including their breasts, genitals and buttocks; pulled their hair; tugged their bodies in different directions; and attempted, in some cases successfully, to remove their clothes. The women were violently dragged while surrounded by the mob to different locations. Such attacks lasted from a few minutes to over an hour, until the women were rescued or the perpetrators abandoned them.[179]

The level of violence increased, and the use of various weapons was a dominant feature: 'at least two women were cut with blades, including on or near their genitals. Other women were beaten and/or threatened with knives, blades and other weapons'.[180] This time, the issue was widely covered in Egyptian media, and it sparked outrage. 'Hundreds' took part in a demonstration organised by OpAntiSH, Nazra and others, entitled 'The Street Is Ours – No to Harassment and Sexual Assault'.[181] Clearly, the regime could not remain silent, but the response given was far from what the groups involved expected. On 11 February the upper house of Parliament discussed the issue. A representative of the ruling Muslim Brotherhood asked how women could expect to be protected when they stood among men,[182] whereupon a Salafi lawmaker argued that women themselves were '100% responsible'.[183] Not surprisingly, the controversial statements sparked outrage, and were condemned in a worldwide demonstration the following day.[184]

On 15 March HarassMap, in cooperation with OpAntiSH and others, launched a new online event, this time aiming to refute excuses for harassment. Using the hashtag #بيتحرش_ليه (Why does he harass), it generated 764 tweets between 15 and 19 March, according to Topsy. As we have seen, 15 March was also the day on which Tahrir Bodyguard and OpAntiSH took part on *al-Barnamig*. During the show, mentions of @opantish increased sixfold.[185]

Violent confrontations between protesters and police continued throughout the spring of 2013, but mass attacks on female protesters like those seen on 25 January did not take place again until the June 30 demonstrations that led to the ousting of the elected president. According to a joint statement by Nazra, HarassMap and many other organisations, a total of 101 assaults took place between 28 June and 3 July 2013, in the context of these demonstrations.[186] Human Rights Watch refers to 91 cases, but relies on the same groups working on the ground. Moreover, they point to the same level of violence in the attacks as seen before, including the use of weapons.[187] Following the military coup, several protests were held in support of the ousted president. These were attacked by the police, but it is unclear whether female protesters were targeted specifically, and the groups studied here did not take part. Since then, mass opposition protests have gradually disappeared. However, when state-sanctioned celebrations were held in Tahrir in the beginning of June 2014 on the occasion of the election of President al-Sisi, female participants were attacked once again. On 8 June, nine cases of assault were recorded.[188] This time, the authorities did provide a response. Seven persons were arrested and given harsh sentences,[189] and President al-Sisi also visited in hospital one of the women who were attacked.[190] A demonstration against the attacks was held in Tahrir, guarded by security forces.[191] Just weeks earlier, the outgoing administration of President ʿAdli Mansur introduced new laws on sexual harassment, although these were seen as inadequate by activists.[192]

In all, more than 500 attacks on female protesters, including assault and in some cases rape, were documented between February 2011 and January 2014.[193] While the sheer scale and severity of these attacks played an important part in bringing the issue to the attention of the Egyptian public, the work of the groups studied here played a crucial part as well, as I will demonstrate in what follows. And even when the attacks on female protesters demanded much attention, the groups continued to work against sexual harassment through online and offline campaigns, media appearances, outreach programmes, documentation and, not least, organisation building. Although some of the groups are older and more established, most were created in the opening up of organisational life that followed Mubarak's resignation. Yet the repressive laws regulating civil society were still in place, and the groups' access to resources often quite limited. Moreover, many of the participants had previous experience with activism, and many knew each other from other groups and initiatives. This might help to explain their ability to respond rapidly in November 2012, when the situation was critical. The groups became part of an established activist scene, of which online work was an integral part. Before I present the analysis of this online work, a brief presentation of the groups included is provided.

The Groups Included in the Case

The groups included in the material are as follows:[194]

نظرة للدراسات النسوية (Nazra for Feminist Studies)

Nazra was founded in December 2007, but was not able to begin working as it does today before 2010. Its aim is to 'build an Egyptian feminist movement, believing that feminism and gender are political and social issues affecting freedom and development in all societies. Nazra aims to mainstream these values in both public and private spheres.'[195] The group is quite professional in its work, and while it is less active online than many others, it is crucial in terms of documenting harassment and violence, and is frequently cited by both domestic and international media, as well as by international rights groups. In addition, the group is central in providing help to those who have been harassed and/or assaulted, and is part of OpAntiSH.

حركة بصمة (Imprint movement)

The group states online that it was founded on 1 June 2012, as a voluntary social group that aims to change 'all that distorts the society of ignorance and backwardness and to support and help develop all that serve society in every field possible'.[196] While concerned with several issues, a clear majority of its activities are related to the fight against sexual harassment, including campaigns on the metro and in downtown Cairo during holidays. The group explicitly states that it will cooperate with various parties, including the police. The group is no longer listed as a part of OpAntiSH on the latter's website, but was identified as such on various other occasions.

خريطة التحرش الجنسي (HarassMap)

The website, which is the foundation of HarassMap's work, was officially launched on 16 December 2010, to coincide with the release of the movie *678*, which raises the issue of sexual harassment. The idea behind the website is to document the extent of sexual harassment by allowing women to report incidents anonymously using various platforms. The group also provides help to those affected, conducts research and holds online events. They are a part of OpAntiSH and work actively together with other groups and initiatives concerned with the issue. The group sees its work as a continuation of the initiative of the ECWR launched in 2005, and one goal is to regain momentum for the cause, arguing for the need to take action on the ground and to fight social acceptance, rather than 'waiting for the government to act'.[197] The group seems to have several core members with extensive experience, and is very active on several platforms online.

قوة ضد التحرش/الإعتداء الجنسي الجماعي (Op Anti-Sexual Harassment/ Assault) (OpAntiSH)

The group was founded in late November 2012 in response to the many attacks on female protesters in and around Tahrir Square. According to one of the founders, it was very much an ad hoc initiative: only 48 hours passed between the birth of the idea and the group's presence on the ground in Tahrir.[198] The initiative seems to have been launched online on 28 November, and on 30 November the group started its Twitter account and held its first patrols in Tahrir. However, the number given as one of the hotlines to which people could report incidents was tweeted by the media collective Mosireen on 27 November, with a text stating that a trustworthy team would come to help.[199] An article in *Egypt Independent* holds that Mosireen was central in founding the group.[200] In either case, what started as a Facebook event soon evolved into a group, consisting of both independent activists and other groups and initiatives, such as HarassMap, Nazra and EIPR. The group clearly had many experienced members and was highly active online.

حماية التحرير (Tahrir Bodyguard)

The organisation was founded in late November 2012 in response to attacks on female protesters in demonstrations. The idea was first raised on Twitter by one activist, and the Twitter profile of the group itself seems to have been created on 27 November. In the beginning, the group worked solely online, giving advice to female protesters, but soon started to work on the ground in Tahrir as well. The group is not part of OpAntiSH. On 31 July 2013, the group announced the formation of another group, called Dignity Without Borders (DWB), also dedicated to combating sexual harassment, but with a broader focus than Tahrir Bodyguard (TBG).

شفت تحرش (I Saw Harassment)

The group was founded in October 2012, to begin its work for the ʿId al-Adha celebrations beginning on 25 October. The initiative sprung out of other initiatives and an NGO named Act. This NGO is among seven groups listed as 'signatories' to the mission statement on the group's old website, which has since been replaced with a new website. The group has organised patrols in downtown Cairo during holidays, often taking journalists with them. In general, gaining media coverage of their work and the issue seems to have been a priority. In addition, the group took part in various demonstrations, held meetings, provided legal assistance, held meetings for new volunteers and was an integral part of OpAntiSH.

The Groups' Work Online and Offline

Before moving on to analysis of the online work of the groups studied, it is important to get an overview of the extent of this work; that is, which platforms were used, how active the groups were, how many followers they gained, and so on. To begin with their online presence, the groups made use of online platforms as shown in Table 4.1.

Clearly, all the groups within the study sought to maintain a broad presence on social media, and each had a Twitter account, a Facebook page and a YouTube channel.[201] Nazra also had an account on Flickr, but this was seldom used. Three of the groups also had their own websites. Whereas those of Nazra and ISH were quite similar, in that they both served to gather information from the groups in one place, the site of HarassMap stands out: for this group, the site is the foundation of their work. It is designed to enable people to report harassment, to document and map harassment and to provide help to those who have experienced harassment. The site is based on FrontlineSMS and Ushahidi. FrontlineSMS is software, first developed in 2005, which enables 'instantaneous two-way communication to any mobile handset',[202] is open source and free to download. HarassMap uses this with the Ushahidi platform, a tool which visualises information through mapping.[203] The two were combined for the new website, free of charge, by NiJeL, an organisation that helps other organisations to develop tools and systems to 'better interact with their data', through visualisations and mapping.[204] The result is a map in which reports of harassment are marked with a red dot, which varies in size according to the number of reports from that area. When one clicks on the dot, accounts of the reported harassment are provided, along with relevant categories, such as 'cat calls', 'comments' and 'touching'. Incidents can be reported anonymously through the website, by email, through social media or by sending a text to a four-digit number. Those who send a text will receive one in return, providing information on legal assistance, counselling and self-defence classes.

Turning to social media, Table 4.2 clearly shows that, while there were similarities between the groups in relation to their selection of online platforms, there were marked differences in the popularity they achieved in terms of followers, likes and subscribers.[205]

On Twitter, two groups clearly stand out, namely HarassMap and OpAntiSH. These were among the most experienced and professional

Table 4.1 Egyptian Platform Selection

Group	Twitter	Facebook	Website	YouTube	Other
Nazra	@NazraEgypt	Nazra	nazra.org	nazraegypt	Flickr (nazraegypt)
Imprint	@Imprint_Mov	Imprint movement	–	Imprint movement	Google+ (not public)[206]
HarassMap	@harassmap	HarassMapEgypt	harassmap.org	HarassMap Egypt	
OpAntiSH	@OpAntiSH	opantish	–	OpAntiSH	
TBG	@TahrirBodyguard[207]	Tahrir.Bodyguards		Tahrir Bodyguard	
I Saw Harassment	@ShoftTa7rosh	Shoft.Ta7rosh	isawharassment.org[208]	Yes[209]	

Table 4.2 Followers on Social Media, Egypt

Group	Twitter followers	Facebook likes[210]	YouTube views/ subscribers	Followers, other platforms
Nazra	7,774	5,071	11,657/121	Not available
Imprint	353	15,282	14,517/81	
HarassMap	17,918	19,474	60,585/153	
OpAntiSH	20,330	34,950	1.5 million/2,570	
TBG	8,923	6,813	2,034/27	
I Saw Harassment	516	12,401	32,998/173	

groups. However, Nazra, both experienced and professional, did not gain so many followers, even though the content they produced was popular in the sense that it was widely disseminated by other groups. This, in turn, is connected to the way in which they used social media, and their lack of capacity to exploit the possibilities inherent in different platforms. Similarly, there is a vast difference between the number of followers of Imprint and ISH on Twitter and Facebook, which is also due to their capabilities in using the platforms. TBG, a group that was started online, was fairly successful on both platforms, but not on the same level as their more experienced colleagues. On YouTube, OpAntiSH clearly stands out, a result which is due to one particular video, as will be discussed below.

One factor that seems to be important in gaining popularity is the level of activity, as shown in Table 4.3.

Table 4.3 Social Media Activity, Egypt

Group	Tweets	Facebook posts	YouTube videos	Other posts
Nazra	438	185	16	121 (Flickr)
Imprint	345	345	20	
HarassMap	3,953	1,228	2	
OpAntiSH	4,035	203	3	
TBG	3,854	1,618	1	
I Saw Harassment	396	1,173	1	

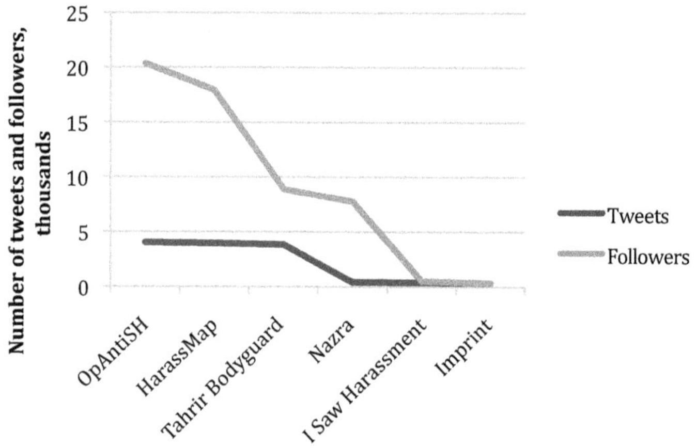

Figure 4.1 Activity and Followers, Twitter, Egypt

The three most popular groups on Twitter are, to say the least, a lot more active than the three least popular groups, as illustrated in Figure 4.1.

Yet, clearly, a high level of activity is, in itself, no guarantee of popularity, although it might seem to be a precondition. The most experienced groups are the most popular both among the top three and the bottom three. However, if we look at Facebook, the connection between activity and popularity is less clear, as shown in Figure 4.2.

Indeed, OpAntiSH is by far the most popular group, but it was the second least active on the platform. Similarly, Imprint was the third least active, but is still the third most popular group. Clearly, there are several factors in play. The two most successful groups offline in terms of volunteers and media attention, HarassMap and OpAntiSH, are also the most successful online. Again, these were also among the most experienced groups. While Nazra also is an experienced and professional group, it is clear from their usage that they did not fully exploit the possibilities inherent in the platforms – gaining followers was perhaps not a priority. While TBG was successful, it could not match the two groups at the top of the profile. As for Imprint and ISH, these groups succeeded on the platform that they seem to have prioritised – Facebook – but not on the other. Thus, experienced groups who prioritise their online work seem to be the

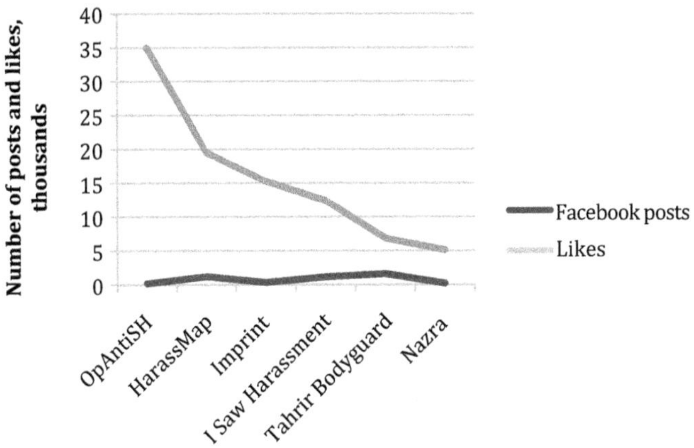

Figure 4.2 Activity and Followers, Facebook, Egypt

most successful, and one factor for success seems to be to maintain a high level of activity.

The coding of the Twitter material from the Egyptian case provided the results shown in Figure 4.3.

The aggregate results reflect a fairly similar level of usage among the groups: the three most frequently employed categories were among the

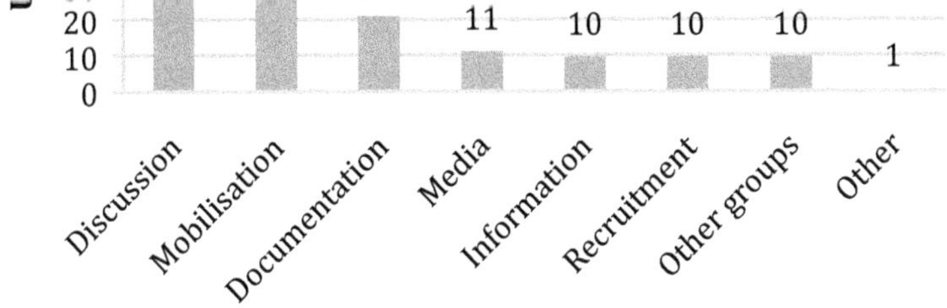

Figure 4.3 Twitter Usage, Egypt

top four categories for five of the groups.[211] However, there were some interesting differences as well, which related to the ways in which the groups worked. TBG spent no fewer than 835 tweets on recruitment, a lot more than any other group. Yet, as the group was started online, and thus had no activist base to begin with, this should not be surprising. Similarly, Nazra, as a relatively professional group focusing on studies and documentation, spent less time mobilising than the others, but more time disseminating information. For their part, ISH spent more time than the others disseminating media attention paid to themselves, as will be discussed further below. For now, the important point is to stress that differences in strategy and background are reflected in the groups' work online, indicating a conscious approach to the use of the platform.

'Discussion' is by far the most frequently employed category, and this is primarily due to three subcategories: 'taking part in a discussion', 'agitation' and 'responding to others'. For one thing, this reflects widespread usage of popular hashtags among most of the groups, with the exceptions being Nazra and Imprint. Still, the groups also spent a lot of time arguing for their cause and discussing various issues, although seldom with people who disagreed. Moreover, they often responded to individual users, which covers no less than 19 per cent of all tweets published. While the groups spent quite some time mobilising for offline events (8 per cent), this category ('mobilisation') primarily reflects mobilisation for and participation in online events (14.5 per cent), as well as encouragement to their volunteers and followers. In addition to live reporting from events and dissemination of pictures and video, 'Documentation' also consists of the gathering and dissemination of testimonies and reports – an important part of the effort to gain acknowledgement of the severity of the problem. While certain groups spent quite some time disseminating media coverage about themselves and on the issue, the 'media' category also covers regular contact between groups and journalists. All groups wrote in both English and Arabic, with TBG perhaps leaning more towards English than the others, and Imprint and ISH towards Arabic. Figure 4.3 shows the aggregate results terms of retweets as opposed to tweets of their own writing.

Figure 4.4 hides an extremely uneven practice among the groups, in which the popular groups (OpAntiSH, HarassMap and TBG) frequently published retweets, and the less popular groups (Imprint, Nazra and

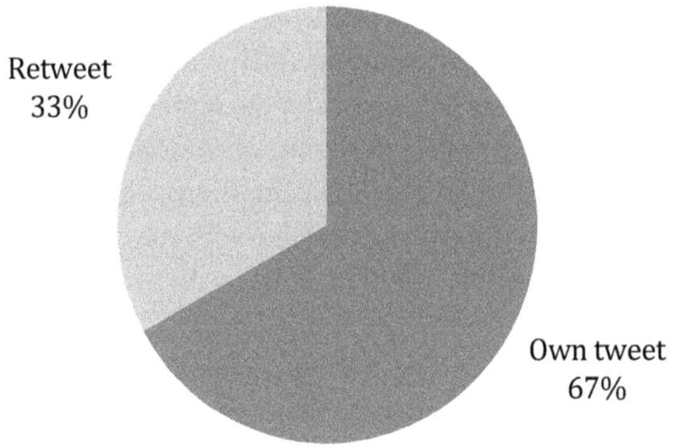

Figure 4.4 Retweets vs. Own Tweets, Egypt

ISH) almost never did so.[212] Seemingly, engagement with followers is closely linked to popularity. In part, this is confirmed if we look at the engagement created by the content published.[213] The exception in this regard would be Nazra, whose tweets were retweeted as frequently as those of OpAntiSH. This should be seen in connection with the widespread dissemination of their reports and documentation by other groups. While popular content was frequently retweeted, it was almost never favourited; OpAntiSH was most popular in this regard with an average of one favourite. On Facebook, OpAntiSH generated the most engagement by far, followed by HarassMap, Imprint, ISH, Nazra and, somewhat surprisingly, TBG. For the most part, this is in line with their popularity in terms of likes, again indicating that engagement is important. The engagement mainly consisted of users sharing content, followed by liking it. In general, the content published generated relatively few comments.[214]

The kind of content that was popular on Twitter, whether retweeted or favourited, was very similar for all groups studied: practical information, warnings and updates from the ground in connection with large demonstrations. In fact, most of the popular content for most groups is even from the same time: the anti-Brotherhood demonstrations of late June and early July 2013.[215] On Facebook, the popularity of content depended – not surprisingly – on whether it was shared, liked or commented upon. The most widely shared content was the kind of content popular on Twitter, as well as media attention to the groups or the issue. The most frequently liked posts usually contained pictures of the groups working, quotes, arguments or media reports – content one would wish to acknowledge and express support for, although there were exceptions. The posts generating the greatest number of comments were more mixed, but often contained questions, claims or stories and testimonies. Not surprisingly, users engage with the content in line with what they seek to achieve, whether it is to disseminate information, express support or answer a question. Finally, TBG was somewhat different in this regard, as very similar content was shared, liked and commented upon. This consisted, most of all, of pictures of their volunteers. This should be seen in connection with the relatively limited engagement created by their content: the figures are so modest that they may, first and foremost, have engaged their own volunteers. The level of correlation between the most popular content and the most published content was not always very high among the groups, particularly not on Twitter. Still, the most popular content – namely live updates and practical information – was also dictated by events offline, and it would hardly make sense for the groups to remain silent between large demonstrations.

The videos published on YouTube were either links to TV segments on the issue or on one of the groups, or videos produced by the groups themselves, usually documenting the problem and their work. The latter gained, by far, the most views, in particular a clip released by OpAntiSH showing an attack on a female protester. In general, however, the videos gained few views, almost no comments and their channels few subscribers. While the groups clearly saw YouTube as a useful platform for publishing, they did not use it for discussions, and it was not the online 'home', or main platform, of any group studied.

The offline events that the groups held or took part in can be roughly categorised into four groups: patrols, meetings for volunteers, outreach campaigns and demonstrations and other meetings. Patrols were conducted by OpAntiSH and TBG at first, and later also by ISH. Both groups organised teams dressed in recognisable T-shirts or vests that patrolled Tahrir, and intervened to rescue protesters that were attacked. OpAntiSH, with help from Nazra and others, also provided medical and legal assistance, and operated a hotline to which attacks could be reported. All groups, including TBG, disseminated information on the hotlines and the help offered, and it seems clear that the groups, at least after a while, coordinated their efforts. However, as discussed below, this coordination did not take place in public online. Both OpAntiSH and TBG asked volunteers to attend at least one meeting before participating on the ground. In addition, as we have seen, ISH held patrols in downtown Cairo, as did Imprint, which also patrolled the metro. Outreach campaigns were held by HarassMap in various neighborhoods, using the information from the website to inform people about the problem. Similarly, several groups disseminated flyers on the issue at universities, on the metro and in the streets.

The groups also helped to organise and took part in demonstrations, including the protests in Cairo on 6 and 12 February, and on International Women's Day, 8 March 2013. Several other groups and political parties also took part, but attendance was limited, judging by the pictures. As for the meetings, these included discussion sessions held by Nazra, an annual meeting held by HarassMap and self-defence classes held by both TBG and ISH, and more. Typically, they were aimed at a particular, interested audience, rather than at mass mobilisation. These events will be discussed further in the analysis below, which is roughly organised around the coding categories. The purpose is to shed light on the groups' usage patterns as well as on the similarities and differences between them. From there, I move on to the question of traceable results offline. First, however, I provide a discussion of which platforms were used and prioritised by the groups, and, in light of the groups' aims and needs, why these were used.

What Do They Want, and What Do They Need?

All groups included in the study can be said to be part of the same general movement, in the sense that they worked towards the same goal, at the same time, and they cooperated to a large extent. All groups sought to end sexual harassment in all its forms, and to end sexual violence against female protesters, with two of the groups initiated specifically for the latter aim. Given the extent of the problem, they faced a formidable challenge. All groups agreed that it would be crucial to break the silence that they perceived had engulfed the issue in Egypt, and to end what they saw as the social acceptability of the phenomenon. For some of the groups, this meant advocating for new laws against harassment. Others argued that this should not be their first priority, and that lack of implementation of existing laws was an equally serious problem. More importantly, all groups agreed that at least part of the solution is social, and that they need to take direct action themselves. This, in turn, is closely connected to the lack of trust in the authorities expressed by most groups. Imprint may be said to have been somewhat different in this regard, and cooperated with the police on several occasions. Many were, however, very sceptical of the authorities, whom they accused of neglecting their responsibilities, and even of being a driving force behind the problem in the 2000s. As a result, although they demanded that the authorities step up to their responsibility, the groups *expected* little from them.

Many of the groups included activists with experience from the days of the Mubarak regime. Most groups were formed following the 2011 revolution, and should be seen in the context of a broadened but contested political space in which many were fighting to preserve the revolution and the right to participate and, not least, to improve their country. Even for those groups which predated the revolution, the new situation must have had an impact in terms of mobilisation and recruitment. As such, the groups sought to fight an almost all-encompassing problem, in a context of increased participation, but with deep-seated mistrust towards the state, and with varying degrees of access to resources. They all seem to have preferred to organise themselves, and to take direct action outside of political channels to reach their goals. As we have seen, the experience from the 2000s favoured a rather loose organisational structure. The groups studied were somewhat more clearly defined and structured, accepting applications from prospective members, providing training and even organising teams and branches. Even so, they remained quite flexible and open. Perhaps more importantly, online platforms had been established over the past decade as an arena for debate and activism, and would be where one could address and mobilise other concerned young Egyptians.

All the groups needed volunteers. For some of the groups, this was a matter of urgency, and time was a crucial factor. They all sought to bring attention to the issue, both by encouraging people to speak up and by reaching out to the traditional media. Some of the groups also focused on influencing how the media dealt with the issue, both in terms of protecting the privacy of those attacked and of paying attention to the language used and how the issue was framed. For the groups working in Tahrir, it was crucial to disseminate information as widely as possible.

Moreover, all groups sought to disseminate information on meetings and other events, and to document their own work. Furthermore, they all seem to have been eager to present their views on the issue, as well as the factual information they had gathered. To carry out these tasks, the groups turned to various online platforms, an accessible and, not least, affordable alternative. As pointed out by Howard and Hussain, the falling costs of internet usage in Egypt meant that one could reach a wider audience.[216] Offline networks were also important to most groups studied, but as I will argue below, the groups successfully employed online platforms to meet the challenges they were facing, and to achieve tangible results. Then again, it would be rather extraordinary if young activists mobilising on an issue chose *not* to use social media in their work, not least following the celebrated use of Facebook and Twitter during the revolution. Yet, while online platforms may have been an obvious choice, the issue here is not that these groups used online platforms per se, but how they used them and, not least, if they helped the groups to achieve their goals. The use of online platforms, like everything else, may be successful, unsuccessful or anything in between. Moreover, there are differences between the various platforms available, in terms of possibilities, local context and reach. Thus, we begin with a brief discussion on the choice of platforms made by the groups.

Websites

Of the three groups that operated their own websites, HarassMap stands out in that their site was the basis for their work. The idea for the site came as a reaction to what the founders of HarassMap viewed as a solitary focus on advocacy for a new law against harassment among NGOs in the late 2000s. In their view, what was needed was instead grassroots work, not least to document and talk about the issue. Online solutions made this possible and, in a sense, the site encompasses many of the positive features of the internet and the international online community that are referred to as tools for social and political change. The group received free technical help from idealists who had developed free, open-source software designed to aid groups such as HarassMap. By using SMS in combination with the website, HarassMap sought to overcome one of the difficulties they faced, namely making it possible to reach those who experience harassment and enable them to report it, thus contributing to breaking the silence and documenting the problem. There are more mobile phone subscriptions in Egypt than there are people[217] and, according to the group itself, half of these subscribers are women. They had identified a problem, and they found a technical solution that was affordable, and that made it possible for them to achieve something they viewed as strategically important in solving the issue. Deservedly, the group received wide media attention, and even international awards.[218] However, while all this is true, in itself it does not necessarily contribute to solving the problem. For one thing, the number of mobile phone subscriptions in a stratified society such as Egypt says nothing in itself about *who* owns a mobile, and how ownership is distributed. Moreover, although the website clearly states that one can report anonymously, understanding and trusting this information is not a given, especially not for those with limited technical knowledge, and especially not regarding a subject that is seen by many as taboo. Access and ability remain problematic, even though mobile phones are more widely distributed than internet access: only about 1,200 reports were registered on the site by the end of the time frame. If up to 99.6 per cent of women in Egypt experience harassment,[219] the website is clearly able to capture only a small fraction of this.

However, the website did not need to capture everything, and it would be extremely optimistic to expect that it would. Rather, the important part is that it captures something, and then how it uses this information. For one thing, up to 1,200 people who reported incidents received an offer of assistance after doing so, which they would probably not have received otherwise. While the alternative earlier most often would have been to do nothing, those who experienced harassment could now do *something*. This kind of empowerment should certainly not be ignored. Second, the group used the information gathered in their offline and online work. Being aware that the site itself reaches only a limited audience, they brought the information with them offline in their community outreach programme, in which they visit neighbourhoods – often low-income areas where internet access may be limited – and discuss the issue directly with people. This was usually done by the group's local volunteers, who were deemed to be more credible than the leadership. According to the group itself, the information gathered online is important for convincing people that the problem is widespread and that it actually happens in their area.[220] They also use the information online, in reports, for advocacy, and in their campaigns.

By referring to the website, the group presents a credible way in which these accounts have been gathered, and a credible basis for their claims. As will be discussed further below, the group was very often referred to in both national and international media, who seem to view it as a credible source.

Whereas the website was part and parcel of HarassMap's purpose, Nazra mainly used theirs as a place to publish information. This was a basic requirement of the organisation, as one of their key goals is to provide documentation, position papers, testimonies, and so on. In order to disseminate this information further, the group made use of social media, namely Twitter and Facebook. Their success in doing so was rather limited, as measured by the number of followers. Moreover, they often neglected to use hashtags, and thus may not have reached many beyond their followers. However, as all the other groups, particularly HarassMap and OpAntiSH, regularly linked to their content, it potentially reached a much wider audience than those following Nazra's accounts. The group was regularly used as a source not only by media, but also by international organisations such as Amnesty and Human Rights Watch. For those concerned with the issue, the website offered large amounts of relevant, credible and unique material, all in one place. The group clearly targeted both an international and a domestic audience, as most content was provided in both Arabic and English.

The third website, operated by ISH, was different. The site hosted two reports, which were disseminated through social media. However, the remaining content – videos, pictures, news items and the description of the group – was also posted on social media. Importantly, the content *itself* was posted on social media, not just links to it. The website was seldom linked to and seldom updated, and following the time frame of this study, the group chose to develop a new website. The original site was hosted on a site run by Act, so its creation may have been dictated more by the opportunity to do so in connection with an already existing site than by the need or wish to do so. Interestingly, the three groups that ran websites were also the three seemingly most professional groups, they were not ad hoc responses to a problem, and they all involved activists with previous experience. In general, websites may be useful and even essential to the groups, even in the age of social media, but more so if used with skill and purpose – in combination with social media.

Social Media and Platform Selection

All groups studied have a Twitter account, a Facebook page and a YouTube channel. The YouTube channels were used in a very limited manner and are not the main online presence of any group, but rather a useful platform for publishing videos, which are then disseminated through other channels. Two of the groups also have Flickr accounts, but these are not their main sites either. Their main presence in social media was and is on Twitter and Facebook, both popular platforms in Egypt with 519,000 and 13.8 million users as of May 2013, respectively.[221] However, some groups clearly preferred one platform over the other, and this had consequences. Whereas most groups had relatively similar numbers of followers on both platforms, Imprint and ISH did not. The former had 15,282 likes on Facebook, compared to 353 followers on Twitter. The latter had 12,401 likes on Facebook, compared to 516 followers on Twitter. Both these groups performed poorly in terms of the success factors on Twitter discussed above: low level of activity; the group seldom retweeted others' tweets; few users who retweeted the group's tweets; and the tweets with the most retweets on their timeline were not written by themselves. Moreover, the groups often published tweets that contained a link and nothing more, whereas the successful groups almost always tweeted comprehensible and appealing sentences. The point, of course, is to stress the difference between *presence on* and *(skilled) use of* social media. Both groups were popular on Facebook, the platform they prioritised, and they received wide media attention. Clearly, many users on Twitter were also interested in the subject, but since the groups merely provided a presence on the platform, they failed to fully exploit the possibilities inherent in it. It should be mentioned that these groups wrote markedly less in English than, for instance, OpAntiSH and TBG, and followers from other countries were doubtless a part of the latter groups' success.

Then again, Nazra used Twitter in fairly a similar way – few retweets, few tweets in general, often containing nothing more than links – but were far more successful in terms of followers and engagement. One obvious point to make in this regard is that very popular groups, such as HarassMap and OpAntiSH, frequently retweeted Nazra, thus making the latter's Twitter account known to a large number of users. Nazra also provided very popular content: they wrote reports, testimonies and position papers that were often disseminated widely and referred to in the media. This should also remind us not to draw a clear distinction between online and offline: Nazra was a group that provided crucial 'expert' services to the operation on the ground, and clearly enjoyed credibility among those involved. There is no reason to believe that Twitter users decide who to follow based solely on what they learn online: it is, of course, also based on what they learn and see offline.

In general, the content published on both platforms was rather similar, but there are some interesting differences as well. First of all, a lot more was published on Twitter than on Facebook: taken together, the groups published 13,021 tweets within the time frame, compared to 4,754 Facebook posts. There are, however, two notable exceptions, related to the discussion above: Imprint, which published equal amounts on both platforms; and ISH, which published three times more on Facebook than on Twitter. Even so, there is a clear trend among the groups that content is repeated much more often on Twitter. At the same time, Twitter was also the platform most frequently used to give updates and information while events were taking place. The same information was usually given only once, and often later, on Facebook. While Twitter's strict limitation on characters in each tweet is certainly relevant, a self-energising effect might have been in play: more activity on Twitter means more tweets in a user's feed, meaning that they are likely not to scroll as far back in time as they do on Facebook, which in turn means that things need to be repeated. In either case, it is clear that the groups, by and large, prefer Twitter during events, rather than Facebook. OpAntiSH, as a group organised to work during large demonstrations, published roughly 20 times more on Twitter than on Facebook.

This is also reflected in which tweets and Facebook posts generated the most engagement. Of the 60 most retweeted and favourited tweets among the groups, 39 were either live updates from the ground during demonstrations or relevant information, such as the number for the hotlines. Of the 90 most liked, commented-on, and shared posts on Facebook, the equivalent is 16, and nine of these are among the most shared. These figures are not very surprising; people would probably deem this kind of information important to others, and thus they retweet it. To the extent that the information is available on Facebook, the equivalent would be to share it. Other than that, there are two features that stand out in terms of generating engagement on Facebook: pictures and videos of the work of a group, and references to media coverage of the group, other groups or the issue. Many of these pictures, which drew a noticeably large number of likes, show members of a group in action or ready for action. This is the kind of content that typically would be popular with members or sympathisers of the group, in that it gives attention to, and credit for, the work that is being done. However, it also shows beyond reasonable doubt that the groups actually do what they claim to do, which may be important for their credibility both in the population at large and among journalists.

Finally, there are two features that are prominent on Facebook, but not on Twitter, namely what I would call general encouragement and shaming. The former typically takes the form of quotes from famous people, inspiring pictures, or the like, as in the following example:

> 'If it would destroy a 12-year-old boy to be called "a girl",what are we then teaching him about girls?' – Tony Porter
>
> TBG on Facebook, 22 May 2013

This was rarely done on Twitter. As for shaming, this also took place on Twitter, usually in the form of a group tweeting a phone number and stating that it is being used to harass. However, it was done far more frequently on Facebook. While phone numbers were disseminated there as well, shaming was often done through pictures taken on the street, showing someone accused of harassment. It is not clear whether or not the groups verified this information themselves, or relied on information that was sent to them. In either case, the practice is highly problematic, but it should be seen in the context of the more or less constant refusal of the police to deal with such incidents.[222] In a similar manner, the practice of organising patrols that intervene in extremely violent situations is also problematic, but is, of course, a result of the same context. In general, there was a difference in how the two main social media platforms were employed, and whether or not they were employed successfully in terms of followers and engagement. These differences will be discussed further as we turn to the thematic discussion.

Discussions, Agitation and Hashtags

Perhaps the most striking feature regarding this subject is that, contrary to what many optimists have pointed to as a key democratising feature of the internet, there is little debate between opposing views. That does not mean that such debate never takes place, but that there are few examples to be found.[223] There are, however, quite a few examples of differing views being presented to the followers of the groups, but this is in the context of displaying what some people actually advocate, which of course is seen as wrong:

> انتو جبهة نسائية ضد التخرش ولا واخدينها ستار لاغراض سياسية @OpAntiSH
> مين اغتصب البنات مش هما متظاهرين التحرير؟
>
> Are you a women's front against harassment or are you using it as an excuse to achieve political goals. Those who are raping the girls, are they not the demonstrators of Tahrir?
>
> @[User 1],[224] Retweet by OpAntiSH, 12 February 2013

HarassMap and OpAntiSH in particular did this several times on Twitter, and a similar post was the most commented-upon on Facebook for HarassMap. Then again, one could argue that there is no apparent reason why these groups should engage opposing views in open debates. Anti-racism groups would hardly spend much time discussing whether or not racists might have a point, as their view is a given, and their purpose is to defeat racism as such. Similarly, an extremely important point for these groups is that whether or not sexual harassment and sexual violence is wrong is not up for debate. Their purpose is to convince people that they are right, not to acknowledge opposing views or seek consensus. This, however, would require quite an effort, as their view of the problem was far from universal in Egypt at the time. Accordingly, while the groups seldom discussed with opponents, they spent much time arguing for their cause. A partial exception was Nazra, which did not do this to the same extent as the others on social media. They did, however, provide reports and position papers, which argue much more substantially for their cause than short tweets or Facebook posts. On Twitter, the agitation generally took the form of short utterances stating that harassment is a crime, that no one would accept it if it was done to members of their family, that it is an attack on the revolution, and so on. These are not posed as questions; they are posed as statements:

> STRESSING: Any assaulted woman is the victim of a criminal act – regardless of what she was wearing, where she was, and what she was doing.
>
> @OpAntiSH, 30 November 2012

The groups, and particularly HarassMap, repeatedly argued against excuses given for harassment, using the data they had compiled as well as arguments provided by their followers and participants in online events to refute misconceptions:

لو التحرش سببه الانفلات الأمني... أمين الشرطة #بيتحرش_ليه؟

> If security issues are the reasons behind increased sexual harassment, why is the policeman harassing?[225]
>
> @harassmap, 16 March 2013

Moreover, the groups frequently argued through retweets, passing on what they deemed good arguments. The three groups that spend the most time arguing for the cause on Twitter are also the groups with by far the largest number of retweets. On Facebook, the agitation often took a somewhat different form, in that it was combined with pictures or illustrations. Regardless of the form, however, any follower of the groups would never be in doubt as to their positions and, perhaps more importantly, would regularly see new arguments, and constantly be reminded that harassment is wrong and it is always the harasser who is to blame. All groups pointed out that women often keep silent about incidents as they fear the reaction of their family, blame themselves or are ashamed. By following the groups, one would constantly be told otherwise: that women are not at fault, that they are not alone and that what they have experienced is wrong and not something they should tolerate:

> You raped her because her clothes provoked you? I should break your face because your stupidity provokes me.
>
> Text on a sign on a picture shared by ISH on Facebook, 8 June 2013[226]

المتحرش جبان, متخافيش وأتكلمى

> The harasser is a coward, do not be afraid and speak up.
>
> @harassmap, 26 May 2013

Furthermore, the groups sought to establish harassment and violence as problems for society and as crimes, to define who is to blame and to fight the silence that engulfed the issue by making it public. This approach was far from accidental:

> As feminist activists, we approach our cause as it is in reality: a public issue that affects all Egyptian women.
>
> Nazra, 4 February 2013[227]

There was, however, some discussion as to how harassment and violence should be fought or, more precisely, if it was acceptable/desirable to use weapons, as in the following examples:

> RT @[User 2]: @TahrirBodyguard Word of advice @[User 3] carrying a knife or weapon can easily backfire & be used against you in seconds.
>
> @TahrirBodyguard, 7 February 2013

> MT @[User 4]: @[User 3] @TahrirBodyguard Let's go to the streets with knives & weapons. Let's start a civil war! Is that the best solution?
>
> @TahrirBodyguard, 7 February 2013

This, however, was not a dominant feature, and discussion for the groups mainly meant arguing for their cause. Yet, while they seldom interacted with their opponents, they did interact directly with their followers, albeit to varying degrees. Mostly, this simply meant providing a response, sometimes to direct questions, but more often just stating that they agreed with someone, that they appreciated their effort or providing encouraging words:

> @[User 5] we need all the help we can. Email us on tahrir.bodyguard@gmail.com
>
> @TahrirBodyguard, 24 January 2013

> @[User 6] and the team appreciate having people like you. A group hug.
>
> @OpAntiSH, 13 February 2013

The groups that did this most frequently on Twitter were also the groups that most urgently needed volunteers, namely TBG, for which it comprises 31 per cent of their tweets, and OpAntiSH, for which it comprises 19 per cent. Surprisingly, Imprint and ISH, which also depended on volunteers, almost never posted this kind of content. For groups asking people to volunteer for a dangerous task on short notice, it makes sense to show how much this is appreciated, and that they are part of the community of the group. For such groups to ignore their followers online would hardly be a successful strategy.

Last, but not least, there is the issue of the use of hashtags. With the exception of ISH, the groups that seldom tagged their tweets – Imprint and Nazra – had fewer followers than those that did – HarassMap, OpAntiSH and TBG.[228] Granted, part of the explanation is that the three latter groups were those mostly known to work with an issue that received wide attention, and which concerned many in Egypt and abroad. Still, the other groups also received widespread attention, but did not manage to translate this into engagement on Twitter. One could argue that these groups did not want their tweets to be read by other than their followers, but this is not only counterproductive in terms of their stated goals, but is also impossible to control, as their messages may be retweeted. Moreover, two of the groups in particular, namely HarassMap and OpAntiSH, managed to utilise hashtags to create online debates and discussions through their days of tweeting and blogging. The use of one of their favoured hashtags, #EndSH, became widespread in Egypt, and even the newspaper *al-Masri al-Yawm* started to employ it repeatedly from 22 August 2012. OpAntiSH and HarassMap also used hashtags when asking for help online, potentially reaching more people that could contribute. OpAntiSH received help to translate the subtitles for their most viewed video,[229] while HarassMap sought support for an online crowd-funding initiative they launched.[230] In both instances, the groups also spoke directly to those who helped. Moreover, HarassMap retweeted calls from various celebrities to help, including TV host Bassem Youssef, Cairokee lead singer Amir Eid, and the activist-celebrity commonly known as Sandmonkey. Similarly, when the group was started, TBG spoke directly to famous Egyptian tweeple asking for their help to gain attention, including Wael Ghonim, Wael Abbas, Mona Eltahawy and Mahmoud Salem (AKA Sandmonkey):

> @Sandmonkey We are trying to keep people in #Tahrir safe, please support us with a RT. Idea is for people to tweet at us and we RT for help.
>
> @TahrirBodyguard, 27 November 2012

This seems to have been successful, as the number of both followers and volunteers increased drastically.[231] The group also sought help online in other respects, both to get messages translated and to gain material assistance with a logo, stickers and even a tent.[232] Utilising these features – hashtags to reach more people, the resources of those they reach and the fame of those known on the platform – is a marked difference between those groups that gained many followers and much attention, and those that did not, with the partial exception of Nazra.

Mobilisation and Recruitment

Mobilisation is the most prominent feature of Imprint's Twitter activities, and it is the second-most prominent for TBG, HarassMap and OpAntiSH. For Nazra and ISH, it was less of a priority, although the latter often writes about upcoming events on Facebook. This category, however, also includes mobilisation for online events, for material support and for followers. In terms of offline events as such, the extent to which groups promoted these was, naturally, dependent on how often such events were held. For instance, TBG held several self-defence courses, in addition to meetings for volunteers, and spent twice as much time publicising offline events as OpAntiSH, which did not hold any such events except for meetings for new volunteers. Then again, other groups which held several offline events, such as Nazra and HarassMap, did not spend more time promoting them than OpAntiSH. This is connected to the fact that many groups disseminated information on each other's events, which account for a large part of all reposts and links to other groups, and which somewhat evens out the numbers, as many people reposted the events of Nazra and HarassMap.

Yet, mobilisation *just* for the offline events is not a particularly dominant feature with any of the groups, for which there may be several reasons. For one thing, given the widespread attention these groups attained over time, they may not have found it difficult to gain attendance. Moreover, as many of those volunteering with the groups probably also went to their meetings, they may have known of the events from other sources, and the closed Facebook groups may be important in this regard. Furthermore, in contrast to their Kuwaiti colleagues, all groups created events on their Facebook pages. These show up in the streams of those following the groups, who are automatically reminded when the event draws near. Moreover, some of the offline events were directed at a particular audience, and may not have been intended to draw as large a crowd as possible. For instance, Nazra held discussion meetings for those who had experienced harassment. In addition, dissemination by their followers – shares, likes, retweets – may also have been important. In either case, the groups spent only a limited amount of time mobilising for what they did offline, with the partial exception of TBG.

As for recruitment, the figures for Twitter usage may be more surprising. Generally, this was not something the groups spent much time on, with the single clear exception of TBG. ISH, OpAntiSH and HarassMap all had a core of engaged activists when they started, or sprung out of other initiatives in which many were involved. As we have seen, this was partially true of Imprint as well, which had several founders, some of whom were involved in the earliest initiatives to safeguard female protesters. TBG, on the other hand, was the result of one person's online initiative. Thus, it should not be surprising that TBG spent more time than others recruiting volunteers: this accounted for 21 per cent of their tweets, in comparison to between 3 per cent and 11 per cent for the others. That being said, all groups did spend time on the issue, both on Twitter and on Facebook. Imprint, which spent the second greatest amount of time on this subject, started early with online forms to be completed by those wishing to volunteer. Following this, the would-be volunteers were contacted by the group and had to attend interviews. Then, lists of those who had been accepted, and the committee within the group into which they were accepted, were published on Facebook:

> Forms submission phase has ended, thanks to all of the people that applied or even encouraged and wished us success. We will contact all the applicants that passed stage one to set date and time for the personal meeting with in the next two hours [. . .]
>
> Imprint on Facebook, 11 April 2013

Other groups also had rather detailed instructions for those applying, with HarassMap and ISH also utilising online forms, whereas TBG and OpAntiSH asked people to contact them by email. The intention, of course, was to ensure that no harassers were able to join any of the groups.[233]

All groups disseminated this information on both Facebook and Twitter, and seem to have been quite successful in their work: HarassMap states that it has about a thousand volunteers; ISH has volunteers in different parts of the country, and has been able to conduct patrols; Imprint has documented through pictures and videos that they have dozens of volunteers at least; and OpAntiSH and TBG managed to organise several patrols in Tahrir over sustained periods of time, several days in a row. OpAntiSH and Nazra, together with other groups, also operated the hotlines and various teams providing legal and medical help. Given the danger these people were exposed to, this was no small accomplishment. Moreover, in the beginning, they were able to organise teams on the ground within days of the inception of the idea. However, during times of demonstrations, the level of violence and the number of attacks took their toll on their teams, and they all, at times, sidestepped their own procedures:

> @TahrirBodyguard and @OpAntiSH are on ground today. Join if u can #endSH
>
> @TahrirBodyguard, 1 July 2013

One could, of course, argue that they did not succeed in terms of recruitment as they were not able to stop attacks from taking place during large demonstrations. Yet, as neither the police nor the army seemed able to control the situation at such times, it would be rather naive to expect these groups to do so. While it is unclear exactly how many women the groups were able to bring away from attacks, it is safe to say that they accounted for dozens of people, if not more.

In all, TBG seems to confirm that Twitter and Facebook can be adequate tools for recruitment, although word probably spread through other channels as well. For the other groups, social media were used actively, but they also had existing offline networks to tap into. While the relative importance of the two is difficult to establish, the combination seems to have been effective, and we should not try to force a clear distinction between the two.

Also included in the category 'mobilisation' are online campaigns, of which HarassMap and OpAntiSH were the foremost proponents. For these groups, mobilisation for and participation in such events account for no less than 30.2 per cent and 15.5 per cent of their total Twitter activity, respectively. Both groups also used Facebook for this purpose, but Twitter was clearly favoured. Most of the tweets included here were part of the organised days of blogging and tweeting against harassment, and include both tweets written by the groups themselves and retweets of other participants using the assigned hashtag:

> #مصر_من_غير_تحرش يعني المجتمع يفهم ان التحرش ملوش علاقة باللي البنت لبساه
>
> #(Egypt without harassment) that society understands that harassment has no relation to what a girl is wearing
>
> @[User 7], retweeted by @harassmap, 24 January 2013

> @[User 8] thank you, but we started the hashtags as well to get more people involved, empower more people, & reflect the situation
>
> @OpAntiSH, 24 January 2013 (during the same online event)

The concept was started before the time frame set for this study, and in the summer of 2011 a joint campaign of HarassMap and Nazra generated over 12,000 tweets and more than 150 blog posts.[234] As we have seen, two online campaigns were held during the time frame, generating more than 2,500 tweets between them. I will argue that these events were important for several reasons. For one thing, they contributed to a sense of belonging and empowerment, and showed those who have experienced harassment that they are not alone, and that many are fighting to put an end to the problem. They certainly contributed to breaking the silence on the issue, particularly when it was covered in the media. Moreover, they offered a very affordable and technically easy avenue for participation and resistance for those concerned, although it may be costly and difficult to talk about the issue. Still, participants could also contribute anonymously, should they wish to do so. Thus, the leap from passive to active participation may have been a short one, giving many a sense of fighting back, and of being part of something bigger. But, perhaps most importantly, they contributed to the crucial leap from private problem to public issue. For instance, while admitting individual poverty might be seen as embarrassing, it is not embarrassing to take part in the fight against poverty. Similarly, when thousands publicly discuss harassment, they are not having their private shame exposed; they are partaking in a political struggle.

Also included in this category is the mobilisation of resources: that is, asking the online community for technical help and material assistance. As we have seen, the groups that were adept in using online platforms were quite successful in this regard. This illustrates an important point, namely that the publicness provided by platforms used was important not only in terms of fundamental issues, such as making the problem public, but also in solving very concrete challenges in their day-to-day operations.

Documentation

Documentation of their own work, of the work of others and of the issue at hand was an important feature of the online work of all groups involved, albeit with some variations in terms of what was documented. Although Twitter was used widely for this purpose, Facebook was perhaps more important because the platform can host pictures and photo albums. Moreover, YouTube was used to host videos, although the groups in general published few of these. I will argue that this documentation was important for several reasons, including providing convincing descriptions of the problem itself and gaining acceptance for their presentation of it, showing the work of their volunteers and demonstrating beyond reasonable doubt that they were credible sources. These features, in turn, were important in gaining media attention, and also in attracting volunteers and in motivating and encouraging those already working for the group.

To begin with the issue of describing the problem, this work was driven by Nazra, along with HarassMap and OpAntiSH, although all groups contributed. On the part of these three, there was a coordinated and continuous effort to collect testimonies from those who had been attacked, those who worked with the groups on the ground and witnesses. Especially following the 25 January 2013 demonstrations, the groups repeatedly told their volunteers that they would contribute considerably to the cause by taking the time to send in their accounts:

> IMP to ALL @OpAntiSH volunteers & all witnesses, plz take time to write testimonies & send them to opantish(at)gmail.com #endSH
>
> @OpAntiSH, 29 January 2013

Testimonies were published separately, but also compiled in reports, analysed and often accompanied by recommendations and political statements. All were anonymised, unless those providing the testimony chose to go public. The groups repeatedly wrote about the importance of letting those who had been attacked make their own decisions in this regard, and they frequently criticised journalists for not being respectful. The reports and testimonies were spread widely through social media, and all groups studied linked to such publications from Nazra and OpAntiSH, which seem to have been the groups considered most credible. OpAntiSH and HarassMap were the groups most eager to disseminate this material online, doing so on almost 400 occasions. The reports and accounts are quite detailed, refer to specific places in and around Tahrir and roughly set the time at which an attack occurred. They also describe how the work of OpAntiSH and TBG was done, and often include what happened afterwards as well. The testimonies are often written in a vivid and emotional language, which leaves the reader in no doubt about how horrifying and dangerous the attack was:

> سأحكي حكايتي التي تشبه الكثير من الحكايات، حكايتي أنا وأنتي، أنا وأنتي نعرف كيف حدث هذا، الموت كان قريبا لكنه لا يأتي، أنا وأنتي نعرف إننا انتهكنا، إننا اغتصبنا في قلب ميدان التحرير بين جموع من البشر لا نعرف دينهم
>
> I will tell my story, which resembles many other stories, my story of me and you, me and you know how this happened, death was near but never came, me and you know that we were violated, that we were raped in the heart of Tahrir among crowds of people that we do not know who are
>
> From testimony published on Facebook by Nazra, 26 January 2013

Anyone reading these reports would have a hard time denying either the seriousness of the problem, the extent of the problem or the importance of the work being done by the groups – especially when they are seen together with the videos and pictures published, which make fabrication all the more unlikely. Attacks on female protesters were documented in two videos. One is the video referred to above entitled 'This is Mob Attack', published by OpAntiSH. The video shows how groups of men encircle a protester, over a prolonged period of time, while volunteers from TBG and OpAntiSH try to interfere using sticks and gas canisters. The video features a voice-over explaining what is taking place and stating that they will resist, as well as dramatic music in the background. It ends with a question to the viewer: Is he or she able to help? If so, it asks them to volunteer and provides contact information. As described above, the video was provided with subtitles in 22 languages thanks to help from their followers online. It was seen more than 1.5 million times, and generated 1,500 comments. The second, published by HarassMap, lasts only 21 seconds, and shows two girls who are dragged screaming by a mob down the entrance of a metro station. The text states that the footage is from the June 30 demonstrations and provides information on how to volunteer, and how to donate. It also says that they were able to rescue the two girls in the video, but that there were others they could not get to. Both videos are extremely disturbing to watch, but leave no doubt as to the severity of such attacks.

Most groups published videos showing their work. For instance, Imprint published several videos, either of their own making or from TV clips, of their work both securing downtown during the holidays and patrolling the metro. ISH also did this, in addition to videos of harassment taking place (but not mob attacks), although, more often than not, they linked to videos uploaded by other users and not by themselves. TBG published a video featuring footage from their self-defence courses, providing tips and asking people to join the classes, all to the sound of Survivor's 'Eye of the Tiger'.[235] Most of all, however, the groups published many, many photos of their work. The pictures were published on Facebook, and links were provided on Twitter. With the exception of Nazra, this accounted for between 5 per cent and 15 per cent of the Twitter activities of all groups. Most of these pictures were either group photos of volunteers ready for work, or pictures of one or more of the volunteers in action, whether patrolling Tahrir, patrolling the metro, handing out flyers, holding a meeting, talking with people on the street or taking part in a self-defence class. I argue that this was important to the groups for several reasons. For one thing, it gave something back to those participating: their work was acknowledged by the group, they could see themselves with their colleagues as part of a community and they probably received praise from others as well. Moreover, for would-be volunteers, these same features must have been appealing. Furthermore, they clearly showed the serious nature of the groups' work, which gave further credibility to their reporting and advocacy. Finally, it also contributed to documenting the problem, and for those reading the reports, watching the videos and seeing the pictures, denial would have become a rather difficult option.

The groups also spent much time providing live updates from meetings, demonstrations and campaigns. This could sometimes involve, for instance, listing the speakers or the arguments presented during the course of meetings. Most of all, however, this was done during large demonstrations, and provided continuous updates on the situation, the number of attacks that had taken place, how many volunteers were working on the ground, and so on:

> 26 cases of mob sexual assault in #Tahrir tonight. We are doing everything we can but the area is not safe at all.
>
> @OpAntiSH, 1 July 2013

Finally, the groups also disseminated testimonies on harassment outside the large demonstrations, and such reports often seem to have been compiled online. For one thing, there was the HarassMap website. Yet all groups published stories of harassment that had been sent to them, presumably by email or direct messages. For the most part, such testimonies were published on Facebook, as in the following example:

> تم التحرش بى فى الشارع ليس ببعيد عن مكان سكنى ولم تكن هذه المرة الأولى
> إنما يحدث هذا بشكل يكاد يكون يومى تقريبا على إختلاف أشكاله وإختلاف
> أعمار المتحرشين

> I was harassed on a street not far from where I live and it was not the first time, it happens almost on a daily basis in different ways and with harassers of different ages.
>
> Testimony published by HarassMap on Facebook, 10 June 2013

To summarise, the groups used social media to host, compile, make available and disseminate documentation of their work and the situation. Crucially, this documentation was frequently picked up by the traditional media.

Media

There are two main features regarding the groups' work with the media online: to gain the attention of the media in the first place, and then to publicise this attention to their followers. To begin with the former, this was seldom done directly online. Most groups did spend some time communicating with journalists, but this is not a dominant feature. Moreover, most of this communication can be linked to a particular subject, namely the perceived lack of media respect for those who had been attacked. OpAntiSH, TBG, Nazra and HarassMap tweeted frequently on this, and they even organised a meeting with journalists to discuss the issue:

> دعوة لاجتماع عاجل مع الصحفيين والإعلاميين لمناقشة كيفية الاستجابة الإعلامية إلي الاعتداءات الجنسية
>
> Invitation to an urgent meeting with journalists and media professionals to discuss the manner in which the media responds to the sexual assaults (with link to invitation)
>
> @NazraEgypt, 30 January 2013

In addition, some of the groups, namely OpAntiSH, HarassMap and ISH, also spent some time disseminating press releases through both Facebook and Twitter. These can also be linked to specific events, and some were given following large demonstrations. These typically provided information on the number of attacks, the groups' assessment of the current situation and contained criticism of the lack of response from the authorities as well as from opposition political parties. Two events in particular created much activity in this regard. The first was the infamous debate in the Shura Council in which Islamist MPs blamed women themselves for the attacks. Naturally, this provoked a fierce response from the groups, and a press release written by OpAntiSH was disseminated widely. The second event is rather peculiar. On the evening of 30 June 2013, as numerous attacks were taking place during the demonstrations preceding the military coup, the state-owned newspaper *al-Ahram* published an article headlined 'I Saw Harassment denies the occurrence of any incidents in the square',[236] even though the group had reported the exact opposite on their Facebook page – repeatedly. The group published a press release denouncing the article; the press release was then disseminated widely by themselves and other groups:

هام / تنفي مبادرة #شفت_تحرش ما اوردته جريدة الاهرام على لسان منسقتها (...) بأن لا تحرش في ميدان #التحرير

> Important / the #(ISH)-initiative denies what the newspaper al-Ahram claimed was said by their coordinator [...] that there is no harassment in Tahrir [a link to the press release was provided]
> @OpAntiSH, 1 July 2013

It is quite remarkable that *al-Ahram* should choose to publish such an article to begin with. If they followed any of the groups studied here online, they must have been aware that they all reported – repeatedly – that attacks were taking place, and that, in fact, the situation had never been worse. Although it seems quite obvious, it is not for me to decide why the newspaper wanted to give the impression that no attacks were taking place. Rather, the important point is to note that it clearly deemed the story more credible if attributed to the group. This, in turn, should be seen in connection with the remarkable success of this group in gaining media attention – even their founding was covered by *al-Masri al-Yawm*.[237] According to the group itself, the reason behind their success was that they were extremely accurate in their reports and could document all their claims. In their view, this earned them the trust of many journalists, who then turned to them for coverage of an issue increasingly on the public agenda in Egypt.[238] As I have argued, I believe this was the case for most groups studied: their extensive work online and offline, meticulously documented, made them credible and accessible sources, able not only to raise the issue, but to affect how it was discussed.

However, given their success, it is beyond the scope of this study to provide a full picture of all media attention devoted to the issue, as it is likely to include outlets in almost all countries worldwide. Even providing a full picture of the coverage within Egypt has proven too daunting. However, I do believe that the examples given here show beyond doubt that the subject became an issue of concern in the Egyptian press and among the wider Egyptian public, and that the press came to treat sexual harassment as a problem. Activities covered by the media included the metro patrols of Imprint, the joint patrols during the holidays undertaken by Imprint and Anti-Harassment, and the holiday patrols of ISH. On several occasions, press releases distributed by the latter group were published almost verbatim by several outlets.[239] In addition, countless meetings, seminars and campaigns held by other groups also received media attention.[240]

By far the most widely covered topic, however, was the attacks on female protesters. As early as 4 December 2012, when OpAntiSH and TBG had barely started, *Egypt Independent* wrote about their work, naming the former specifically.[241] Their work was also covered in foreign outlets from early on.[242] Following the 25 January 2013 demonstrations, the groups were widely used as sources providing facts and figures about what had taken place, although more frequently in the foreign press than in domestic outlets.[243] Even the United Nations referred to these figures in condemning the attacks.[244] Moreover, while the Egyptian newspapers may have been slow on the uptake, several reports were made on television, as well as interviews featuring activists from the groups. When Egyptian newspapers eventually picked up the issue, they included many outlets that were condemned by activists for neglecting or avoiding the attacks that took place in 2005 and 2006, such as *al-Dustur*, *al-Gumhurriyya* and *al-Ahram*.[245] In addition, there were countless pieces in both the domestic and the foreign press focusing on the groups themselves, who they were, how they worked, and so on.[246] From the spring of 2013, if not earlier, instances of sexual harassment were widely reported, and the groups were routinely used as sources. As we have seen, even the Islamist-dominated Shura Council felt compelled to discuss the issue, albeit in a shamefully disgraceful manner. The office of the president repeatedly released statements on the issue, and claimed that a new law was in the making.[247]

The groups were interested not only in gaining media coverage, but also in how the issue was presented in the media. This included fighting sensationalist reporting and defending the privacy of those attacked. Additionally, they were concerned with the language used to describe the situation. For one thing, they were clear that it was not a matter for debate whether or not this was a problem, and this does not seem to have been debated by the media. Moreover, they frequently argued for the use of the word *nāgiya*, which the groups themselves translated as 'survivor', rather than *ḍaḥiya*, meaning victim. To a certain extent, they seem to have been successful in this respect. A search on the Arabic term yielded numerous results, including articles in *al-Masri al-Yawm*,[248] *al-Watan*,[249] *al-Yawm al-Sabi'*,[250] *al-Gumhurriyya*,[251] *BBC Arabic*[252] and the Kuwaiti outlet *al-Ra'y*.[253] A search on the English term produces similar results, including outlets such as *Al-Jazeera*,[254] *Al-Arabiya*,[255] the *Guardian*[256] and *Haaretz*.[257] Also, international NGOs picked up these terms, including Human Rights Watch and Amnesty. The same organisations also used the Egyptian groups as sources on several occasions.[258] However, a search of the terms they sought to avoid, both in Arabic and English, produces more results, and includes most of the outlets, and even the organisations, listed above. Obviously, these are not scientific results as to the distribution of the various terms. Rather, the point is to illustrate that, while these groups could not control media coverage as such, they were able to gain a lot of attention, they were able to gain trust as sources and they were able to affect how the issue was framed and presented.

There are several factors to address in this regard. First, the opening up of the media in Egypt following the revolution was clearly important: not only were there more news outlets, but outlets that had been silent on the issue during the days of Mubarak now wrote about it. Second, the nature of the issue at hand demands media attention; these are horrific attacks on female protesters taking place in one of Egypt's most public and revered places. Finally, there were important offline links between journalists and activists. For instance, the appearance of OpAntiSH and TBG on *al-Barnamig* was the result of such ties, not online activity.[259] Still, the online activity undoubtedly had made the groups well known and therefore interesting guests to feature on the show. As we have seen, while there are relatively few people in Egypt who frequently use Twitter and Facebook, such usage is correlated with higher education and socio-economic background, which in turn makes journalists likely users. Moreover, TBG, OpAntiSH and HarassMap frequently responded to journalists on Twitter, often providing contact information in order to set up interviews.

Then, there is the issue of disseminating media coverage of oneself. Interestingly, the groups that seem to have received the most attention, HarassMap and OpAntiSH, spent much less time on this than the other groups, particularly TBG, Imprint and ISH. Whereas the former spent only 1 per cent of their tweets on this, the latter spent between 4 per cent and 15 per cent, as in the following examples:

> حركة بصمة هتكون موجودة على قناة القاهرة (تردد 11227 أفقي) في برنامج صباح القاهرة بكرة الساعة 10:00 صباحاً...
>
> Imprint movement will be on the Cairo channel (frequency 11227) on the program Cairo Morning tomorrow at 10:00 am (link to Facebook)
>
> @Imprint_Mov, 10 April 2013

This, of course, may be connected to the background of the groups. Imprint and TBG did not have the same base of experienced activists as the others, and did not have the same offline networks. As such, building trust and confidence in their own organisation may have been seen as important, and media coverage contributed to this. Moreover, media attention contributes to increased awareness of a group, which in turn could lead to volunteers and followers. However, dissemination of such attention on social media would primarily reach those already following the group or certain hashtags, so the issue of credibility might have been more important than the attention itself.

Guides and Instructions

In general, all groups spent quite some time disseminating important information, more so on Twitter than on Facebook. Whereas such messages account for between 6 and 14 per cent of the Twitter activity of the other groups, they account for almost one-third of Nazra's writings on the platform. This is due to the wide dissemination they conducted of their guidelines on how to deal with those who had been attacked. These were easily accessible guides that stated how to be of help, what to do, what not to do, who should be contacted, and so on. During large demonstrations, several groups distributed warnings, usually on areas to avoid:

> There are men with sticks at the entrance of the metro station across from KFC in #Tahrir who are attacking women. Please avoid.
>
> @OpAntiSH, 1 July 2013

The rest of these tweets are predominantly made up of information on the numbers to the hotlines, mainly those operated by OpAntiSH and Nazra, which were also disseminated by TBG. The number of a hotline solely operated by ISH was also disseminated widely. On Facebook, these numbers were usually posted in poster-like pictures. The groups' live reports during the demonstrations suggest that there was much activity on these hotlines, which indicates that they were known to quite a few people. Apparently, this was at times due to journalists using these numbers to get information:

> Our Hotlines in cases of mob sexual assaults NOT FOR the media please [numbers provided] #Tahrir#Egypt#Jan25 @OpAntiSH
>
> @Harassmap, 25 January 2013

However, the groups also distributed leaflets containing these numbers in Tahrir, so social media were not the sole channels through which they were made known. Moreover, some of the teams working on the ground patrolled the area and identified attacks in this manner. Finally, social media in themselves were almost never used to directly *report* attacks. This, in turn, indicates that the hotlines were reasonably effective in identifying and locating attacks, and the groups' priority online during demonstrations seems to have been to disseminate the numbers.

Communication Between Groups

The last feature included here was not a dominant feature, which is exactly why it is included. The groups *did not* use social media to communicate and coordinate with each other to a large extent. They frequently linked to each other's reports, testimonies and offline events, and they sometimes provided encouragement and praise for each other's work:

> @TahrirBodyguard please give our hugs to your team! The battle continues.
>
> @OpAntiSH, 1 July 2013

Yet, there are hardly any examples of the groups communicating directly or coordinating online, although they sometimes provided supplementary information to each other's tweets. However, in sharp contrast to the praise given above, OpAntiSH and TBG engaged in a rather heated argument in late January and early February 2013, on the perceived lack of cooperation between the two and an alleged attack on one party by the other:

> @OpAntiSH @[User 9] @[User 10] @[User 11] yes, there was a public attack. you can check Twitter & Facebook. Or we can show you, as you wish
>
> @TahrirBodyguard, 31 January 2013

> Again, @TahrirBodyguard there has been NO direct/indirect attacks from OpAntiSH's Facebook nor Twitter nor press releases!!!!
>
> @OpAntiSH, 31 January 2013

Fortunately, the groups soon were on amicable terms again. Yet, even though the groups did not communicate and coordinate using social media, they clearly did so through some other channel. For instance, I have found no evidence that cooperation connected to the operation of the hotlines and the provision of legal and medical help, which involved Nazra, OpAntiSH and several other groups, was negotiated or initiated online. As discussed above, offline networks were clearly important to the groups. As seen in what follows, a partial exception was TBG, which in the beginning frequently contacted HarassMap on Twitter and stated their interest in cooperation. This group did not know those involved, coming from the outside, so to speak, and a public invitation may have been the only, or at least the most obvious, choice:

> We need to work together under one umbrella. Unite our efforts against sexual harassment in #Egypt. Working on that @OpAntiSH @harassmap
>
> @TahrirBodyguard, 27 Novermber 2012

However, as cooperation became established, TBG did not do so any more. Once offline contacts were established, there would be no need to make public this kind of contact, which only needs to involve a few individuals and is of a private nature. Yet, voicing criticism and disagreements was another matter, and when one group – TBG – felt wronged by another group – OpAntiSH – they chose to say so in public. While there may have been many arguments offline as well, TBG clearly felt the need to display the perceived injustice in public. As we shall see in the following chapter, a similar mechanism was in play in Kuwait: activists generally preferred and were able to coordinate in private, but disagreements were sometimes made public if one party felt wronged.

Problems Solved and Offline Results

Certain problems and challenges dictated by the context were relevant to all groups studied, albeit to varying degrees. The groups needed to be able to communicate their views, to mobilise for their events and, not least, to recruit volunteers, and they needed to do so at a low cost. Two of the groups were ad hoc initiatives, created in response to an ongoing and critical situation, and they needed to do all this as fast as possible. One of these, namely TBG, started almost as an utterance of despair online, and then evolved quickly into an organisation capable of operating on the ground. Moreover, the groups, and particularly Nazra, HarassMap and OpAntiSH, wanted to reach those who had experienced harassment, without, of course, knowing who they were. In other words, they needed to make themselves and their work known to as many as possible, and to be accessible to those with something to tell. All groups wanted to make the issue as public as possible, and wanted the Egyptian public to be made aware of the extent of the problem. Some groups advocated legal reform, but they do not seem to have prioritised this aspect in their work. All groups also needed to be able to publish texts, videos and pictures, and to disseminate these as widely as possible. In addition, all groups wanted to be able to generate direct action to confront the problem.

Many of these challenges were solved through the use of online platforms – Twitter and Facebook in particular. These social media provided a platform for both publishing and disseminating their material, for discussing the issue and for recruiting volunteers and mobilising for events. They did not, however, reach everyone through online channels, but the groups seem to have been well aware of this aspect. Thus, they also conducted campaigns to gather and spread information offline, as well as to discuss the issue and, not least, to take direct action through patrols, demonstrations, and the like. Moreover, they did reach quite a few online, most of whom seem to have been people who, to varying degrees, agreed with them – crucial for any group seeking to mobilise support for an issue. The groups quite clearly seem to have been able to recruit enough volunteers to conduct their work. Moreover, they reached an international audience, through which they were able to generate material support in the form of crowd-funding, translation, technical assistance and attention to the issue. Finally, they seem to have reached and/or been accessible to journalists, both foreign and domestic.

For most of the groups, Twitter was the preferred platform, at least for providing updated information, agitation and discussions. They seldom debated the issue with those advocating opposing views, but they frequently engaged with those who shared their point of view. Not least, they spent much time presenting their understanding of the problem. However, it is clear that utilising social media is a skill, and this skill was not equally distributed among the groups. The most successful groups were also the most active, the ones that routinely used hashtags, provided complete and understandable messages and offered popular content. Offline networks seem to have been important, and those who were the most successful online were also the most successful offline. The most successful groups also seem to have been those with the most experience. Thus, while these platforms provide an extremely cheap solution for the challenges they faced, this does not mean that they override offline differences.

The groups did not succeed in ending sexual harassment in Egypt, nor its social acceptability. They did not succeed in ending the attacks on female protesters or making it completely safe for women to participate in demonstrations. However, they could hardly be expected to do so either, and they were remarkably successful in many respects. To begin with the latter issue: they were able to save dozens of women from attacks, and proved to Egyptian society that such attacks would not take place without a response. Moreover, women did not stop going to demonstrations, and were not excluded from public political participation, although the number of women taking part in Tahrir may have declined. They were able to document the severity and the extent of the problem, and they were able to gain the attention of the traditional media with their findings. Herein lies perhaps their biggest success: sexual harassment and sexual violence became subjects of public debate in Egypt, that is, in newspapers and on television, as a problem that needs to be addressed and solved. As Fraser points out, previous victories in solving problems that had been neglected by the public at large, such as domestic violence, began by gaining public acceptance of the existence of the problem *as* a problem.[260] Importantly, the severity of the problem is such that, once it is accepted as true, it cannot be dismissed. Political parties, the government and even the president all felt compelled to comment on the issue, and to show that they were doing something to solve it. Yet, how they would act was not a given, and it was of great importance that the groups were also able to affect how the issue was discussed, including the words used and how it was framed. For instance, they managed to mobilise widely against Islamist MPs' attempts to make the issue a question of morals.

Following several attacks on women during the celebrations in Tahrir of President al-Sisi's election, the president visited in hospital a woman who had been attacked, highly publicised arrests were made and new legislation imposing harsher punishments and clearly defining sexual harassment as a crime was promptly pushed through. Moreover, female police officers were dispatched to downtown Cairo to apprehend harassers.[261] On the one hand, this demonstrates success in establishing sexual harassment and sexual violence as problems of public concern, to which the representatives of the state must respond. On the other, many met these efforts with understandable scepticism, given the track record of the authorities.

Moreover, such efforts clearly fall short of the more comprehensive discussion sought by the groups on the issue as a public problem: while increased penalties and police efforts may be necessary, a narrow focus on these measures frames the problem as a simple question of security. Taken together with the much-publicised presidential visit to the hospital, it may signal the regime's appropriation of the issue for its own purposes, with the state assuming the role of protector, as described by Amar with reference to the 2000s.[262] Thus, as we shall see in the Kuwaiti case, gains are not necessarily made once and for all. Nevertheless, by the end of the time frame, the groups had achieved considerable success, and we should bear in mind that the groups are still active. Online platforms effectively solved many of the challenges faced by the groups, and were crucial in achieving their aims.

CHAPTER 5

THE KUWAITI CASE: THE CONTEXT, THE ISSUE, AND MY FINDINGS

On the evening of 15 October 2012, Musallam al-Barrak, widely seen as the leader of the Kuwaiti opposition, spoke to a defiant crowd of some 5,000 protesters.[1] The emir had recently dissolved the Parliament, in which the opposition enjoyed a majority. Even worse, he now threatened to increase the number of electoral districts, in effect crushing the victory of the 2006 Orange Movement. Not surprisingly, the crowd cheered as al-Barrak stated that power in Kuwait lies with the people, and that each and every one are the source of political power. Then, he did what no one had dared before him, he spoke directly to the emir: 'we will not let you, your highness the Emir, to rule this country on your own'.[2] The sense of liberation in uttering those words is quite evident both with the speaker and the crowd, which exploded in applause, chanting 'We will not let you'. Over the past year, the opposition had successfully demanded the resignation of the prime minister; they had won an election, were able to mobilise tens of thousands to the streets, publicly demanded constitutional reform and a full parliamentary system, and now they even challenged the emir directly. Seemingly, the opposition was able to break all the established rules of Kuwaiti politics in their bid for democratic reform. However, later that night, security forces violently broke up the demonstration and several participants were arrested.[3] Al-Barrak himself was later sentenced to two years in prison for his speech,[4] and the government by and large succeeded in crushing the opposition by early 2013. Clearly, the regime sought to push the opposition back across the red lines of Kuwaiti politics that they had crossed.

In the following, I will present the Kuwaiti case studied; that is, the spectacular rise and fall of the opposition movement in Kuwait over the past few years. I will argue that the youth movement was a driving force in challenging the established rules of Kuwaiti politics, and in reformulating the demands of the opposition. This youth movement grew out of an online, activist environment that came to the fore in 2006, and began organising online again in 2009, forming the groups studied here. Below, a detailed description is given of the genesis of this movement and the campaign from 2009 until 2013. As I have argued, proper contextualisation is key in order to understand and interpret the work of these groups, and not least the significance of their aims and the results they achieved. Their main aim concerned the political system of the country, and their work interfered with the established practice of politics in Kuwait, and so I begin with a brief discussion of the historical background. From there, I detail the issue at hand – democratic reforms – before I present the campaign studied. I then give the analysis of my material and the initial findings.

The Kuwaiti Context: Historical Background

The time frame for the Kuwaiti case stretches from November 2009 until March 2013. Although the campaign has its roots in previous activism in the country, it took a distinct turn beginning in 2009, openly challenging the established practice of politics in Kuwait. At the same time, previous initiatives and campaigns had laid the groundwork and provided invaluable experience for the protagonists, and these will be included in the discussion. However, at the heart of the current political conflict lies a question that has haunted the Kuwaiti state throughout its modern history, namely that of power sharing between the ruling family and its subjects.

The Al-Sabah and the Kuwaiti State

The literature on Kuwait states that the Al-Sabah was established as the ruling family by the middle of the eighteenth century.[5] Furthermore, there is broad agreement on the nature of the family's ascendance to their position: they were selected from among the powerful merchant families in the area to rule among equals, in consultation with those merchants.[6] According to Herb, the merchants in fact held the upper hand, as they kept the ruling family dependent on their own voluntary donations for the state's and the ruling family's income.[7] This situation changed at the end of the nineteenth century, during the reign of Sheikh Mubarak ('the Great', 1896–1915), who initiated a series of important changes, and who is today seen as the founder of the modern state of Kuwait. According to Salem, Sheikh Mubarak 'broke' the spirit of consultative rule and sought a more 'authoritarian style of politics'.[8] To weaken the merchants' power, he imposed a series of new taxes and took control of state revenues, a control that the ruling family has retained ever since. The merchants organised in protest and Mubarak eventually backed down. This was the first of many times during the twentieth century in which the merchants would organise in opposition to the ruling family.[9]

When Mubarak died in 1915, he was succeeded by the brief rule of his two sons, Jabir (1915–17) and Salim (1917–21). During the rule of the latter, a key event in Kuwaiti history took place, namely the battle of al-Jahra' and the construction of the city wall. Relations between Ibn Saʿud and the Kuwaiti emir had been deteriorating, and on 10 October 1920 the Wahabi Ikhwan forces attacked. They were met by the Kuwaitis in al-Jahra', just outside Kuwait city. The Kuwaitis prevailed, and an important national myth was born. Those who took part in the defence of the city and the construction of the wall have since been seen as the original Kuwaitis, whose loyalty to the state has never been questioned.[10] However, for those who did not take part, and even those who took part but have not been credited for doing so, the event carries a different meaning. One stark division in Kuwaiti society today runs between the *ḥaḍar*, that is, the city dwellers whose ancestors are said to have defended the city in 1920, and the *badw*, those of tribal origin, many of whom were granted citizenship in Kuwait at a later stage. While there certainly were *badw* who took part in the battle,[11] they have not been given the same credit as the *ḥaḍar*, and have at times been viewed with suspicion by the latter. Then, when the throne became vacant in 1921, two of Mubarak's grandsons sought power: Ahmad al-Jabir (son of Jabir) and ʿAbdallah al-Salim (son of Salim). However, Sunni merchants also seized the occasion and organised themselves into a council, demanding the right to advise both on 'the administration of the country' and on succession.[12] Ahmad al-Jabir was elected in line with their advice. This election instituted a power-sharing arrangement within the ruling family that is valid to this day: that the position of emir is reserved for the descendants of Mubarak's two sons (the Jabir line and the Salim line), and should alternate between the two.[13]

Independence and the Constitution

When Kuwait gained independence from Great Britain in June 1961, her citizens had already seen the rise and fall of their first representative assembly. In the summer of 1938, discontented merchants and notables drew up an electorate, consisting solely of their own peers, which elected a 14-member legislative assembly headed by Sheikh ʿAbdallah al-Salim.[14] The council passed a 'constitutional document', which held that 'the people were the source of all authority, represented through the elected deputies'.[15] Thus, the council, albeit short-lived, set an important precedent before it was dissolved in December of the same year.

Moreover, when Sheikh Ahmad al-Jabir died in 1950, it was Sheikh ʿAbdallah al-Salim who ascended to the throne, remaining emir until his death in 1965. Thanks to increased oil production, the new emir had a degree of financial leeway his predecessors would have envied, which gave rise to an ambitious development programme. However, spending was not tightly controlled and the merchants voiced their opposition to reckless spending and corruption and, perhaps most of all, to not receiving what they deemed to be their fair share of the spoils. The excessive spending took its toll on the emir's finances as well, and by 1953 he even had to borrow from the merchants. Seeking to free himself of their influence, the emir struck a deal with the merchants in 1954: 'In exchange for receiving a sizeable portion of oil revenues, the merchants renounced their historical claim to participate in decision making'.[16] In doing so, he provided the merchants with a powerful economic argument for retaining the political status quo. Financial leverage has since been employed to foster support in the population at large through wealth distribution, resulting in a monolithic economy in which more than 90 per cent of the labour force is employed by the state.[17]

When independence was declared, the emir announced he would establish a new constitution, providing for an elected assembly. The new constitution was drawn up by a constituent assembly consisting of 20 elected members and eleven government ministers from the royal family.[18] According to Alnajjar:

> [t]he deliberations took the form of negotiations between the elected members on one hand, and a representative of the ruling family (the current [at the time of his writing] Crown Prince and Prime Minister, Sa'd Abdallah Al-Sabah) on the other, over the amount of power that the ruling family would concede to the elected assembly,[19]

a point reiterated by Herb.[20] As a result, compromises are a dominant feature of the constitution. For instance, whereas article 6 states that the 'system of Governance in Kuwait shall be democratic', and that the people are 'the source of all powers', articles 50 to 78 heavily favour the emir in terms of executive and legislative powers.[21] In general, it 'falls short of true constitutional democracy', but is 'unparalleled among monarchies in the region'.[22] Not surprisingly, the interpretation and practical employment of the somewhat ambiguous text would prove to be a contested issue in the years to come.

Under the new constitution and the law on elections, five MPs were to be elected from each of ten electoral districts and, in addition, 15 members of the appointed cabinet would also hold seats in Parliament. The first elections, held in 1963, returned a government-friendly majority, but also a very vocal nationalist/pan-Arabist opposition. Then, in 1965, Sheikh 'Abdallah died, and was replaced by the then-prime minister, Sheikh Sabah al-Salim, ignoring the rule of alternation between the two eligible lines of the family. According to Alnajjar, Sheikh 'Abdallah's death represented a blow to the democratic project and marked the beginning of increased government interference in parliamentary life and elections.[23] This interference began in the 1967 elections, in which the regime used various means to achieve an opposition-free Parliament, including ballot stuffing and gerrymandering.[24] More importantly, the government naturalised thousands of *badw* in order to gain new, loyal allies. As a result, the electoral power of this group expanded rapidly, from 21 per cent of the electorate in 1963 to 45 per cent in 1975.[25] However, the absence of any opposition in the 1967 Parliament – despite being of their own making – made the royal family 'uncomfortable',[26] and relatively free elections were held in 1971 and 1975.[27] Then, the government's most dramatic interference to date took place, as the emir dissolved the assembly.

The Struggle for Parliament

According to article 107 of the Kuwaiti constitution, the emir is entitled to dissolve Parliament, but should then call for new elections within two months.[28] In 1976, however, the royal family set aside the constitution, and dissolved Parliament without any immediate calls for new elections. For the following five years, Kuwait did not have an elected assembly. Before parliamentary life was reintroduced in 1981, the regime wanted to rewrite the constitution, but backed down in the face of public opposition.[29] The regime did, however, succeed in changing the electoral districts, increasing these from ten to 25, which later would prove to be the rallying cause of an opposition campaign. Even so, the reintroduction of parliamentary life was not to last and, in 1986, the regime once again dissolved the assembly.

In both instances, there were several reasons behind the dissolutions, including regional events and the Parliament's interference in foreign policy.[30] However, perhaps most importantly, Parliament in both cases crossed the government too often, while at the same time lacking public support.[31] According to Herb, this is a crucial point as it goes to the heart of the regime's strategy, in which 'the pattern of openings and closings [of Parliament] is best understood as a strategy by the Al-Sabah to retain the support of moderate public opinion, while isolating radicals'.[32] That being said, the 1986 closure was soon met with organised opposition, but expressing political opinions at that time was not as easy as it had been; in 1985, the government had outlawed public gatherings of more than three persons,[33] and along with the dissolution itself came government censorship of news outlets.[34] In addition, the government kept tight control over voluntary and civil organisations.[35] Yet, there were two protected spaces readily available, namely mosques and private homes, which were exempt from the law on public gatherings.[36] Private homes were, and are, particularly important in this regard, as they are the site of the *dīwāniyāt* – 'the traditional meeting area adjacent to a Kuwaiti home'.[37] Although considered a social institution, and not entirely free from government interference, these institutions had been the site of important political deliberations throughout Kuwaiti history, and they retain this role today.[38] In December 1989, the opposition began their so-called 'Monday *dīwāniyāt*', attracting thousands of participants demanding the reopening of Parliament. The government responded in two ways: the security forces cracked down on the meetings[39] and a new council with restricted powers, *al-Majlis al-Waṭanī*, was established.[40] The opposition boycotted what they saw as an attempt to legitimise autocratic rule, but before the power struggle was settled, Iraqi forces invaded, on 2 August 1990.

The royal family's performance during the war was not viewed too favourably by Kuwaitis. Insofar as people's everyday needs were met during the occupation, this was not attributable to the royal family in exile, but to local, informal networks. This created a problem for the regime in terms of legitimacy, and something needed to be done. A conference was held in Jedda in mid-October, and what Herb terms the 'obvious deal' was struck: Kuwaitis would support the government in exile and the royal family, who in turn pledged a return to the constitution and parliamentary life.[41] Following liberation, the royal family kept their promise and, on 5 October 1992, new elections for the National Assembly were held. The elections returned an opposition majority, and, interestingly, 'a number of traditionally loyalist Bedouin districts returned opposition candidates'.[42] Originally intended as a counterweight to opposition forces, the influence of the Bedouins increased following the war as voting rights were expanded in 1994.[43] According to Salem's estimate, they constituted 65 per cent of the population as of 2008.[44]

In spite of the opposition's majority, the early 1990s were a period of relative calm in Kuwaiti politics, and the 1992 Parliament completed its four-year term. However, the 1996 Parliament did not. In fact, of the 17 Parliaments elected since 1963, only six have completed their terms, that is, about 35 per cent. The royal family has repeatedly demonstrated its willingness to interfere with parliamentary life and even suspend the constitution, while the opposition has demonstrated its ability to successfully campaign in favour of its reintroduction. As Tétreault rather eloquently argued:

> [t]he repeated recurrence of broadly similar situations and strategies indicates the inability of Kuwaiti rulers to 'go back' to a stable autocracy just as it reveals the inability of pro-democracy forces to 'move forward' to a stable rule of law. How to get off the horns of this dilemma is the fundamental issue to be resolved in Kuwaiti politics today.[45]

2006: The Rise of Youth Groups and Popular Mobilisation

Between 2006 and 2015, Kuwait has seen no fewer than seven elections and 14 cabinets. In order to understand this period of unprecedented conflict, two things deserve particular attention, namely the constitutional institution of *istijwāb*, and the events of 2006. To begin with the *istijwāb* (pl. *istijwābāt*, meaning interpellations, often referred to in the English-language press in Kuwait as 'grillings'), articles 100–102 of the Kuwaiti constitution state that every MP has the right to question a minister on any subject relating to his portfolio in the cabinet. This questioning might be followed by a vote of no confidence should at least ten MPs demand it; in such a vote, a simple majority is enough to unseat the minister.[46] The use of the *istijwāb* has increased drastically since 2006: from 2006 until July 2014, 55 *istijwābāt* were presented in Parliament, whereas the entire period of parliamentary life before that (1963–2006) only witnessed 33.[47] Moreover, while a total of five *istijwābāt* (15 per cent) were directed at the royal family before 2006 (and none against the PM), no less than 38 (69 per cent) have been directed at the ruling family since 2006, of which 17 (31 per cent) addressed the PM.[48] Most *istijwābāt* are presented by opposition MPs, and are often based on accusations of corruption, a key issue for the opposition. As observed by Herb, the interpellations provide the MPs with a powerful tool: 'it [the Parliament] has the ability to stymie government action without the responsibility for rule that would come from the formation of the government by parliamentary parties', with the end result often being 'political deadlock'.[49]

The events of 2006, Kuwait's 'Annus Mirabilis',[50] began on 15 January when the emir died. The crown prince, Sheikh Sa'd al-ʿAbdallah al-Salim, was very ill, and he was in effect deposed by Parliament and replaced by the then-prime minister, Sheikh Sabah al-Ahmad al-Jabir. While the Parliament's successful interference in the succession in itself was remarkable, the move had other, more sinister, consequences. As Sheikh Nawwaf al-Ahmad al-Jabir was named heir apparent and Sheikh Nasir al-Muhammad al-Ahmad al-Jabir prime minister, the al-Jabir branch of the royal family gained all the most influential positions at the expanse of the al-Salim branch, setting the stage for very public conflicts within the family in the years to come.[51] Importantly, the positions of PM and crown prince were kept separate, which made it possible for the opposition to criticise the PM. Prior to 2003, both offices were held by one person. This placed the PM outside the bounds of opposition criticism, as he one day would become emir, and the emir should not be criticised.

The succession crisis, as it was referred to, would also prove to be the beginning of a youth movement known both as Nabiha Khamsa[52] (We Want Five) or al-Haraka al-Burtuqaliyya (the Orange Movement, henceforth referred to as OM). The movement started with a blog that at the time provided news on the succession crisis when the traditional media did not.[53] By providing news on the issue, the blog in question had an audience in place when, later that year, the authors decided to start the campaign to change the electoral districts. Arguing that the 1981 increase in the number of electoral districts facilitated gerrymandering and vote buying, the authors of the blog Sahat al-saffat (known in English as Kuwaitjunior) in the spring of 2006 launched a campaign to reduce the number of districts to five (hence the name). By early May they held their first offline demonstration, a significant development as the ban on public gatherings introduced in the 1980s had been lifted by the constitutional court only days earlier.[54] The campaign managed to obtain the support of many established politicians, and when the government proposed in Parliament to ask the constitutional court to look into the issue in an attempt to sideline the issue, 29 MPs left the negotiations, rendering the assembly without a quorum. As a majority of the current Parliament seemed to support the campaign, the emir dissolved the assembly and called for new elections. Following a determined campaign by the OM supporting any candidate who embraced their suggestion of five electoral districts, the Kuwaiti electorate returned a clear majority in favour of reform and, on 17 July 2006, a new law instituting five electoral districts was passed nearly unanimously.

Two more important events took place in Kuwait in 2006: women participated for the first time in the parliamentary elections on an equal footing with men, and Sheikh Nasir al-Muhammad began his extremely troubled premiership. Following the 2006 elections, it did not take long before opposition MPs presented new interpellations against cabinet ministers, accompanied by the implicit or explicit threat of votes of no confidence. Through fear of losing such votes, interpellations often led to the pre-emptive resignation of either the cabinet or the minister in question.[55] This would prove to be a recurring pattern, leaving Kuwaiti politics in a dysfunctional pattern of cabinet reshuffles and early elections. While this might be seen as obstructionist behaviour on the part of the parliamentary opposition, it is also a reflection of the political tools granted to MPs in the constitution, which are 'largely negative'.[56] From their point of view, the continued attacks through interpellations were an attempt to pressure the government in the direction they sought. While the opposition hardly had a unified programme, there were three issues that were of particular importance, namely the fight against corruption, the fight for democratic reform (albeit vaguely articulated at the time) and – increasingly until his resignation in 2011 – a demand to remove Prime Minister Sheikh Nasir.

The Volatile Context of the Campaign Studied

This was the chaotic state of affairs of Kuwaiti politics when young activists again started to organise in 2009, and the time frame set for this investigation began. Following a period of relative calm in the 1990s, the opposition increasingly, and more directly than before, challenged the government in the Parliament, and with it the accepted limits of opposition politics in the country. Kuwaiti history shows that there are clear limits to what the royal family will tolerate, and that one challenge too many might lead to the suspension of parliamentary politics. On the other hand, the royal family had never been able to abandon representative practices altogether, and the opposition successfully mobilised popular opinion in favour of restoring the Parliament both in the late 1970s and in the late 1980s. Thus, it may not be surprising that, ever since independence, the opposition had framed their democratic struggle as a defence of the constitution. Still, this strategy had not produced any democratic gains, and the fundamental question of power sharing remained unresolved.

Throughout the 1990s and the 2000s, the composition of the opposition changed. In the years following independence, secular liberal and pan-Arab *ḥaḍar* formed the challenge to the regime, and Bedouins were naturalised to form a counterweight. In the 1980s, the regime also supported Islamists for the same reason, who often allied with conservative, tribal politicians. Following the war, tribal districts returned their first opposition politicians to Parliament and, by the late 2000s, tribal and Islamist MPs would come to dominate the parliamentary opposition. Similarly, whereas the 2006 OM was dominated by liberal *ḥaḍar* activists, later youth movements came to be dominated by tribal activists. Importantly, while the opposition still includes *ḥaḍar* activists and politicians, we have seen that the *ḥaḍar/badw* split runs deep in Kuwaiti society, beginning with the battle of al-Jahra'. The different social and political standings of the two groups are relevant both in the composition of the opposition and in their dedication to democratic reform – the issue at hand for the groups studied.

The Issue: The Fight for Democratic Reform in Kuwait

The tribal population has suffered discrimination in favour of the *ḥaḍar* population. According to Al-Nakib, the government from the beginning sought to exclude this group both socially and geographically, most importantly through their housing policies from the 1950s until the 1980s.[57] The newly naturalised, as well as those who were not yet naturalised, were settled in their own areas, at quite some distance from the city centre, with inferior housing and services. At the same time, they were politically integrated, so that the regime could secure a loyal group of voters not influenced by opposition elements in the city. In Al-Nakib's view, this explains why the regime heavy-handedly interfered when one of the so-called Monday *dīwāniyyāt* of the 1989 pro-democracy movement was held in the tribal areas, as it was 'putting its residents at risk of political contamination'.[58] However, over time, and not least through a new generation of well-educated tribal citizens, an increasing number of people saw that they were supporting a regime that did not support them equally.[59] In a similar vein, Tétreault argued in 1995 that the tribal population had a 'general lower socio-economic status' than the *ḥaḍar*.[60] In her view, Kuwait at the time did far better in terms of positive liberties than negative liberties, yet even these were 'enjoyed disproportionally more by the economically and socially better off Kuwaitis'.[61] If, however, larger parts of society were to be included, this could bolster the democratic development of the country:

> Democratization is constrained by the common interests shared by the ruling family and social groups that already dominate politics, economics, and society in Kuwait. What could move Kuwaiti politics off this equilibrium is the strengthening of additional groups whose interests diverge from those of the other two.[62]

In these groups she also includes the younger generation of Kuwaitis. Still, she warns that the inclusion of new groups provides no predictable end result: 'there is no guarantee that an increase in political participation by any of these new groups, would automatically promote democratization'.[63]

Still, if the tribal parts of the population were to affect this equilibrium, reform of the political system was needed. Even though the tribal population now constitutes the majority of the population, this has not been reflected politically: following the 2006 reform of the electoral law, the two tribal districts elect 20 MPs on behalf of 209,598 voters, whereas the three *ḥaḍar* districts elect 30 MPs on behalf of 175,192 voters.[64] Democratic reform was needed to ensure equal representation, and the results achieved by the opposition working for such reform over several decades within the framework of the current constitution were hardly impressive. While it was a gradual process, it is not difficult to see why impatient young tribal (and some *ḥaḍar*) activists concluded that a more democratic system was needed, and that this would entail changing the constitution. According to the opposition, this was also necessary in order to deal with two other issues with which they were concerned, namely corruption and the premiership of Sheikh Nasir. Thus, there is an anti-establishment element to the opposition and their issues of concern or, to put it differently, as a privileged minority and the beneficiaries of the 1954 historic compromise with the royal family, the *ḥaḍar* elite would have much to gain from retaining the status quo. In a simplified description of the competing sides in the country's current political conflict, one could say that the opposition mainly consists of tribals and Islamists, whereas the pro-government side is composed of *ḥaḍar* and the Shi'a (who are also *ḥaḍar*). However, there are very important exceptions and, no less important, there are varying stances within both the opposition and the pro-government camps. There were several liberal *ḥaḍar* politicians who took part when the opposition boycotted the December 2012 elections, and even some who support the demand for a constitutional emirate. However, there were many more *ḥaḍar* who supported the opposition in their fight against changes to the electoral law imposed by the government in the autumn of 2012, changes that were seen as restricting the democratic rights enjoyed by the Kuwaiti population. In other words, both the government and the opposition found it difficult to gain wide support for their more drastic measures and positions, but were able to do so for their more moderate stances. As we have seen, this struggle for public support has been key for both the opposition and the regime throughout Kuwaiti history. Finally, the youth movement has been a driving force within the opposition over the past few years, and when young activists entered the political stage in 2006, they sought to build as wide a coalition as possible.

The Genesis of the Online Youth Movement

Internet was introduced in Kuwait following the Iraqi occupation, and the government actively sought to provide access to its citizens. As of 2014, the International Telecommunications Union (ITU) estimates that more than 78 per cent of people in Kuwait use the internet.[65] This is an increase from 28 per cent in 2006 and 50.8 per cent in 2009.[66] It is unclear, however, if this number refers to Kuwaiti citizens or to all people living in the country. Kuwait has a substantial number of foreign workers, as well as a large stateless population known as *Bidūn*. There is every reason to believe that the number of internet users is higher among Kuwaiti citizens than within the total population of the country, as citizens have free access to education, health services and public employment. Kuwait is a very wealthy country – GDP per capita is about the same as that of the United States[67] – and illiteracy is not a major problem.[68]

When the 2006 movement began to organise, the Kuwaiti blogosphere was seen as unpolitical.[69] Having built a readership during the succession crisis, the liberal *ḥaḍar* bloggers behind Sahat al-Saffat started to discuss the issue of the electoral districts in April. A campaign site was set up, with information on the issue and on how to lobby MPs and other influential figures. Other blogs also took part, but the main site for debate was the comments on Sahat al-Saffat. In a debate in the comments to a post published on 3 May 2006, one user suggested they should take to the streets and, on 5 May, they did.[70] Then, when Parliament was dissolved, various blogs were used to support all candidates that agreed with their position, to mobilise for demonstrations, expose alleged corruption and, not least, to support and encourage the unity of the activists who took part, of both tribal and *ḥaḍar* background.[71] As we have seen, the movement was successful and the number of electoral districts was reduced to five. While the regime was clearly forced to do something it did not wish to do, it should be noted that the reform was well within the boundaries of the constitution, and did not challenge the position of the royal family directly.

The Orange Movement gained several advantages by organising online. For one thing, to establish a traditional, offline organisation was problematic, as the government kept tight control over voluntary and civil organisations.[72] A partial exception would be the student unions, which at times have taken part in the opposition campaign, and key organisers had experience from Kuwaiti student unions abroad.[73] However, these unions had the obvious restriction that they only include students, and had been dominated by Islamists since the late 1970s.[74] Moreover, public gatherings were outlawed in the mid-1980s. When the *dīwāniyya* movement challenged this, the government replied with force. Thus, as an established and legitimate method of political expression, the status of demonstrations was somewhat unclear in 2006, even following the verdict by the constitutional court. It was hardly an alternative to begin their organisation offline. When they *did* move offline, they knew that they would not be left alone facing the police as they had already organised online. Importantly, the reintroduction of public mobilisation as an avenue for protest was one of the lasting changes that the OM achieved in Kuwaiti politics, as argued by Diwan: 'Political change requires a cultural change: to convince Kuwaitis that protests are a right'.[75]

As we have seen, previous opposition campaigns in Kuwait had been centred around the *dīwāniyyāt*. However, for several reasons, these traditional gatherings would hardly have been suitable for the organisation of a youth movement. For one thing, they – at least the most popular ones – are usually hosted by men of a certain social and political standing. While there are *dīwāniyāt* for young people as well, these are typically not of a political nature.[76] Moreover, they are the traditional domain of men, not women, although this convention has been changing.[77] Finally, attendance is based on invitation, although politicians sometimes announce open invitations.[78] A central feature of the online activist environment in 2006 was that many of them did not know each other prior to the OM, as pointed out by one participant: 'bloggers before the beginning of the Orange [M]ovement were total strangers yet became close cyber-friends, and that was the beauty of that group'.[79] Online platforms seem to have enabled young activists to go public, take initiatives and cooperate across traditional boundaries, based on shared interest in a subject rather than an invitation to an offline gathering.

In 2006, internet usage in Kuwait was limited, and the activists in the OM predominantly communicated with each other via the blogs. However, one of the lasting changes to Kuwaiti politics effected by the OM was the introduction of online platforms as tools of activism and arenas for political debate. Over the past few years, online platforms, particularly Twitter, have become not only an arena for dedicated activists, but also a part of the 'public at large', as discussed in Chapter 2. In fact, the country has the highest number of Twitter users per capita in the world.[80] Influential figures in Kuwaiti society are highly active on the platform, and media in the country routinely refer to debates that take place on Twitter. Ahead of the July 2013 elections, hopeful candidates reportedly spent up to US$35,000 to hire help in communicating on the platform, as it was seen as 'a favorite platform to promote political campaigns'.[81] Established politicians, intellectuals, journalists, analysts, some members of the royal family and activists engage in political exchanges that are at times heated. Interestingly, the discussion is not only among those who already agree with each other, and there are also several examples of people from different sides engaging in direct debate. One of these debates even moved offline, with two activists defending opposing views on a particular matter, represented by the hashtags employed by the two sides.[82] However, these debates were hardly in line with Habermas's force-of-the-argument ideal, and often took the form of competitions between the positions being advocated. Testament to the importance of the platform, the government has increasingly persecuted activists for opinions expressed on the platform, even revoking citizenships.[83]

Interestingly, Tétreault pointed to the need for new public platforms in 1995. In her view, as the press at times faced severe restrictions, the *dīwāniyyāt* and the mosques were the only protected space for political deliberation. This, however, was problematic, because '[e]ven though Kuwait is small, it is not small enough for all Kuwaitis to share the same space of appearance when that space is private rather than public'.[84] While she emphasises that the press is 'the largest public forum in the country' when it is allowed to function, she argues that, even at the best of times, there are restrictions on what can be published. In the example she provides, a journalist solved this by 'simply fax[ing] the article to several diwaniyyas', which 'is only a second-best solution from the perspective of democracy, because it partially privatizes political discourse and limits the points of view reflected in the public arena'.[85] It is important to note here that, following a liberalisation of the press law in 2006, many new media outlets have been started in Kuwait, and as such might provide an expansion of the public sphere. Yet, as shown by Selvik et al., many of the new outlets are owned by members of the royal family or businessmen sympathetic to the royal family, and proved to be biased against the tribal population in their coverage of the 2009 elections.[86] Not surprisingly, the opposition campaigns studied here frequently expressed their distrust in what they termed the 'corrupt media' and seldom sought their attention,[87] as will be discussed below. The exception, however, would be the two online newspapers *Alaan.cc* and *Sabr.cc*, which were clearly sympathetic to, and trusted by, the opposition.[88]

By late summer 2006, the OM had succeeded in their campaign, and had demonstrated the abilities of young activists – not least their ability to lead. According to Tétreault and al-Ghanim, this led to young Kuwaitis being given more responsibility in civil society organisations in the years that followed.[89] Perhaps more importantly, youth groups since then have simply taken the lead themselves, and established politicians – many of whom cooperated with the OM – have listened. Furthermore, they had introduced online platforms as an arena for debate and activism, and a community of online activists had been formed. This community – veterans from the OM – would prove to be the starting point when young activists once again organised online, in 2009.

The Campaign Studied: The Youth Movement from 2009 to 2013

Activists, and everyone else in Kuwait for that matter, witnessed three politically turbulent years from 2006 until 2009, with the parliamentary opposition increasingly assertive and determined to challenge the boundaries of acceptable opposition behaviour using interpellations as their weapon.[90] In March 2007, oppositional MPs demanded a vote of no confidence following the interpellation of a minister from the royal family. Knowing they would lose the vote, the government resigned.[91] A vote *was* allowed to take place in January 2008, but the minister in question was not from the royal family, and she survived comfortably.[92] On 17 March 2008, the government handed in its resignation, citing lack of cooperation on the part of the Parliament. The emir accepted the resignation, dissolved Parliament and called for new elections on 17 May. However, if the regime hoped for a more compliant assembly, it was disappointed and, by November, the first interpellation against the PM was presented. Predictably, the government resigned, only to reappear with minor changes. This spectacle was repeated in March 2009, when three different interpellations were filed against the PM. This time, no new government was appointed, as it was clear that the ongoing situation with repeated government resignations was untenable. On 16 March the emir once again dissolved the National Assembly, and called for new elections on 16 May. The voters were said to be tired of the continuous fighting in the political arena, and a more compliant Parliament was the result. Still, the opposition was far from eradicated, and on 8 June a new interpellation was submitted against the interior minister, a member of the royal family. This time, the government chose to face both questioning and a vote of no confidence, thereby setting a new precedent.[93]

Parallel to the struggle in Parliament, the young activists, now frustrated with both the prime minister and the continuing political deadlock, started to move online. On 14 October 2009, a well-known blogger, who three years earlier was the one who suggested that the OM should take to the streets, published a post entitled 'To the Kuwaiti blogs, with greetings'.[94] In it, the author argued that Kuwait belongs to all its citizens, whether *ḥaḍar*, *badw*, Shi'a, Sunni, liberal or Salafi, and that they should work together to improve their country. This entailed working for a more democratic political system, and not least removing the unpopular, and in their view corrupt, prime minister. He asked his colleagues (other Kuwaiti bloggers) to take part in this struggle, and a debate, though limited in terms of participants, took place, involving several activists involved in the OM. On 27 October the movement 'Irhal, nastahiqq al-afdal' ('Leave, we deserve better') was launched simultaneously on at least 16 blogs.[95] The group started a Facebook group on 27 October,[96] and launched its own blog on 9 November.[97] The movement held several demonstrations, the first on 16 November, but they seem to have been limited in size. It is also clear from the beginning that they, or at least parts of the movement, held meetings with opposition politicians,[98] although it was stated that they did not agree with them on every aspect of the political struggle.[99] At around the same time, opposition MP Faysal al-Muslim submitted an interpellation against the prime minister, on charges of corruption.[100] This time, as with the minister of the interior, the government chose to face both questioning and a vote of no confidence in Parliament, though only after securing the support of 30 of the 50 MPs eligible to take part in the vote.[101] While the new campaign demonstrated outside Parliament, confidence in the PM was renewed by a comfortable margin. Still, this meant that the 'right to question ministers was successfully broadened to include interrogation of the Prime Minister',[102] and further interpellations would follow.

The spring and summer of 2010 would prove to be a calmer period in Kuwaiti politics. A new interpellation against the PM was discussed in Parliament in June, but when a majority voted to close the session, the interpellation was withdrawn. In August 2010, what appears to have been a short-lived activist initiative, 'Iradat al-Sha'b' (The Will of the People), was formed and published a declaration on Facebook with five demands, arguing for an elected prime minister; that is, a PM heading a government based on a parliamentary majority, on the basis of the constitution.[103] In fact, the five demands presented not only speak of the democratic features of the constitution, but also argue for the need to revise the paragraphs in question. In other words, the document goes a long way towards presenting the same demands that the larger part of the opposition youth movement would endorse a year later, though not in the same words. While the declaration published on the Facebook page was not signed, the same demands were also published in the online newspaper *Alaan.cc* on the same day, with 21 individuals signing on, mostly tribal and Islamist activists.[104] However, the initiative does not seem to have gained a wide following. This does not mean that activists were satisfied with the outcome of their struggle for democratisation so far, but rather that they were otherwise engaged, namely in campaigns to defend other activists persecuted by the authorities.

On 22 November 2009, lawyer, journalist, blogger and activist Muhammad al-Jasim was arrested on accusations of 'libel and slander', following the criticism and charges of corruption against the prime minister that he voiced at a *dīwāniyya* at the end of October.[105] Many activists, as well as the 'We Deserve Better' campaign, took up the issue as a question of freedom of speech. At around the same time, a number of bloggers were allegedly threatened by members of the state security services, which sparked a reaction from their colleagues.[106] On 30 November/1 December, a number of politically involved blogs 'shut down' for 24 hours as a protest.[107] On 11 May 2010, al-Jasim was arrested again, and on 18 May the 'We Deserve Better' campaign held a demonstration in support of him at the square opposite Parliament, referred to as Sahat al-Irada (Square of the Will), in addition to several other gatherings organised by others. On 24 June the campaign site Aljasemcase.com was created to advocate his case, and on 28 June he was released on bail.[108] However, only two days later, Khaled Alfadala, secretary general of the National Democratic Alliance and one of the heroes of the Orange Movement, was sentenced to three months in jail, again because he had accused the PM of corruption in a speech. A campaign site was promptly set up, as well as a YouTube account, a Twitter account and a Facebook page,[109] under the slogan 'Kulluna Khaled Alfadala' (We Are All Khaled Alfadala).[110] He was released after serving only ten days, but it seemed clear that the government intended to use a more severe approach towards the opposition.[111] This willingness to punish those criticising the government would soon escalate the conflict further.

New Movements are Launched

On 1 December 2010, 23 members of Parliament released a joint statement announcing the formation of the campaign 'Illa al-Dustur' (Only the Constitution).[112] The campaign came as a response to the government's attempt to make the assembly lift the parliamentary immunity of one opposition MP, Faysal al-Muslim, so that he could be prosecuted for revealing confidential information. This information consisted of cheques, allegedly proving the corruption of the prime minister, presented during the 2009 interpellation of Nasir al-Muhammad.[113] According to Diwan, this was seen in connection with yet another arrest of al-Jasim on 22 November.[114] The first meeting of the campaign was held on 4 December, at the *dīwāniyya* of prominent opposition MP Ahmad al-Saʿdun, and the second on 8 December, at the *dīwāniyya* of MP Jamaʿan al-Harbash.[115] This time, the security services struck, injuring as many as 14 persons, including four MPs,[116] and arresting a renowned constitutional scholar. The attack sparked outrage among the opposition in a country not accustomed to the use of violence as a means to silence critical voices, and 'united all the Parliament's opposition groupings – liberal, Islamist, and tribal populist – in criticism of the current Government'.[117] An interpellation against the prime minister was promptly submitted, resulting in a vote of no confidence that he barely survived – 25 to 22 – on 5 January 2011. This would also be the spark that led to the creation of a number of new youth movements, that is, those studied in this investigation.[118] On 25 December, the group al-Sur al-Khamis (The Fifth Fence) was formed, and a Twitter account created. The group called for a demonstration to coincide with Parliament's first discussion of the abovementioned interpellation on 28 December, under the slogan '*al-Taʿāwun Tahāwun*' ('Cooperation is Neglect'). The group was said to consist primarily of tribal activists, including veterans of the OM. A statement regarding the first demonstration was published on the online forum of the Mutayr tribe.[119] On 28 February 2011, a new group, Kafi (Enough), was formed. A demonstration was planned for 8 March but, according to Diwan, cohesion turned out to be a problem, as the movement 'fragmented into two and later three separate organizations',[120] and indeed, new movements were created. On 6 March, 'Hamlat Nurid' (the 'We Want' campaign) was announced in a declaration published by *Alaan.cc*, in which three demands were articulated: a new government, a new prime minister and a new 'approach', taken to mean a more democratic form of governance on the part of the regime.[121] On 7 March, yet another youth movement was formed, namely Shabab al-Hurriyya (Youth of Freedom), which stated its goals in a series of tweets, including an 'elected government' and the legalisation of political parties. On 8 March, al-Sur al-Khamis, Kafi and Hamlat Nurid jointly held the planned demonstration, demanding a new PM and a new Parliament.[122] However, the demonstration had to change its location, as the Ministry of Interior prohibited the organisers from gathering at Sahat al-Irada. Nevertheless, several prominent political figures participated in the demonstration.[123]

During March 2011, a number of interpellations were presented against three ministers, all members of the royal family, which led yet again to the resignation and reappointment of very similar governments. On 22 June, the PM once again faced a vote of no confidence, which he survived by a comfortable margin.[124] Interestingly, an interpellation was also presented by two pro-government MPs against the PM's main rival within the ruling family, Ahmad al-Fahd. As pointed out by Coates Ulrichsen, conflict within the royal family over the distribution of various important offices following the 2006 power grab by one branch of the family led to tensions that 'intersected with the volatile political scene', adding to instability in the country.[125] For their part, the youth movement continued to put pressure on the PM in the streets, with regular demonstrations on Fridays.[126] On 27 May, a 'Friday of Wrath' demonstration was called for, with the activists of Kuwait seemingly taking cues from demonstrators in other Arab countries. While Kuwaiti activists were inspired by the so-called Arab Spring, it is clear that their campaigns and conflict with the regime predated the Tunisian uprising, as has been shown here. Nevertheless, the government did provide their citizens with a 'generous hand-out' in early 2011 to pre-empt 'any spread of unrest'.[127] This attempt at appeasement was, however, not successful. When the prime minister responded to the 'Friday of Wrath' by stating that the demonstrators did not express the view of the people, al-Sur al-Khamis, the 'We Want' campaign, and others held a 'Friday of Answer [to the PM]' demonstration on 3 June. According to the newspaper *Al-Watan*, the protest drew a crowd of up to 1,500 people.[128] By the end of the month, two more movements had been formed, namely Shabab al-Taghyir wa-l-Tatwir (Youth for Change and Development) and al-ʿAdala al-Dusturiyya (Constitutional Justice), with the latter being announced on the YouTube channel of the ʿUtayb tribe.[129] Then, corruption charges against the prime minister were fuelled as new evidence was presented. In 2009, evidence had first surfaced that the PM had made payments to supportive MPs and other influential persons in Kuwait. On 30 August 2011, the campaign site 25millionkd.com was launched, in an attempt to expose the members of Parliament who might be implicated. According to Tétreault, 'local banks were reported to be preparing to refer between 15 and 20 members of Parliament to the public prosecutor to be investigated for money laundering [...] the suspicious deposits began to look like bribes and the bribes seemed to be coming from the Prime Minister'.[130] While the youth movement hardly needed any further reason to campaign for reform, they did up the ante with a demonstration planned for 16 September.

On 10 September, the formation of a new movement, or rather a coalition of movements, was announced in a statement published by

Alaan.cc. The new group, called the September 16 coalition, presented four demands for democratic reform, including a demand for a *īmāra dustūriyya* – a constitutional emirate. Moreover, they explicitly stated that they wanted the constitution to be reformed in line with their demands.[131] The new coalition was formed by some of the recently established youth groups, namely al-Sur al-Khamis, Kafi, al-ʿAdala al-Dusturiyya, Shabab al-Taghyir wa-l-Tatwir and Shabab al-Hurriyya.[132] The demonstration itself, however, was not particularly successful, as fewer than 300 protesters took part.[133] Nevertheless, the government seemed to take the threat posed by the activists seriously, as two of them were detained in early November for writing tweets deemed offensive to the emir – hardly unrelated to their political project.[134] Yet, while the demands presented might have been too radical at the time, there was no escape for the prime minister following the latest revelations. Several demonstrations were held in the following weeks, with one on 19 October described as the 'largest to date', allegedly drawing as many as 12,000 protesters.[135] There was movement in Parliament as well, and by early November it was clear that enough former supporters of the government had switched sides to provide the opposition with the votes needed to remove the PM. On 15 November, three MPs submitted the interpellation. However, the government had one last card to play. Earlier, they had managed to make Parliament send a request to the constitutional court regarding the legality of questioning the PM, using the 15 cabinet members able to vote in Parliament in order to do so. The court deemed the practice unconstitutional in October, thus providing yet another possible lifeline for al-Muhammad.[136] Not surprisingly, this provoked the rage of the opposition, resulting in a demonstration on 16 November, ending with some protesters storming the Parliament and crowds chanting *al-shaʿb yurīd isqāṭ al-raʾīs* (the people want the downfall of the prime minister [literally 'the president', but meant to refer to the PM]), a message difficult to misunderstand in the midst of the so-called Arab Spring. The emir heard the message loud and clear and, on 28 November, Nasir al-Muhammad handed in his last resignation. The opposition had not only crossed several red lines of Kuwaiti political practice – they had achieved an important goal in doing so. Skipping the al-Salim line once again, former defence minister Jabir Al-Sabah was named PM on 1 December, the National Assembly was dissolved and new elections were called for 2 February 2012.

The Peak and Fall of Popular Mobilisation

Opposition candidates fared well in the February 2012 elections, and won 35 of the 50 seats in the National Assembly.[137] However, the parliamentary majority did not bring the democratic reform that many wanted. One important victory was achieved when the new prime minister was questioned in an open session on 28 March, the first interpellation of a PM to be discussed in an open session in Kuwaiti history. Yet, much time was spent on narrow religious issues, including attempts to make sharia *the* and not *a* source of legislation, and to introduce the death penalty for blasphemy. Such moves were hardly encouraging for liberal *ḥaḍar*, and they did not meet the expectations of the pro-democracy youth activists in general, resulting in growing distrust between MPs and impatient activists.[138] Nevertheless, the spring of 2012 was a relatively calm period, with the youth movements focusing on their own organisation. On 27 and 28 February, the 'founding conference of the youth movement' was held, following a call from various organisations.[139] In the words of the newspaper *Al-Qabas*, the conference 'gave birth to a political movement', namely al-Haraka al-Dimuqratiyya al-Madaniyya (Hadam) (the Civil Democratic Movement).[140] The movement stated its general goal as working towards a more democratic society, including a more democratic electoral system. A rather complex structure was set up for the organisation, with accompanying and similarly complex statutes.[141] A leadership was elected, including activists with experience from the OM and later movements.[142] The logo, website and other visible symbols of the new group were all mostly orange, evoking memories of the 2006 movement. Moreover, the movements Kafi, Shabab al Taghyir wa-l-Tatwir and al-ʿAdala al-Dusturiyya became part of the new group, while al Sur al-Khamis stayed outside, although its representatives were present at the conference.[143] Thus, the new group did not encompass the entire opposition youth movement, and it was also the subject of criticism from other activists.[144] In general, many discussions took place online in the spring of 2012, as Twitter became *the* arena of political debate on central issues. The debates were organised by hashtags, and at times generated thousands of tweets, involving known activists, movements, politicians and even members of the royal family.[145] In April, a debate was started using the hashtag #ليش_منتخبة (why elected), on the issue of why Kuwait was in need of an 'elected government'. Other debates included the hashtag #مواد_الدستور_الجديد (the articles of the new constitution), on propositions for a new constitution (December 2012), various debates on whether or not to attend particular demonstrations and the rather interesting #علمت_من_الربيع_العربي (I learned from the Arab Spring), on lessons learned from the Arab Spring (October 2012). These debates drew attention also outside Kuwait and, on 3 September, *al-Arabiyya* claimed that 'everyone' in Kuwait took part in, or at least read, these discussions.[146]

Even though the opposition majority in Parliament did little to further the cause of reform, the emir soon decided that the political situation was untenable. On 7 June, a staunchly anti-tribal and pro-government MP submitted an interpellation against the minister of the interior,[147] and on 18 June the emir dissolved the Parliament for a period of one month, which is within his powers according to the constitution. It is difficult to imagine that these events were not related. Two days later, the constitutional court dissolved the 2012 assembly altogether, arguing that the dissolution of the previous assembly, the one elected in 2009, had been unconstitutional.[148] The opposition was understandably furious, and those elected to the old assembly refused to take part in any new sessions. The old speaker of Parliament was nevertheless reinstated, but was unable to mobilise a quorum. Even so, a new cabinet was sworn in, headed by the same PM. A new election was bound to be announced, but this was viewed with scepticism by the opposition as rumours said that the emir would change the electoral system. This was confirmed in early August when the cabinet agreed to ask the constitutional court to review the 2006 reform.[149] The opposition, for their part, mobilised in protest both against any changes to the electoral law and against the dissolution of the 2012 Parliament. On 26 June, more than 5,000 people gathered to protest against the return of the 2009 Parliament.[150] Subsequently, a series of meetings took place at various *dīwāniyyāt*, referred to as Monday *dīwāniyyāt* in reference to the 1989 protest movement, in which both activists and the politicians of the 'majority' – the opposition majority of the 2012 Parliament – took part. On 15 July, a declaration was released by this 'majority' calling for an elected government, one electoral district, legalisation of political parties and a constitutional emirate – the demands presented one year earlier by several youth movements.[151] Not surprisingly, this step was controversial within the opposition; 15 members of the 'majority' voted against the declaration, and several activists withdrew and released their own statement of protest.[152] Yet, when it became clear that the government was serious in its attempt to change the electoral law, all parts of the opposition joined together in the protest. On 27 August, a demonstration called for by the 'Nahj' movement[153] drew a crowd of more than 2,000 protesters against changes to the electoral law, calling for an elected government and for a constitutional emirate.[154] Further protests were held during the following weeks, until the constitutional court declared the 2006 reform constitutional in late September.[155] On 7 October, the emir finally dissolved the 2009 Parliament.

However, on 20 October, an emergency decree was issued and approved by the cabinet, reducing the number of votes each person could cast from four to one. The move was anticipated by the opposition, which predictably opposed such a clear-cut attack on the victory of the 2006 Orange Movement. On 15 October, more than 5,000 Kuwaitis gathered in protest and Musallam al-Barrak gave his famous speech, known as the '*lan nasmaḥu laka*' (We will not allow you [the Emir]) speech. The aforementioned heavy-handed response of the regime did little to deter protesters and a new demonstration was planned for 21 October, organised by Karamat Watan (Dignity of a Nation), a new group with the sole purpose of organising protests. The demonstration itself turned out to be an unprecedented success in terms of numbers, drawing a crowd estimated at between 50,000 and 150,000,[156] including liberal *ḥaḍar* activists. While the demand for a constitutional emirate might have been too radical for many, it seemed that most parts of Kuwaiti society could agree on the struggle to preserve their already established political rights. However, the regime had no intention of allowing such an opposition display. Riot police used tear gas, rubber bullets and truncheons to break up the march, and several activists were arrested.[157] Yet again, the deterrent effect was limited, and the autumn of 2012 was a time of unprecedented popular mobilisation in Kuwait. Moreover, most opposition movements and politicians, including the liberal forces, declared that they would boycott the upcoming elections. On 5 November, the 'Popular Committee for the Boycott of the Elections' was founded, with the aim of organising the boycott and also observing the elections themselves, in order to establish the turnout.[158] The large demonstrations continued, including two more organised by Karamat Watan. Although the police dispersed the first of these, the following demonstration was allowed to take place in peace. This might have been related to a 'veiled criticism' voiced by the United States, reminding their ally of the right of all citizens to express their opinions.[159] That being said, the government still sought to crack down on its opponents, arresting several activists on 7 November for criticism expressed online, including two members of the royal family itself.[160] Understandably, the attacks on freedom of expression online angered Kuwait's seasoned blogging community and, on 16 December, prominent bloggers released the 'blogger's statement', condemning the government's behaviour.[161] By the end of the year, in spite of US criticism, *Kuwait Times* reported that an unprecedented number of 491 people had been 'trialed for riots'.[162]

On 1 December, the elections took place. Not surprisingly, voters returned a much more compliant assembly from the perspective of the regime. However, the opposition claimed victory as well, arguing that the boycott had succeeded. According to their estimate, the turnout was as low as 28 per cent, whereas the regime claimed that 43 per cent of voters had taken part.[163] Whatever the truth, turnout was markedly lower than in previous elections.[164] The opposition itself saw the boycott as a success, and made sure to say so online: the hashtag #المقاطعة_نجحت (the boycott succeeded) generated more than 3,000 tweets within 24 hours of the election. Yet, even as the opposition claimed victory, they were left outside of formal politics. Thus, they once again took to the streets, and the fourth Karamat Watan march was held on 8 December, drawing up to 4,500 participants.[165] This obviously concerned the authorities, and on 16 December the *Arab Times* reported that 'foreign bodies' were behind the Twitter account and the demonstrations, seeking to 'tamper with the security and stability of Kuwait'.[166] Although hardly the result of such rumours, the opposition did find it difficult to mobilise popular support in the weeks that followed. Three more Karamat Watan marches were held in January, but turnout was low. The marches were held outside the city centre, and the security services reverted to their harsh approach.[167] The regime also demanded that activists obtain a permit to demonstrate, which they refused to adhere to. As well as struggling to mobilise popular support, the opposition reportedly disagreed on how to proceed.[168] Recognising the dangers of a divided opposition, on 14 January young activists and bloggers called for the formation of an opposition coalition.[169] The coalition was announced on 3 March, with the stated goal of an elected government and, of course, the dissolution of the December 2012

Parliament. The declaration was signed by 15 members of the majority of the February 2012 Parliament, as well as a number of youth groups, including al-Haraka al-Dimuqratiyya al-Madaniyya (Hadam).[170] However, by this time, the opposition was, at least for the moment, no longer able to mobilise popular support in the streets, and made no attempt to do so. The formation of this coalition also marks the end of the time frame set for this investigation. Since then, the opposition has not managed to mobilise as they did in the autumn of 2012. New elections were held in the summer of 2013, and this time the opposition was divided on whether or not to boycott. Moreover, the regime has continued its heavy-handed approach to criticism, even going as far as revoking citizenship to punish opposition voices.[171]

This does not mean that no demonstrations have taken place in Kuwait since March 2013; quite the contrary. In particular, the two-year sentence handed down to Musallam al-Barrak following a lengthy court battle has proved to be a potent rallying call to dedicated oppositional activists[172] and several demonstrations have taken place.[173] Attendance, however, has been quite modest, at least compared to the autumn of 2012. Moreover, with few exceptions, the demonstrations have been met with violence from the riot police and numerous activists have been arrested.[174] Thus, while oppositional mobilisation still takes place, and while the autocratic moves made by the regime are contested by the opposition, I will argue that there are two fundamental differences in comparison to the autumn of 2012 and the massive popular mobilisation that took place. First, it seems that it is predominantly dedicated oppositional activists who now take part, and few others. While still substantial, the number of protesters is nowhere near that of the autumn of 2012 and, more importantly, nowhere near the numbers needed to force the hand of the regime. As argued above, the ability to muster the support of the middle ground of Kuwaiti popular opinion is a crucial goal for both the regime and the opposition and, as of April 2016, it seems that the regime is the party with the ability to do so. Second, the regime is willing to meet all opposition demonstrations with violence and arrests. Again, this is connected to popular opinion, as the regime is able to do so without provoking widespread indignation. Yet, as the fundamental questions of power sharing and corruption have not been resolved, it seems unlikely that this setback for the opposition should prove permanent, as argued below.

The Groups Included in the Case

The work of eight of the different youth activist groups that were formed during – and took part in – the campaign described above is the subject of study in this investigation. Some of these groups had ended their activities by 2013, but others were still active. All operated both online and offline, and were in general agreement on the need for a more democratic Kuwait – although there were some differences in terms of focus, strategy and ideology. The eight groups included are as follows:[175]

السور الخامس (al-Sur al-Khamis) (The Fifth Fence) was founded on 25 December 2010. The group presented itself as a group of Kuwaiti youth from different parts of society, brought together by the goal of defending the constitution and general freedoms. They use the slogan 'New Government – New President [meaning PM] – New Approach [meaning a more democratic approach]', which was widely used until the autumn of 2011. They are said to have primarily recruited members from the tribal part of the population. They took part in/supported the September 16 coalition, demanding a constitutional emirate. They did not become a part of Hadam in February 2012, although there has been no activity either on their website or on their Twitter account since.

كافي (Kafi) (Enough) was, it says, founded on 28 February 2011. It refers to itself as 'the Kuwaiti Youth Movement (Kafi)', and argues in its founding statement in defence of the constitution, in line with other groups at the time. It is more concerned with issues pertaining to civil society, freedom of expression and organisation than other groups. It also expresses concern regarding the unity of the country, an issue that is recognisable from earlier writings of its founder. In February 2012, the group joined Hadam, and has not been active online since.

حركة شباب الحرية (Harakat Shabab al-Hurriyya) (Youth of Freedom Movement) was founded on 7 March 2011, through a Twitter account in which their goals were stated. The group is clearly based within the Islamist camp of Kuwaiti politics and seems to be closely related to Salafi leader Hakim al-Mutayri and his Hizb al-

Umma (the Umma Party), both of whose tweets they constantly retweeted. Their demands stated on Twitter included the legalisation of political parties, an independent judiciary and an 'elected government', but also demands pertaining to issues such as unemployment, citizenship and housing; that is, more practical demands than the constitutional struggle mainly occupying the opposition. They took part in the September 16 coalition but did not join Hadam in February 2012.

شباب التغيير والتطوير (Shabab al-Taghyir wa-l-Tatwir) (Youth of Change and Development) was founded on 12 June 2011. The stated goal of the group was reform of the three branches of power, which includes dissolution of the 2009 Parliament, changes to the way in which the government is selected and a reform of the judiciary. The group was clearly based within the Islamist camp, and was at times quite sectarian in its rhetoric, although it claimed not to be so. They took part in the September 16 coalition, demanding a constitutional emirate. As for Hadam, the group's position is somewhat unclear. While all newspaper accounts and statements say they joined the new group, they themselves say they withdrew from the proceedings. Nevertheless, the online work of the group was discontinued a few months later.

العدالة الدستورية (al-ʿAdala al-Dusturiyya) (Constitutional Justice) was founded on 25 June 2011, through a video published on the YouTube channel of the ʿUtayb tribe.[176] It is it unclear if the group was solely the domain of this particular tribe or if membership was wider. The goals stated by the group are similar to those of other groups and include political reform towards a more democratic society. It also expressed concern over issues of racism, sectarianism and class struggles, which should not be surprising, given the exclusion of the tribes discussed above. The group was part of the September 16 alliance, and joined Hadam in February 2012.

الحركة الديمقراطية المدنية (حدم) (al-Haraka al-Dimuqratiyya al-Madaniyya [Hadam]) (the Civil Democratic Movement) was, as discussed above, founded following a conference held on 27/28 February 2012, and can be seen as an attempt at unifying the youth movement. The goal of the group is a more democratic Kuwait, which entails a constitutional emirate. The group is also concerned with the issue of democratic culture and of establishing a 'civil' state, reflected in a focus on the inner workings of the group. However, at the end of September and the beginning of October 2012, the group did experience trouble within its ranks. At the time, there were contradictory reports on how the organisation dealt with the trouble, who led the group and, not least, which account represented the group online. This last point seems to have been a part of the initial problem, as there were complaints about some of the statements made through the Twitter account. In a report on *Sabr.cc* on 30 September, it is claimed that the leader was fired, a point which is reiterated in a statement given on the Twitter account on 3 October, which claimed that this happened at an extraordinary conference of the group.[177] However, in a report provided by *al-Ra'i* on 4 October the situation is given as the exact opposite, with the leader remaining the same and some of those involved in the statement of 3 October being excluded.[178] The last account seems to be the correct one, as the leader is quoted *as leader* in a statement published on the website on 8 October and has figured in this capacity repeatedly since. In March 2013, the group joined the opposition alliance.

كرامة وطن (Karamat Watan) (Dignity of a Nation) published its first blog post on 11 October 2012 and a Twitter account was created on 13 October. However, the writings on both the blog and on Twitter make it seem as if the march, which was the sole purpose of the group when it was established, might already be known to its readers. Its purpose was to organise demonstrations against the changes in the electoral law in the autumn of 2012, which it saw as a breach of the constitution, as the constitution states that the people are the source of all power. The authorities sought to expose the identities of those behind the movement, but did not succeed in doing so. The group itself was concerned with issues of anonymity and advised its followers on Twitter on how to conceal their identities.

مقاطعون (Muqati'un) ([We Are] Boycotting/Boycotters) was founded on 5 November 2012. The group also had a blog. It was an ad hoc response to the elections of December 2012, which the opposition boycotted. It organised various local committees tasked with overseeing the election in their respective communities. The group's intention was to provide an uncensored figure of voter participation, as they clearly did not trust the government.

The Groups' Work Online and Offline

When analysing the work of the different groups online, we first need to gain an overview of their presence on various platforms, their levels of activity, their popularity and levels of engagement with followers and, not least, how – that is, for which purposes – they made use of online platforms. To begin with their online presence, Table 5.1 details how the groups made use of online platforms.

Clearly, Twitter was by far the most popular platform among the groups and was used by all of them. Interestingly, whereas all the groups in the Egyptian case made use of both Facebook and YouTube, these were hardly used at all in Kuwait. The two groups who did use YouTube generated very few views, and both abandoned the platform rather quickly. Similarly, of the two groups using Facebook, only one (Kafi) can be said to have made a serious attempt at utilising the platform, but it gained only half as many followers as on Twitter, and soon left the platform. Five of the eight groups studied had their own websites or blogs; these were predominantly used to publish statements given by the group, as well as practical information. Finally, two groups made use of additional platforms, namely Yfrog and Instagram, not surprisingly for the purpose of disseminating pictures.

There were clear differences in terms of the popularity attained by the different groups online, that is, the number of followers, likes[179] and subscribers they gained on the various platforms, as shown in Table 5.2.

Two groups quite clearly stand out: Karamat Watan, which gained over 80,000 more followers than the second most popular group, and al-ʿAdala al-Dusturiyya, which only gained fewer than 7 per cent of the number of followers of the second least popular group.[180] As I will argue below, I believe the popularity of Karamat Watan was due to the popularity of the issue it raised – defending the constitution and the victory of the 2006 OM – and its skilful work online and offline. In a similar vein, the work of Muqatiʿun can also be seen within the

Table 5.1 Kuwaiti Platform Selection

Group	Twitter	Website/blog	YouTube	Facebook	Other
al-Sur al-Khamis	@soor_5	soor5.com	–	–	Yfrog
Kafi	@Kafi_Q8	kafiq8.blogspot.com	KafiQ8	kafiq8	–
Shabab al-Hurriyya	@shbabq8	–	–	–	–
Shabab al-Taghyir wa-l-Tatwir	@mohafedheen[181]	–	–	Yes, شباب التغيير والتطوير	–
al-'Adala al-Dusturiyya	@aladalh2011	–	–	–	–
Hadam	@CDMkuwait[182]	cdmkw.com	CDMQ8	–	Instagram, cdmkuwait
Karamat Watan	@KarametWatan	karametwatan.wordpress.com	–	–	–
Muqati'un	@kwboycott	kwboycott.wordpress.com	–	–	–

attract more followers, given its high levels of activity. However, this group, along with the other Islamist group, conducted its work online differently in comparison to other groups, and was more oriented towards its existing followers rather than a potentially much wider audience, as will be discussed below. Nevertheless, although a certain level of activity seems to have been important in Kuwait as well, the connection between activity and popularity is not as explicit as in the Egyptian case.

The coding of Twitter material from the Kuwaiti case provided the results shown in Figure 5.2.

The results reflect very similar usage among the various groups, and the three top categories in the aggregate results were also the three top categories for all groups but two; al-ʿAdala al-Dusturiyya and Karamat Watan. For the former group, 'media' was the second most coded category. However, as it only published 44 tweets in total, this was merely the result of a few tweets referring to the same item on the group. As for Karamat Watan, 'information' was the second most employed category. This was due to a large number of tweets containing practical information published ahead of their demonstrations, as will be discussed below.

The most employed category by far is 'discussion', and this is primarily due to two subcategories, namely 'taking part in a discussion'

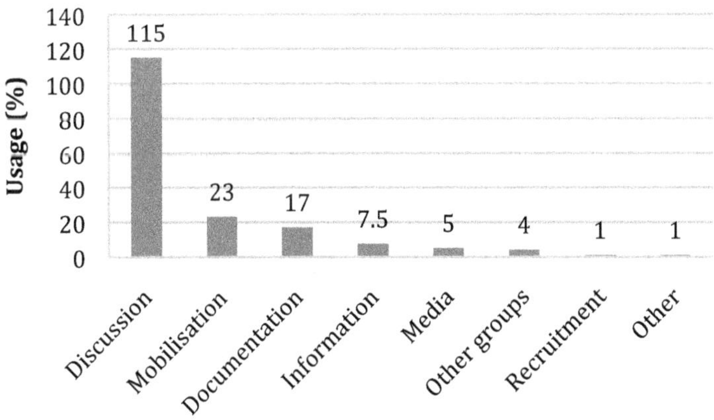

Figure 5.2 Twitter Usage, Kuwait

and 'agitation'. The first of these subcategories mainly covers the use of popular hashtags among the groups, which in general was done in between 75 per cent and 85 per cent of all their tweets. The clear exceptions were the two Islamist groups, which almost never made use of hashtags. In addition, this subcategory also covers responses and engagement with individual users, which was a frequent feature of the Islamist groups' usage, as well as done frequently by Karamat Watan. The second most employed category, 'mobilisation', first and foremost covers mobilisation for offline demonstrations. In contrast to the Egyptian groups, mobilisation for and participation in online events was almost non-existent. The tweets coded as 'documentation' are primarily made up of tweets disseminating pictures and videos from demonstrations, as well as live reporting in text from offline events. As for 'media', the tweets that make up this category mainly linked to statements released by the groups published in the two online newspapers sympathetic to the opposition, *Alaan.cc* and *Sabr.cc*. Finally, almost no tweets were spent on communicating between the groups or on recruiting volunteers for the groups. In terms of retweets as opposed to tweets of the groups' own writing, the aggregate results for the Kuwaiti case is shown in Figure 5.3.

This figure, though remarkably similar to that covering the Egyptian case, hides a rather uneven practice among the Kuwaiti groups. By and large, Kuwaiti groups almost never published any retweets, and retweets

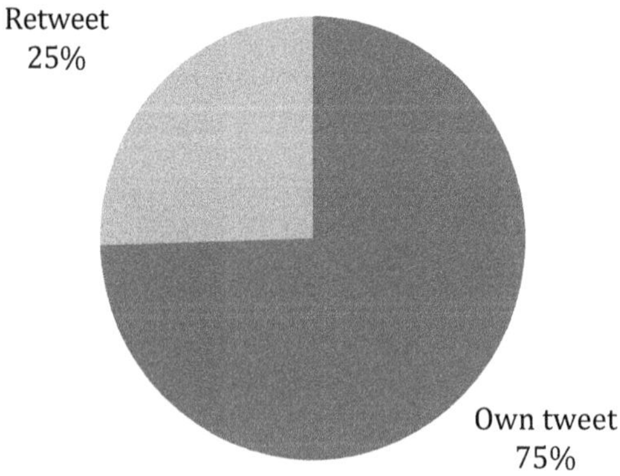

Figure 5.3 Retweets vs. Own Tweets, Kuwait

account for less than 5 per cent of the Twitter activity of most of the groups studied, with two clear exceptions: Shabab al-Hurriyya and Shabab al-Taghyir wa-l-Tatwir. For these groups, retweets accounted for 52.5 per cent and 50 per cent of the tweets published, respectively. Again, we see that the practice of the two Islamist groups is markedly different from that of the others.

There were substantial variations in the popularity of the content provided by the groups or, if you will, the level of engagement created by said content. While the tweets published by Shabab al-Taghyir wa-l-Tatwir were, on average, retweeted three times and favourited 0.01 times, the corresponding numbers were 9 and 0.2 times for al-Sur al-Khamis and Kafi, and 17 and 0.5 times for Hadam. However, by far the most engaged groups online were Muqatiʿun and Karamat Watan, which received an average of 55 and 203 retweets, and 2.5 and 5 favourite markings, respectively. Thus, the most popular groups in terms of followers also provided the most popular and engaging content.

The kind of content that was most popular in terms of retweets is fairly similar across the groups: it was concerned with offline protests and contained either a call for participation, practical information or in-the-moment updates. The partial exception was Muqatiʿun, whose followers also retweeted arguments and agitation for the cause. However, in terms of favourite markings, which were used a lot less frequently than retweets, the popular content is more mixed. It contained statements of support for arrested activists, information on how to remain anonymous online, agitation, pictures from demonstrations and links to media items. Thus, and perhaps not surprisingly, it seems retweets were used mainly to disseminate content deemed important by the users, whereas favourite markings were given as a sign of support or appreciation, in much the same way as 'likes' on Facebook. In fact, the most liked and commented upon content on the Facebook page of the one group that made a serious effort to utilise the platform, Kafi, is quite similar to the most favourited content on Twitter. None of the Facebook posts of the group were shared by their followers.

Demonstrations were the main offline activity pursued by the groups studied, and public displays of support for their cause were their main strategy to incite change. In a sense, their online activities can be said to have been designed predominantly to support these protests, as the groups spent much of their time mobilising, documenting and providing information on these demonstrations. However, the groups also invested a lot of time in stating their views online, often participating in wider debates through the use of designated hashtags. Thus, it seems the participants deemed both the online and offline work to be important. Moreover, we can hardly draw a clear distinction between online and offline, and discussions took place in both contexts. Many of the groups regularly held small seminars on the issues in question, referred to as *nadwāt*, which were announced online. On some occasions, people were explicitly invited to participate in open debates at offline gatherings, but these do not seem to have been particularly well attended. One debate between those who supported the boycott of the December 2012 elections and those who did not support the boycott even moved from online to offline on 21 November, when a debate was held at Kuwait University 'between' the hashtags 'سأشارك' (I will participate [in the elections]) and 'مقاطعون'[187] ([We are] boycotting). Muqatiʿun also launched an offline campaign in which people were asked to submit photos of themselves (or others) wearing orange, which were then disseminated to their followers on Twitter.

Two of the groups, Hadam and Muqatiʿun, also held internal meetings to organise the groups' operation and elect its leadership, or to organise specific offline activities. Most of the other groups do not seem to have been particularly concerned with their internal organisation or with recruiting volunteers. There were, however, some meetings between the groups, but these were seldom announced online. Rather, it seems that other means of communications were used, and that there were offline connections between the groups. Naturally, more meetings may have been held between the groups than were made known online. Similarly, there may have been more internal meetings within the various groups than I have been able to document. Such offline networks may also have been important in terms of mobilisation for offline protests, as will be discussed in my analysis below. The analysis of the material presented will be roughly organised around the categories used, but the groups' choices concerning platform selection will also be the subject of some deliberation. Moreover, some of the material referred to above that is not strictly part of the case will also be discussed, namely the individual blogs involved early in the campaign and the Twitter debates organised around hashtags. I begin, however, with a brief discussion of the aims and needs of the groups studied, in order to properly contextualise their work and internet usage.

What Do They Want, and What Do They Need?

All groups sought what they perceived to be further democratic development of Kuwait, which for most of the groups meant political reform leading to what they termed a 'constitutional emirate'. For others, however, it meant preserving the rights secured by the constitution in its existing form and defending this against perceived attacks by the regime. While this did reflect genuine differences of opinion, it was also connected to the opposition's development over time and its changing fortunes. Their work began with what appears to have been a rather unifying position: that the then prime minister, Nasir al-Muhammad, should resign. This, in turn, was related to the extremely unifying issue of fighting corruption, which has been central to the opposition since before independence. Following several successful marches, the youth movements moved on from their demand for an 'elected government' to demanding constitutional reform resulting in a constitutional emirate. Yet, as we have seen, mobilisation around these demands was not particularly successful. Still, when the regime dissolved the opposition Parliament, even established politicians supported this demand. However, just weeks later, as the regime sought to change the rules of the game by changing the electoral law, the opposition rallied around the constitution in its existing form, an effort which also was markedly more successful in terms of popular mobilisation. Following the regime's crackdown on the demonstrations in January 2013, there have been few manifestations of popular dissent in the country. Moreover, the opposition did not manage to remain unified in its boycott of elections under the new electoral law throughout the summer of 2013. In short, when the opposition seemingly had the upper hand, the youth movements went further in their demands. When the opposition Parliament was dissolved, the MPs responded by supporting these demands. However, when it became clear that there was a real possibility that political participation in the country could be decreased rather than increased, they rallied around their existing rights. While mobilisation in support of such demands was highly successful, their attempt to block the proposed changes was not. Thus, after five years of popular mobilisation and political conflict, the opposition was left with a new prime minister, but with an unfavourable electoral law.

As the situation changed, the practical work of the opposition changed with it. From the beginning, popular mobilisation offline was their key tool. At first, this was directed against the prime minister, in parallel to opposition MPs' filing numerous interpellations in the assembly. When opposition voices were persecuted by the authorities, focus changed towards defending them. Then, following the events of December 2010, more comprehensive political demands were presented, although the demand to remove the PM was still key. Further demands were presented in the summer of 2011, as popular mobilisation grew in tandem with the escalating corruption scandal involving the PM himself. When the regime sought to avoid a vote of no confidence that they would have lost, the opposition escalated the situation further. That is, when they saw what they perceived as disregard for their constitutional rights, they escalated the situation by storming the Parliament. The opposition was successful, as the prime minister stepped down. Then, as new elections were called for, the youth movement – naturally – supported opposition candidates. When victory was achieved in these elections, the youth movement focused on its own organisation, gathering several groups into Hadam. Then, when this victory was taken away from them, they again altered their focus. Following a few demonstrations against the dissolution of the Parliament, the Karamat Watan demonstrations were organised to defend the electoral law, which was not only important for opposition representation, but also represented the spoils of the 2006 campaign. As these changes nevertheless became a reality, focus changed once again, this time to the issue of boycott. Having organised and monitored its own boycott, the opposition claimed success. However, when the regime paid little attention, the Karamat Watan marches continued. When these died out, focus once again turned inward, leading to the launch of the 'coalition of the opposition' in March 2013. In other words, while there have been differences of opinion all along, and while the focus in terms of practical work has changed over time, the common denominator of the opposition in a broad sense has, since the beginning, been popular mobilisation aiming at political reform. At times, the opposition had the initiative, but towards the end, they were usually responding to the actions of the regime. This underlines an important, if obvious, point in the analysis of their work: both goals and strategies were continually adjusted to their ever-changing context.

All groups studied made extensive use of online platforms in order to achieve these goals, and to conduct their work. However, as with the Egyptian case, it would have been extraordinary had they chosen not to do so. Kuwait is a small country, and there cannot have been many who did not notice the Orange Movement's successful utilisation of the blogs. Moreover, many of those involved had prior experience from the OM, and the groups studied here started among such activists. Furthermore, as a clear majority of Kuwaiti citizens are online, online platforms are a rather obvious tool to make use of. Moreover, civil society is formally quite tightly regulated in the country, but the Orange Movement had demonstrated that a more ad hoc and loosely organised initiative could be not only successful, but also tolerated by the regime. While access to resources would be a smaller problem in Kuwait than in Egypt, there would hardly be any other accessible tools or channels that could match the potential reach of Twitter, blogs and YouTube. In addition, the opposition was highly critical of the traditional media in Kuwait, and online platforms offered a cheap alternative for disseminating their version of events, not least concerning alleged corruption, as well as their accounts of their offline activities. Finally, there is a dimension whose importance is hard to assess but which is a factor that must be taken into account when studying Kuwait, namely the facilitation of contact between people of different social backgrounds, and between the sexes. As discussed above, the *ḥaḍar* and *badw* populations have been separated not only in socio-economic terms, but also physically, although this situation has changed over time. Similarly, Kuwait is a conservative country, where even liberal candidates separate men and women during election campaign events. Such barriers are not as present online, however, which has been a feature of Kuwaiti internet use since the 1990s.[188] While men dominated the leadership of the groups, there were also many women involved, particularly in Hadam.

Some of the main features of the groups' internet usage seem to fit well with the challenges presented above, namely agitation, documentation and mobilisation/organisation. That being said, offline networks also played an important part. It is clear that several groups coordinated their work, for instance ahead of the 8 March 2011 demonstration, but this coordination did not take place publicly on social media. The groups clearly had contact with well-known politicians from the outset, but this was not negotiated publicly online either. Granted, there were some online attempts at engaging politicians directly in political debate, or at least making them aware of a group's work. Shabab al-Taghyir wa-l-Tatwir called publicly for other groups to take part in a conference to coordinate their work during the spring of 2011. Yet, as with the Egyptian case, there would hardly be any reason for the groups to conduct this kind of coordination in public, and it is clear that they generally wanted to be public online. They had no incentive to make public negotiations or any quarrels taking place, at least not as long as they managed to achieve agreement. When they did not, however, some parties felt the need to let their side of the story be known, or even to try to use publicness as a means to gain an advantage. For instance, when conflict was running high in Hadam, both sides went public with their version of events. Similarly, when Shabab al-Taghyir wa-l-Tatwir disagreed with the founding principles of the Hadam, they made sure to say so in public. It should be noted that, as a new group integrating a number of movements whose leaders undoubtedly saw themselves as entitled to leadership positions, Hadam was perhaps bound to face this kind of conflict. Still, we observe a similar pattern to that in the Egyptian case: coordination and negotiation is done offline as long as such links exist, but when disagreements occur, some groups deem it necessary to go public with their views, or with accusations against others.

Finally, as the situation changed, so did the needs of the groups. When activists were arrested in 2009 and 2010 for what they said online, the reaction of other activists was outrage, almost indignation, that the authorities dared to do what they did. Campaigns were promptly launched, typically stating 'we are all' the person in question. When sanctions against Twitter users were tightened throughout 2012, such campaigns were still launched but did not gain the same attention. Moreover, while activists remained defiant, some of the indignation seemed to be gone and to have been replaced by a certain level of fear and sober pragmatism: freedom of expression was no longer taken for granted. For instance, when Khaled Alfadala was arrested in 2010, one of the first tweets of the campaign for his release was as follows:

> Khaled AlFadala, the victim of an unjust sentence of 3 months in jail for the absurd accusation of slandering
>
> @kalfadala, 2 July 2010

In contrast, when Twitter was used to collect bail money for arrested activists in December 2012, many expressed gratitude for the contributions rather than indignation at the situation:

تم تجميع المبلغ بالكامل واطلاق سراح الشباب, الف شكر لمن تبرع #كفالات_الشباب

> The entire amount has been collected and the youth have been freed, a thousand thanks to those who contributed
>
> @{User 13}, 5 December 2012

Clearly, it makes sense to thank those who contributed, but it also shows how the focus shifted from the illegitimacy of the actions of the regime to being able collectively to solve the problems caused by a repression that no longer surprises them. Yet, even in this situation, Twitter remained a powerful tool.

While the campaigns of 2009 and 2010 had been successful, it was clear in 2012 that the regime had adopted a tougher approach. The question of anonymity became important, and some groups started spreading tips and links to software designed to protect such anonymity. The Karamat Watan initiative was also led anonymously, and managed to keep it that way in spite of persistent regime efforts to reveal the leaders' identity. Thus, the needs of the groups changed with the situation, but they continued to use the online tools even in the face of potentially severe punishment. While there certainly is a political principle at play, the situation is also indicative of the importance or even the necessity for the groups to have an online presence. Naturally, there were several online platforms available to the groups, and before moving on to the thematic discussion of how they were used, a look at the platform choices made is necessary.

Platform Selection: Were Blogs Still Relevant?

We have already seen that activists' choice of platforms is dependent on the local context; although Facebook was actively used in Egypt, it does not seem to have been favoured in Kuwait. However, platform selection is also dependent on time and development; as new platforms are launched, activists can utilise new features and possibilities. Yet, this does not happen automatically, and not all new platforms gain popularity. For instance, Google+ does not seem to have caught on among activists in either Egypt or Kuwait, in spite of the favourable 'review' given by the famous Egyptian activist Tarek Shalaby.[189] Moreover, a new platform does not necessarily replace an old one and make it irrelevant; it is not a zero-sum game, although this certainly has happened.[190] The point here is that blogs still seem to be relevant in Kuwait, in spite of numerous predictions of the death of the platform.[191]

Having said that, there is no doubt that the introduction of new platforms – particularly Twitter – has changed the online habits of Kuwaiti activists. During the Orange Movement campaign of 2006, months before Twitter was launched, debates took place through the comments on the blogs, as well as in discussion forums. Throughout the three most active months of the OM – May to July 2006 – no fewer than 6,500 comments were posted on the main blog alone. I have not systematically gone through the comments posted on the blogs involved during the time frame of this study, but the numbers do not seem to be remotely close to those of 2006. Rather, debates have taken place on Twitter, organised around particular hashtags. I have identified 29 large-scale debates on the issues of concern for the opposition that took place on Twitter within the time frame, involving more than 86,000 tweets, according to Topsy.com.[192] There is substantial political discussion taking place online in Kuwait, but it seems to have moved from the blogs to Twitter.

Still, the blogs do seem to have been important, particularly in the beginning. The community of bloggers established through the Orange Movement was still in place, and they were directly addressed when a blogger first proposed what would become a campaign to remove the prime minister:

> أول شي السلام عليكم ورحمة الله وبركاته, هذه رسالة من زميلكم (...) إلى المدونات الكويتية جميعها أخوة وأخوات
>
> First of all, May Allah's peace, mercy and blessing be upon you, this is a message from your colleague [...] to all the Kuwaiti blogs, brothers and sisters
>
> Altariq2009.com, إلى المدونات الكويتية مع التحية, 14 October 2009[193]

This does not seem to have been a wide debate in terms of the number of participants, but rather a targeted debate, involving bloggers with previous experience who were known for their political activism. When the abovementioned group 'Irhal, nastahiqq al-afdal' was formed, it was launched on 16 blogs simultaneously, and within days managed to hold offline demonstrations. Offline networks undoubtedly played an important part, for instance in contacting established politicians, who seem to have been involved from the beginning. Clearly, it is difficult, if not impossible, to establish the relative importance of the online part of their work. Still, if nothing else, it is evident that those involved deemed it worthwhile, and that it is seen as an important arena for political work in Kuwait, as was confirmed by several activists.[194] Interestingly, the debate was not to foster consensus on all issues, and the community formed in 2006 seems to have been divided over the past few years, something which has also been confirmed in interviews.[195] To some extent, the same issues that are seen as divisive in Kuwaiti society at large were involved. For instance, when Hadam was formed in 2012, it was criticised as being too Islamist. Also, when activists saw themselves and their freedom of speech threatened in December 2009, not all bloggers from the OM were equally convinced of the problem, a critique that seems to have been influenced by the *ḥaḍar/badw* divide. Finally, the sectarian divide between the country's Shi'a and Sunni populations seems to have been problematic, particularly following the somewhat sectarian agitation by some of the more Islamist-leaning groups.

Yet, the bloggers also were able to unite on certain issues, in particular those involving arrests and attacks on freedom of speech. A case in point in this regard was the arrest of liberal activist Khaled Alfadala, which seems to have provoked widespread reactions online. Moreover, for those that did agree, the blogs seem to have been important in formulating their position and plan of action at an early stage. Finally, the citizen journalism blog AlziadiQ8 continues to be one of the most popular sites in Kuwait.[196] Again, this should be seen in connection with the opposition's sceptical view of the traditional Kuwaiti media. Yet, it is also clear that following the dramatic events of December 2010, and the establishment of the groups studied here, Twitter has been the most important platform among Kuwaiti activists.

The Popularity of Twitter

Twitter has gained fame as an arena for political debate and activism in Kuwait over the past few years, and there are several factors that give evidence of this. For one thing, all groups studied here used Twitter as their main platform online, which they probably would not have done had it not been effective in reaching possible sympathisers and fellow activists. Most activists, politicians, commentators and even some members of the royal family make wide use of the platform as well, and Twitter discussions frequently receive media coverage in the country.[197] Moreover, the regime's harsh reactions to critical utterances on the platform clearly show that they also view it as an important arena. Finally, the importance of Twitter as *the* platform for political deliberations in Kuwait was also expressed in the interviews conducted, a claim also reported by the state-run *KUNA* news agency.[198]

As we have seen, some of the groups also made use of Facebook, but only to a very limited extent. The group Kafi made perhaps the most sincere attempt at utilising the platform, but only gained about half as many followers as they did on Twitter. Al-ʿAdala al-Dusturiyya also created a page, but only published four posts and gained just 32 followers. Lastly, both the 'nastahiqq al-afdal' campaign and the 'Iradat al-Shaʿb' campaign used Facebook groups, but this does not seem to have been particularly successful either. While these results show the importance of the local context online, the big question is why Facebook is widely used among activists in Egypt, but not in Kuwait. Facebook is a far more popular platform than Twitter in Kuwait in terms of users, with estimates given at almost 900,000 users for the former,[199] compared to 225,000 for the latter.[200] The answer given in the interviews was that Facebook *is* popular in Kuwait, but as a more private space. Moreover, in spite of the lower number of users, Twitter is extremely popular in Kuwait in comparison to other countries. According to *Arab Social Media Report*, the country accounts for 10 per cent of the tweets written in the Arab region and is the country with the highest number of Twitter users per capita in the world.[201] Thus, while there may be more people using Facebook than Twitter in the country, there are certainly enough Twitter users to make the platform important. As the political use and importance of the platform was made well known by the traditional media in the country, everyone who was interested knew where to go. Which brings us to an important point in terms of platform selection: you need to know that you are reaching the people you want to reach, meaning that popularity in the sense of who is using which platform may be just as important for platform selection as the features inherent in the platform itself. There are several features provided by Facebook which may have been useful to the Kuwaiti groups, such as the capacity to publish photo albums, to create event pages and to comment directly on a post. Yet, they still chose to use Twitter, and found other solutions to the features that were lacking, for instance through the use of Twitlonger and Yfrog.

The Use of Websites, Blogs and YouTube

Even though Twitter was the most important site for the groups, we have seen that other platforms were used as well. The two websites and the three blogs used by the groups served one common main purpose, namely as hubs of information. The possible exception was the blog of the group Kafi, which also contained a post arguing that former Emir ʿAbdallah al-Salim would have disapproved of Prime Minister Nasir al-Muhammad. However, this blog contained only two posts, and the other was the first statement given by the group, which is similar to the content provided by others. In general, two kinds of information were provided: the statements given by the groups and practical information related to the work done by the groups, most often demonstrations. This covers all the content provided on the websites and blogs of al-Sur al-Khamis, the Karamat Watan campaign and the boycott campaign. It also covers the website of Hadam in the beginning, but this group has later added detailed information on the group itself, as well as some links to news items, a membership form and political texts explaining their positions. As such, it still serves the same function as the other sites described above, namely to gather relevant information from the group in one place online. One would expect the groups to actively disseminate the location of these sites, and refer to them for further information. Yet, with the exception of Karamat Watan, they almost never did. Al-Sur al-Khamis did so on six occasions, Hadam on four occasions, Kafi on 11 occasions and the boycott campaign only on one single occasion. Rather, they seem to have preferred to disseminate practical information directly in tweets and statements through applications such as Twitlonger or the media. This latter practice may not be surprising, as even online outlets may carry more authority than a website or a blog. Still, it seems that some of the potential of having one 'go-to' place for those interested in a group is lost when the site is not actively promoted. The Karamat Watan campaign, on the other hand, actively utilised social media to promote its blog on no fewer than 124 occasions. This was also by far the most successful group in terms of attracting support both online and offline. I do not claim that this was due to their ability to link to their blog; rather, it was the other way around. As I will argue below, I believe the campaign was run more professionally and more efficiently than the other groups, and this is just one example of how the group made good use of the possibilities inherent in the platforms employed.

As for YouTube, only two groups created their own channels: Kafi and Hadam. These two channels can only be said to have been moderately successful in terms of views and subscribers. The channels were only active for a short period of time and most of the videos published have been seen by very few. A great majority of the videos provided coverage of their own events, although there also were some presenting their views, their previous work, media coverage or even a different issue. Given the short period of time during which the channels of both groups were in use, and the relatively low number of views, both instances may have been attempts at utilising an additional platform, which were abandoned when it proved ineffective. Whatever the case, YouTube was not a widely used platform among the groups in terms of creating their own channels. They did, however, frequently link to videos published by others. These were usually from a demonstration, from media coverage of an event or of the issue itself, or from meetings and seminars held by the groups or others. Thus, the groups did not object to the platform as such, and although Kuwait is known for YouTube censorship, it does not seem to have been an issue in this regard. Rather, it may seem that the groups did not see it as necessary or meaningful to create their own account, or that they did not primarily film their own events themselves but relied on others to do so. Still, documentation of their own work was important to most of the groups studied, as will be discussed below. First, however, we turn to what was by far the most dominant feature of their online work: discussion and agitation.

Discussions, Agitation and Hashtags

The category 'discussion' was by far the most comprehensive in terms of the groups' online activities. For most of the groups studied, this was driven by the use of popular hashtags. There were, however, two exceptions: Shabab al-Hurriyya and Shabab al-Taghyir wa-l-Tatwir. These groups only used hashtags in a small proportion of their tweets, although both demonstrated that they were familiar with the practice.

This is particularly interesting given that debates organised by hashtags were such a dominant feature of the Kuwaiti Twitter-sphere. Both of these groups spent most of their time agitating for their cause – this accounted for around 50 per cent of their tweets – but chose to do so without using hashtags. There are several factors that may be at play here. For one thing, they may not have seen this as important or necessary, or even desirable. Yet, when mobilising for the 16 September 2011, demonstrations, both groups saw the value of using the 'assigned' hashtag, in a situation where their goal clearly was to reach as many as possible. They could, of course, have forgotten to use hashtags at other times, but this does not seem likely. They may have wanted their tweets to be more or less secret, but in that case they should not have published them on Twitter to begin with. Rather, it seems that the way in which these groups discuss online is key. These two groups conduct their discussions using more religious language and arguments than others, and often on religious subjects as well. They were concerned with a greater variety of subjects than the other groups, not least the situation in Syria. The following examples are illustrative of their online habits:

نصرتك لإخوانك السوريين واجب شرعي وحق دستوري, شارك غدا في الاعتصام السلمي عند السفارة السورية للمطالبة بطرد الشبيح

Your help to your Syrian brothers is a religious duty and a constitutional right, take part in the peaceful protest at the Syrian Embassy to demand the removal of the phantom[202]

@shbabq8, 8 August 2011

مسؤولية التغيير تبدأ من الفرد. فكل القوانين الكونية تدل على ذلك. وإذا ساد هذا المفهوم عند الأسرة ثم الجماعة ثم المجتمع ثم الدولة تنهض

The responsibility to change begins with the individual. All existing laws point to that. If this understanding prevailed in the family, then the community, then the society, then the state would be reborn

@youthchangeQ8, 9 July 2011

When they engaged in discussions, they seem to have done so with a more targeted audience than other groups. They very often included the usernames of individual users in their tweets, to speak to them directly. Moreover, these two groups together responded directly to other users almost four times as often as all the other Kuwaiti groups combined. Similarly, whereas the other groups almost never retweeted other users, such messages account for about half the Twitter activity of both these groups. Rather than seeking to reach as many as possible with their views through hashtags, they seem to have targeted their followers, and to have engaged with them and some particular users – often well-known Islamists. When they *did* use hashtags, it was not to argue for their cause, but rather to mobilise for an event. As such, the groups reached out when mobilising around their more 'mainstream' views, which were shared by other groups. In other words, most of their debates are public yet somewhat internal, or at least targeted, not unlike the famous debate on the programme of the Muslim Brotherhood that took place online in Egypt in 2007.[203]

That being said, one might question the extent of sincere debate in a Habermasian sense that took place between opposing views on Twitter in general. Although different views were presented, for instance through the hashtags #مقاطعون and #سأشارك, these had the form of campaign and counter-campaign rather than an attempt to reach some common ground. Yet, as discussed in the previous chapter, this would not be the goal for those initiating these debates either, or for the groups studied. Rather, the goal would be to convince others of one's position:

> #مقاطعون لأننا نؤمن بدولة مؤسسات مدنية تحت ظل الدستور
>
> #[we are] boycotting because we believe in state of civil institutions under the protection of the constitution
>
> @kwboycott, 16 November 2012

> لايماني في الدستور في جميع مواده, في 1 ديسمبر سأشارك #سأشارك
>
> For my allegiance to the constitution and all its paragraphs, I will participate on December 1
>
> @[User 14], 23 October 2012

Still, for those who were undecided, many of these debates may have provided useful arguments one way or the other – though mostly in favour of the opposition. Clearly, many Twitter users in Kuwait deemed such debates worthwhile. This may not be surprising, as they had, to some extent, to redefine the political solution sought by the opposition in the country, namely to move from defending the constitution to changing the constitution. Views related to this particular change were expressed in numerous Twitter debates, using hashtags such as #حكومة_منتخبة (elected government), #مواد_الدستور_الجديد (the articles of the new constitution) and #ليش_منتخبة (why [we need an] elected [government]). To give a few examples:

> #ليش_منتخبة ؟ لأننا نحن "الأمة" مصدر السلطان, كل السلطات! #حكومة_منتخبة
>
> #(Why elected)? Because we 'the Umma' are the source of powers, all powers! #(Elected Government)
>
> @[User 15], 26 April 2012

> يجوز للنائب في مجلس الأمة ان يكون عضوا لدورتين فقط (8 سنوات) ولا يحق له الترشيح لدوره ثالثه #مواد_الديتور_الجديد
>
> It is permitted to the deputy of the Parliament to be a member for two periods only (8 years) and he is not entitled to run for a third #(The articles of the new constitution)
>
> @[User 16], 4 December 2012

While people participating may naturally use the hashtags to express differing views, the hashtags themselves quite clearly set the tone. Moreover, they helped redefine the boundaries for the opposition debate: while constitutional reform may not have been a topic raised in the traditional media, it clearly was here. Similarly, anyone seeking to redefine the problem and/or the solution in such a manner would need to gain the attention of the public, unless they were able to impose change autocratically. Given the wide usage of Twitter in Kuwait, and the attention some debates received from the traditional media, raising these debates on the platform certainly makes sense from this perspective. Through Twitter, opposition activists could initiate public debates on topics of their own choosing, within boundaries set by themselves. Such debates could also be of a practical nature, and Karamat Watan invited people to discuss how to conduct their protests using the hashtag

#اقتراحات_كرامة_وطن5 (Suggestions for [the demonstration] Karamat Watan 5), although participation was quite limited.

All groups studied used Twitter to argue for their cause, not only those with an Islamist orientation. For these other groups, between a quarter and a third of their tweets were spent on agitation. Again, the tone was hardly one designed to reach consensus, and the groups usually just stated their position, for instance declaring that Kuwait deserves better, that they need a new prime minister or simply asking the prime minister to step down:

> سمو رئيس الوزراء .. الشعب لا يريدك #soor5
>
> Your highness the Prime Minister . . The people do not want you #soor5
>
> @soor_5, 4 March 2011

This was also frequently done through statements, which were often published by one or both of the two online newspapers clearly sympathetic to their cause. The statement given ahead of the September 16 demonstration, which called for a constitutional emirate, received wide attention from other outlets as well. Naturally, this must have been important in encouraging public debate concerning their views.

The majority of the tweets coded under this category, however, were so coded due to the use of popular hashtags. With the exception of the two groups discussed above, all groups studied used hashtags in a great majority of their tweets. Often, they used their own name as a hashtag, which in turn was picked up by other users. The groups did so regardless of the content in question, be it agitation, mobilisation, documentation, practical information or something else. However, even though this was a common feature, there was great variety in terms of their success in attracting followers and engaging with their readers. The two most popular initiatives in terms of followers and engagement with their readers, Karamat Watan and the boycott campaign, not only made continuous use of hashtags, but also utilised hashtags that were already popular. Still, although Shabab al-Hurriyya hardly ever used hashtags, they had more followers than either Kafi or Hadam. Thus, the picture is not black and white, which leads us to some perhaps rather obvious observations. For one thing, some are more skilled than others at utilising social media, and this seems to have an effect. Yet there are important offline factors that must be considered as well, and the popularity and urgency of the issue at hand also plays a part. As we have seen, *defence* of the constitution seems to generate wider support in Kuwait than *change* of the constitution. However, the relative success of Shabab al-Hurriyya may suggest that different mechanisms are at work for those on the fringes of mainstream debates, and concerned with a more specific, in this case Islamist, public.

In summary, Twitter seems to have been an important arena for discussion and agitation, mainly aimed at providing convincing arguments for one's cause. Whereas most groups tried to reach as wide an audience as possible through the use of hashtags, the two Islamist-oriented groups did not, at least not when engaging in discussion. Statements published online and in newspapers also seem to have been an important vehicle for the groups to make their views known. However, perhaps the most important and visible tool used by the groups was popular mobilisation offline.

Mobilisation and Recruitment

The main strategy of all groups studied was popular mobilisation offline, so it should come as no surprise that this was a dominant feature of their online activities. Similarly, it may not be surprising that recruitment seems to have been relatively unimportant to the groups, given that their goal was to encourage people to take part in demonstrations, not necessarily to participate in the work of the groups. Granted, there were a few tweets provided by some groups, for instance Kafi, detailing how one could volunteer and most groups provided contact information. Still, this was clearly not a priority, which may indicate that the groups themselves were not particularly large entities, with the possible exception of Hadam. For instance, while most groups published several pictures of attendance at their meetings and demonstrations, some also published pictures of 'their' people at such events, and these photos generally did not include many individuals. The relative ease with which several groups could come together and form Hadam does not suggest that large numbers of members needed to be convinced. Moreover, since Hadam *was* formed, they have spent much time publishing the names of those holding positions within the group, as well as the rules and statutes governing their work. This is markedly different from the practice of other groups, who never did any such thing, except to refer to their leaders. As such, one does get the impression of several small groups with few members working for the same issue. This impression is consistent with information gathered through interviews, which suggested that the presence of some rather strong personalities might perhaps be part of the reason why there were several groups. As we have seen, when some groups did come together in Hadam, it was not long before this created personal conflicts. Moreover, given the way the groups worked, one might also ask why they would need or want many members or volunteers; their aim was public displays of opinion. However, there are some interesting differences between the groups in terms of mobilisation and recruitment that require attention.

For one thing, it is sometimes difficult to classify tweets as one thing or the other. Karamat Watan was formed with the sole purpose of popular mobilisation, so everything they write might be considered mobilisation. Moreover, the initiative to boycott the elections spent a substantial amount of time mobilising online, mainly promoting meetings held in the different electoral districts. Their purpose was to organise efforts to monitor the elections and, as such, may be seen as recruitment rather than mobilisation. A distinction is nonetheless made, in order to provide more detailed accounts of their work. Second, there were differences in how these groups mobilised for offline events. Most made use of particular hashtags associated with the events, particularly in advance of large demonstrations, including #sep16, #16/9,[204] and #ساحة_الارادة (the name of the site of most protests, understood as a reference to protest as such):

> لأني لا أقبل أن يقتل مواطن أثناء التعذيب ولا أن يسحب جناسي المواطنين أتوجه لساحة الصفاة #16/9
>
> Because I don't accept that a citizen is killed through torture or that the citizenship is taken from citizens, I am heading to Saḥat al-Saffat #16/9
>
> @youthchangeQ8, 16 September 2011

Although Shabab al-Hurriyya demonstrated familiarity with this practice, they also chose to use an extremely inefficient method, tweeting the same message several times directly to various users:

اثنين 10/10 (حق الشعب) شباب 9/16 مطلبنا حكومة منتخبة قانون [User 17]@
الأحزاب دائرة واحدة هيئة انتخابات مستقلة منطقة فهد الأحمد الساعة 8 مساء

Monday 10/10 (the right of the people) the youth of 16/9 our demand elected government legalization of parties one electoral district an independent elections committee the area Fahd al-Ahmad 8 in the evening @[User 17]

@shbabq8, 7 October 2011

However, this should be seen more as an attempt to gain the attention of these users than anything else. Karamat Watan, as mentioned, used an already popular hashtag that generated 1,700 tweets on 15 October 2012:

#انتخابات_بلا_عبث #الكويت خارطة #مسيرة_كرامة_وطن

#(elections without interference) #(Kuwait) map of #(the dignity of a nation march) https://karametwatan.wordpress.com/[205]

@KarametWatan, 13 October 2012

For most groups, there is little to differentiate between agitation and mobilisation, as most calls to demonstrations were accompanied by slogans or short arguments:

سمو رئيس الوزراء .. الكويت بحاجة إلى رئيس وزراء قادر إدارة البلد,
إرحل فقد فشلت , موعدنا 8 مارس #Soor5

Your Highness the Prime Minister . . Kuwait is in need of a Prime Minister capable of running the country, leave, you have failed, our appointment is March 8 #Soor5

@soor_5, 1 March 2011

The initiation of a demonstration was usually started by the release of a statement by one or several groups, which provided further reasons why one should take part, and which often gained attention from the traditional media. As we have seen, tweets calling for participation were also among the most popular messages in terms of retweets, particularly among the first groups formed, such as al-Sur al-Khamis, Kafi and Shabab al-Taghyir wa-l-Tatwir.

The groups were, at times, spectacularly successful in terms of popular mobilisation – some more so than others. While the figures concerning the first Karamat Watan march were somewhat contested – there was a difference between government-friendly sources and opposition sources – there is no doubt that this was the largest demonstration to date in the country. Yet, while the Karamat Watan campaign was by far the most successful initiative in this sense, the others certainly saw some highlights. The 'Will of a Nation' demonstration held on 11 November 2012, is reported to have drawn a crowd of up to 50,000 people,[206] and the one held on 19 October 2011, up to 12,000 people. In general, however, participation varied between a few hundred and up to 2,000, but given the number of protests held, this still amounts to a substantial display of popular mobilisation. We should bear in mind that participation seems to have depended, at least partially, on the issue in question, and should therefore not be seen as a simple function of the effectiveness of the mobilisation involved. As for the offline meetings and seminars held by the groups, these were usually part of a demonstration, mainly the smaller ones, or they were held in connection with *dīwāniyyāt*. Thus, participation was either dependent on the demonstration in question or, in the case of the latter, restricted by the limits of the venue. The aim does not seem to have been to gather as many people as possible, which is also evident in their documentation of such events: focus was on the speakers and what they said, not on the number of participants.

Still, even though mobilisation was a dominant feature in general, it may not have been as dominant as one would expect. For most groups, mobilisation for offline events accounts for between 10 per cent and 15 per cent of their published messages. There is some variation, however: Kafi and al-Sur al-Khamis spent about every third tweet in this manner, and it accounts for almost half the tweets of the boycott campaign. The question, of course, is how important and effective this online mobilisation was. While this is an extremely difficult question to answer, there are some interesting clues in the data discussed here. By far the most successful group offline was the Karamat Watan campaign, and this was also the most successful group online. With over 100,000 followers, it seems plausible, to say the least, that their mobilisation on

Twitter had an effect. Their tweets concerning demonstrations were frequently retweeted by other users – in all, the group received more than 200,000 retweets within the time frame. Granted, this group mobilised on a very pressing issue and received quite a lot of attention from the traditional media, as well as from the regime. Furthermore, all other opposition groups supported the initiative, along with many well-known politicians, who probably contributed with their networks. Nevertheless, this group was the most successful in terms of mobilisation both offline and online, a connection which very probably goes both ways. Offline success must have gained them followers online, and online success must have gained them participants offline. When the group had to change a demonstration's meeting points at the last minute due to police interference, this was announced online, and the update seems to have been disseminated efficiently. While offline networks certainly played their part, it is clear that what the group announced online worked offline. Online and offline networks are not mutually exclusive, and we should not seek to force a clear distinction between them.

Offline networks and contacts seem to have played an important part for other groups as well. In general, coordination between the groups took place outside the public channels online. Although some groups made an effort online to gain the attention of well-known politicians and intellectuals, there were clearly a number of pre-existing contacts. I have found no evidence of the groups asking such personalities to attend their meetings, yet well-known politicians and intellectuals took part even before the first group studied here was formed. While the names of these politicians in themselves might have drawn additional participants to meetings and demonstrations, they may also have contributed by mobilising participants with their own offline networks. Moreover, the *dīwāniyyāt* played a part, particularly as venues for seminars and organisational meetings for the boycott campaign. These venues proved themselves capable of drawing large crowds long before the age of social media, for instance during the Monday *dīwāniyyāt* movement of 1989. It should be noted that the youth groups at this stage had proven themselves as activists, and might therefore have been able to enter the *dīwāniyyāt* on more equal terms than had previously been the case, as discussed above. However, as attendance at protests varied greatly, and was seemingly connected to the demands put forth, the loyalty of offline networks was clearly not the only factor in play. Rather, it seems that people may have been made aware of demonstrations from various sources, and then made up their mind as to whether or not they should attend.

Whatever the case, the limited number of tweets that most groups spent on mobilisation is somewhat surprising, given that most people do not read their Twitter feeds continuously: possible participants might miss important information about a demonstration simply because they weren't online at the right time.[207] In this regard, Facebook provides some clear advantages over Twitter as a platform: if you are invited to an event, you receive a notification. If you accept the invitation, you will get a reminder as the time draws close. Twitter does not provide similar features. However, as argued above, it is equally important to be active on the platform that enables one to reach the people one wants to reach and, in Kuwait, this would be Twitter. Moreover, through the use of hashtags, retweets, favourites and, not least, the organisation of particular hashtags in which 'Top Tweets'[208] are listed first, the risk of missing important information is diminished. Those interested in the issue in Kuwait know that they can find relevant information on Twitter, and the groups in question know that they can find people interested in the issue there. Again, it may not be useful to distinguish between online and offline networks, but rather to speak of which means are used to reach people: one might very well reach one's offline network through Twitter, and a person's offline network may, of course, be influenced by who they have reached on Twitter. In either case, Twitter was the main tool used for what was, at times, highly successful popular mobilisation.

Documentation and Media Attention

A third dominant feature common to all groups was documentation of their work, which was mainly done either through live updates in text or by publishing pictures and links to pictures and videos. On average, this accounts for about a quarter of the tweets published, but there are some clear differences between the groups. Moreover, this activity seems to have been motivated by different needs among the groups, or to fulfil different functions.

For many, and particularly at the beginning of their work, this documentation seems to have been primarily aimed at their own followers, members or those with knowledge of and interest in the issue at hand. For instance, Kafi, al-Sur al-Khamis, Shabab al-Hurriyya and Hadam spent a lot of time providing live tweets from events. Often these were not particularly informative for those unfamiliar with their work, and simply stated the names of various speakers, or provided very detailed information as to what they were doing or where they were heading:

ثاني المتحدثين الشباب (speaker) #soor5

The second of the youth speakers: (speaker) #soor5
@soor_5, 8 March 2011

The value of such updates will be limited unless you know the group, the speakers, the event in question and the subject matter. Thus, such tweets may have been primarily aimed at followers who were unable to attend a particular event, or people engaged in the issue but not yet with the group in question. It may even have been of interest to followers who actually were present, who then saw that their work was made known to the Twitter-sphere. One should keep in mind that, until late summer 2012, the groups in the campaign were both plentiful and concerned with the same issue. Although there were important differences among the groups, it would be surprising if there was no competition between them for attention from the media, established politicians, the Twitter-sphere in general and, not least, potential participants. Particularly for Hadam, a group that was very concerned with its own organisation, showing off its work surely must have been important. Not surprisingly, pictures disseminated by the group often showed enthusiastic members taking part in their activities. Similarly, other groups linked to both pictures and videos from their events, showing the attendance, posters used, slogans shouted and speeches given. While this also serves the function of disseminating their views, it was hardly lost on the groups that such displays make both them and their message seem more attractive and convincing.

However, there is another important element to this, connected with the opposition's less than favourable view of the media outlets in the country. The opposition generally expressed distrust of the media, and labeled it 'corrupt'.[209] That is not to say that the media did not cover the work of these groups, but rather that the groups may not have seen the coverage as positive or, in their eyes, fair. The two online newspapers sympathetic to the opposition, *Alaan.cc* and *Sabr.cc*, gave broad coverage to their work, both publishing their statements and frequently providing live coverage of demonstrations.[210] The live coverage featured both constant updates through text and several photos from the events, often focused on prominent participants:

19.32: بدأ توافد المواطنين إلى ساحة الإرادة (...)
(pictures)
20.02: انطلقت فعاليات تجمع "قاطع" في ساحة الإرادة (...)

> 19.32: The arrival of citizens to Sahat al-Irada has begun [...]
> 20:02: The activities of the group 'boycott' has begun in Sahat al-Irada [...]
>
> *Alaan.cc*, 18 November 12[211]

Large demonstrations were also covered in other outlets, both TV and newspapers, but the organisers almost always disagreed with the attendance figures given. However, the opposition also seems to have felt the need to provide their own coverage, particularly when the police started to crack down on protests in the autumn of 2012. In a country not used to police violence, it was important for the opposition to show the heavy-handed approach being used by the regime – the images of the attack on the *dīwāniyya* in December 2010 had proved to be a potent rallying call. Moreover, in the eyes of the opposition, this proved the illegitimacy of the regime's conduct, in a country that should be based on democracy and not force. Furthermore, there is no reason to doubt the opposition's genuine anger and contempt towards the violence used, not least following alleged attacks on female protesters during a demonstration on 19 December 2012. This last incident sparked a heated debate on Twitter, centered on the hashtag #ضرب_بنات_الكويت ([the] hitting of Kuwait's women). A battle of blame was taking place as well, with media outlets close to the regime often referring to 'elements' within demonstrations attacking the police, or castigating entire groups as villains, such as Karamat Watan. In the face of such allegations it is not difficult to see the need for documentation, not least of the fact that thousands of ordinary Kuwaitis took part. As we have seen, the videos uploaded by the groups themselves did not gain much attention and it was, by and large, clips published by other users which were used. The aforementioned blogger AlziadiQ8, often referred to as the online activists' own 'minister of information', was particularly important in this regard.

As for the differences between the groups studied, these seem to be related to the different motives for providing documentation. Unlike the others, Karamat Watan almost never provided pictures and videos. While this group was anxious to gain media attention, they were not concerned with showcasing their work. For one thing, they knew that they would gain massive media coverage if they were successful. Moreover, they were not interested in building an organisation and so did not need to compete for attention. Rather, they only needed the media to be aware of their events, and then to be successful in mobilising participants. Thus, they repeatedly contacted journalists and outlets directly ahead of the first march:

> Kuwaitis call for #March_of_Dignity on Sunday 21-10-2012 @ap @reuters @afpfr @BBCWorld
> @TWCable_NYC @cnn pic.twitter.com/P2WJQHaf
>
> @KarametWatan, 20 October 2012

Yet, when violence erupted, it was important for them to make it known that they were peaceful but were nevertheless attacked, and on several occasions they provided live updates relaying the actions of the police:

> القوات الخاصة تستخدم القنابل الصوتية أمام ساحة الإرادة #مسيرة_كرامة_وطن
>
> The special forces are using sound grenades in front of Sahat al-Irada #(the dignity of a nation march)
>
> @KarametWatan, 21 October 2012

As for the campaign to boycott the elections, one would expect continuous updates on their work, particularly during the election, but these were not provided. They did, however, publish several pictures documenting the campaign in which people were asked to wear something orange, as they surely knew this would not gain the attention of the traditional media. More importantly, such a campaign was probably intended as a source of motivation, and would not be effective unless the results were made known.

Thus, documentation was important to all groups studied, but for slightly different reasons, and it changed over time. In the beginning, it seems to have been important to the groups to display visual evidence of the work they conducted, as it was for Hadam slightly later when they sought to build their organisation. When the lines hardened between the youth movements and the regime, it became all the more important to publicise their side of the story and to show people how the authorities were abusing their powers. Still, while this must have been a powerful impetus for mobilisation for those most involved, it does not seem to have had the desired effect on the public at large. As we have seen, the demonstrations died out in January 2013, as the police continued to meet the protesters with tear gas, sticks and arrests. This is, in many ways, remarkable: not only could the regime's response provoke anger in itself, but this also followed the elections that were held according to rules which 10 per cent of all Kuwaiti citizens deemed it necessary to protest against in public. Granted, the wear and tear of seven years of political chaos and two years of more or less continuous protests must have taken its toll, but it is surprising that the regime's policy of ignoring both the large protests and the rather successful boycott did not provoke a greater reaction. In this regard, the regime's willingness to use violence as well as the media's vilification of the opposition may be important aspects of the explanation. As such, the groups' attempts to provide an alternative narrative can hardly be seen as successful.

The strained relationship between the youth movements and the media may help to explain why media attention constitutes such a small part of their online activities when compared to the Egyptian case. In general, the groups studied seldom linked to stories in the media covering their own activities. The few times they did so, they usually provided links to statements published in either *Alaan.cc* or *Sabr.cc*:

> #soor5 http://bit.ly/hBacsQ بيان السور الخامس حول جلسة 8 فبراير
>
> #soor5 [URL] Statement from al-Sur al-Khamis on the session [of the Parliament] on February 8
>
> @soor_5, 1 February 2011

It may, of course, be a result of the groups' inability to gain the attention of the traditional outlets or their lack of interest in doing so. Yet, the abovementioned online newspapers also published coverage of the demonstrations, as did many other outlets. The groups hardly linked to these news items at all. Moreover, the groups almost never linked to pieces on the issue itself, although the issue essentially was the political situation and the political system of the country, subjects which naturally received massive coverage. A partial exception should be made here for the two Islamist groups, which did link to news items on the issue on a number of occasions. However, as we have seen above, 'the issue' was somewhat different for them, and even so, it only accounts for between 2 per cent and 4 per cent of their online activity. Similarly, the groups almost never communicated with media outlets or journalists, with the exception of the Karamat Watan initiative.

This, in turn, provides important clues to the groups' use of online platforms. First of all, it seems that their distrust of the media was heartfelt, to the extent that they did not prioritise it as a channel to reach the public. There may, of course, have been no love lost on part of the media as well, to the extent that they deemed it unnecessary to provide coverage to groups that had proven their ability to mobilise large parts of the public. Although I have not systematically examined all Kuwaiti media during the time frame of this investigation, it seems clear that the focus is on the demonstrations, not on the groups calling for them, although some of the groups have taken part in discussions on television. This, in turn, may indicate that such coverage might have been seen as negative, or of little importance, with the exception of the statements. Moreover, it speaks to the importance of Twitter as a platform for political debate in Kuwait, as well as the importance of offline meetings and demonstrations. These groups were able both to mobilise widely and to affect opposition policies, while gaining – or seeking – only limited attention from the media. At the very least, it testifies to the belief of these groups in the platform they used – they sought to affect public opinion, and seem to have been content with Twitter as a vehicle to do so.

Information and Instructions

In general, the groups spent almost no time disseminating practical information and instructions, with one very important exception: the Karamat Watan campaign. This group spent almost a third of its tweets providing such content, and this also accounted for their most popular messages in terms of retweets and favourites. I will argue that this was not only an essential part of their work, but also an essential part of their success. The group disseminated detailed descriptions and maps, so there would be little doubt as to when and where participants in demonstrations should gather. By designating various meeting points based on geographical background, the group created an easily understandable system, which made attempts by the regime to prevent protests all the more difficult. Moreover, the group provided backup plans in case of various scenarios. Followers online were told to check the account for alternative meeting points in case of police interference and, as we have seen, this worked efficiently when employed. Fearing that the government might 'shut down' internet access in the areas of protest, the group even developed an SMS service designed to provide information without internet access. These detailed directions not only made the organisational skills of the group visible and convincing, they also made it easy to take part. Furthermore, the group carefully explained the security precautions that were in place: a member of the organising team would be present at each meeting point, and would take command if unforeseen circumstances arose. A medical team would accompany the march, as well as representatives of human rights organisations and a media team documenting all that happened:

> تعليمات #مسيرة_كرامة_وطن سيرافق كل مسيرة فريق طبي #انتخابات_بلا_عبث #الكويت
>
> Information on #(the dignity of a nation march) a medical team will accompany all marches #(elections without interference) #(Kuwait)
>
> @KarametWatan, 13 October 2012

> تعليمات #مسيرة_كرامة_وطن سيرافق كل مسيرة فرق إعلامية لتتواصل مع المؤسسات الإعلامية المحلية والدولية #انتخابات_بلا_عبث #الكويت
>
> Information on #(the dignity of a nation march) media teams will accompany all marches to liaison with domestic and international media institutions #(elections without interference) #(Kuwait)
>
> @KarametWatan, 13 October 2012

Thus, participation would be not only easy, but low risk as well. Moreover, the group framed the issue as a defence of their existing rights, not as a demand for new ones. They encouraged people to wear the colour orange, evoking memories of one of the most successful political campaigns in Kuwait in the twenty-first century and, crucially, a campaign that had not escalated into violence, and that had ended with the organisers meeting with the emir – a peaceful, favourable result.[212] It was a skillfully organised campaign and the most successful in terms of mobilisation both online and offline. It seems clear that the organisers had extensive prior experience, which, as with the Egyptian case, appears to be important.

Yet, the campaign did not end well. Following the initial success, the regime made it clear that this was not a form of dissent they would tolerate. Although this was temporarily toned down following US criticism, it did not take long before the regime returned to its heavy-handed practices. These included the use of violence against protesters, often followed by arrests, as well as persecution of opposition criticism online. Nevertheless, the group responded through their preferred medium, Twitter. For one thing, they documented police violence along with other groups, and they also argued strenuously for their right to hold demonstrations. However, while people following may have found their arguments convincing and the actions of the police appalling, this did not make the very real offline consequences any less dangerous. There is a clear difference between making your voice heard with little risk and making your voice heard when the risk is high: you certainly need more motivation for the latter. As a precaution, the group disseminated links to anonymising tools, and these messages were among the most favourited ones. Yet, while applications may help one to conceal one's identity online, they also raise the level of technical know-how needed to take part. For instance, although the use of Tor may make it possible to criticise even the most autocratic regime with a limited risk of repercussions, not many people do so. For one thing, it is beyond the knowledge and ability of most users. Second, the knowledge needed to *trust* such an application is also not widely distributed, and it may not seem a convincing option to everyone. Thus, when the regime simultaneously increased the risk of both offline and online participation, and thus also increasing the knowledge needed for more or less secure online participation, the group was no longer able to mobilise large crowds. This happened at a time when the regime showed far more contempt for the constitution and Kuwaiti citizens than had previously been needed to provoke a forceful response. While this does not provide the complete explanation for the end of two years of nearly continuous popular mobilisation in Kuwait, it does provide a sobering argument as to the possibilities *and* the limitations inherent in social media and other online platforms.

Problems Solved and Offline Results

All groups studied have one central feature in common: they sought to use popular pressure to either provoke political change or to hinder changes initiated by the regime, with the aim of either producing a more democratic political system or preventing a more autocratic one. As such, they took part in the essential conflict of power sharing that has been a feature of Kuwaiti politics since long before independence. There has always been an opposition present, and by and large it has framed its struggle as a defence of the constitution; most of the time, this has been a defence of the constitution also in practice. Most of the groups studied here came to disagree with this viewpoint, and demanded changes in the constitution rather than its mere preservation. Therefore, they sought not only to effect political change in the country, but also a change of policies within the established opposition, and to widen the scope of political solutions open for public debate. Their main tool in doing so was offline demonstrations, combined with online organisation, mobilisation and debate. They sought to do so in the context of a country that is wealthy but divided. Moreover, the regime has not always respected civil liberties, such as freedom of expression and assembly, and has sought to tightly control civil society. Importantly, these opposition groups did not trust the country's media.

In practice, the work of the groups involved changed over time, depending on the political situation. It involved various campaigns and aims, including forcing the resignation of a prime minister, supporting the opposition in an election, making the groups' demands heard in public, reacting to and protesting against moves made by the government and boycotting and monitoring new elections. What all this work shared was the need to mobilise as many people as possible, and therefore to convince as many as possible of the groups' views, to provide coverage and documentation of their own work and to disseminate information and instructions rapidly when needed. Moreover, they needed platforms for the groups they formed, which were rather informally organised. In general they were relatively small organisations: they needed protesters rather than volunteers. As we have seen above, online platforms, predominantly Twitter, seem to have provided what they needed. Twitter gave them a platform for mobilisation and agitation, which was how they mainly used it. They also seem to have successfully employed it to deliver rapid instructions and messages, and to disseminate documentation of their work. Much of this could also have been done on Facebook but, as we have seen, this was not a preferred platform in the country. Aside from reminding us of the importance of the local context in internet studies, this also gives us a clue to the success in using Twitter: although it may not have had all the ideal features, this was where they could reach the public to which they spoke. While most groups frequently linked to YouTube videos, only two groups created their own channels, and these were not particularly successful. While the groups were in need of documentation of their protests, they clearly preferred to leave this task to others.

The first, main aim of the groups was to force the resignation of Prime Minister Sheikh Nasir al-Muhammad, and this came about on 28 November 2011. Again, many factors were in play, not least the incompetence of the person in question, as well as conflict within the royal family. However, judging by the number of second chances given to al-Muhammad by the emir, his resignation would hardly have been accepted had the royal family not felt compelled to do so. Although MPs did exert pressure inside Parliament through numerous interpellations, it is hard to imagine that the popular mobilisation was insignificant; it was, after all, what directly preceded the PM's resignation. At the same time, the 2009 Parliament was dissolved, also a key demand of the youth movement. In the following elections, the opposition gained a majority, which also should be seen in connection with the surprising decision to dissolve Parliament and call for new elections at a time when popular discontent was running high. Preceding the PM's resignation, the youth movement had formulated the demand for a constitutional emirate, and following the dissolution of the new Parliament they gained support from many prominent and experienced opposition politicians. However, there may, of course, be two sides to this story. For one thing, these politicians might have supported such a view all along, but preferred that the youth movement air it in public before they made their position known. Or the politicians might have used the radical positions of the youth movement as leverage, and then given these positions their support when the regime took away their victory.

It is clear that, from the beginning, there was close contact between prominent politicians and activists offline, so there would have been several occasions on which to conduct strategic discussions. Yet, the youth movements deemed it necessary to spend much time discussing the issue online. This clearly involved 'their own public'; that is, people who seem to have been at least sympathetic to their cause in general. This indicates that support for such a view was not guaranteed within the opposition. However, given the popularity of Twitter in Kuwait, these debates could potentially involve large parts of the population. As such, the groups made their demand both public and political. When they gained some support, the regime reacted with unprecedented harshness and vilification of the opposition – clearly, it had no intention of accepting such a demand as a legitimate topic for public debate. Judging by their ability to mobilise offline, the groups did not succeed in convincing many of the population at large.

Thus, as the attacks by the regime became more threatening, the opposition and the youth groups reverted to their initial position of defending the constitution, and were able to mobilise effectively in support of this cause. Even though offline networks and the traditional media played their part, the Karamat Watan campaign seems to have been spectacularly successful in this work, mainly using Twitter. This, in turn, underlines a point also made in the previous chapter: there is skilled use of social media, and there is less skilled use. That they defended a more popular view does not diminish the organisational skills of this group, and it was hardly irrelevant to their initial success. In a similar vein, the boycott campaign spent substantial amounts of time explaining their work, their organisational structure and how one could contribute, and the offline result was in line with their aim.

In all, there seems to be an online political public in Kuwait, or perhaps rather several publics that in part overlap: opposition, Islamist, pro-government, the 'public at large', and so on. The youth movements were able to address and mobilise these publics predominantly through the use of Twitter. This also seems to have been the main aim, or predominant feature, of the groups' use of online platforms. While there were opposing views present in Twitter debates, any discussions between the two sides were more akin to competitions than to rational-critical discourse, and predictably so given that their aim was to gain acceptance for their views. While the impact of political debate online is difficult to assess, it seems to be a factor in Kuwaiti politics that is taken seriously by all parties involved, as will be discussed further in Chapter 7. Online platforms, and most of all Twitter, seem to have provided the groups with an indispensable tool to solve their organisational and social challenges, and a comprehensive arena for public debate. Even so, the groups were not able to withstand the repressive tactics employed by the regime.

CHAPTER 6

COMPARING THE CASES

The aim of this comparison is to establish what can be considered general features of online activist work in the cases studied, and what can be identified as results of the particular contexts within which the activists worked. Naturally, this dictates close attention to the relevant contexts, the issues the groups were concerned with and how they conducted their work. Thus, before we move on to a comparison of their online habits, a brief discussion of the differences and similarities in the factors that may have shaped those habits is needed.

Comparing the Contexts

In Chapters 4 and 5, we have seen that there were similarities, but also clear differences, between Egypt and Kuwait in political participation and freedom of expression. However, we have also seen that both countries have been changing following the so-called Arab Spring of 2010/11. Freedom of expression and of assembly increased in Egypt following the revolution, at least in practice if only partly on paper, although it has decreased again following the time frame of this investigation. In Kuwait, we have seen how the opposition first expanded the sphere of political participation and 'shattered' the boundaries of permissible opposition,[1] only to face a backlash in the form of increased repression starting in the summer of 2012. From this point, the regime increasingly used violence and persecution to hinder the opposition, both online and offline. Yet, also in Egypt, although public political expression reached unprecedented heights after 2011, the risk of reaction by the regime was always present, and repercussions were often more severe than in Kuwait in terms of lives lost.

The issues at hand in the two cases must also be considered in this regard: while activists challenging the political system and the regime in Egypt frequently faced difficulties, the groups working to combat sexual harassment do not seem to have been seen as a threat to the same extent. Then again, groups in Egypt concerned with human rights in a wider sense, such as the Egyptian Initiative for Personal Rights (EIPR), did face reactions. Throughout the autumn of 2012, the Kuwaiti groups were increasingly hindered by the regime in conducting their work, to the point that they were unable to mobilise effectively offline by March 2013. The Egyptian groups were not hindered directly in their work by the regime within the time frame, although activists in Egypt in general still faced violent repression. This is a contextual difference that may affect the groups' use of online platforms. Arguably, regimes in both countries were authoritarian at the time, although the Egyptian regime appeared to be liberalising whereas the Kuwaiti regime appeared to be becoming more authoritarian. This difference may shed light on how repressive a regime must be in order to hinder effective use of online platforms.

The formal and organisational status of political and social activist groups can be said to have been unclear in both countries. Groups in Egypt were formally subject to the restrictions specified in Law 84 of 2002, although more loosely organised initiatives were tolerated. As for the Kuwaiti groups, the most relevant organisational structure may have been that of political parties, but these are not permitted in the country. Nevertheless, groups in neither country seem to have faced formal difficulties during the time frames studied.[2] Another common feature was distrust of the authorities, although for different reasons and to different extents. While there were some internal differences in this regard among the Egyptian groups, most viewed the regime, and not least the police, with scepticism and low expectations. Moreover, some saw the authorities as an intrinsic part of the problem. This was due to the state's use of sexual violence as a weapon, and acceptance of or denial of sexual harassment as a societal problem. In Kuwait, the regime was viewed as corrupt and flawed, and the activists actively sought to change both key powerholders and the foundation of the regime's power. As violence was increasingly deployed against protesters, the state was seen as illegitimately employing its power. Groups in both countries did not trust the regimes, they did not believe that the regimes could understand and take seriously the problems they described and they did not expect anything from them in terms of a solution, so they would have to provide one themselves. These are features that the two contexts shared.

However, there were several clear differences as well. For one thing, the level of violence in Egypt was far more severe than in Kuwait. Although state violence did not target the groups studied here, they were most certainly exposed to violence. In addition, whereas the political situation in Kuwait during the time can be described as chaotic, it was unstable and volatile in Egypt. Throughout the period of this study, Egypt did not have an elected lower house of Parliament,[3] and violent demonstrations and street battles were occurring almost daily. The Egyptian regime did not survive the time frame set for this investigation, and was forcibly removed by its own army. Certainly not unrelated, living conditions varied greatly between the two countries. Whereas Kuwait is ranked as number 48 in the United Nations Human Development Index, Egypt is ranked as number 108.[4] Similarly, GDP per capita in Kuwait was more than ten times that of Egypt in 2013, according to the IMF.[5] This is an important aspect of the contexts for several reasons, including internet access in the population, the ability to use the internet, the ability to devote time to the cause in question and willingness to take risks. Access to resources was clearly an issue for all groups involved in Egypt, and several groups actively used online platforms to gain material assistance and help. In the Kuwaiti case, it does not seem to have been an issue to the same extent. All groups were able to provide equipment for demonstrations, venues for meetings and various products marked with their logo, particularly Hadam. Still, the Kuwaiti groups did not spend lavishly, and mostly made use of resources accessible in many countries, such as computers, posters, banners and sound equipment. Either way, while access to resources clearly was an issue for the day-to-day work of the Egyptian groups, it was – at least – not raised as one in Kuwait.

Perhaps the most obvious and visible difference relevant for this study was internet access. Approximately three-quarters of the Kuwaiti population has access to the internet, compared to about half the Egyptian population. Taken together with the differences in the standard of living, it is clear that the internet involves a larger part of the Kuwaiti population than the Egyptian one. Moreover, there were clear differences in terms of social media usage. Whereas Kuwait is the top-ranking nation worldwide in Twitter users per capita, the situation is very different in Egypt. According to the Arab Social Media Report, the number of Twitter users in Egypt is roughly double that of Kuwait, in absolute numbers. Given that Egypt's population is somewhere between 80 and 90 times that of Kuwait, the relative difference is substantial. Similarly, the number of Facebook users is relatively much lower in Egypt than in Kuwait.[6] Quite clearly, activists can potentially reach a larger proportion of the population online in Kuwait than in Egypt.

Moreover, as noted above, the differences in living standards between the two countries may be important in terms of the risks activists were willing to take. Increased risk of excessive violence does not seem to have hindered recruitment in Egypt. Although it may have hindered popular mobilisation in the sense that fewer women may have taken part in demonstrations, it did not stop women from participating altogether, and it did not stop large demonstrations from taking place. In Kuwait, increased risk of violence and persecution seems to have hit popular mobilisation hard, as demonstrations died out in January 2013. While many factors undoubtedly were in play in both cases, the statistics suggest that those participating in Kuwait – on average – may have had more to lose materially than those participating in Egypt. Such factors have been seen as crucial in explaining collective action in studies of activism and internet usage in the Middle East.[7] Then again, we should also keep in mind the data on Egypt presented in Chapter 4, which shows a correlation between social media usage and high levels of income and education. Those participating online in Egypt were hardly a cross-section of the population at large in socio-economic terms, but a relatively affluent public. While I do not know the background of everyone participating in the Egyptian campaign, it is clear that many were recruited from among the middle class or upper middle class. Finally, the risks one is willing to take are inevitably connected to the issues in question, and these also demand our attention.

Comparing the Issues

Although seemingly very different, there are several similarities between the two issues of concern for the groups studied. For one thing, both contained elements of both long-term strategic work for change and ad hoc work to counter critical situations created by others. In the Egyptian case, the groups studied sought to fight sexual harassment in Egypt, a deep-rooted feature of society that affects almost all women on a regular basis. However, when targeted attacks against female protesters began, the groups organised a response to this particular phenomenon as well. While clearly connected to their overall work, it also demanded a particular response, which differed from the way the groups usually worked, and sparked the creation of two new initiatives. As for the Kuwaiti case, their long-term goal was reform of the country's political system in terms of increased electoral control of all branches of government, as well as increased transparency. However, they also had short-term goals that were direct responses to others' actions, namely the demand to remove the PM due to his alleged incompetence, to dissolve one Parliament and to reinstate another, to block any changes to the electoral law and to boycott and monitor the elections of December 2012. Granted, the overarching goals of all groups can be said to be responses as well, to sexual harassment in one case and to an undemocratic system in the other. Yet, there is a difference between seeking to create social and political change and seeking to hinder specific actions by others. In both cases the activists' work changed over time, and contained components of both long-term strategic work and ad hoc responses. This, in turn, affected their work online, and also had implications for whether or not they were successful.

Second, I argue that in both cases, the groups studied sought democratisation through the issues they were concerned with, as these were demands for increased participation and equality. Clearly, in the Egyptian case, they also sought to prevent what in most countries is considered a crime, and which arguably was also seen as such by Egyptian law at the time. Thus, they were seeking to fight a social problem that the state should have fought, but was not able to and/or not interested in taking seriously. The Kuwaiti case also contained similar factors, in that socio-economic differences between the tribal population and the rest of the population seem to have been important for opposition organisation, although, as we have seen, this certainly did not explain opposition mobilisation as a whole. But, in both cases, they clearly also fought for the right to participate: in Egypt, this meant the right of women to participate not only in demonstrations and public political expression, but also in society in general. In Kuwait, the fight was for the right of the country's citizens to participate and influence the executive branch of government. That being said, the demands of the Kuwaiti groups did not entail increased participation for all of Kuwait's inhabitants: although some groups did argue for the rights of stateless Kuwaitis, no group showed any concern for the rights of migrant workers. Still, it is difficult to describe popular control over the executive branch of government and increased transparency as anything other than democratic goals.

In both cases, the groups conducted their work through political mobilisation and public participation, which, as argued in Chapter 2, in itself can be a democratising feature in that more people take part in the political process. Moreover, in both cases, they did so from a position of relative marginalisation. Youth in both Egypt and Kuwait were, by and large, excluded from politics, although they did make their voices heard through activism and protests. The tribal population in Kuwait was marginalised both in economic and political terms, but came to form the driving force of the opposition nonetheless. In Egypt, women deemed their country the worst in the Middle East in terms of equality and rights, and the state not only ignored the problem they sought to solve, it actively contributed to it. Thus, the groups working on the issue not only had to try to solve the problem; they had to convince the public that it *was* a problem, and one that needed solving. As for Kuwait, the question of power sharing between the people and the royal family is indeed an old one, and gaining acceptance for the idea that corruption and democratic shortcomings were problems may not have been so difficult. However, the solution these groups came to propose, namely that of a constitutional emirate, was not one championed by the opposition traditionally. Thus, in both cases, the groups worked for increased social and political participation by demanding that society treat the problems they had identified as political issues, and by seeking to convince the public at large of the solution they proposed. They did not represent the dominant forces in their societies, and presented their demands from a subaltern position.

Even though there were important similarities, however, there were also substanital differences. For instance, the reforms advocated by the Kuwaiti groups could, in theory, have been enacted fairly easily if the relevant legal changes had been passed by Parliament and signed by the emir. Naturally, the realities of such a struggle are far more complex, but a successful outcome of their fight would most probably have ended in this manner, if not in revolution. For the Egyptian groups, the situation was quite different. Recognising that the state would not be willing or able to end the problem, they sought to end what they deemed the social acceptability of the problem, which is quite a different story. This entails changing the norms of society at both a collective and an individual level. While passing and enforcing legislation are key components in this regard, this would demand a dedicated effort from the state and, even then, it might not solve the problem in itself. This tells us something about the nature of the problems involved and the scope of solutions proposed, relevant to how the groups worked online.

Moreover, sexual harassment is a more international problem than the democratic shortcomings of the Kuwaiti constitution, as is evident from the international attention gained by the two cases. Although the issue of democratisation in Kuwait is of interest outside the country, perhaps particularly in the other Gulf Cooperation Council (GCC) countries, the issue of sexual harassment is something women experience in all countries in the world, and it is acknowledged as a problem internationally. In addition, the sheer scale of the problem and the level of violence seen in Egypt were bound to draw international attention, not least because they were taking place in a country whose revolution was followed on Twitter, Facebook, YouTube and satellite TV all over the world. Such international attention is important both to the outcome of the campaigns in question and to the way the groups studied worked both online and offline.

Furthermore, this universal character of the issue in question in Egypt also has domestic ramifications. As we have seen, practically all women in Egypt have experienced harassment, and while they may envisage different solutions, many may have been motivated to dedicate time and effort to fighting the problem. In addition, there are, of course, men who are concerned about the issue as well, and who also are affected by it. As for Kuwait, the tribal population does constitute a majority among the citizens of the country. The opposition was more than a tribal rebellion as there were *ḥaḍar* who supported it as well, but the tribal population formed the backbone of the campaign. However, it would be hard to imagine that they all feel equally marginalised or envisage the same solution to their marginalisation. Although many may be willing to protest against a lack of opportunities or services, this does not mean that they necessarily want to protest against the form of government. Kuwaitis of tribal origin also led materially quite comfortable lives, and would probably continue to do so even if the opposition failed in their efforts for political reform.

Egyptian women, however, are still affected by sexual harassment every day. Thus, one could argue that those involved in the Egyptian case had more to lose from *not* acting than their Kuwaiti counterparts. The Egyptian groups continued their patrols in Tahrir in spite of extreme levels of violence. In Kuwait, violence proved an effective regime tactic against demonstrations, although it was hardly the only factor that led to the end of popular mobilisation. Again, this may be related to differences in what people are willing to risk for the issue in question. However, it also points to a contextual similarity, and another difference: from the autumn of 2012, activists in both countries risked facing violence when participating offline. Whereas the state was the perpetrator in Kuwait, it remains unclear who was behind the attacks in Egypt. In all, while the issues raised in both countries were, in essence, demands for increased participation and equality raised by subaltern groups, there were important differences relevant to how the groups conducted their work.

Comparing How They Worked

From the outset, gaining public support was, naturally, at the heart of the work done in both countries. In Kuwait, the main tool used was popular mobilisation, along with massive efforts to disseminate the views of the groups online. The groups also frequently held offline meetings and seminars and, as we have seen, it is clear that they coordinated with each other as well as with opposition politicians through channels other than social media. In Egypt, the groups did mobilise popular support offline in the form of demonstrations, but their main concern was to document and speak about the issue, and to disseminate this as widely as possible both online and offline. This entailed gathering information, holding meetings, gaining press coverage and conducting outreach programmes and online campaigns. Several groups held events in which the metro or certain areas of downtown Cairo were safeguarded, which clearly also included an element of drawing attention to the issue and documenting the problem in addition to the very particular task of securing the given area.

Therefore, the Egyptian groups were more dependent on volunteers being willing to invest time and effort with the groups than on getting as many people as possible to attend a particular event. The situation for the Kuwaiti groups was quite the opposite: they worked through small organisations seeking as large an attendance as possible on given occasions. The difference between volunteers and participants in protests is understood as follows: volunteers commit themselves to work with a group in the manner established by the group, preferably over an extended period of time, and with training. Participation is simply understood as taking part in an event, supporting the demands put forth on that particular occasion.

As the groups responded to changing circumstances in both countries, their work changed. Yet, it did not fundamentally alter the way they operated. The groups working to prevent attacks on female protesters in Egypt were perhaps even more dependent on volunteers, and in this context volunteering entailed intervening in dangerous and violent situations. Similarly, in reacting to the perceived autocratic actions of the regime, the Kuwaiti opposition responded once again with popular mobilisation. The campaign to boycott the elections, however, *did* need volunteers to take part in monitoring the elections, but achieving this does not seem to have been particularly problematic. Yet, when these responses failed to hinder the moves made by the regime, and when the regime tightened its grip even further, the opposition proved unable to respond. While many reasons were undoubtedly involved, this may indicate a fundamental problem with the strategy of popular mobilisation: as long as the regime is in control of its security apparatus and is willing to use violence, demonstrations may be quelled – at least in the short term. In doing so, the regime increases the cost of participation, and makes it easier for itself to treat and portray the demonstrations as questions of security rather than of politics.

The different modes of operation are, naturally, related to the issues of concern in each case. The Kuwaiti groups sought to convince as many as possible of their view, and to force the regime to reform the political system in line with their demands through popular mobilisation and protest. The Egyptian groups, for their part, did seek to affect public opinion and to alter the norms of society, in addition to the very concrete efforts to hinder and intervene in attacks on female protesters. In all, while there are clear similarities between the groups, there are also clear differences in context, issues and, not least, methods of operation that must be taken into consideration when we seek to distinguish between general and context-specific features of online activism in the two countries.

Internet Usage: Common Features vs. Context-Specific Features

Comparing internet usage in the two cases naturally involves looking not only at what they did but also at how they did it and, not least, where they chose to do it – that is, which platforms they chose to use.

Platform Selection

The most obvious difference between the two cases is that of platform selection and the use of social media. Although all the Egyptian groups studied made extensive use of Facebook, the Kuwaiti groups did not. Granted, two of the groups seem to have experimented with using this platform, as did the initial campaign against the then-prime minister. Yet, these early attempts at utilising the platform do not seem to have been considered a success, and the pages and groups were quickly discontinued. As we have seen, this was in spite of the fact that more Kuwaitis were active on Facebook than on Twitter, and that features available on Facebook but not on Twitter might have been useful to them. Both platforms could be used in Arabic at the time in question, both provided their services free of charge and both were accessible in the two countries. Moreover, Facebook had previously been employed successfully in other more autocratic settings, not least in Egypt during the days of Mubarak.

This, in turn, brings us to a potentially crucial point: local practice and precedents. By the time the groups studied in Egypt began their work, Facebook had been established as a proven platform among activists in the country through, for instance, the April 6 Movement. The 2011 revolution and the widely celebrated 'We Are All Khalid Saʿid' page had given further credibility to the platform. To my knowledge, the Kuwaiti activists did not have similar experiences. Rather, they had seen how blogs played a central role in their most celebrated success, the 2006 Orange Movement, which may help to explain why political blogs are still a dominant feature of the Kuwaiti online sphere. However, blogs are not ideal in all repects, for instance when it comes to discussion and rapid dissemination of information, and it would be astonishing if Kuwaiti activists had not adjusted and adopted new platforms as they became available. Moreover, while lacking their own successful experiences, they might nevertheless have been influenced by activists in other countries, such as the much-discussed 2009 Iranian 'Twitter revolution'.

Still, the point here is perhaps not so much why one particular platform was chosen over another, although this certainly is interesting in its own right, but rather the more general issue of being able to reach those you seek to reach. Shouting political statements randomly online would hardly be any more effective than doing so offline; you need to target those who might be receptive to your message. In Kuwait, Twitter was not only extremely popular, it was also widely used for political deliberations. In Egypt, on the other hand, the groups seem to have reached their audience on both Twitter and Facebook. This can be seen as a context-specific feature of online usage: activists need to go where their audience is, and that particular platform may vary from country to country. This warns us against the danger of discarding one platform, such as blogs, because new ones become available, such as Facebook and Twitter. Platform selection is not just a function of features available among various services; it is also affected by practice within the audience one seeks to address. The platforms used may change and, over time, Twitter may not retain its prominent role in Kuwait. However, we should not assume that such a change will take place just because a new platform with improved features is launched. Rather, we must consult the practice in any given context.

Nevertheless, there are some general elements inherent in the use of Twitter which are common to both cases studied. Although the Egyptian groups also used Facebook, they used Twitter *more* in a quantitative sense, with two exceptions, namely I Saw Harassment (ISH) and Imprint. While Twitter's strict limitation on how many characters each post can contain should be considered in this regard, there may be something more to it: Twitter seems to be the preferred platform for providing live updates and time-sensitive information. As discussed above, this is evident both in what the groups publish and in what generates engagement among their readers. There are some rather obvious factors that may be in play here, such as ease of use from a mobile device, which is what most people participating in a demonstration would be using. Moreover, there may be an economic component as well, as Twitter might require less material to be downloaded than Facebook. While any definitive conclusions would require more data on the habits of users in both countries, the material seems to partly confirm Eaton's observation that '[c]ertain platforms lend themselves to specific tasks'.[8] However, even though platform selection seems to relate to the type of content one intends to disseminate, it is also dependent on the local context.

Two of the groups studied in Kuwait created their own websites, as opposed to three of the Egyptian groups. Whereas three of the Kuwaiti groups made use of their own blogs, no Egyptian group did so.[9] While one could argue that this highlights the importance of blogs in Kuwait, it may also be a feature of those working against harassment, just as much as a feature of the Egyptian online sphere. Kuwaiti blogs have been central in discussing various political issues and, as discussed in Chapter 4, this was true in Egypt throughout the 2000s as well. As demonstrated by Pepe, blogs still constitute an important scene for literary production in the country.[10] Moreover, the use of both websites and blogs is quite similar in both countries, in that they primarily provide information, with one exception, namely HarassMap. For this particular group, the website was the central idea of their operation, and is itself part of the solution to a problem they had identified. Yet, even HarassMap's site also provided extensive information on the group, their work and their findings, and this seems to have been the central feature of the other websites and blogs created: they were hubs of information.

While there were differences between the sites in question, they all share the common feature of providing information on the groups, their activities and their positions. The five websites all provided contact information and, to varying degrees, further information on the work of the group, how to join the group or even the rules regulating the internal organisation of the group. The blogs contained fewer of these particular details, although they did contain links to the groups' presence on other platforms, as did the websites. The Kuwaiti websites and blogs contained much information on the views of the groups in question, particularly in the form of statements. Similar content was published by the Egyptian groups as well, although more in the form of position papers and reports. Detailed information on upcoming events was disseminated through these sites in Kuwait, particularly from al-Sur al-Khamis, Karamat Watan and the boycott campaign. Similarly, both

Nazra and HarassMap did provide details on their offline activities, although Facebook seems to have been the preferred platform in this regard in Egypt.

However, there were some important differences as well, both within each case and between the cases. First, the websites seem to have been more of a 'home' online to the groups in question, whereas the blogs were purely a platform to disseminate information. Second, there were clear differences in how successfully the groups managed to employ the websites and blogs as homes or hubs of information. For instance, Nazra's site was widely disseminated, most of all by other groups. It became a point of reference for many of those involved in the fight against sexual harassment, and a source of information for both the media and other organisations. Similarly, HarassMap's site was widely disseminated and people were encouraged to report any cases of harassment. In Kuwait, the Karamat Watan initiative also seems to have been successful in spreading the word about their blog, mostly through their own tweets, which were frequently retweeted. The other Kuwaiti groups, however, did not seem particularly concerned about their own sites, and frequently either used other platforms altogether or linked to other sources for content that was also published on their own website. In Egypt, ISH did not seem particularly concerned with the matter either, although this might have changed when they created a new website. Interestingly, those that seem to have been most successful in the use of their websites/blogs are also the groups that seem to be those with the most experience and/or better access to resources.

Naturally, the use of websites and blogs as informational archives is related to the platforms themselves. As has been discussed widely in the literature, websites are publishing tools, unlike social media, which are communication tools. Blogs, in a sense, are in the middle, but given that no comments were made to any of the posts in the material, they can hardly be seen as anything but a publishing tool in this particular context. Moreover, much of the content in question was also published on Twitter and Facebook, such as testimonies, statements and practical information on demonstrations. One might therefore question the value of operating both the blogs and the websites. Even so, for the groups providing valuable material for both the media and activists, such as Nazra, HarassMap and the Karamat Watan initiative, it must have made their work easier to be able to gather much of it in one place.

Twitter Usage

There were clear differences between the groups within each case in terms of how they made use of Twitter, and how successful they seem to have been in their online endeavours. However, given that the groups in each case worked with the same issues under the same circumstances, comparing the two cases taken together is key in identifying the general and the context-specific elements, and directs our attention towards important differences and similarities. The coding of the material taken together provided the results shown in Figure 6.1.

As can be seen, the three most prominent features are common to both cases, and the fourth and fifth are also identical, although in reverse order. These similarities also extend to the issue of own tweets versus retweets published on the timeline, as is evident from Figure 6.2.

Twitter seems to have been employed in a strikingly similar fashion in both countries, and there certainly are important similarities, or what we might consider general features. However, there are important differences as well, which become evident when we take a closer look at the activities grouped together in the categories given in Figure 6.1. For instance, although 'discussion' was by far the most central feature in both cases, this was partly due to different subcategories, as is evident in Figure 6.3.

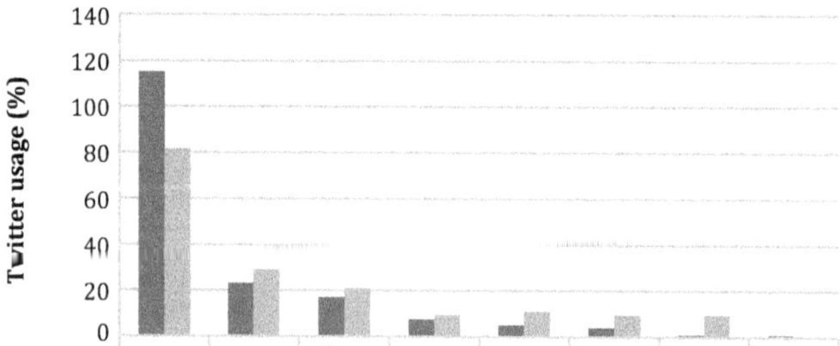

	Discussion (%)	Mobilisation (%)	Documentation (%)	Information (%)	Media (%)	Other groups (%)	Recruitment (%)	Other (%)
Kuwait	115	23.00	17	7.50	5	4	1	1
Egypt	81.50	29	21	9.50	11	9.50	9.50	0.50

Figure 6.1 Twitter Usage, Both Cases

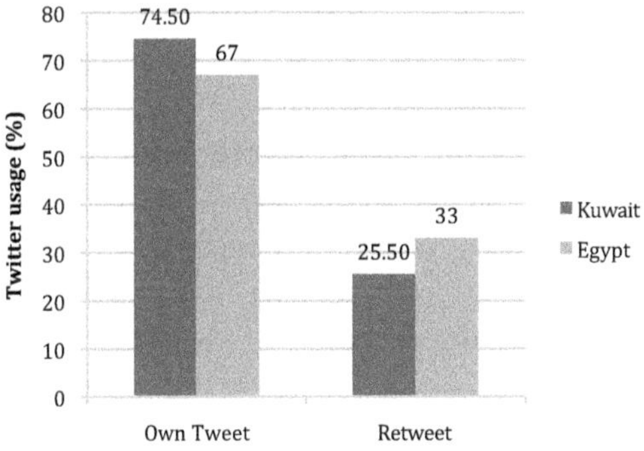

Figure 6.2 Retweets vs. Own Tweets, Both Cases

Groups in both countries made extensive use of popular hashtags. As we have seen, some of the groups studied in Kuwait frequently used their own name as a hashtag, a feature shared with some Egyptian groups. Moreover, many Egyptian groups were quite skilled in employing particular hashtags as part of online events and to disseminate their content. This was also done by some of their Kuwaiti counterparts, who at times made good use of the hashtags of the many Twitter debates taking place in the country. However, there were some

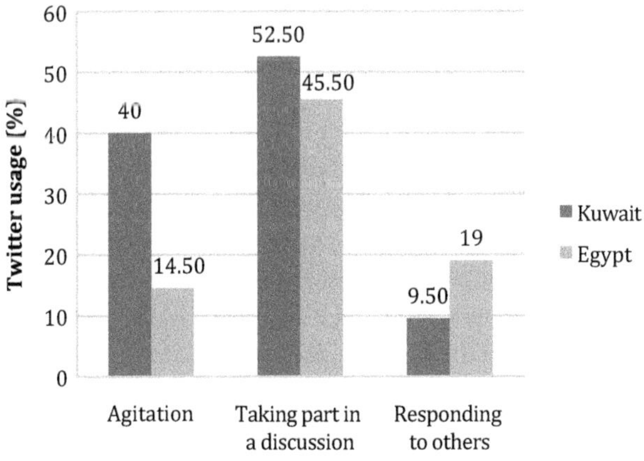

Figure 6.3 Discussion Subcategories, Both Cases

groups in both cases that seldom made use of hashtags. It should be noted that the Kuwaiti groups for whom this is relevant were also among the most productive, and therefore have a clear impact on the overall Kuwaiti numbers, as opposed to the Egyptian groups in question, which were among the least productive. Nevertheless, the majority of groups in both countries frequently employed hashtags to reach as many as possible, and to take part in or initiate discussions on Twitter. The groups that most frequently did this were also the most successful ones in terms of followers and activity, with the partial exception of Shabab al-Hurriyya in Kuwait.

What was not equal, however, was the time spent on agitation for their cause, as well as on responding to followers. I will argue that there are several factors that we need to take into consideration if we are to provide an explanation for these differences. For one thing, Twitter was widely used as an arena for political debates in Kuwait. That is not to say that the Egyptian groups did not feel the need to state their views – they most certainly did – but rather to point out that Twitter does not seem to have had the same status as such an arena in Egypt. Interestingly, groups in both cases predominantly argued in a manner that sought to impress their views on others, rather than to discuss and then reach a conclusion or a consensus. As we have seen, they were not often met with counterarguments, suggesting that they mainly reached those inclined to agree with them. However, in the Kuwaiti case, there were several levels of agreement, in the sense that many may agree with the general opposition stance of the youth movements, but perhaps not with their more radical suggestion of changing the constitution. Thus, the Kuwaiti groups may have felt a more pressing need to convince their own, so to speak, than did the Egyptian groups, who clearly needed to convince outsiders. Therefore, the outreach campaigns and attention from the traditional media may have been more important tools in Egypt. It should be noted that the Egyptian groups were not only more active than the Kuwaiti groups online, they also spent more time on features that were not central in the Kuwaiti case, which naturally contributed to lowering the relative amount of time spent on agitation. Nevertheless, it was a more dominant feature among the Kuwaiti groups, and this may be part of the explanation. As such, the differences would be both circumstantial – related to Twitter as an arena for political debate in Kuwait – and dependent on the issue at hand, in the sense that the position of the Kuwaiti youth groups was more controversial *among their own* than was the case for their Egyptian counterparts.

Moreover, the Egyptian groups spent markedly more time than their Kuwaiti colleagues responding to their followers. This finding may be affected by how online debates are conducted in the two countries; whereas the Kuwaiti Twitter-sphere is dominated by hashtag debates with many participants, it may be that the Egyptian debates involve fewer people and were more easily conducted in a more direct manner. However, as we have seen, there were several debates in Egypt that were also organised around hashtags, and there were some Kuwaiti groups that frequently debated by responding directly to others, particularly the Islamist groups. A more convincing explanation may be related to the way they work, namely that the Kuwaiti groups predominantly sought popular mobilisation, whereas the Egyptian groups predominantly sought volunteers. What they asked of their volunteers was not insignificant: from taking part in violent confrontations in Tahrir, to securing parts of downtown Cairo, to asking people to share what may have been painful and traumatic experiences, even if they were shared anonymously. Moreover, they asked them to take part in a steep uphill battle, namely to fight a problem that dominated society and largely was not even seen as a problem. Granted, the magnitude of the problem provided powerful motivation in itself, but it should not be surprising that these groups took the time to answer questions, to respond to positive feedback and to give praise to their volunteers. As we have seen, two of the most successful groups in Kuwait, namely the Karamat Watan campaign and the boycott campaign, also spent more time than others responding to their followers in this manner.[11] Thus, the most successful groups in gaining volunteers and participants took the time to reassure, motivate and value individual followers.

Similarly, there are also important differences between the two cases when it comes to 'mobilisation'. While this clearly, and predictably, was a dominant feature both in Kuwait and Egypt, a closer look at the activities of the group provides the results shown in Figure 6.4.

First of all, the Kuwaiti groups spent more than twice as many of their tweets mobilising for offline events as the Egyptian groups. This may not be particularly surprising, as the main tool employed by the Kuwaiti groups was popular mobilisation. The Egyptian groups also held offline events, including meetings and demonstrations, but most of

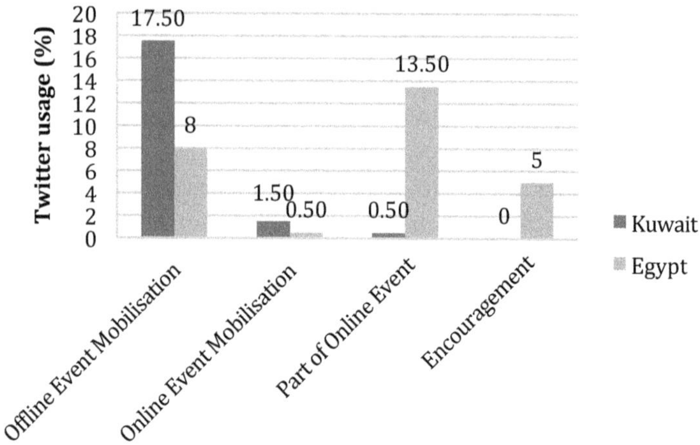

Figure 6.4 Mobilisation Subcategories, Both Cases

their offline work was carried out by volunteers. Consequently, they focused on recruiting volunteers. Moreover, their meetings often targeted a specific audience rather than as many people as possible. In addition, the Egyptian groups also made use of Facebook, creating events for their meetings and demonstrations there. Still, it is quite striking how little time was spent asking people to take part offline, also by the Kuwaiti groups – not least given that they were, at times, highly successful. Naturally, this speaks to the importance of offline networks and mobilisation through other channels. In either case, it seems that even groups that depended on attendance of their events deemed the time spent on this aspect to be sufficient. Moreover, it illustrates that these same groups do a lot of other things besides just mobilising online, and that Twitter is not merely a mobilisation tool.

Then there are the online events, which on several occasions were initiated by Egyptian groups, mainly HarassMap and OpAntiSH. This was almost never done in Kuwait, and when a group did call for online action, it was of a less sophisticated nature than that enacted in Egypt. One could argue that the online debates in Kuwait are comparable to the online events in Egypt, and that the difference is merely a matter of the name ascribed to them. However, this would be misleading in both instances. The Egyptian campaigns were initiated by the groups themselves, with a specific aim in mind, be it to break the silence surrounding the issue or to raise funding for an initiative. These aims were explained when people were asked to participate. The campaigns were also followed up by the groups, and contributions were reposted, or gathered and disseminated. Throughout the crowd-funding campaign, the group constantly thanked their donors and asked others to join them. The debates in Kuwait were quite different. Usually they were not initiated by the groups, and on many occasions, the groups did not participate, though key activists did so as individuals. The debates sometimes emerged as reactions to offline events, and other times as discussions of more general issues of concern for the opposition, such as the possible content of a new constitution. This points to an important difference: the online campaigns in Egypt were initiatives started by the groups to achieve specific goals, whereas the Kuwaiti Twitter debates were held outside the framework of the groups' activities. That being said, the Egyptian online campaigns created to discuss the issue shared an important feature with the Kuwaiti Twitter debates: the issues of concern were articulated and raised in public.

At least one of the Egyptian online events gained the attention of the traditional media. Yet, in general, the campaigns aimed at discussing the issue seem to have been aimed towards, or at least gained most participants from, those who already agreed with the groups. As such, they may also have been important in terms of affirmation and belonging. As for fundraising, this was not a concern for the Kuwaiti groups. Interestingly, neither the groups in Kuwait nor those in Egypt spent much time mobilising for online events. Although the Kuwaiti groups, surprisingly, spent more time on this than their Egyptian colleagues, it was not a priority in either country. This suggests that the involved groups did not consider it necessary to spend much time inviting and reminding people when mobilising online. Given their relative success in encouraging participation in these events, it seems they may have been right in this assessment.

The last category included in Figure 6.4, namely 'encouragement', also seems to be connected to the difference between recruiting volunteers and mobilising popular support. The Egyptian groups probably considered it important to show that they appreciated the work of their volunteers, to reaffirm that they were part of a group and part of a community – all the more so, perhaps, given that they were fighting against a practice which was widely accepted, and which most of them had experienced. In such a situation, it is not difficult to see that positive examples are important, to show that things might get better and that they are not alone in facing the problem. As for the Kuwaiti case, these groups also made use of emotional and symbolic references, such as the use of the colour orange. By and large, however, they did not prioritise cultivating the relationship with their supporters to the extent that the Egyptian groups did, nor did they ask as much of them as the Egyptian groups did.

The third most dominant feature in both cases was documentation, for both similar and different reasons. For the Egyptian groups, a crucial point was to document the extent and the severity of the problem, through the HarassMap website, through videos and pictures and, not least, through testimonies and compiled reports. In the beginning, this was not as important to the Kuwaiti groups, who were more concerned with disseminating their views and their solution. In terms of documentation, they seemed more concerned with depicting the work they themselves did offline. The Egyptian groups also felt the need to document their own work, both in order to attract potential volunteers and to show that they were credible sources: as I have argued, documentation was important for the Egyptian groups in order to attract attention from the traditional media. The Kuwaiti groups, on the other hand, seemed little concerned with such attention. Clearly, this is related to their distrust of the media, with the exception of *Alaan.cc* and *Sabr.cc*. For this very reason, documentation took on another function as time passed: to back up their own claims both of attendance and of how the authorities reacted, as they argued that reports in the media were incorrect.

However, it may also point to a contextual difference: as Kuwait has the most Twitter users per capita in the world, the platform may, in that particular context, offer direct access to the public at large. In Egypt, attracting media attention may have been more pressing in order to affect public debate. There were clearly important offline connections between activists and journalists, as seen for instance with regard to the appearance on *al-Barnamig*. According to Faris, important ties were forged between activists and journalists in Egypt during the 2000s, and these have been vital in disseminating content provided by the activists.[12] An exception in the Kuwaiti case was the Karamat Watan campaign, which actively contacted journalists in order to encourage coverage of their planned marches. Yet, as we have seen, there were several differences between this and the other groups in terms of how they worked and also of how successful they were.

There was also a clear difference between the two cases in terms of disseminating media attention:, as shown in Figure 6.5.

Concerning recruitment, we have seen that this difference is related to how the groups worked: whereas the Egyptian groups depended on volunteers, their Kuwaiti colleagues were more concerned with attendance. Then, there is the issue of contact with other groups, with which the Egyptian groups seem to have been more concerned than were their Kuwaiti counterparts. Yet groups in both countries clearly coordinated their work, whether in the form of joint statements, joint demonstrations or joint hotlines. In both cases, this coordination seems to have largely taken place offline. Still, there was some communication between the groups publicly online as well, particularly in Egypt. This was mainly in the form of encouragement, some discussion, comments on each other's events and work and some direct communication during large demonstrations. However, it is clear that in both countries the important coordination took place either offline or through other channels.

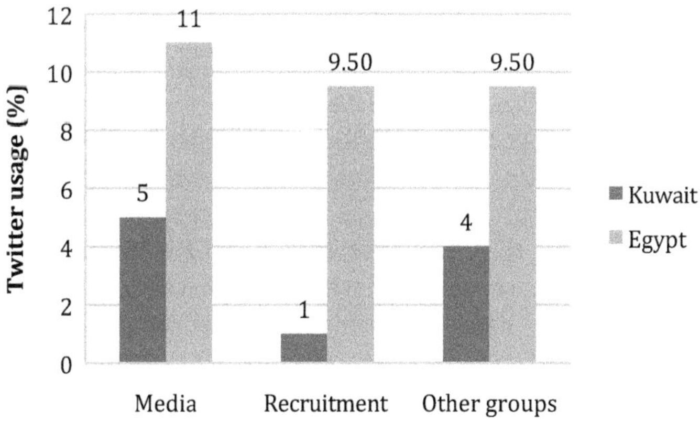

Figure 6.5 Remaining Features, Both Cases

Finally, groups in both countries seemed to be equally concerned with disseminating important information but, in the Kuwaiti case, this is solely due to the work of the Karamat Watan campaign. Although one Egyptian group spent more time on this than the others, namely Nazra, it was, by and large, fairly equally distributed. In Kuwait, however, the groups spent almost no time at all on this, with the exception of the Karamat Watan campaign, which was also the most successful Kuwaiti group in terms of mobilisation. Similarly, the Egyptian groups managed to prevent the attacks on protesters from discouraging female participation altogether, and it is difficult to imagine that their efforts, and the wide dissemination of the information on the hotlines and on their work, were not an important factor in this achievement. The material at hand does suggest a connection between the provision of ample and convincing information and people's willingness to take part in what might be controversial or dangerous events. Again, those who are skilful in providing such information are also successful in attracting participation, even in difficult circumstances.

YouTube

As shown in the previous chapter, YouTube was widely referred to by the Kuwaiti groups, but only two groups had their own channels. Both channels were discontinued after a short time. Moreover, the videos uploaded generally received very few views. The Egyptian groups, in contrast, all had their own YouTube channels. Many of the videos uploaded received quite large numbers of views, but there was wide variation between the groups, and between the videos uploaded by each group. A clear difference between the videos that *were* uploaded in both countries was the quality and the level of professionalism. Most of the videos linked to or published on their own channels in Kuwait were either footage from demonstrations, often apparently shot with cell phones, or videos of speeches that seemed to have been edited only minimally. In addition, there were some links to footage from TV shows. Clearly, there were plenty of videos with similar content which were linked to in Egypt, not least from TV shows, but there were also well-produced short 'documentaries' or advocacy videos published by some of the groups, including OpAntiSH, HarassMap and Imprint. As discussed in Chapter 4, it is clear that the self-described 'media collective' Mosireen[13] was concerned with the issue, and they may have been involved in the production of some of the videos. OpAntiSH mobilised the resources of their online followers as well, to provide subtitles in a number of languages for one of their videos. The videos of Imprint were also markedly better produced and more professional in form than those of the Kuwaiti groups. Whether this is a question of priorities or access to resources and knowledge is difficult to determine, but it constitutes a marked difference, which is mirrored in the number of views and subscribers, in favour of the better-produced Egyptian videos.

The most popular video from OpAntiSH garnered almost 1,500 comments on YouTube but, aside from that, little engagement was created by the clips published. Rather, they were discussed on other platforms, such as Facebook. The same goes for the two Kuwaiti groups in question here; their YouTube channels were used only as a publishing platform for their videos, which they could link to on Twitter. This seems to be a general feature: YouTube was a useful platform – and given its popularity probably the only realistic alternative – for publishing videos, but nothing more.

Comparing the Cases

There are both clear differences and clear similarities between the online activities of the groups studied in the two cases, and these seem to be related to all three factors discussed above, namely the context, the issues at hand and the way the groups did their work. This should not be surprising; the groups would hardly be oblivious to such factors, but would rather try to utilise the tools available in the best possible way. However, not all were equally successful in doing so, and there were marked differences between the groups in terms of followers online and results offline. The most successful groups seem to have certain features in common: experience and professionalism; skilled use of social media; ample and reassuring information provided to their followers; and, perhaps, access to resources. The groups that are the most successful online arguably seem also to be the most successful offline, although this depends on how one defines offline success, as will be discussed in the following chapter. Baym and Boyd have pointed to the importance of skill in using social media and addressing publics,[14] and the material studied here supports this observation: there is a marked difference between more or less skilful and, not least, strategic use of social media.

In other words, social media do not in themselves compensate for lack of previous experience and knowledge.

Some of the differences discussed above concern internet usage directed towards the *same* aim through *different* strategies. For instance, groups in both cases sought to turn public opinion in their favour, but they used different means to achieve this, which in turn affected how the groups worked online. In both cases, the most successful groups online, namely OpAntiSH and the Karamat Watan campaign, were created as responses to the actions of others. This suggests that it may be easier to mobilise against perceived wrongs – in this case the attacks on female protesters in Egypt and the regime's interference with the elections in Kuwait – than to create engagement through one's own initiative.

The differences in usage are also visible in terms of engagement with their followers. Whereas the most popular tweets in the Egyptian case were concerned, by and large, with live updates and practical information relating to large demonstrations, followers of the Kuwaiti groups were, to a greater extent, concerned with calls for protests and agitation. However, practical information also seems to have engaged Kuwaiti tweeple. Moreover, the popularity of different content changed over time, as did the context and the work of the groups. Thus, as the authorities tightened their grip in Kuwait, content providing links to VPN clients and other practical information became more attractive.

Platform selection is dependent on the local context, as a key criterion is a platform's ability to reach the desired audience. This is not entirely decided by technological possibilities and development, but also by the preferences and experiences of the intended audience. Twitter seems to have a special status as a political arena in Kuwait, and this was reflected in platform selection among activists. However, there is no reason to declare either websites or blogs dead, as they seem to be used as hubs of information. The introduction of a new platform should not automatically lead us to assume the death of older alternatives. YouTube, for its part, does not seem to be the online 'home' of any of the groups studied, or the site of active deliberation with others. Rather, it is simply a publishing platform. The Egyptian activists seem more concerned with the quality of the videos published than their Kuwaiti colleagues, and their videos also generated far more views. The Egyptian groups were also more concerned with publishing videos on their own channels.

While the Egyptian groups all made use of both Twitter and Facebook, Twitter seems to be the preferred platform for live updates and disseminating vital information. Twitter is also used more, in a quantitative sense, and there are several features of Twitter usage that are common between the two countries. Most of all, it is widely used in both cases to agitate, discuss and mobilise for the cause in question. In terms of discussion, the groups seldom speak *to* those who disagree with them, although they often speak *about* them. This may include specific references to persons or institutions, but most often it is references to opposing views in general, or to the fact that not all agree with their view. Thus, the groups not only get to express their positions, but also to stress the importance of their work: people disagree and things will not change by themselves. They also get to mark the difference between inside and outside; that is, to contribute to a sense of belonging among them and their supporters, as distinct from those who disagree. There does seem to be some discussion within this 'in-group', or among those who, in general, agree on the issue at hand. The most successful groups take care to use known and popular hashtags to disseminate their arguments, which makes it easier to reach those interested in the issue.

An exception was the two Islamist groups studied in Kuwait, who seemed to prefer to target their own followers and certain persons directly rather than to use hashtags and thus make the topic and one's views the criteria for participation. Granted, many, if not most, participants and readers were very probably also followers of the groups when hashtags were used, since interest in the topic would make it logical to follow the groups concerned with it. However, there is a difference between seeking those interested in a topic through hashtags, and just speaking to and/or with your followers. For instance, without hashtags, one can hardly participate in a trending discussion either locally or internationally, and thus the discussion may fail to reach many potential supporters. While this seems to have been a conscious choice for the Islamist groups, there were also groups that seemed to seek as wide an audience as possible, but made little use of hashtags. Not coincidentally, these groups were less successful online.

In terms of mobilisation, online work was adapted to how the groups worked offline: while the Kuwaiti groups mainly mobilised for demonstrations, the Egyptian groups spent more time seeking volunteers. Yet, in both cases, the groups spent less time doing so than might be expected, given the centrality of these features for their work. This indicates the importance of offline networks and other channels, but it may also suggest that social media are a time-efficient means of mobilisation, provided one is able to reach the intended audience. Documentation of their work was important to groups in both cases, although how they did it, why they did it and how they used this documentation was in part adapted to need as dictated by their context, in one case the relationship to the traditional media. Common to both cases, however, was the need to present the work they do, often in a manner that would be appealing to possible participants and volunteers. Finally, dissemination of detailed information on their work was a common, albeit unevenly distributed, feature of the work. It seems clear that skilful use of social media combined with convincing displays of organisational knowledge and experience correlates with success both online and offline.

A number of features to which the Egyptian groups dedicated quite some time were almost absent among the Kuwaiti groups, namely online events, media relations, communication with other groups, responses to followers and encouragement. This is related to how the groups in both cases worked, which in turn was related to the issues at hand. In a sense, this will probably always be the case when groups working on different issues are compared. The Egyptian groups deemed it necessary to document and define their issue of concern as a problem, but this seemed less important to the Kuwaiti groups. The Egyptian groups certainly aimed at the public at large, but they also sought to influence people at an individual level, and they saw a change of social norms as part of the solution. The Kuwaiti groups, on the other hand, sought to pressure the political regime into making concessions. Thus, it is not surprising that they worked in different ways, and that this affected how they operated online.

Yet it seems that online platforms provided the solution for quite similar contextual problems, namely reaching their intended audiences, or at least a sufficiently large audience. This may have been difficult due to contextual restrictions, such as lack of resources, unfriendly media, lack of democracy, a patriarchal public sphere, problems or even prohibitions against forming formal organisations and general ignorance of the problem at hand. The solution, in both cases, seems to have been provided, at least in part, by the groups' use of social media, which made it possible to reach their audiences and which made it possible to make their issues and their views public. However, when the Kuwaiti context changed, as the regime sought to crush the opposition movement in 2012, the groups were unable to withstand the pressure, in spite of social media. Clearly, there is a limit to how unfavourable and repressive circumstances online and offline activism can be conducted within. This will be discussed further as we turn to the issue of whether or not the campaigns managed to have an impact.

CHAPTER 7

ASSESSING THE CAMPAIGNS

In the following, I employ the framework presented in Chapter 3 in order to assess the impact of the campaigns studied. The framework identifies seven features, or *dimensions* as I have termed them, drawing inspiration from Dahlgren,[1] that are crucial in terms of being able to effect social and political change. A central element is to understand and interpret the campaigns within their relevant contexts, as what constitutes such change only can be understood in relation to the particular context in question. Furthermore, I seek to link online and offline work and, of course, to link online work to tangible offline results. However, the framework is also concerned with the impact of the campaigns in a wider sense than simply realising their specific goals, including experiences and expectations gained by the protagonists and changes in social relations. Thus, it provides a structure for a comprehensive assessment of the impact of the campaigns. This, in turn, will be crucial when I engage, in the following chapter, with the theoretical approach discussed in Chapter 2.

Evolution of the Campaigns

The first dimension deals with questions concerning the growth of the campaigns: their ability to attract followers over time; whether the issues and viewpoints were developed over time; and their ability to gain attention from the traditional media.

To begin with the Egyptian case, the assessment of these issues is, in general, quite positive. First of all, all the groups included in the case seem to have grown over time, in one form or another. The clearest examples are to be found in the groups responding to the attacks on female protesters. OpAntiSH started as a Facebook event and grew into a group able to mobilise several teams taking part in high-risk patrolling, and with thousands of followers online. One of its videos gained more than 1.5 millon views and the group became a widely used source in domestic and international media. Again, when assessing these impressive figures, we should bear in mind the offline networks and the experience of those who started the group. Still, Tahrir Bodyguard (TBG) started as a Twitter account created by one person and went on to conduct regular patrols, hold regular self-defence courses and be followed by almost 7,000 and 9,000 people on Facebook and Twitter, respectively. One could argue that OpAntiSH indicates the groups' ability to adjust to their circumstances, as many other groups joined the initiative. However, although many were engaged in various groups, the initiative came from individual activists. OpAntiSH was formed with one clear aim; it operated only during large protests and remained dormant between them. TBG, on the other hand, sought to expand its activities, through holding self-defence classes and later by forming Dignity Without Borders (DWB) as a group with a more comprehensive approach to sexual harassment and sexual violence.

The other groups also seem to have grown and developed. Imprint was formed in the summer of 2012 and, within weeks, they were able to conduct their patrols on the metro. They then moved on to secure an area of downtown Cairo during the holidays in cooperation with the group Anti-Harassment, while continuing their metro patrols. By spring 2013, the group had 55 members, in addition to volunteers who took part in specific campaigns.[2] I Saw Harassment (ISH) began by conducting patrols and documentation of an area of downtown Cairo during the holidays, but then expanded. They held self-defence classes in the spring of 2013 and operated their own hotline during larger demonstrations. Apparently, they were also in charge of their own area around the Presidential Palace during such protests. The group also held meetings outside Cairo, and a sister group has even been formed in Tunisia following online contact with the Egyptian organisers.[3]

HarassMap had been working longer than the other groups and was already quite well established by the time this investigation started. Nevertheless, the group continued to grow online, increasing its followers on Twitter and Facebook from March until August 2013 with 4,518 and 8,284 new followers, respectively. The group launched a series of new campaigns, including the ambitious initiative to raise funds for air time on nationwide TV. The group stated that it had about 1,000 volunteers by the spring of 2013, but it is unclear whether or not this represented an increase. As for Nazra, it is clear that the group had already expanded quite a bit before the time frame set for this investigation, and the group did not seek volunteers and members in the same way as the other groups. Moreover, they clearly managed to adjust their work during the period, supplying much of the knowledge, help and the guidelines provided to female protesters who had been attacked. They did grow online in terms of followers, gaining 2,384 new followers on Twitter and 2,207 new followers on Facebook between March and August 2013.

As we have seen, the groups in general were spectacularly successful in gaining the attention of the traditional media. In terms of policy adjustments, some changes did occur. For instance, some groups did call for legal changes as an important means to fight the problem and, while none of these groups explicitly changed their minds, they did talk a lot less about the issue. Moreover, there was some debate online about the use of violence, in particular the use of knives, which many warned against. While it was necessary to use force in order to help female protesters who were attacked, no group made use of knives. Public shaming of alleged harassers online increased over time, but again there was no stated change of policy. Given the extent and severity of the problems the groups were facing, it is quite remarkable that they did not adopt more radical stances. In all, they seem to have generally agreed on the problem and its solutions, and any changes that took place seem to have been in the direction of aligning more closely with the dominant groups, OpAntiSH, HarassMap and Nazra. The partial exception would be Imprint, which stuck to its policy of cooperating with the metro police.

In the Kuwaiti case, the development throughout the given time frame seems to have been more varied. All groups included were created within the time frame, and their mobilising capabilities developed quite rapidly to the impressive levels achieved at their height. However, all the groups collapsed during the time frame as well, with the exception of Hadam and Shabab al-Hurriyya.[4] The early groups, such as al-Sur al-Khamis, Kafi and Shabab al-Hurriyya experienced a rapid growth in early 2011, and managed to mobilise offline within a matter of days of their creation. They also seem to have been able to meet with established politicians from the very beginning. During the summer of the same year, two more groups were formed – Shabab al-Taghyir wa-l-Tatwir and al-ʿAdala al-Dusturiyya – although the latter did not manage to develop a following of any importance, at least not online.

However, following the election of an opposition majority in February 2012, things changed, as most groups joined forces in Hadam. Al-Sur al-Khamis chose to continue on its own, but has not been active since. Shabab al-Hurriyya, at least after a while, did continue on its own, and did continue to grow. More specifically, they had gained 6,742 new followers on Twitter by the end of the time frame in March 2013. Hadam, for its part, grew both online and offline from the beginning, but seems to have been more focused on its own organisation than on popular mobilisation, at least during the time of the opposition majority in the Parliament. Although the group was plagued by internal disagreements and had to create a new account on Twitter, their number of followers increased from 630 on 15 October 2012, to 4,500 a year later, and has since grown further. The group has expanded its website and is still active as of November 2015. Nevertheless, they were not able to take the lead on popular mobilisation when the opposition Parliament was dissolved and throughout the course of the dramatic events that followed.

The Karamat Watan initiative was launched in October 2012, and experienced the most spectacular and rapid growth. From about 2,500 followers on 18 October, the group soon reached more than 100,000 followers on Twitter – unprecedented among the Kuwaiti youth movements. Moreover, they managed to mobilise similar numbers of people in the streets, also an unprecedented occurrence. However, as the authorities cracked down on their activities, the group was unable to maintain momentum, and the demonstrations died out in March 2013. Nevertheless, the group is still active online, and has now reached 120,000 followers. A further demonstration was held in July 2014, but although attendance seems to have been relatively good, the march was violently broken up by the police.[5] Finally, the boycott campaign was launched in response to the elections of December 2012, and quickly gained almost 20,000 followers online. The group was able to conduct monitoring of the elections themselves and gain international media coverage of their work. However, as an initiative launched with such a specific goal, the group ceased its activities following the elections, although they attempted to resume them for the July 2013 elections.

Thus, the Kuwaiti groups involved all experienced rapid growth and decline during the period. Yet, if one looks at the opposition youth movements as a whole, their initial success was quite spectacular. From the launch online of the campaign against the PM in 2009, they moved on to sustain popular mobilisation for more than two years throughout 2011 and 2012, breaking all previous records of attendance in the process. Their downfall was quite striking as well; when the regime decided to quell the protest movement and became willing to use violence and autocratic means in doing so, they succeeded. The youth movement did not prove able to adjust to these circumstances. They did, however, adjust their views and goals during the process. As we have seen, the rallying call from the beginning was the removal of the PM, the fight against corruption and political reform. In the summer of 2011, several groups managed to come together and release a joint statement demanding a constitutional emirate. Importantly, this came at a time when the opposition was on the offensive, and the regime made concessions. When the regime turned the situation around, the focus for the opposition changed from demanding new rights to defending existing ones. While this was more successful in terms of mobilisation, it was not successful in terms of political results: the change to the electoral law is still in place and the February 2012 Parliament has not been reinstated. The change of focus does not necessarily signal that the groups studied had a change of heart, but that the regime rather than the opposition began to set the agenda. Thus, their views did evolve on their own initiative, but they also had to make tactical adjustments as demanded by the situation. At the same time, one can argue that their own initial views represented a miscalculation: by challenging the hegemonic order and demanding changes to the constitution and the status quo, everything came into play. The groups ended up losing, and when the hegemonic forces reasserted themselves, they increased their power at the expense of the opposition. This may be the result, not only of strategic misconceptions, but also of the groups' abilities, or specifically their ability to run effective campaigns.

Intra-Campaign Build-Up and Evolution

This dimension deals with the internal workings of the group, whether they provided training, how they recruited, their skill in employing online platforms and if these features were developed over time.

Starting once again with the Egyptian case, some interesting changes can be observed. For one thing, the process of recruitment did change, but not permanently and not under all circumstances. In the very beginning, TBG and OpAntiSH simply asked potential volunteers to contact them, or to meet at a given location at a given time. However, quite quickly, they began to give more detailed information about what personal information would-be volunteers should provide, and stated explicitly that they screened those wishing to take part. OpAntiSH insisted that all volunteers attend at least one meeting, to make them aware of what they would be taking part in. Other groups, such as ISH and HarassMap, asked people to contact them, but also provided online forms that new volunteers could complete. Imprint was perhaps the most vigorous group in this regard and their process of recruitment included a form, a phone call, an interview and the public announcement of new members accepted into the group. The rationale behind these measures is quite easy to comprehend: they needed to make sure that no harassers infiltrated the groups, and it is quite clear that the groups picked up hints from each other. However, when the need was urgent, such as during the 25 January and 30 June demonstrations in 2013, OpAntiSH and TBG disregarded their own procedures and asked anyone present and able to help.

The work of the groups also evolved over time. OpAntiSH and TBG had no clear plan of action when they were started, and much was decided as they went along.[6] This process happened quite rapidly, and by the time they started to operate on the ground, several things were in place: volunteers wore identical and easily recognisable clothes; they were organised in teams; the hotlines were operating; and support was also offered to those who had been attacked. Both OpAntiSH and TBG held regular meetings for their volunteers, particularly before large demonstrations, but it is not clear if this included any training beyond instructions as to how they would work. HarassMap *did* hold meetings and seminars/courses for their volunteers, as did Imprint and ISH. HarassMap continuously launched new campaigns, although this did not signify changes in their work mode, but was rather the nature of how they worked. Still, they did introduce new *tools* as they went along, including online events, art exhibitions and crowd-funding. Imprint expanded from patrols on the metro to downtown patrols and information campaigns at universities and ISH expanded from downtown patrols to self-defence courses, demonstrations and patrols during large demonstrations.

As a more 'professional' organisation, Nazra was a bit different. They held open meetings where people could talk about the issue, meetings for journalists, video courses and several other activities. Yet, all these were quite similar in the sense that the group was concerned with disseminating its knowledge and providing assistance and help, as well as the opportunity to talk to those who needed it. As such, it represented not so much new modes of working as a diversification of what they were already doing. In any case, it is clear that some groups possessed a great deal of knowledge and experience to begin with. The methods used evolved, and the groups learned from each other. Most of all, this was a period of expansion for all the groups studied, and their activities were affected by this. It should be noted that, although the work and visibility of these groups clearly was a reason for this expansion, the extent and severity of the problem in Egypt at the time must also have played a part.

In their use of online platforms, some were more skilful than others, and interestingly, this does not seem to have changed much over time. OpAntiSH, HarassMap and TBG consistently used hashtags on Twitter, wrote mostly in complete sentences and included an explanatory text when disseminating links to content on other platforms. Nazra, Imprint and ISH did not do this to a great extent from the beginning, and they did not do so towards the end of the time frame either. Granted, Imprint and ISH clearly prioritised Facebook as a platform, and Nazra probably saw that their content was disseminated effectively by others. Nevertheless, they must have noticed the differences between their own usage and that of the others, and they must have seen the differences in terms of followers and reach. TBG's practice of contacting famous Twitter users to gain attention was not picked up by other groups. However, there is a dimension of sharing responsibilities and fields of activity involved as well. For instance, the documentation conducted by Nazra, HarassMap and OpAntiSH was important in terms of their credibility as sources for the traditional media. The fact that other groups did not pick up this practice is probably not the result of failure to grasp its potential, but rather that they saw that these groups were doing it perfectly well. Instead, they conducted their own work, which gained attention in its own right. That being said, it is remarkable that the groups were not even more similar online, given the close contact between them.

In terms of innovation online, HarassMap seems to have been the leader. For one thing, they initiated the website, variations of which are now in use in other countries.[7] Moreover, together with Nazra, they initiated the online events, later picked up by a group called the Uprising of Women in the Arab World.[8] Finally, they used online platforms to mobilise assistance and resources, as did TBG and OpAntiSH. Some groups were also quite successful in attracting the support of other skilled activists and artists, as is evident, for instance, in the OpAntiSH video and in the art exhibition held by HarassMap, which further strengthened their campaigns both online and offline. In general, however, the groups' use of online platforms was quite consistent over time.

As for the Kuwaiti case, all groups stuck with the strategy of popular mobilisation throughout the period studied here. For the first groups, organisation does not seem to have been a main concern, at least not on the surface, although it was discussed. According to one prominent activist, disagreements as to whether a lasting movement was needed as opposed to more loosely organised initiatives were part of the reason that al-Sur al-Khamis was joined by two new groups before the 8 March demonstration in 2011.[9] Still, until February 2012, all the active groups seem to have been small, loosely organised initiatives. This changed, however, after the PM resigned, the opposition won the elections and the youth movement could turn its attention inwards. In February 2012, the founding conference of Hadam was held, with deliberation both on how the group should be structured and on the positions they should advocate. The result was a rather elaborate set of rules and statutes.[10] Moreover, the leadership of the group was quite extensive, perhaps as a necessary means to accommodate the leaders of several initiatives, and the first board consisted of no fewer than 14 people.[11] According to a central member of the group, it was intended as something lasting, which might over time perhaps become a political party representing the youth,[12] although it soon faced internal strife.

Then came the dramatic autumn of 2012, and the leading role was taken up by Karamat Watan and the boycott campaign. These groups clearly had learned from previous experience with activism in the country. Both were more skilled in their use of online platforms than earlier initiatives, and both made explicit references to the 2006 Orange Movement. As we have seen, Karamat Watan took several organisational steps to make participation an easy and safe option. Yet, there is no fundamental difference between their work and that of their predecessors, and many of the same people were probably involved. Rather, they just did the work a bit better; they framed it better, they organised it better, they used social media more competently, and they did it at a time when public engagement was higher. This therefore illustrates that online activism develops over time. This points to an important observation that can be made from the recent history of both Kuwait and Egypt: online activism *takes* time. The level of public engagement seems to have been crucial, in the sense that the groups studied in Kuwait acted in tandem with the political situation in the country, mutually affecting each other. When the level of public engagement was high, the groups did an important job in further strengthening it and organising it into political expressions of opposition. But they were also hampered by their circumstances, and lost their momentum by late 2012.

The desire to create something lasting is understandable, and it may be that Hadam will prove to be a success. Shabab al-Hurriyya also survived this intense period and still does its work online. As we have seen, this group is connected to the Umma Party in Kuwait, which by no means represents mainstream political expression. As such, their ability to work or mobilise may not change much depending on the political situation in the country: they have their dedicated followers in either case, and they do not generate wider support as easily as others.

Finally, the fact that the groups were dependent on their context does not mean that they were a simple function of it: they were able to affect it, and they were able to amplify and direct whatever opposition sentiments existed. Of course, others were also able to affect the context, not least the regime itself. As such, they were able to bring about change, just not under any given circumstances. Recognising this, the regime did seek to change these circumstances to the disadvantage of the youth movements, which in turn brings us to the next dimension, namely reactions and adjustments.

Reactions and Adjustments

This dimension concerns the following questions: Did the campaign provoke any reactions from the government and/or from opponents? Did other forces adjust their view due to the campaign, either to accommodate it or to stand as a clear alternative to it? This is understood in relation to the groups' work both online and offline.

The issue of sexual harassment and sexual violence did provoke massive reactions in Egypt during the period studied, in no small part due to the work of the groups studied here. The most obvious reaction was from the traditional media, but the groups also generated direct reactions from various forces and institutions in society. The Imprint campaign on the metro took place with the cooperation of the metro police. According to the group itself, neither the police, the metro company nor the private security company hired by the metro company liked the idea to begin with.[13] However, following pressure from the group, and not least the occurrence of harassment while they were negotiating, the above-mentioned bodies decided to participate. According to Imprint, this has been vital for their work, and has produced tangible results. The metro company now operates a hotline in case of harassment,[14] and female police officers have been dispatched to prevent harassment and keep men out of the women-only cars.[15] It should be noted that other groups also held campaigns in the metro, and this naturally also affected the reactions of the authorities. While these changes clearly are to be seen as *results* of the campaigns, they also testify to the *reaction* sparked by the work of the groups, which, judging by the history described in Chapter 4, might have been different had it not been for the 2011 revolution. This was far from the only reaction sparked by the groups studied, and even the Islamist-dominated Shura Council discussed the issue in February 2012. All groups reacted with contempt to the utterly careless and misogynist manner in which the subject was raised and the attempt to turn the problem into a question of morals. Yet, it also illustrates that even these hostile forces felt compelled to address the problem, and they would hardly have done so on their own initiative.

Frequently, the groups studied called for the opposition political parties in the country to accept their share of the responsibility for the security of the participants in the demonstrations the parties supported. However, these calls largely went unanswered in terms of concrete steps, with the exception of some young members of the Social Democratic Party, the Dustur Party, the Socialist Party and some other parties who participated with the groups on a couple of occasions.[16] However, the political parties did address the problem in their statements, and they could hardly have abstained from doing so given the work of the groups studied and their explicit calls to the parties: it was an obvious and pressing problem in the country at the time.[17] It should be noted, however, that these opposition parties also took the opportunity to point to the ruling Muslim Brotherhood as the responsible party, at a time when they were using every occasion possible to attack the government.

Following the coup in July 2013, the regime, which had failed to react to the problem before, started to respond. The interim government declared that new legislation on the issue was on the way, and following attacks on female participants in the large celebration of the inauguration of President Sisi on 8 June 2014, several steps were taken by the regime. Seven persons were arrested for the attacks, the president visited in hospital one of the women who had been attacked,[18] new legislation was introduced[19] and the police announced the formation of a department to work on the issue.[20] It should be stressed that these are the reactions of a post-coup regime that many compared to the old Mubarak regime, and of the unreformed institutions of that regime. Thus, even though one of the articles given as a source here claims that groups fighting sexual harassment were ecstatic, this was not the case: they reacted with scepticism. The regime only spoke of the issue in terms of increased security, whereas in fact reform of the security services would be one of the most important steps to combat the problem.[21] Had the regime been serious in its desire to fight the problem, it could have reacted much earlier, and it remains to be seen whether these promises will lead to tangible results. Still, it does bear witness to the fact that the groups studied here had succeeded in breaking the public silence on the issue and establishing it as a political problem, thus embarrassing the regime and forcing a reaction. In an interview with *MadaMasr*, a representative of the Egyptian Initiative for Personal Rights (EIPR) stated that the new laws should be 'celebrated, but we should also claim this victory as it is a result of years of struggle and pressure', further arguing that '[t]he amended wording is an improvement as it is not morally charged and more gender-sensitive'.[22]

A final reaction that can be mentioned in this regard, although one that was not particularly important or decisive, took place on 2 July 2013.

The groups had frequently complained about callers who harassed the hotlines and routinely shamed them in public. During the 30 June demonstrations, however, the problem seems to have become a more serious challenge to the groups' ability to do their work, and they started demanding that phone companies do something to prevent this from happening. Several of their supporters joined in and, within hours, Mobinil, one of Egypt's largest phone companies, responded, providing numbers for the police departments to which harassers could be reported. This did not cost the company much, and it hardly solved the problem. Still, Mobinil, as any company, is very concerned with its own image, and seems to have deemed it harmful to be seen as inattentive or negligent on the issue. This, in turn, says something about the groups' success in terms of establishing the issue as a problem in the eyes of the Egyptian public.

Within the time frame, the groups did not provoke any organised and explicit negative reaction to their work, aside from the comments made in the Shura Council and similar expressions made online. However, the targeted attacks on female protesters may be seen as such, even though it is unclear who was behind them. They clearly targeted women, and sexual violence was their means of attack. These might also be seen as attempts to create disorder, to undermine the regime, to hinder protests, to deny women political participation or to remove women from the protests so that the remaining men could be attacked more directly, as was the case with the 2005 attacks. Yet, it seems to have been more a question of the groups studied reacting to these attacks, rather than the attacks being a response to the work of the groups. Finally, all activist groups in Egypt may face reactions in the time to come, as the current authorities are targeting NGOs and human rights defenders.

Their Kuwaiti counterparts faced severe reactions from the authorities, and these increased over time. In a sense, reactions from the government had been a part of their issue from the very beginning: bloggers launched a protest against online attacks on freedom of speech in 2009, and the police's heavy-handed breakup of a *dīwāniyya* was the event that led directly to the establishment of al-Sur al-Khamis, although the groups clearly were built on long-standing grievances. Since then, the youth movement has faced increasingly harsh reactions from the authorities. The protest planned for 8 March 2011 had to be moved, due to restrictions put in place by the regime. In December of the same year, several activists were arrested following the storming of the Parliament by the opposition. It should be noted, however, that the storming probably constituted a breach of Kuwaiti law: the Parliament was closed, and the activists forced their way in. Moreover, all charged were eventually acquitted, although this did not happen until December 2013.[23] The regime then started to prosecute activists on the basis of statements published online, particularly on Twitter, and even sought to punish dissenting members of the royal family. This actions increased in the autumn of 2012, in parallel with violent crackdowns on demonstrations. Following a brief pause in this practice as a result of US criticism, the regime managed to quell the protest movement by January 2013. Since then, as we have seen, the regime has been willing to use even more drastic means to silence its critics, including revoking citizenships, which naturally has substantial repercussions for those targeted. Several factors need to be taken into consideration relating to these measures.

For one thing, throughout the years following the 2006 Orange Movement, there has always been a threat of reactions from the regime hanging over activists in the country. However, these have usually taken the form of targeting particularly outspoken activists, most often by incarcerating them for a limited period of time then releasing them. This tactic was not used against 'ordinary' protesters, as long as they were Kuwaiti citizens, and it did not involve such serious consequences. Then the regime saw what was happening in Bahrain, and perhaps also in Egypt, and was disinclined to take any chances. Moreover, the regime knew perfectly well that what they did in the summer of 2012 was widely seen as illegitimate, and that the protest movement would grow if it were allowed to do so: according to one activist, the regime found itself in a crisis of legitimacy.[24] Perhaps most importantly: the regime knew that it was on the defensive and needed to take action if it was to retain its position. It was clear to everyone in Kuwait that the regime had been forced, in public, to dismiss the prime minister in November 2011. The protest movement had infringed on the emir's power and privilege to change the head of the government. This constituted an obvious threat to the royal family's rule, not least because it was combined with explicit demands to remove much of their power.

At the same time, the regime also knew perfectly well that most Kuwaitis were well-off and were not likely to risk their lifestyle, and that clashes with the police could also serve to delegitimise the protest movement. The violence employed also made it easier to treat the protests as a matter of security. Moreover, efforts were made to further depoliticise the demands of the opposition by portraying these as part of a sectarian pro-*badw*, anti-*ḥaḍar* conflict. In a telling incident from the February 2012 election campaign, the well-known pro-government politician and notorious anti-*badw* troublemaker Muhammad al-Juwaihil made derogatory remarks about the largest tribe in Kuwait. Young members of the tribe took the bait, and burned down his campaign tent.[25] Similarly, on 18 January 2013, the emir's sister went on record stating that those participating in the opposition movement were not 'real Kuwaitis',[26] provoking thousands of tweets denouncing her under the hashtag #تصريح_فريحة_الأحمد (the statement of Fariha al-Ahmad). Clearly, the sectarian anti-Shiite sentiments expressed by parts of the opposition did not make things better.

As we have seen, the regime succeeded in repressing the protest movement. As will be discussed in the following chapter, this illustrates how hegemonic forces fight off challenges. It also illustrates the ability of activists to operate online and offline in contexts of varying degrees of authoritarianism. A central feature of such activism often referred to by observers, and by myself in this study, is the ability to document the wrongdoings of the regime and thereby spark reactions. The Kuwaiti groups *did* document the violence of the regime, but aside from some US criticism, which was soon ignored, it did not spark major reactions or outrage, either in Kuwait or abroad. A similar situation occurred when the Egyptian authorities used extreme violence to crush the protests of the Muslim Brotherhood in the summer of 2013: they were not stopped even though the violence was documented. Obviously, the value of such documentation is diminished when it does not spark a reaction from a party which is able to intervene or affect the situation.

I suggest that a crucial contribution of online platforms is that they enable excluded groups to raise their political concerns in public. However, the ability to do so is also dependent on the context, and there seems to be a crucial threshold in terms of the freedom needed for these mechanisms to function: it must be possible to voice in public a view on an issue that is not in line with the state's own version of the problem, and to receive responses to this other than mere repression. This includes raising issues that the state does not want discussed, but it does not have to be issues that challenge the state directly. When this no longer is possible due to fear, lack of venues, repression, or the like, these counterpublics will not be able to challenge the hegemonic order of societal discourse and thus not able to effect change. This would indicate that, when identifying possible successful movements, we should look at their discourse and their ability to raise conflicting views and information in the public arena.

However, through such absolute repression, the regime may pay a high price in terms of international standing and internal legitimacy. Moreover, experiences and expectations gained from activism may prove more difficult to quell than a demonstration. Furthermore, crushing a protest movement in this manner means relying on its coercive apparatus, which may also be problematic. In either case, online platforms have their limits, and should not be expected to supersede their online and offline contexts. Clearly, the regime took the opposition groups in Kuwait seriously, to the extent that they were willing to use hitherto unheard-of measures to suppress their protests. This, naturally, speaks to the impact of the youth movement.

Importantly, the youth movement managed to change the positions of others, as prominent opposition politicians came to endorse their goal of a constitutional emirate. According to one of the key activists of the youth movement, they were the first to raise this issue, and the politicians did indeed follow their lead after some time.[27] There may have been other mechanisms at work as well, but it is clear that the youth movement first publicly championed a radical idea that was later endorsed by more established opposition forces. As I have consistently argued, this represented a shift from a line held by the opposition since independence. One may, of course, wonder why experienced politicians would endorse a radical idea that proved not to enjoy wide support – as discussed in Chapter 5, both the opposition and the regime have been concerned with staying within the bounds of the 'acceptable' in Kuwaiti politics in order to retain popular support. One factor would be anger caused by the dissolution of the February 2012 Parliament, and perhaps hubris following their successful removal of Prime Minister Nasir al-Muhmmad. At the same time, one should also consider the possibility that very active youth activists dominating a Twitter-sphere that is ascribed much importance but perhaps is not quite representative of the population at large may have caused a glitch in the assessment made by experienced populist politicians.

Offline–Online Relations

This dimension deals with questions regarding connections between online and offline activities, including whether or not there were any connections between suggestions and decisions reached online and actions offline, if the groups documented their offline actions online, if growth online materialised offline and if links between offline events, achievements and the like can be traced to activity online.

The first point to address in this discussion would be the futility of upholding a strict separation between online and offline. Such a separation is increasingly seen as artificial, and the material presented here points in the same direction. It would be meaningless to try to decide whether these groups were offline movements that also worked online, or online movements that also worked offline, regardless of where they were started. Hardly any youth activist group would choose not to use social media, and we should not make this feature of their work exotic by ascribing some special importance to the decision to use online platforms in itself. Moreover, although there clearly are campaigns that predominantly work online, and do not seek offline mobilisation in any form, they do seek offline change, and we cannot disregard a priori the importance of offline networks and contacts just because they mainly work online. This is not to say that the ability to export online engagement offline is not important, or that everyone succeeds in doing so. Neither is it an argument to diminish the importance of online platforms. On the contrary, the point is to stress the importance of these factors, by emphasising that they must be the focus of empirical and detailed investigation, and not to fall victim to a focus on the decision to use online platforms in itself as a 'new' and 'important' feature. Most activists can and will be active both online and offline, but not all will do so successfully, and it is this aspect that we need to assess.

Most of the links between online and offline work are not particularly explicit, and exemplify the difficulties in sustaining the separation. For instance, if a woman experiences harassment, reports it to the HarassMap site and receives assistance from the group, then the group publishes the testimony online, uses it in a report picked up by a newspaper and uses it offline in their outreach programmes, whereupon one of their followers online reads it and feels compelled to volunteer with the group: this is not online or offline activism, it is simply well-functioning activism which naturally involves both online and offline activity. Most of the success of the groups studied in Egypt lies in similar work, which is the result of both offline and online efforts. Importantly, the groups in Egypt were neither online initiatives unable to make an impact offline nor offline groups that merely had an online presence, they combined both, albeit with varying degrees of success, as I have documented in the previous chapters.

That being said, the Egyptian groups studied were clearly able to translate online engagement into offline action. Most groups asked for volunteers online, and each was able to mobilise dozens of volunteers within a short period of time. Offline networks clearly played an important part in this, but it seems quite clear that, for instance, Imprint managed to recruit online, as no alternative to the online form was offered as a way of joining the group, and they even announced their new members on Facebook. Similarly, TBG was started online, recruited online and *then* moved offline. Obviously, there is no one-to-one relationship between followers online and volunteers, and the groups do not need this to be the case. Their online work is valuable in many respects other than simply gaining volunteers. Rather, the important point is that they were able to reach *enough* volunteers, and they seem to have succeeded in this regard.

Moreover, the groups' utilisation of their online followers' resources did provide tangible results offline, both in the case of the crowd-funding campaign and in the efforts to translate the OpAntiSH video. Similarly, TBG received help in providing a logo and material for the group after asking for it online. The documentation provided online, combined with other aspects of the groups' work, did produce coverage offline, to the extent that the traditional media can be termed 'offline'. Moreover, offline demonstrations were announced online, which probably resulted in increased attendance. Finally, following Harass-Map's publication on Facebook of downloadable files for new stickers that they had made, they followed up with pictures of these stickers being used in various locations in Egypt. While these stickers could have been spread through other channels, it seems likely that they were adopted and used by activists obtaining them online. In general, however, the interconnectedness of online and offline is the central point, and the groups could hardly have conducted either their online or their offline work without the other.

Similarly, the Kuwaiti groups cannot be said to have been strictly online or offline, although their main tool was offline mobilisation. Therefore, one could argue that the online work was merely supporting the offline work, but we would then have difficulties incorporating the online debates into our analysis, and they do seem to have played an important part. Moreover, we have seen that the groups were concerned with documenting their offline activities and disseminating this documentation online, which was particularly important given their strained relationship with the traditional media. Most importantly, one may argue that the entire opposition youth movement started online, in the Kuwaiti political blogosphere. In 2006, the Orange Movement started with the authors of one blog asking their readers if they were ready to take action. In 2009, the same blogger who had suggested offline demonstrations in a comment in 2006 asked on his own blog if people were ready to take action once again, which eventually led to the campaigns studied here.

One could argue that this was, to a large extent, due to the determination of one person, as one particular activist was central in no fewer than five of the initiatives and groups founded since 2009. However, while in no way diminishing this person's efforts, I argue that such a conclusion would fail to grasp the workings of the Kuwaiti activist sphere, both online and offline. For one thing, several other groups were formed within the same time span, initiated by others. The various groups seem to have cooperated extensively, although not always without problems, and it is rarely the case that one person leads the way for everyone else. Rather, there is an online political public to which the groups seem to have close links, and from which they managed to mobilise, also offline. The fact that offline popular mobilisation was the central tool for all groups should not be particularly surprising given the Kuwaiti experience. The success of the Orange Movement was familiar to everyone, as were probably the 1989–90 protests to reinstate the constitution and the Parliament. Thus, working both online and offline would be the 'natural' work mode for young activists in the country.

That is not to say that the use of online platforms has not been important, and it would be difficult to imagine that the groups could have worked as effectively in any other manner. Among other things, it created a 'home' for the groups, a platform from which they could stage their bid to influence politics. Traditional politics is anything but welcoming to young people, as a look at any given Parliament since independence will confirm, especially considering that the majority of the population is under 25 years of age.[28] Whereas the 1989–90 protest movement was led by established politicians, young activists took the lead in 2006, and again in the years since 2009 – this time with leading figures from the tribal population. As we have seen, the traditional media could hardly have served as a platform for their work. As such, online platforms have been important for making their claims both among 'their own', that is, the opposition, and in the Kuwaiti public at large. A similar point can be made about the Egyptian case; the issue at hand was not only neglected or not spoken of in the public at large, but existing women's movements were unwilling to engage with the problem. Many of these movements were connected to the state. Thus, in addition to the various concrete beneficial features discussed, this overarching ability to create a platform should not be disregarded, and even though these platforms may be located online, they should not be seen as separate from the offline work of the groups.

There are concrete examples of the online–offline connection from the Kuwaiti case as well. For one thing, the online mobilisation seems to have had an effect, particularly in the latter part of the campaign. The up to 100,000 participants in the first march held by Karamat Watan were hardly all mobilised through offline networks. Moreover, debates held online moved offline, and offline debates moved online. Following the now famous speech by opposition leader Musallam al-Barrak, 6,000 tweets were written discussing it online, using as the hashtag the phrase which is commonly used in referring to the speech, namely #لن_نسمح_لك (we will not allow you).[29] In early December 2012, following the arrest of many young activists, a campaign was started on Twitter to raise bail money for those apprehended, under the hashtag #كفالات_الشباب (the bails of the youth). Following several hundred tweets over a few hours, it was said to have collected about KD2,000, roughly US$6,670.[30]

An interesting difference between the two cases that should be noted is that the Kuwaiti groups not only wrote less online than their Egyptian counterparts, they also wrote less during periods of low activity. While this may seem rather obvious, the point is that, while the Egyptian groups – with the partial exception of OpAntiSH – may have deemed it necessary to provide a steady flow of content, the Kuwaiti groups seemed confident that their followers would be receptive to their calls for participation following periods of inactivity. Most of the groups were primarily active in the early spring of 2011 and during the autumn of 2011, and relatively quiet in between. Granted, the Egyptian groups conducted more varied work than the Kuwaiti groups, and perhaps more continuous work as well. Nevertheless, it is clear that in terms of instrumental use of social media aimed at offline actions, the Egyptian groups published a lot of material in between offline events. This was important in and of itself, to maintain momentum and to keep volunteers engaged. That the Kuwaiti groups managed to pick up where they left off after calmer periods should be seen in connection with all the discussion that continuously took place online regardless of what these groups were doing: the online political public was still present and ready to mobilise when they returned. In any case, the groups studied in both countries were able to mobilise both online and offline.

Goal Realisation (In Degrees)

This dimension is concerned with whether or not the groups were able to achieve their goals, either completely or partially. Moreover, it includes questions such as whether or not others were convinced by the campaigns, if the issue at hand was raised in the public at large and if they were able to keep their supporters engaged with the cause.

The Egyptian groups studied did not realise their goal of eradicating sexual harassment and sexual violence. Nor did they succeed in ending the social acceptability of these acts or in ending attacks on female protesters. They did, however, make substantial gains towards realising these goals, not least given their starting point. They did help dozens of women who were attacked in Tahrir, rescuing them from attacks and providing legal and medical assistance. If it were not for these groups, these women would not have been helped by an organised response, although individuals might have tried to intervene. Moreover, the organised response provided may have discouraged additional attacks, although this is impossible to assess: we cannot quantify this kind of non-action, but we have reason to believe that the situation might have been worse if not for the actions of the groups studied. Similarly, although the number of attacks seems to have increased from November–December 2012 until the 30 June 2013 demonstrations, this should also be seen in connection with the increased effort to document attacks and the fact that the help given by these groups provided a reason for those attacked to report it, which they may not have had before. This was also a period marked by a general lack of security and increased polarisation within Egypt, which created an extremely volatile situation. While the number of attacks that took place during the celebration for the new president in the summer of 2014 was substantially lower than the number of attacks a year earlier, the security situation in general was very different.

At the same time, while the police may have felt compelled to be sincere in their efforts to make the celebration of their new president secure, there is nothing in the history of the issue in Egypt to suggest that the police in general would take harassment seriously. The numbers of both attacks and instances of harassment seem to have decreased, but the changing circumstances must also be seen as part of the explanation. Crucial in this regard is the new law that prohibits demonstrations, such as those held in 2012 and the spring of 2013. Nevertheless, due to the work of the groups studied, neither of these problems went unanswered in Cairo, and those committing these crimes were more likely to face some sort of reaction than before. Finally, women did not stop participating in large demonstrations, and women did not stop going downtown during the holidays.

In terms of ending the social acceptability of harassment, I have no basis for claiming that the groups have succeeded in doing so, although the material suggests they have made substantial gains. As we have seen, previous instances of mob attacks, such as those seen in 2005 and 2006, were met with silence and denial from both the state and most of the media. In general, the issue was not spoken about in public and not seen as a problem. This view is further strengthened by the UN report stating that practically *all* Egyptian women experience harassment. Had it been seen as a problem, this would have demanded wide media attention and swift government action. This situation has changed following the campaign studied here. The issue has been widely covered in domestic as well as international media, political parties have felt compelled to take a stance, the government has felt compelled to show action, as have the police, the metro company, the universities and other societal actors. Most media coverage has not questioned whether or not it is a problem; it has discussed why it happens and how it can be fought. When a female student was harassed at Cairo University in March 2014, a video of the incident went viral and was picked up by the media. When a university official hinted that the girl's attire was the reason for the harassment, he was met with fierce reactions and within hours he apologised and claimed to have been misunderstood.[31] While such comments might have met little resistance some years ago, the wave of public reaction now resulted in them being retracted almost instantly; it is no longer acceptable to blame women for being harassed. This change has not happened due to the benevolence of dominant politicians or the goodwill of the regime. It has happened because young activists, mostly women, have demanded that it be seen as a problem.

One could, of course, argue that the extent and the severity of the attacks in themselves would gain the attention of the press. Yet, there is no guarantee that attention from the press or the authorities in itself would lead anywhere: we have seen how the Shura Council responded. While the revolution in 2011 and the opening up of the media market clearly played a part, these are changes in the context more than anything else and do not in themselves guarantee a particular outcome. It is the combined work of the groups studied that not only created various concrete results, but also affected or even caused this conceptual change in how the problem is viewed in Egypt. This has also entailed a linguistic change in how it is discussed, both regarding protesters that were attacked and in discussing all forms of harassment *as* harassment, and harassment as a crime. While this in itself does not eradicate the problem, it is a necessary first step. As pointed out by one activist; the solution lies in creating public pressure against harassment.[32] Furthermore, some of the groups did demand legal changes that would clearly state that harassment is a crime and would stipulate harsher punishments. This demand was met, although the groups were not unequivocally positive in their response.

Finally, there is the question of whether or not the groups managed to keep their supporters engaged with their cause and their work. Within the time frame, all groups did expand, and it seems quite clear that they did not lose support. Following the time frame, there have been fewer demonstrations attended by the groups.[33] Moreover, the context has changed, and it is not clear if the groups will be allowed to work as freely as they have done so far. All groups are still active online, and the groups that conduct downtown patrols did so also during the holidays in the summer of 2015. Most groups have also continued to grow online, in terms of number of followers. However, as I have not systematically studied the groups since 1 August 2013, it would be difficult to provide an accurate assessment of their current work. Suffice it to say for now that they seem to have experienced continuous growth throughout the period studied.

The Kuwaiti groups were both successful and unsuccessful in achieving their goals. They were able to sustain popular mobilisation for over two years. They demanded Prime Minister Nasir al-Muhammad's resignation, which came on 28 November 2011. Only days later, the 2009 Parliament was dissolved, another important demand presented by the youth movements. The opposition victory in the February 2012 elections was naturally not one of the overarching aims of the groups, as they could not have known at the outset that this would take place, but it was, of course, viewed as a success nonetheless. From that point, however, their fortunes seem to have changed, and most of their gains were reversed – quite literally reversed with regard to the 2009 Parliament, which was reinstated. Following the dissolution of the February 2012 Parliament, the electoral laws were changed, and the opposition was unable to prevent this, in spite of unprecedented popular mobilisation. While the boycott of the elections of December 2012 was claimed as a success, the regime did not seem to mind, and a new Parliament, free of opposition elements, was elected. During the same period, hundreds of opposition activists were detained, both for their participation offline and for their writings online. The opposition alliance was formed in March 2013, but it does not seem to have been able to make much of an impact. In the summer of 2013, Kuwaiti voters once again voted for a new Parliament, and this time the opposition did not manage to stand united in its boycott, with some liberals and candidates from smaller tribes participating.[34] Moreover, voter turnout increased markedly from the level of the December 2012 elections.[35] While the opposition has held several demonstrations since, particularly in support of former MP al-Barrak, these do not seem to have been particularly effective.

These losses may, in part, be related to the success of the opposition youth movements. The groups managed to gain the support of established politicians for their demand for a constitutional emirate, and the change from *defending* the constitution to actively seeking to *change* the constitution touched a nerve with the regime. Since independence, the regime had, at most, been pressured to revoke autocratic measures it had taken and reinstate the constitution. When the opposition got out of hand or became too involved in the affairs of the royal family, the regime could take autocratic measures again. Had the opposition realised their new goal of a constitutional emirate, there would have been no going back because the royal family would no longer have had the power to undo it. Moreover, while these demands were dangerous in themselves, they also set a dangerous precedent: that it is acceptable to call for the de facto end to the current regime, although allowing it to retain symbolic significance. Naturally, the opposition's frequently impressive ability to mobilise made them all the more dangerous; with time they might have gained wider support even for their more radical positions. Thus, while the royal family could sacrifice one of its own – the prime minister – they could not sacrifice their position. In this uncomfortable situation it is perhaps not surprising that they chose to dissolve the opposition Parliament, even though this Parliament had taken few concrete steps towards democratisation. When opposition politicians responded by endorsing the demand for a constitutional emirate, there can hardly have been many within the royal family who deemed it wise to allow the opposition another victory, which in turn might help to explain why they stood firm on their changes to the electoral law, even in the face of unprecedented mobilisation.

There was, however, an element of the opposition movement that was perhaps even more dangerous than their demands, namely their ability to mobilise the tribal population. This marginalised and formerly loyal part of the population comprises the majority of Kuwaiti citizens, and successful mobilisation on their part could be seen as a threat not only to the royal family but to the *hadar* population – a narrative that was cultivated by pro-regime forces and members of the ruling family. Similarly, their Islamist compatriots may have an equally deterrent effect. While there were many pro-democracy liberals who worked together with the rest of the opposition, the prospect of more influential tribal and Islamist politicians seems to have generated much fear and resentment as well: at least, the regime's heavy-handed repression did not spark general outrage in the country.

One repressive measure used by the regime was to revoke the citizenship of individual activists. This was, of course, not coincidental:

the tribal population was given their citizenship by the royal family, and it can be taken from them by the royal family. It is a very literal way of reasserting the hegemonic order. At the same time, the royal family has shown that not all citizens are equal and have placed themselves firmly in the way of further democratisation, a step which might be ill advised, given the demographic composition of the population. While Davidson's assessment of the almost imminent breakdown of the GCC regimes seems overly drastic to this author,[36] it is equally difficult to see the opposition settling for the current situation. If the royal family then seeks to hinder further reform rather than to find a place for themselves within it, they may face many difficult battles in the years to come. The opposition has set a new precedent of challenging the royal family and the emir directly and, if Kuwaiti history is a guide, it seems likely that they will do so again. Thus, while the youth movements achieved only a few of their goals, they did succeed in setting the agenda and changing the practice of opposition politics in Kuwait, which in itself is no small thing. Crucially, this involved mobilising previously loyalist parts of the population.

Experiences and Expectations (Changes in Social Relations)

This dimension is concerned with whether or not new social groups were mobilised, meaning parts of society that were previously not active and visible in the public and in political life. Naturally, this also entails questions of whether new topics were raised in public, if those who were mobilised changed their practices or gained new experiences and expectations, and how they perceived their own work. In short, it is concerned with any change in social relations that may have taken place as a consequence of the work of those studied.

Neither the issues of concern in Kuwait nor those in Egypt were raised overnight: it was a long process that culminated in the activism studied here. Similarly, the mobilisation of those involved grew over time and was affected by a variety of factors. Nevertheless, the agenda of public debate was changed due to the campaigns studied, and other parts of society had to adjust accordingly. To begin with the Egyptian case, we have seen that sexual harassment and attacks on women came to the fore in 2005, but they were not dealt with. A few activists started working on the issue in the mid-2000s, and were also central in some of the groups studied here. Thus, one might argue that the actions of particular individuals seem to have been decisive, and they undoubtedly were important. Still, the movement grew to be something much bigger, and the fight against sexual harassment and sexual violence became a larger movement that, in part, was self-driven, although some groups and individuals were more influential than others. Moreover, we have seen that young activists came to be an important force throughout the 2000s, with online platforms an integral and important tool in their work. Furthermore, female activists have naturally played an important part during the same period, in both the blogosphere and the pro-democracy movement and during the revolution of 2011. Finally, the revolution of 2011 changed the circumstances within Egypt in that political debate expanded to unprecedented levels, an opening up of the press took place and people seemed more willing to engage in political work. According to one activist, not only were people more engaged, they also expected to be able to demand what they saw as their rights.[37]

Thus, when the time frame set for this investigation began in the summer of 2012, the issue of sexual harassment was not unknown, online activism was not unknown, and the mobilisation of young female and male activists was not unknown. Moreover, it was a period of unprecedented levels of political engagement in general. Yet, the groups studied here did fundamentally alter the perception of the issue and the debate surrounding it. This is not to say that the 2005 and 2006 scandals were not important, or that the work done by activists in exposing them was irrelevant. According to Faris, the number of articles on sexual harassment in the Egyptian press 'jumped from 33 stories in 2004 to 173 in 2006 and 171 in 2007'.[38] Still, while this amply illustrates the importance of the work at the time, it also shows that it received nowhere near the kind of attention that it has over the past few years, and the authorities now clearly feel compelled to provide some sort of response. I have not found anything in the material presented here that indicates that this was the predetermined outcome of the events that would have taken place if not for the work of these and other groups. The results, as we have seen, are quite compelling, and Egypt has come under international pressure to do more, as seen in the United Nations periodic review in Geneva.[39] The point, naturally, is that, while it clearly was important to expose the problem in the mid-2000s, the recent campaign has made it a problem of public concern, with the resulting consequences for the authorities. At the same time, we cannot say how many *individuals* have actually been convinced, so if the position of the media and state institutions were to shift back to ignorance and denial, it may have severe negative effects.

In terms of mobilisation of new groups in society, young activists have been active for quite some time in the country. Moreover, judging by the data presented on internet usage in Egypt, it might appear that activist groups are dominated by the middle class or upper middle class, and thus it is hardly the silent masses that are in motion. Moreover, Egypt has traditionally not been the most conservative country in the region and the previous regime, and particularly the first lady, were at least in theory concerned with issues of gender equality. Yet, there is a fundamental difference between benevolent rulers 'handing favours' to their subjects on the one hand, and citizens organising and mobilising to define and demand their rights on the other. Equally important, there is a fundamental difference between the pro-democracy stance of the activist movement of the 2000s and the issue of sexual harassment; namely, that 'democracy' as a concept is something that few claim to be against. That does not mean that a democratic system will be introduced, and there were many who argued against the pro-democracy movement, claiming either that Egypt was already a democratic country or that it was not ready to become one. Very few, however, argued against democracy per se. This was different with the issue of sexual harassment: many argued sincerely that it was not a problem, and among those who believed it was, 'nobody understood the magnitude of the problem'.[40] In this sense, a new mobilisation took place, in that some of those affected by harassment organised and defined it as a problem, then demanded the attention of the public at large, and got it.

We have seen how some activists benefited greatly from their previous experience, and there is no doubt that many involved have gained valuable experience from their work in the groups studied. Many organisers and volunteers must have gained much practical experience from setting up patrols, operating hotlines, providing legal and medical assistance, writing press releases, compiling reports, appearing on TV, initiating online events, mobilising on various platforms, using the features inherent in these applications, and so on. These skills and experiences will not be lost, even if the groups in question should stop their work. In other words, many activists have gained the practical know-how to conduct similar campaigns in the future. Perhaps more importantly, many have seen that there is no reason to stay silent about such a problem, and that proper organisation can lead to results, even on a sensitive subject. The inclusive nature of the online work may mean that this holds true for far more people than those active on the ground: many participating online may also feel ownership of the issue, that they have engaged with the issue and that this has produced tangible results. Crucially, many have seen that they themselves can help to define what constitute public, political problems. As pointed out by Filiu, the days when young citizens in the Middle East silently listened to father-like statesmen are gone,[41] and while the circumstances may change drastically, those involved in this campaign know what they are capable of.

As for Kuwait, the issue of power sharing between the people and the regime has been contested for decades. Young activists had already proven their ability to organise and mobilise through the 2006 Orange Movement. Moreover, Kuwaiti students had for a long time been engaged in the students' unions, which since the late 1970s had been dominated by Islamists.[42] Increased access to education in itself is also an important factor in terms of youth mobilisation, especially as the Kuwaiti economy did not manage to produce a sufficient number of relevant jobs for the mounting number of graduates.[43] One key activist considers education a crucial factor for tribal mobilisation as well, as it became increasingly available to larger parts of the population.[44] Moreover, the tribal population has suffered discrimination for a long time,[45] and their political mobilisation should not come as a surprise. Thus, the issue at hand in a wide sense was known, as was youth mobilisation. There were also structural features of Kuwaiti society that encouraged increased participation from the groups in question. However, a fundamental change occurred due to the campaign studied here.

For one thing, some of the *demands* raised were new in Kuwait, namely those concerning a constitutional emirate. Moreover, whereas the youth movement in 2006 had mobilised on one specific subject for a very limited period of time, activists now managed to sustain popular mobilisation on a broader spectrum of issues for more than two years. Crucially, whereas the issue championed in 2006 would not, in itself, have threatened the royal family, these issues did. And whereas the youth movement in 2006 fought for a cause that had been discussed repeatedly, the concept of altering the constitution was a new one for the opposition. The tribal population had mobilised politically on previous occasions, for instance holding primaries in advance of elections to maximise the impact of their vote. However, tribal youth had not previously mobilised on their own initiative, through their own movements, online and in the streets, and so the activists were challenging patriarchal structures on several levels. Clearly, the regime felt compelled to adjust, and reacted harshly – which proved successful. As such, one might argue that, instead of raising the issue of a constitutional emirate, the youth movements killed it. At the same time, the royal family also demonstrated beyond doubt that the only path to democratisation is to take power away from them, thus confirming the accuracy of the youth movements' demands. The groups did manage to make their demands known to the Kuwaiti public, and to convince established politicians of their view and thereby alter the established practice of the parliamentary opposition. However, they did not manage to convince the Kuwaiti population at large.

In terms of experiences and expectations, the lessons learned must be many for those who took part. For those on the fringes of the movement, who at most took part in the larger demonstrations, the lesson seems to have been that there are certain red lines that it is better not to cross. For those central to the groups studied, the lesson may be quite different. From their perspective, the regime was not playing by the rules, and in its current form it is an obstacle in the path to democratic reform. Their desire to curb the powers of the royal family and the loyal political elite has hardly been diminished by the events described here. However, there are some clear strategic lessons for the activists as well. For one thing, some issues are more popular than others, it is easier to mobilise *against* repressive measures than *for* positive change and the support of established opposition politicians does not equal the support of the population. The groups became more skilled at mobilisation as time passed, and the success of the Karamat Watan initiative will not be lost on others.

In all, youth activists proved not only that they could be a part of Kuwaiti politics, but that they could influence Kuwaiti politics and, indeed, set the agenda. Moreover, the tribal population has demonstrated both their ability to participate in public and their determination to improve their situation. While the regime may seek to defuse such a threat through lavish benefits, it seems quite clear that the youth movements and, not least, the tribal youth are now factors to take into account in Kuwaiti politics, and that their defensive stance on the constitution is no longer a given.

Copying/Follow-ups

This dimension is concerned with the continuity of the work of the groups studied, and the issues they were concerned with. Thus, it deals with whether or not the groups and initiatives evolved into something lasting, if new groups formed on a similar basis or if others picked up the same issues.

The period studied was a time of expansion for the Egyptian groups, many of whom were created during this period. According to HarassMap, Anti-Harassment, one of the groups not studied here, was founded by a participant in one of its meetings and was directly inspired by its work.[46] It is clear that the groups have been inspired by each other and that they, to a large extent, saw each other as part of the same general struggle.[47] Some groups, such as Nazra and Harassmap, also helped new ones to set up shop, with the latter having the creation of an Egyptian feminist movement as one of its stated goals.[48] Throughout their work, the groups have received support from a wide range of well-known Egyptian activists who have argued for their cause, including Sandmonkey, Wael Abbas, Mona Eltahawy and Mona Seif. Political parties have also 'adopted' the cause, in the very limited sense that they have described sexual harassment as a problem that must be solved. However, judging by the parliamentary elections of October 2015, the political parties that are currently legal in Egypt are both weak and tightly controlled by the state.

This leads us to a central point regarding these questions: as of late November 2015, the prospects for activism in Egypt are grim. Following the revolution of 2011, a number of initiatives were launched to reform the regulation of NGOs and to change the much-criticised Law 84. In the summer of 2014, a new draft for a law regulating civil society was discussed, which was met with fierce resistance from various organisations. An amendment to the penal code was issued by President al-Sisi in September 2014, introducing even more repressive regulations and punishments for NGOs.[49] According to *MadaMasr*, 380 NGOs were dissolved by the regime in the two first months of 2015,[50] most of which seems to have been connected to the Muslim Brotherhood. It is clear that civil society will be not be allowed to operate in the future as it did following the revolution, and the post-coup regime in Egypt has made it extremely clear that they will tolerate no form of public dissent.

All groups are still operating as of April 2016, with the partial exception of OpAntiSH and TBG, which do not engage in offline activities in between large demonstrations.[51] Importantly, as large demonstrations attended by the groups no longer take place, the urgency of this particular aspect of the work may have passed for the time being. TBG has created a new group, Dignity Without Borders (DWB), meant to present a more extensive approach to sexual harassment and related issues. It is clear that none of these groups were short-lived initiatives that were not able to operate offline, or did not survive the initial phase, but it seems too early to draw conclusions about their ability to sustain activity and operations over an extended period.

Most of the Kuwaiti groups studied are no longer active, with the sole exceptions being Hadam and Shabab al-Hurriyya. The Karamat Watan initiative did organise a protest in the summer of 2014, so they may perhaps more accurately be described as dormant rather than non-existent. Moreover, many of the groups were absorbed into Hadam and thus were not shut down per se. There is, however, no doubt that the groups were hit hard by the regime's harsh reactions, and that they lost momentum as well as the ability to mobilise broadly. It seems clear that the loosely organised groups they relied on to begin with, while beneficial for many reasons, could also disappear quite quickly, which may explain the desire to form something more lasting through Hadam. As of late November 2015, no mobilisation is taking place that is comparable to the activity seen between 2011 and 2013. Moreover, while the groups did succeed in convincing others to adopt their stance, there is no similar debate in Kuwait at the moment in favour of a constitutional emirate. On the contrary, the opposition seems to be weaker than it has been for several years. That being said, Kuwaiti politics post-independence have been characterised by this power struggle, and the opposition has been met with severe restrictions in the past as well. Thus, the current setback may be a temporary one, and changing circumstances may see the opposition regain the initiative.

The difference this time will be that the youth movements have proven their ability, that they have made the idea of a constitutional emirate a part of the discussion and that they may still be organised – at least partly – in Ḥadam. Given that the various grievances raised have been crushed rather than solved, it seems highly unlikely that Kuwaiti politics will prove peaceful and stable over an extended period of time. Still, the initiative gained in 2011 was lost by the opposition, and they did not prove able to institute formal, lasting changes.

Assessing the Impact

By and large, the groups were able to continue past their initial phase and grew both online and offline, with the possible exception of al-ʿAdala al-Dusturiyya in Kuwait. This is important to show that the groups studied were not simply a Facebook page or a Twitter account established at a given time, unable to evolve into something bigger which might have influence. If a campaign were to take place at a point in time when changes relevant to the issue of concern were about to occur in any case, we might be tempted to assign more importance to such an initiative than we should. When instead we see that the groups were able to grow and evolve, it makes their ability to have an impact more plausible. Similarly, the groups were able to develop their methods and their organisational skills, further substantiating such plausibility. Crucially, both the Kuwaiti and the Egyptian groups did provoke reactions and adjustments from other forces in society. These were both positive and negative, and stemmed both from the regime and from other parts of society. The groups were clearly not irrelevant, and they were not ignored. Moreover, the groups were able to mobilise and work both online *and* offline. As such, they were neither just a toothless campaign site nor a more or less private offline club; they were able to publicly and effectively work within their contexts, which meant working both online and offline. Not all goals were realised in either case, although important steps were taken towards achieving them. The practical, short-term results in the Kuwaiti case were negative. Still, both the Egyptian and the Kuwaiti groups were able to state their claims in public and successfully demand that society listen and react.

All groups studied in Egypt are still in operation, and although the urgent attention to the issue of attacks on female protesters dropped, they continued to be able to gain the attention of the traditional media.[52] In Kuwait, most of the groups are no longer operational, and those that are still functioning seem to be cautious and are not making any attempts at popular mobilisation. However, we have seen the value of previous experience in both cases studied and many activists have gained valuable skills and practical know-how that may be employed at any time for a given cause. Many more have, in some form or another, participated in political activism that led to tangible results, and learned that their engagement can make a difference. In both cases, the groups have shown that disadvantaged groups in society can successfully organise and state their claims in public, thus taking part in defining the boundaries of public debate and of the political. Moreover, they have shown that they can achieve tangible results, and that they have the ability to effect political and social change.

The groups studied in both cases did have an impact. While there were clear differences between them, they were collectively able to reach, organise and mobilise activists who shared their views, both online and offline. They were able to state their claims in public and to force a reaction from the authorities and other dominant forces in society. This had concrete effects on the issues at hand, and will most likely have long-term effects for the participation of those involved and those who followed them.

CHAPTER 8

UNDERSTANDING ONLINE ACTIVISM

In Chapters 1 and 2, I argued that in order to gain a more comprehensive grasp of online activism we need detailed, empirically based studies with which to revise our theoretical understanding of the phenomenon. I have provided such an empirical study, and demonstrated how both the campaigns studied managed to have an impact on their respective contexts. Moreover, I have argued that, while the notion of the public sphere remains crucial, we should depart from Habermas's deliberative public in favour of Mouffe's less normative agonistic pluralism. Below, I engage with the empirical findings through the framework of counterpublicness presented in Chapter 2. In doing so, I aim to move beyond the debate between optimists and sceptics, and the vagueness that such a debate entails. I have hypothesised that the central contribution of online platforms is the publicness they provide and facilitate, which in turn enables activists to conduct their work and to have an impact. Thus, I begin with a brief discussion on the relationship between the public and the private in the cases studied.

The Public and the Private

As pointed out by Baym and Boyd, the boundaries between private and public are blurred in social media.[1] Yet, it is an important distinction for this study in many ways, perhaps most of all in terms of private or public issues and private or public discourse, but also in terms of private or public work. My central argument is that online platforms help the activists as they facilitate publicness, but it seems clear that the groups also conducted work of a more private character. This, in turn, raises the question of what constitutes private and what constitutes public.

In the Egyptian case, we have seen that several organisations created closed Facebook groups. The content of these groups is not part of the material, but it has been described in interviews as an initiative motivated partly to disseminate information, but mainly to sustain engagement among volunteers in between other activities. This was clearly also an important feature of the public work conducted online, and we have seen that the most active groups were also, by and large, the most successful groups. However, the open online channels were seldom used for communication between volunteers on the ground and those in the operations room, who were manning the hotlines and directing help and assistance, to report critical situations or to convey practical information to those who were already registered volunteers. Moreover, there was communication between those in leading positions within a group as well as between the groups that was not conducted in public. Furthermore, it seems extremely likely that personal, offline networks were important, for instance in establishing OpAntiSH, although this was also *announced* publicly. As such, closed channels and private networks seem to work in tandem with the publicly disseminated information, and to be important for organising and facilitating some practical work. In other words, communication did take place outside the open channels, and decisions were probably made outside open channels. In short, parts of the practical work that the various groups considered necessary was conducted in more private spaces, and could probably not have been done productively in public in the sense of involving all who wished to take part. These were the many practical tasks that enabled the groups to go public, and they do not counter the fundamental argument of publicness as the central mechanism through which the groups effected change. It simply indicates that, for practical reasons, some tasks were performed outside the open channels.

Similar observations can be made for the Kuwaiti case. The groups discussed in public, called for participation in public and documented their work in public. However, it is also clear that they did work outside public channels: there seems to have been coordination between groups of which no trace can be found online; there seems to have been communication with established politicians beyond the online contact; and it is not clear who was invited to the founding of Hadam, and on what basis. Moreover, Hadam stipulates certain criteria for joining the group, and it seems clear that their meetings are for members only. Although the calls for new members are disseminated in public, the details of all of their meetings are not. Moreover, those responsible for the Karamat Watan initiative chose to conceal their identities. From what we have seen, it seems overwhelmingly likely that, had they not done so, they would have been arrested, and the account would have been closed. Thus, it was a necessary precondition for their work. Moreover, the group did ask for their followers' suggestions for how at least one of the protests should be organised. Still, both this and other groups seem to have had a leadership which conducted practical work and made decisions more privately. Yet, as with the Egyptian case, this does not counter the argument that most groups sought to go public with their views, and worked to reach as many people as they could. Partial exceptions are the two Islamist groups included in the study. As we have seen, these seemed more concerned with their own followers than with reaching as large an audience as possible. Their activities still took place publicly and openly, but they did perhaps seek to address a more specific and limited public.

In general, the groups studied were not private groups, and they did not conduct their work in private, although some practical decisions were made outside the open channels. They were public groups who worked to raise their demands in public. As I have argued, this involved engaging with *a* public, 'their own' public, that is, those concerned with the same issue. It further involved engaging with *the* public, or the public at large, in order to effect change. In both endeavours, the use of online platforms was crucial.

Reaching *a* Public

The groups did reach a substantial number of people concerned with the issues they raised, and they were conscious in their efforts to do so. Offline networks undoubtedly played an important part in their work, but there is no doubt that they reached beyond these connections through the use of online platforms; it seems unlikely that their offline networks included tens of thousands of people – or, in the case of

Karamat Watan, more than 100,000 people. Given the contexts within which they worked, they could not have done so in any other way: there was no realistic alternative through which they could disseminate their content to so many, so rapidly and at a cost they were able to afford. The reverse holds true as well: there was no realistic alternative for people to access this content either. This, in turn, underlines an important aspect of the public character of their work: that it concerns not only the groups' ability to reach out but also other people's ability to reach them and to take part. There is nothing from the empirical or the contextual material presented so far that suggests that all the people who took part in one way or another would have been able to do so without the online platforms employed.

The groups addressed a relatively large audience, which seems to have been made up predominantly of people who agreed or were inclined to agree with their views and their concerns. This audience was hardly representative of their contexts as such, but was perhaps all the more motivated to invest time and effort in the issue. Moreover, as we saw in Chapter 4, there is a correlation in Egypt between the use of the online platforms in question here and the level of education and social status. Thus, these audiences, or at least the Egyptian one, may have been not only motivated, but also relatively resourceful. Moreover, the material suggests that it may not be important that they did not reach 'everyone'. In fact, it might have been counterproductive had they done so. What they needed to do was reach those sympathetic to their views, and for those people to be able to reach them should they wish to do so. The use of various hashtags, as well as the ability to gain likes, retweets, and so on, was important in this regard. These features demonstrate how the platforms in question, when utilised with skill, are well suited to reach and organise a particular public.

Referring to the US feminist movement as an example, Fraser demonstrates how subaltern groups come together and discuss, define and raise their issues of concern.[2] Having organised online, the groups in Egypt and Kuwait proceeded in the same manner. The history of the issue of sexual harassment in Egypt suggests that it was not accepted by the public at large as a problem prior to 2012 or 2013. While it was raised by activists in both 2005 and 2006, the belated and negligent response from the state, as well as the lack of outcry from the public, suggests that it was not taken seriously. Similarly, findings presented in the UN Women report indicate that harassers do not perceive what they do as wrong, and that they blame the women themselves. They state that the lack of modesty in clothing and behaviour is the reason behind harassment, although this is not supported by the other findings of the report.[3] Furthermore, many tweets written as part of the online events held by HarassMap and others clearly show that the problem is not new in Egypt, as many participants recount their first experiences with harassment as having happened during their childhood.

As demonstrated above, the groups working on the issue in Egypt actively sought to fight these attitudes and misconceptions, and to define harassment, violence and abuse as problems of public concern. While there were few debates with opponents, there were several discussions in which their own arguments were reaffirmed. The groups also developed language to accurately describe their reality. Those who were attacked were not 'victims' as some would have it; they had survived attacks in the same manner as any male protester who had fought the police, thugs or the army. Moreover, they defined all forms of harassment *as* harassment, as feminists in Fraser's example defined all forms of violence, including domestic violence, *as* violence.

One can, of course, question whether or not women should be seen as a subaltern entity in Egyptian society. Faris argues that women, along with other groups such as the Copts and the Baha'i, are 'challenging received notions of identity and exclusion that have been foisted upon them by the state and its allies'.[4] Both Nazra and Fu'ada Watch, a group closely related to I Saw Harassment, have documented that women are underrepresented in politics and, as we have seen, women themselves perceive their situation in Egypt as worse than in any other Arab country. Moreover, as will be discussed further below, it seems quite clear that the groups involved did not have the power to define the agenda of public debate; they had to fight to get others to listen. Had they been able to dictate public debate – that is, been a part of the hegemonic order – they would hardly have needed to organise online to raise their concerns.

In Kuwait, however, the situation seems clearer in this regard, as it is well documented that the tribal population has suffered discrimination over a long period of time.[5] Still, the youth movements did not exclusively recruit from the tribal population, and their issues of concern – corruption and power-sharing arrangements – were hardly new to the

Kuwaiti public. Yet, while their issues were familiar, their solutions were not. Moreover, they combined these familiar issues with the grievances of the tribal population. Their conclusion seems to have been that the system itself was the problem, and therefore the system needed to be changed. Thus, they were able to provide their own understanding of the familiar problems, and their own solutions. The tribal population went from grateful subjects to citizens demanding their rights, although this was hardly due to the youth movements' work alone. As with the Egyptian case, there were a lot of discussions on the issue online, again confirming the views put forward rather than challenging them. The Kuwaiti groups also employed their own terms, such as *ḥukūma muntakhaba* (elected government) and *imāra dustūriyya* (constitutional emirate). While I cannot categorically state that these groups invented these expressions, they were the ones who raised them in the Kuwaiti public. The former is particular to the Kuwaiti context, in that it does not make sense in and of itself. The government itself is not elected, and no one called for such an arrangement. Rather, it was used to describe a parliamentary system in which the elected majority formed the basis for the government. Thus, in both cases, online platforms made it possible for those affected by an issue to reach each other and organise. However, while it is important that they were able to reach a sympathetic audience, it was also crucial that they were able to reach the public at large.

Reaching *the* Public

As is clear from both the material presented here and the literature, there is no single public sphere, but rather several publics.[6] Yet, there is no doubt that extensive public debate takes place in all societies, even autocratic ones, and that pressure generated by these debates may affect political and social change. There is a larger sphere in which issues can be raised, and which may affect policy. This is what Warner refers to as the dominant public,[7] what Habermas originally referred to as *the* public and what I have referred to as the public at large. The discourse of this public, as argued by Mouffe, is determined by the hegemonic forces in a society, and it is against this public that subaltern groups organise in *counter*publics. Thus, as noted by Matar, the counterpublics are directed back at the wider public[8] and seek to affect the issues discussed and the opinions formed. These opinions, which Habermas referred to as *public* opinion, may in turn affect political decisions, depending on a variety of factors, including whether or not the power-holders agree with the views presented, if they fear the consequences should they not respond positively or if they might feel obliged to give in to what is perceived as public will. The important point is not to identify or demarcate this sphere, but to understand the mechanisms in play, which are central to our analysis. Similarly, when discussing the relevance of counterpublics, the point is not to claim to have 'found' or 'identified' such publics, as if starting at one Twitter account and ending at another.

It is important for those concerned with the issues to engage with each other, but it is also important to engage with the public at large, as this is a necessary step in bringing about change. Faris stresses this point in his 2013 study of online activism in Egypt, and argues that a few prominent and well-connected individuals are essential for this transition: 'Connectors or network hubs are far more likely to have their arguments heard, and to organize successful campaigns around particular issues in authoritarian systems like Egypt', as 'journalists read the power-bloggers and use them to generate story ideas'.[9] This, in his view, is consistent with the mechanisms regulating the internet as such: 'the internet (and thus digital activism more generally) is governed by power laws that make it easier for some individuals to be heard, and makes it vastly more complicated for non-connected individuals to use these technologies effectively'.[10] Similarly, Wilson and Dunn also pointed to the importance of 'power users'.[11]

The empirical evidence from this study, however, does not unequivocally support such a conclusion. Granted, starting with the Egyptian case, we have established that there were clear differences between the groups in terms of attention from the traditional media, and that this seems to correlate with both experience and skills. Moreover, the offline contacts between activists and journalists described by Faris were also evident, for instance with regard to the much-referenced appearance on *al-Barnamig* by two of the groups. We have also seen that use of the platforms in question is limited, but is more widespread among those with higher socio-economic standing, from which group many activists and journalists hail. Finally, we have seen that TBG successfully utilised attention and support from the very 'power-bloggers' Faris identifies in his study.

On the other hand, none of the groups in question were created or led by any of these power-bloggers. While some had more experience than others, all groups were relatively successful in gaining attention from the traditional media, including Imprint and TBG – seemingly, those groups with the least experienced core members. Thus, a similar mechanism to that described by Faris seems to be at work, but with an important qualification: those with most experience seem to have been the *most* successful, but they were not the *only* successful ones, and they were not necessarily successful at the expense of the less experienced groups. While 'power-bloggers', or in this case the more experienced groups, gain more attention from the press, other groups may also succeed in doing so through their own work and on their own initiative. As such, the difference is perhaps more a relative one than anything else.

The power-bloggers identified by Faris talked about subjects that the official media neglected; they provided evidence, and were probably seen as credible sources of information, at least by the journalists to whom he refers. These are, as I have argued, central features of the most successful groups studied here as well. Naturally, Faris points out that new activists may rise to positions of power online. The journalists who followed these particular individuals would probably be inclined to follow new individuals and groups that gain attention on social media, such as the groups studied here. Moreover, we have seen that some of the groups gained wide attention not only in Egypt, but internationally. While foreign journalists certainly may have followed particular influential activists as well, it does show that successful groups may attain a wide reach in and of themselves.

The attacks on female protesters were so extensive and severe that they probably would have gained some media attention in any case, but for journalists investigating the issue, it would be easy to come across the groups studied, to see that they were present on the ground, knew what was happening and were making a serious effort to document it and combat the problem. The journalists could see that the groups enjoyed wide support, were credible and constituted the dominant response to the problem in the country. Moreover, they would see how these groups framed and discussed the issue, and in some cases pick up on the language employed by the groups. This would not be how every journalist dealt with the issue, but it illustrates the importance of the groups' ability to organise and do their work in public. It was a conscious effort made by the groups to document and articulate the issue, and to convey this to the public at large through the traditional media. While some may have had better connections with journalists than others, this does not seem to be the only deciding factor in gaining attention.

The Kuwaiti groups chose a different strategy to reach a wider audience, namely popular mobilisation. Given that many of those involved had gained experience during the 2006 Orange Movement, this tactical choice should not be surprising. Moreover, given their strained relationship with the traditional media, they did not have much of a choice. That being said, there were two online newspapers that were sympathetic to the opposition movements, and that frequently published their statements or detailed updates on their offline endeavours. However, the effect of this seems to have been quite limited: groups that spent a lot of time disseminating this attention, such as the September 16 coalition, al-Sur al-Khamis and Kafi, were not more successful than other groups, such as Karamat Watan and the boycott campaign, but rather quite the opposite. While attention from these outlets may have been important in terms of building credibility among those supporting the opposition, the material does not suggest that it helped them to reach a wider audience, although this should be studied in more detail before any definite conclusions are made. Offline demonstrations, on the other hand, did gain the attention of society at large, including politicians, the government, the newspapers, the TV stations and the police. In a similar vein, although one can criticise the unlawful storming of the Parliament by protesters, it did attract attention to the issue. Offline popular mobilisation does not just happen by accident, however, and a certain audience is needed to be able to muster a protest.

Offline networks certainly played their part in this, not least those linked to the tribal origin of many of the groups studied. The tribal parts of the population have demonstrated their ability to organise politically, for instance through the primaries conducted within each tribe prior to elections in order to maximise their electoral impact. Election results from before the controversial change to the electoral law demonstrate that this collective organisation was heavily in favour of the opposition; in the February 2012 elections, 18 of the 20 MPs elected from the two main tribal districts were part of the opposition.[12] This would suggest that the tribes were both able and inclined to support the opposition youth movements in their work, using networks that predate social media.

However, had the tribes, who constitute a majority of the population, thrown their full support behind the groups from the beginning, their protests should have been a lot bigger. For instance, the protest held on 3 June 2011, drew a crowd of 1,500, the 16 September protest drew only 300 and the 19 October protest the same year drew as many as 12,000. The point is not that tribal networks were irrelevant, but rather that mobilisation was not simply a question of asking the tribes to take part.

Moreover, it seems that Twitter itself also played an important part in reaching a large audience. We have seen that Kuwait has more Twitter users per capita than any other country in the world, and we have discussed the extraordinary standing that Twitter has as an arena for political debate in the country. Therefore the Kuwaiti groups may have been less dependent on the traditional media for gaining attention and for putting pressure on the regime than their Egyptian counterparts. If this holds true, we see a different mechanism at work than that described by Faris in Egypt – one in which social media can reach a broader audience more directly. The contextual differences between Egypt and Kuwait are important in this regard; Kuwait has a much smaller population, it is much wealthier and its citizens have much better access to the internet. Some of the mechanisms discussed above do seem to be relevant: some groups were more successful than others, gained many more followers and were therefore able to reach a broader audience. In both cases studied there seem to be some mechanisms for filtering content that relate to the skill of those involved as well as to the general interest in the issues raised. Yet, it also seems clear that the local context is important, and that we cannot establish valid rules or predictions as to how this would play out regardless of context. Thus, a general feature is that social media are important both for reaching and organising one's supporters and for reaching a broader audience, but the specific context influences how this plays out in practice. Moreover, there are some common mechanisms that can be identified as we turn to how the publicness described above helps the groups in question to effect social and political change.

No Habermasian Public Sphere

Empirical evidence is crucial for theoretical development. Thus, while I argued for a departure from Habermas's normative model of the public sphere in Chapter 2, I should also confront my assertions with my empirical findings. Habermas holds that a functioning public sphere is crucial for a democracy, as it legitimises decisions and gives citizens political influence through deliberation. He further contends that 'the internet' holds 'unequivocal democratic merits' in authoritarian contexts as it hinders censorship and enables the formation of public opinion, but that it may lead to negative fragmentation in functioning democracies.[13]

The material studied, however, does not present evidence for a public sphere in line with Habermas's normative model. For one thing, we have seen that there clearly is more than one public, as Habermas himself also recognised.[14] While there is a dominant public that may affect policy, access to this public is not 'guaranteed', and the issues discussed are not universally given 'issues of public interest'. Rather, groups in both countries worked tirelessly to gain the attention of the public at large, and fought to gain acceptance for the issues they raised precisely as issues of public interest, and as political issues. It follows that they had no interest in seeking consensus with a public from which they had been excluded on an issue that this public did not recognise as political. This is quite evident in the material studied, and the discussions that took place bear little resemblance to Habermas's rational-critical debate. The groups clearly did not present their arguments with the aim of meeting counterarguments and then reaching consensus on a modified position; they did so to state their views, and hopefully convince as many people as possible. Moreover, they also seem to have sought to reinforce and confirm the views of their followers, or to articulate what their supporters might be receptive to but had not yet stated.

That is not to say that there were no debates and discussions, but rather that these were mainly of a strategic or practical nature, or were between participants who fundamentally agreed on the issue in question. As for debate with those who did not agree, this took place only to a limited extent, and not in the form envisioned by Habermas. As we saw in the Kuwaiti case, there were instances where opposing views were presented at the same time on the same platform, and in one case even moved the debate offline, but these were more akin to competitions between supporters of these views, with different hashtags applied by each party. Similarly, the Egyptian groups did, on some occasions, engage with those who opposed them, but this was principally to tell them how wrong they were or to expose them as wrongdoers. Opposing views were also presented by the groups themselves to their followers, sometimes asking them to provide an answer, with the implication that this was what they were up against.

Habermas further stipulated that relations of power should be neutralised because the weight of the argument itself should be decisive in the public sphere, not the status or the resources of its proponent. Yet, power was clearly not overlooked in the cases studied: it was fought by the groups studied and it was actively employed by their counterparts. This also relates to the issues of access and subjects of discussion. The Egyptian groups raised an issue that had previously been neglected or ignored in the public – the former minister of the interior denied its very existence. When the issues *were* raised as a political problem to be solved, it was due to their successful organising and campaigning: they were able to gain support and pressure the state into taking action. Even then, they met resistance, when Islamist MPs sought to make the issue a moral and not a political one. Similarly, the opponents of the Kuwaiti groups also sought to depoliticise the issue but, in this case, the use of power was even more blatant as the regime turned to outright repression and violence. The offline results gained by the groups were not the product of objective appreciation of their arguments alone; they were the product of skillful activism and sustained pressure over time.

One could also argue that power relations were of importance among the groups studied in each case, as some groups seem to have been more influential than others. While one might argue that these groups would also be best positioned to present the most compelling arguments – which they might have been – status and experience may also have been influential factors. Similarly, the issue of access is also relevant to the counterpublics of the groups studied: while they sought to reach as many as possible, internet access and usage is limited in both countries, albeit to different extents. Moreover, each group's number of followers was, of course, nowhere near the estimated number of users of each particular platform in their respective countries, meaning that they were addressing only a small portion of the already limited number of people who use the platform. This, in turn, highlights a fundamental point: the groups were able to raise an issue in the public at large and effect change, yet we do not observe the features that Habermas associates with such public deliberation. As discussed in Chapter 2, Habermas's concept is intended as a normative model against which actual practice may be compared.

Yet, even as a model it is problematic, because it misdirects us in the search for the central mechanisms at work. This argument is supported by the empirical evidence: features that are discarded by Habermas, such as relations of power, competition and conflict, and publics that are not all-inclusive, seem to be at the heart of the work done by the groups studied and at the heart of the mechanisms through which they effect change. Thus, as argued in Chapter 2, we must move beyond Habermas's normative concept.

Counterpublicness, Agonistic Pluralism and Democratisation

Mouffe argues that there are no given or universal issues of public interest, nor is there any such thing as universal access to the public: both access and agenda are products of the hegemonic order at any given time. As such, power is not overlooked: the dominant public *is* power exercised. The boundaries of public discourse are set so as to hinder any challenges to the ruling order, and issues that may be damaging and fall outside these boundaries are cast as something other than politics. Those excluded must organise themselves and demand that the public at large treat their issues of concern as political problems – they have to fight for them. Once they reach the public, they would hardly have an interest in reaching a consensus based on the current order, given that the main function of this order is to maintain the power of the hegemonic forces. Mouffe argues that counterhegemonic forces need to 'disarticulate the existing hegemony and to establish a more progressive one'.[15] While the need to create a more 'progressive' public would depend on one's political orientation, the need to fight the boundaries of the existing hegemony remains valid. As Warner points out, when a public becomes the dominant one, the 'limitations imposed by its speech genres, medium, and presupposed social base [. . .] invisibly order the political world'.[16] The limits set by the hegemonic public are the limits of the political, and must be challenged and fought by those seeking social and political change. It follows that we can expect the hegemonic order to fight back, and to seek to depoliticise the new issues raised.

The Egyptian groups raised an issue that was not considered a subject of public interest. It had previously been met with public silence, with denial, with outright hostility, with moralism or been seen as a private issue. This is a central mechanism through which the hegemonic public rebuffs challenges: issues are termed private. The examples referred to by Fraser, such as domestic violence, are typically issues that were dismissed as a private matter until the feminist movement successfully demanded that they be seen as political. In her study of Heya TV as a feminist counterpublic, Matar points to the centrality of giving a voice to 'alternative perspectives on what constitutes the private and the public and what constitutes the political'.[17] When the issue is private, claims can be made about it that will not be countered in public, similar to the 'conventional wisdom' of a hegemonic order referred to by Mouffe. In Egypt, sexual harassment could be dismissed as 'flirtation', or said to be caused by indecent clothing; it was made out to be something shameful that one should not talk about. The previous regime of President Mubarak actively employed harassment and sexual violence as a means of repression, and only considered the issue worth discussing when it could be appropriated to support the security apparatus of the state. In this situation, those who experience harassment will hardly speak up and demand that something be done, which in turn demonstrates the importance of organising to raise an issue as a political problem. For instance, while it may be difficult or embarrassing to talk of being poor, it would not be embarrassing to be part of a political struggle against poverty.[18] Similarly, while it may be difficult to talk of one's own experience with sexual harassment alone, it would be less difficult to take part in a political struggle against the problem. Thus, the groups studied made the crucial transition from private problem to public issue: they addressed those concerned with it, discussed it and articulated the problem and their demands, documented the extent of the problem, refuted the misconceptions and moralistic claims made about the problem and demanded that Egyptian society deal with it as a political problem that had to be solved.

The issues raised by the Kuwaiti groups were also a challenge to the hegemonic order of discourse in the country – quite literally, as the order of discourse they challenged was given in writing: the Kuwaiti constitution. Since independence, the constitution had provided the accepted framework for opposition politics in the country. Although one could argue, as the opposition had previously done, that the constitution was not fully respected and thus could facilitate a more democratic system, it *does* grant substantial powers to the royal family and the emir

– the very powers that enable the royal family to rule autocratically. As the framework of the hegemonic order, it is, of course, intended to preserve this hegemonic order. While the victory of the 2006 OM undoubtedly was a hard blow for the ruling family, it was a victory within the boundaries of the constitution and, as such, did not fundamentally alter the political order. The youth movement came to realise this, and gradually saw the need to present a more direct challenge. At first, this meant challenging the sovereign right of the emir to appoint and dismiss the PM, as well as to dissolve an elected assembly. With time, it came to mean changes in the constitution which, in effect, would end the autocratic rule of the royal family and thus alter the political order in the country. Naturally, the youth movement would not be 'given' access to the public to present such demands; they had to fight for it, as they had to fight for their own views rather than seek compromise within the very framework they sought to replace. Thus, the groups addressed those concerned with the issue, organised, discussed, articulated their demands and raised these demands with Kuwaiti society at large.

We have seen that the manner in which demands are raised in the public at large varies and is dependent on the context. However, the steps to be taken before entering this public arena seem to be common, and to be facilitated by online platforms: those concerned with an issue find together, address each other, discuss and articulate their demands in their own words and, in the Egyptian case, document the extent and severity of the problem. As such, the online platforms enable counterpublicness in a very concrete way: the ability of excluded groups to actively come together and organise, articulate a political demand and raise and fight for this issue in the public at large. Moreover, online platforms are also crucial in addressing the public at large, although in different ways. In Kuwait, they were important in mobilising offline protesters, but also in raising the issue directly on Twitter. In Egypt, they were crucial to mobilising volunteers to conduct their work, to disseminate their material and to document the issue and their work as well as providing accessible and trustworthy sources for the traditional media. The groups managed to fight their way into the public at large and to raise their issues, and online platforms were crucial also in this regard.

In doing so, the groups were able to effect change in a democratising manner. For one thing, the goals of the groups in both countries were, as

I have argued, democratising. In Egypt, they fought for the right of women to take part in public political expression, and to take part in working life and education, to use public transport and so on without the risk of harassment. As such, they are demands for increased participation and equality. Similarly, the Kuwaiti groups demanded political reforms that would shift power from an unelected authority into the hands of an elected authority, and which also gave all Kuwaiti citizens fair representation in the elected assembly. Moreover, groups in both cases raised issues on behalf of excluded groups in public that the regimes themselves did not wish to discuss, at least not in the manner demanded by the groups. In practical terms, they increased participation in public, political debate in terms of both participants and issues discussed. They successfully challenged the boundaries of the hegemonic public – boundaries intended to prevent any change to the political order from taking place. Thus, challenging these boundaries is a necessary step towards democratisation, although it does not guarantee a democratic outcome. They practised the right to publicly disagree with the regime – a fundamental democratic feature.

Crucially, groups in both cases managed to pressure the regimes into responding. In Egypt, even the Islamist-dominated upper house of Parliament felt compelled to address the issue, albeit in a misogynistic manner, and the post-coup regime has introduced new laws and a new police task force, and apprehended and sentenced suspected harassers. In Kuwait, the prime minister resigned, the 2009 Parliament was dissolved and the opposition MPs supported the demand for a constitutional emirate. These demands had been raised in public, and it was clear to everyone that the official responses were just that: responses to public demands. This, of course, is a central democratic feature: to be able to raise a concern with the authorities and provoke a response. In the autocratic settings of Egypt and Kuwait, it also entails taking power from the regimes, as their policies become the product of public demand rather than their own, sovereign decisions. As such, the campaigns studied presented challenges to the hegemonic order and, as predicted by Mouffe, the hegemonic forces fought back.

In Egypt, as we have seen, the Islamist Parliament sought to depoliticise the issue by making it a question of morals. Clearly, women's political participation was seen as a threat, and morality was employed as a means of both debunking their demands and, by extension, keeping women out of public, political demonstrations. This tactic, however, did not succeed, as the groups fought back. The Egyptian media continued to give attention to the groups after the parliamentary debate, and the issue continued to be treated as a problem that should be solved. As we have seen, when one university official later sought to blame harassment on a woman's attire, he was met with outrage, and soon retracted his statement. It was no longer politically acceptable to treat the issue in this manner: the groups had succeeded in fundamentally altering how the problem was perceived. Similarly, when a controversial TV host in October 2015 blamed a woman's attire for the harassment she experienced in a mall, it provoked outrage online.[19] A campaign was initially started by the well-known activist Wael Abbas, which soon developed into a concentrated effort to make companies pull their advertisements from the show in question. One prominent participant was former TV host Bassem Youssef, who on 30 October announced that 17 companies had heeded their call.[20] The same day, the TV station on which the show in question was aired, al-Nahar, announced that the programme had been suspended, stressing its 'respect for all women and girls'.[21]

This does not mean that all Egyptians have accepted the problem as presented by the groups, but it does seem that, by and large, and not least in the media, it is now treated as a political problem. Following the 2013 coup, we have seen that the regime has introduced new legislation against harassment, as well as establishing a new police task force. While this should be seen as a positive result of the work done by the groups, it was nevertheless met with considerable scepticism. The regime treats the issue solely as a matter of security, even though the security services have been at the heart of the problem for many years. Moreover, the regime has previously appropriated the issue in order to legitimise its own repressive security measures, and may be doing so again.

The new regime has made it very clear that it does not allow any political challenges, which highlights a central problem: Mouffe based her analysis on well-established European democracies. While the democratising features she identifies are also democratising in the authoritarian contexts studied here, challenges may be rebuffed by autocratic regimes in a very different manner than in a democracy. The final outcome may therefore be very different, as is even more evident in the Kuwaiti case.

The Kuwaiti groups were also met with attempts to depoliticise their demands. As we have seen, individuals very close to the regime sought to turn the question of democratic reform into a sectarian conflict between *ḥaḍar* and *badw*. While important in itself, this stance also helped to legitimise more repressive and violent means. When the Kuwaiti state was unable to reassert itself through hegemonic power, it turned to outright repression and violence. This violence further helps to divert attention from the political demands raised, as demonstrations can be treated as questions of security. This is the crucial difference between the democracies referred to by Mouffe and the authoritarian regimes studied here: authoritarian regimes may resort to repression and violence. In Kuwait, they succeeded: the opposition movement was crushed, without causing an outraged response that could threaten the regime. Many factors may have been involved in this autocratic success, as has been discussed in the previous chapters. In either case, it does show the limitations of online platforms in terms of effecting social and political change along the lines raised by Faris: they may be more suitable for raising an issue than for determining an outcome. Then again, we have no reason to expect that online platforms somehow should supersede their contexts and prevent autocratic regimes from doing what they do: remain in power by repressing political challenges. Moreover, we have no reason to expect democratisation to be a linear, uninterrupted process, and setbacks may occur even when the final outcome is positive. A democratic transition in any of the countries studied would require not only that autocratic regimes waive their absolute powers, but also that society agree on an alternative system: hardly the responsibility of a subaltern group demanding its rights. Finally, these limitations do not mean that the campaigns studied did not have an impact, or that they did not contribute to democratisation.

For one thing, online platforms may actually help to prevent autocratic regimes from repressing political challenges, given that they facilitate documentation and contact with international media. However, for this to have any effect, outside forces must be willing and able to exert pressure on the regime in question to change its ways. Since 2012–13, the international community seems to have accepted that dictators in the Middle East suppress their populations as they see fit, at least in Kuwait and Egypt. Still, the suppression of the Kuwaiti opposition movement does not eradicate previous gains. The groups have shown that the prime minister may be removed by the people, they have shown that excluded groups can successfully organise and voice their demands and they have shown that the boundaries of Kuwaiti politics – the constitution – are not sacrosanct. Similarly, the Egyptian groups have shown that how an issue is treated in public is something that they can determine themselves, that excluded groups can organise and demand that society discuss their problems as political issues. In addition to gaining very practical experience, the participants in the campaigns studied have probably also changed their views and habits in terms of political participation. As argued in Chapter 2, online platforms may contribute further to democratisation in this manner by providing important experiences and expectations: not by enabling deliberations in a Habermasian manner as argued by Dahlgren and Olsson,[22] but by enabling groups and individuals to fight for their cause in the agonistic manner described by Mouffe.

Online platforms are crucial for activists in that they provide a very concrete form of counterpublicness that enables excluded groups to address each other, to organise, to articulate their demands and then turn to the public at large. By abandoning Habermas's normative ideal, we see the centrality of power relations in this struggle, we see how subaltern groups actually connect to the public at large and seek to affect their circumstances and we see why online platforms are crucial. While the architecture of the internet may not facilitate a Habermasian public and rational-critical debate, it does facilitate such counterpublicness. How activists reach the wider public is dependent on the particular context, but online platforms played a crucial role in this regard in the two cases studied here, although the skill and experience of those involved, as well as the nature of the issues at hand, also were important. In doing so, the groups studied challenged the hegemonic order of the public, and the hegemonic forces expectedly sought to reassert themselves. This took the form of both attempts to depoliticise the issues raised, and also through outright repression. In Kuwait, the groups studied were not able to withstand the repressive tactics employed by the regime, indicating that, as stated above, online platforms may be more important in raising an issue than in controlling the outcome. Nevertheless, the campaigns successfully raised their issues in public and expanded political participation through the use of online platforms.

CHAPTER 9

ONLINE ACTIVISM IN EGYPT AND KUWAIT: CONCLUSIONS

This investigation began with the rather general question of whether or not the internet can facilitate social and political change in the Middle East. From there, I narrowed the general query down to specific research questions, selected suitable cases to study and provided a research design capable of answering the research questions posed in Chapter 3. The main aim has been to provide an empirically based study of how activists in Egypt and Kuwait actually employ online platforms, and to identify how this usage has helped the groups studied to realise their aims. The intention has been to focus on the utilisation of online platforms by activist groups, not to use examples of activism to focus on online platforms. The analysis of the cases was provided in Chapter 4 and 5. In Chapter 6, I compared the two cases in order to separate contextually influenced patterns of usage from more general, common features. In Chapter 7, I employed the framework given in Chapter 3 to demonstrate and substantiate the fact that the campaigns studied were able to effect change. Finally, in Chapter 8, I engaged with the empirical findings through the theoretical approach presented in Chapter 2, with the aim of contributing towards a more comprehensive theoretical understanding of online activism. I argued that the main benefit gained by activists from online platforms is the counterpublicness such platforms provide, which enable excluded groups to organise, articulate their demands and fight for these within their national publics. In the following, the conclusions drawn from this work will be presented, and

I begin by answering the research question and the sub-questions given in Chapter 1.

Answering the Research Questions

The research questions were as follows:

– How are various online platforms utilised by the groups and organisations working in Egypt and Kuwait, and are online platforms beneficial for the groups in terms of realising their goals, and if so, how?

The sub-questions were as follows:

– Which platforms are used, for what purposes and what is the intended audience?
– What has been made possible that would otherwise have been impossible, and what has been made significantly easier through the use of the internet?
– Can any factors for success be identified?

We have seen that three dominant features of usage were found in both cases, namely discussion, mobilisation and documentation. These features were appropriated differently in the two cases, in accordance with their work mode, the issue in question and the context. Thus, whereas the Kuwaiti groups spent most of their time mobilising participants for protests, the Egyptian groups were more concerned with recruiting and retaining volunteers. Whereas groups in both countries were concerned with documenting their work, with their own supporters as an important part of the intended audience, we have seen that the Egyptian groups also used this documentation to reach out through traditional media, while the Kuwaiti groups were more concerned with correcting such media reports. Discussion was *the* dominant feature in both countries, but there were few exchanges with those of opposing views. Rather, their positions were reinforced and reiterated, the problems clearly defined as problems, and new expressions were introduced: the Egyptian groups stressed that harassment *is* a crime, and their Kuwaiti counterparts argued that a popularly sanctioned government *is* the solution.

For the Egyptian groups, an important point was to break the silence and provide an arena where the issue could be discussed and, accordingly, they held several online events to raise awareness. Similarly, they spent a lot of time compiling reports and testimonies to demonstrate that their description of the problem was consistent with the reality experienced by Egyptian women. The Kuwaiti groups were, first and foremost, engaged in disseminating their political views, around which they mobilised for offline demonstrations. Most groups actively used hashtags on Twitter to reach a wider audience, with the exception of the two Kuwaiti Islamist groups, which seemed content with talking to their followers and some prominent personalities whom they addressed personally. In Kuwait, numerous debates were organised around hashtags that were not initiated by the groups, and the reach of the platform in itself seems to have been far wider than in Egypt, which also might have helped to compensate for the lack of media attention.

The Egyptian groups also used online platforms for purposes not prominent among those of their Kuwaiti colleagues, such as disseminating vital information, communicating with other groups and recruiting volunteers. Communication with other groups, however, seems to have taken place mainly offline or through other channels. The groups clearly coordinated their work, but there are few traces of this online. Moreover, although Twitter was the preferred platform for the dissemination of updates and information during large offline events in both countries, it was not widely used to communicate with those on the ground or to report attacks on female protesters. Furthermore, some Egyptian groups spent a lot of time circulating media coverage of themselves and their work, but this was not done equally by the different groups within the case. Those groups that received the most attention from the traditional media also spent less time sharing this with their followers, suggesting that they perhaps felt less need to demonstrate their credibility in this manner, as it was already widely known.

Moving on to the first sub-question, we have seen that platform selection differed in the two cases. Facebook was used by all groups in Egypt – as the main platform for two of them – but was not used at all in Kuwait, following some early, unsuccessful and quickly abandoned attempts at utilising the platform. Twitter was the preferred alternative, although Facebook has more users in the country and contains functionality that clearly could have been beneficial to the groups.

Instead, the groups used additional platforms like Twitlonger and Yfrog to compensate. The reason seems to have been the special standing of Twitter in the country. Thus, it is not only technical possibilities, novelty or popularity in itself that inform platform selection, but also the ability to reach the desired audience, or to go public in a meaningful and effective way. This is dependent on the particular context in question. Similarly, while blogs may not be as prominent as they were some years ago, they still retain a function, as we have seen from the Kuwaiti case. The discussion conducted on blogs by the Orange Movement of 2006 has moved to other platforms, but blogs are still used for longer texts, to provide more extensive information and to provide a 'home' for the groups online. Whether or not they actively use and disseminate this content varies from group to group.

Likewise, there is no reason to declare websites redundant due to social media, and they were used by five of the groups studied, and in both countries. Again, they served as a home online and provided relevant information on the group and its work. Some groups, however, utilised their websites for more than that: HarassMap built their group around the technical solutions employed on their website, and Nazra's site functioned as a hub of information disseminated not only by them but by other groups as well. Clearly, some groups made more purposeful use of their sites than others. YouTube, on the other hand, was not the online 'home' of any group, although it was used by many. It was not a platform for discussion or the place where groups provided their vital information, and it was generally the least visited platform employed by the groups.[1] For all groups studied, it was a publishing platform, with the content *disseminated* through other sites. There was, however, a marked difference between usage in the two countries. The Kuwaiti groups primarily used YouTube to publish more or less unedited short videos from offline events, and more often than not these videos were uploaded by others and then linked to by the groups. Their main concern was to disseminate the images, and it was not important that they be credited with the footage. In contrast, the Egyptian groups published several well-produced videos, often more like short documentaries than clips. These groups all did so through their own channels and had more views and subscribers than their Kuwaiti counterparts. Ownership of the videos, as well as their quality, seems to have been more important, perhaps due to the groups' need for both volunteers and credibility among the public at large. Clips from TV shows were disseminated in both countries, through both their own channels and others, but more often in Egypt than in Kuwait. It should also be mentioned here that the online Kuwaiti activist-sphere has its own 'minister of media' in the blogger AlziadiQ8, which may have made the groups' need for their own YouTube channels more or less redundant.

Looking at the Egyptian case, in which both Facebook and Twitter were used by all groups, it is possible to identify some clear differences in how the platforms were utilised. Twitter was used far more than Facebook in a quantitative sense; more posts were published on Twitter than on Facebook. While the 140-character limit was clearly relevant, this was also linked to how the platforms were employed. Twitter was the preferred alternative for disseminating live updates and important information during large protests, that is, during times of high activity on the part of the groups. Such content was also, by and large, the most popular content on the platform. Facebook was different in this regard, and the most popular content there was more varied, with live updates and information accounting for only a small proportion. Instead, links to media coverage of the group, longer texts and, not least, pictures and videos of their work generated the most engagement. Many of these pictures were encouraging displays of the work done by the groups' volunteers, which were important both to demonstrate their credibility and to encourage and retain their members. Encouragement as such was, in fact, a prominent feature on Facebook, in contrast to Twitter, often in the form of inspirational pictures and quotes. Moreover, shaming of people accused of harassment was carried out routinely on Facebook, but not on Twitter. Still, the content published on both platforms was, in general, quite similar (although not in a quantitative sense), but there seems to have been an inclination to use Facebook for content that would be of most interest to those supporting or volunteering with the groups. Interestingly, on both Twitter and Facebook in Egypt and Twitter in Kuwait, there is generally a correlation between the most popular content and the content prioritised by the groups. This, of course, may be the result of skilful use of the platforms on the part of the groups, interests shared by their audience or the audience adjusting to what was available to them.

Moving on to the second sub-question, there are clearly aspects of the groups' work that were made substantially easier through the use of online platforms. Although it is possible, it is difficult to imagine that

HarassMap could have gathered 1,000 testimonies without their website, or that all those submitting the testimonies would have been able to reach someone similar with their story through other channels. Karamat Watan clearly would have found it difficult to provide practical information to its 100,000 followers if not for Twitter, and 12,000 tweets would obviously not have been written as part of HarassMap's online campaign. In short, the wide, instantaneous reach provided by online platforms is hard to match. This had several implications for the groups studied. For one thing, they could reach those who agreed, sympathised or were interested in the issues and who were online; this would not be *everyone*, but it seems to have been a sufficient number to allow the groups to conduct their work. By using online platforms, they could engage with people in real time, give instructions, mobilise and do all the other things they did, to thousands of people at a relatively low cost. This may seem a rather obvious point, given that the topic at hand is online platforms, but that does not diminish its importance.

While leaflets could have been handed out, they do not provide a commentary function, to borrow the language of Horkheimer and Adorno.[2] Information could, of course, be passed on face to face, by phone or by email, but locating those interested would have required a huge amount of work. While well-connected foreign journalists might have been able to cover the groups' work without social media, it would obviously have been more difficult, and it would have been more difficult for the groups to correct any perceived mistakes in the media. This, in turn, points to another central feature: online, the groups are able to articulate and disseminate their message directly, independent of other parties, such as journalists, who may alter or affect said message. We have seen that a crucial feature of both campaigns was precisely to articulate their issues of concern. Language was important, be it to term harassment a crime or to describe an alternative political system: online platforms gave the groups the opportunity to do so in their own, unfiltered words to their followers and others. There are, in concrete terms, no realistic alternatives that match the reach, speed, cost and communicative nature of online platforms. At the very least, online platforms make the work of the groups substantially easier.

If not for online platforms, many features of the work studied would have to have been conducted in a very different manner, if they could have been conducted at all. Tahrir Bodyguard was born and raised online, and the crowd-funding campaign of HarassMap would have been much more expensive, to say the least, were it not for social media. In general, ad hoc responses to a critical situation seem to have gained a lot from the use of online tools. Within a matter of days, TBG and OpAntiSH had volunteers on the ground, Karamat Watan had tens of thousands in the streets and the Kuwaiti boycott campaign could monitor – by their own account – all polling stations. This is related to the observation that online the groups mainly reach those who agree with them or are concerned about similar issues – these would also be those individuals most likely to respond quickly to such calls. When depending on their 'own public', so to speak, the online platforms seem to be sufficient. Such rapid responses would have been difficult without social media, although perhaps not impossible, as demonstrated by the importance of offline networks in the start-up of OpAntiSH. For those less well-connected offline, such as Tahrir Bodyguard, their work might have proven impossible.

Both the Egyptian and the Kuwaiti regimes have sought to tightly control civil society. Starting an initiative online is, nevertheless, quite easy, although harsh reactions may be imposed later. While some of the groups have their own offices, an online 'home' is an affordable, visible and, not least, unbureaucratic alternative. Online platforms made it possible for those concerned to organise, discuss and mobilise even in the controlled and patriarchal contexts within which they operated. Such contextual difficulties may certainly be imposed not only by the regimes in question, but also by society, or by groups seemingly allied with the activists. For instance, the Kuwaiti groups faced not only a society in which joint activism by men and women is problematic, but also an established opposition that for years had engaged with the issue at hand. However, this opposition had not proposed the radical solution that the youth movement deemed necessary, and which they were able to raise themselves through their organisation. Similarly, the Egyptian groups were concerned with an issue that society at large hardly viewed as a problem, and that women's organisations previously had been unwilling to engage with – organisations that were of an 'elitist nature' and had 'difficulty connecting with ordinary Egyptian women'.[3] Thus, online platforms helped to solve some of the contextual difficulties faced by the groups in both Egypt and Kuwait – difficulties caused both by repressive regimes and by patriarchal structures.

In the case of Kuwait, however, such difficulties were not resolved permanently. As we have seen, online platforms cannot be seen as separate from their offline context, and there is a limit to how repressive this context can become before online platforms can no longer solve the problems faced by activists. Kuwait in 2011 was a particular context within which the groups worked, but this context changed in 2012 as the regime repressed the opposition movement. Similarly, Egypt of 2012 and pre-coup 2013 was a specific context which offered the activists particular possibilities and challenges. The Egyptian context has since changed, which in turn may affect the ability of activists to continue their work in the future. Thus, depending on the context, online platforms may help to solve such difficulties faced by activists, but the regime in question may also change these circumstances in such a manner that online platforms no longer provide a solution.

In all, the online platforms employed made the work of these groups substantially easier, and made possible what would otherwise – at the very least – have had to be done in a markedly different manner, which might not have been equally effective. Moreover, there was no reason for the groups studied here *not* to employ online platforms; these were tried and tested tools of activism in both countries. While it is clearly important to be able to work both online and offline, the separation between the two seems constructed, at least for the groups in question. They did not work offline to support their online work, and they did not work online solely to support their offline work: both were important arenas for their activism, and they functioned in tandem.

It seems clear that whether problems are solved and whether the groups are able to realise their goals also depends on *how* the platforms are utilised, and the material suggests that certain factors for success can be identified. First, those who provided the most content online were also the most successful in gaining and engaging with followers. Those who utilised the possibilities inherent in Twitter were the most successful users of the platform. This meant employing popular hashtags to reach a wider audience than just their followers and writing meaningful messages using complete sentences, not just publishing a link with no explanation. Those who were most successful online were also the most successful offline. In Egypt, offline success was understood as gaining attention from domestic and international media, recruiting volunteers, being able to carry out their offline activities, and being able to reach a broader audience with their description of reality, that is, being used as credible sources and even being able to introduce specific language to the debate. In Kuwait, it first and foremost meant being able to mobilise as broadly as possible offline. One could argue that some of the groups that did not have the greatest number of followers online were still the most successful offline, in that they gained support from established politicians for their demand for a constitutional emirate. However, as we have seen, they were not able to mobilise successfully around this demand.

The most successful groups were also the ones that seem to have had the most experienced and knowledgeable core members. Consequently, it can be argued that online platforms do not compensate for offline differences. On the other hand, even the most successful groups did not come from dominant groups in society, and inexperienced groups also achieved considerable success. Thus, online platforms may help to compensate for differences in access to resources and power but, at the same time, there are clear differences between skilled and less skilled use of online platforms. The groups that were most successful in mobilising protesters in Kuwait and volunteers in Egypt spent more time than other groups speaking directly to followers, reassuring and encouraging them and providing detailed and convincing information on their operation. In other words, the groups that made participation easy, rewarding and safe gained the most participants. The most successful groups, particularly in Egypt, seem to have been dominant within the campaign, and to have been able to provide the most sought-after content and the most organised and complex offline operations. Those who did the most skilled work were also the ones that were most successful, both online and offline. Furthermore, it was clearly important that the issues raised were of concern to many, and in Kuwait we have seen that the less radical positions were more successfully championed than the more militant ones. It also seems clear that it was easier for the groups to mobilise in response to perceived injustices inflicted by others, than in support of new positions raised by themselves. This may be a more universal observation, not confined to the use of online platforms. Then, if nothing else, the material suggests that this observation also holds true when online platforms are used to mobilise.

Thus, with regard to the third sub-question, certain factors for success can be identified. Skill is clearly of great importance, both in employing online platforms and in organising the work of the groups more broadly.

As has been discussed in detail above, several features of skilful use of online platforms are common to both cases studied. The issue at hand is also of importance, and it appears to be easier to mobilise against perceived injustices than in favour of one's own initiatives. Convincing documentation of the issues at hand, the work of the groups and the reactions they face is crucial, not least in order to build credibility and trust among their followers and others. This, in turn, is important both for mobilising volunteers and participants, and, in the Egyptian case, for gaining attention from the traditional media. As we have seen, such attention was not a priority for the Kuwaiti groups studied due to their strained relationship with most news outlets; they reached a broader audience through other means than their Egyptian counterparts. It follows that successful groups must not only be able to adjust to their particular context, but also to utilise the possibilities inherent in it. What these factors have in common is that they enable what I suggest is the central benefit to be gained from utilising online platforms: the publicness these platforms provide.

This, in turn, brings us to the final question of whether or not online platforms helped the groups to realise their goals, and if so, how. The short answer would be yes, through the publicness they provide. While none of the groups succeeded in realising all their goals, they made substantial – and impressive – gains. In Chapter 7, we saw not only that the groups were *capable* of affecting change, but also that tangible, offline results can be traced to their online activities: they did have an impact. In Kuwait, the prime minister resigned, and the 2009 Parliament was dissolved – as demanded by the groups studied. Moreover, they articulated the radical demand for a constitutional emirate, and gained support from established politicians. As such, they challenged the hegemonic framework of politics in the country, and indeed *changed* the established practice within the opposition. The groups managed to mobilise not only the tribal population, but at one point up to 10 per cent of all Kuwaitis. Then, as we have seen, the regime struck back, and by the end of the time frame studied, the opposition campaign was crushed and Kuwait had become a more autocratic country. Clearly, online activism is dependent on its context.

The Egyptian groups did not manage to end sexual harassment, the acceptance of sexual harassment or the attacks on female protesters. They did, however, manage to help dozens of protesters who were attacked, and women did not stop taking part in demonstrations altogether. They documented the severity and extent of the problem, as they did with the harassment Egyptian women face every day. They reached out to the Egyptian public as well as to an international audience, and gained massive coverage in both domestic and foreign media. They were able to break the public silence on the issue and to affect how it was discussed: as a crime, and as a political problem. They fought off attempts to turn the issue into a moral question, and it was clear that, from the summer of 2013, the state felt increasingly obliged to respond to the problem. Many remained sceptical, however, as the state predominantly dealt with the issue as a matter of (state) security.

The work that caused these results, in the manner it was conducted, was made possible through the use of online platforms. As we have seen, this meant many different things in practice: from providing online 'homes' to enabling online events, from sharing pictures on Facebook to giving encouragement on Twitter. The usage was adapted to the particular context within which the groups worked, and it was affected by the skills and experience of the groups. In sum, the platforms enabled the groups to organise themselves, to discuss and articulate their demands and to raise these demands in the public at large, albeit in varying ways depending on the context. As such, online platforms did help the groups towards realising their goals and the central contribution was the counter-publicness they provided.

Online Activism and Counterpublicness

By raising their demands in public, the groups studied were able to make the crucial leap from private concern to public issue. This meant that their volunteers and supporters were able to endorse their views in public and to make what might have been their own private concern into a public campaign demanding a solution. Along with several others, Faris argues that the use of online platforms may help to lower the threshold for people to take part in, say, a demonstration, as they can see that they clearly are not alone. This is also relevant for people's threshold in terms of speaking up about an issue and taking a stance. The issue of sexual harassment has long been engulfed in silence, but when people see that others are speaking their mind, they may be persuaded to do so themselves, for instance during online events. Similarly, frustrated

Kuwaitis may dare to state their opposition in a Twitter debate where hundreds of others do the same. Through the use of online platforms, the groups both reached out to and were available to those concerned with the issue. From being private concerns, the issues at hand became the positions of organised groups, or collective positions and demands that the groups fought for in campaigns in which thousands of people took part in some way.

Groups in both countries were able to reach the public at large and set the agenda for public debate. They did so in quite different ways: in one case through popular mobilisation and in the other through traditional media. These strategies were, in turn, affected by their contexts, and could hardly have been switched: the tightly controlled government-friendly Kuwaiti media would not have provided sympathetic coverage to the idea of curtailing the powers of the royal family, and the Egyptian groups would not have been able to reach the same audience through offline demonstrations alone. Moreover, the Kuwaiti groups also reached a wider audience directly online; one activist even argued that Twitter made the traditional media redundant.[4] Quite clearly, context is of great importance for online activism, and the groups need to be able to appropriate the online tools in accordance with their surroundings.

In Chapter 1, I hypothesised that publicness is the central contribution of online platforms, and that the ability to transform online engagement into offline engagement is the biggest challenge in terms of affecting social and political change. My findings, however, indicate that this latter point requires some revision. Clearly, the ability to work offline is important: the campaigns studied here could not have been conducted solely online, and they would hardly have sparked the same reactions within their contexts if not for offline practical work, documentation and, not least, displays of support. It can also be a challenge: the Kuwaiti groups clearly struggled to mobilise protesters in support of their most radical demands. However, we have also seen that the way in which the groups raise their concerns in public depends on the context. It may be through the traditional media or even directly on Twitter, which in neither case *necessitates* offline engagement.

When the groups raise their issues in public, they challenge the hegemonic order. As we have seen, this sparked reactions through which the hegemonic forces sought to reassert themselves and which represented formidable challenges for the groups. These reactions may take the form of depoliticising or appropriating the issues raised, as happened in both cases. However, if the regime is not able to control the situation through such subtle means, the hegemonic order may be reasserted through outright repression, as in Kuwait. The ability to withstand such countermeasures may perhaps represent an even more decisive challenge to the groups' ultimate success, and points to the difficulties in controlling the outcome noted by Faris.[5] Then again, the groups would hardly have been able to raise their issues convincingly and spark such reactions if not for the ability to work both online and offline. Therefore, offline work is both challenging and important, but once the campaigns have succeeded in raising their demands in public, other equally crucial challenges arise.

Online platforms enable activists to reach out publicly to others concerned with an issue. While access remains a concern, these platforms are cheap and easy to use compared with any alternatives, to the extent that any realistic alternatives exist. This enables counterpublicness: it allows subaltern groups to organise and articulate their concerns, which are transformed from private problems into political public issues as these groups raise them as demands in the public at large. How they enter the dominant public depends on the context, and whether or not they succeed depends on the groups' abilities, their experience, the issue at hand and – again – the context. In doing so, they challenge the hegemonic order of public discourse, which, in autocratic countries, is intended as boundaries to inhibit political challenges. Thus, it is a struggle, not an endeavour aimed at achieving consensus. This activism is democratising, also in autocratic contexts, in several ways: it expands participation in public deliberations beyond the hegemonic order; it expands the issues of public interest; it enables those involved to demand action from the regime on an issue with which they are concerned; and, if they succeed, they demonstrate to the public that they have infringed on the regime's sovereign power to decide policy on the matter in question. The hegemonic forces they challenge may fight back and reassert themselves, and in autocratic contexts this may entail the use of brute force. Yet, even if successfully repressed, campaigns such as those studied here provide experience and raise expectations, which may prove far, far more difficult to suppress than a demonstration. The groups studied here were able to effect social and political change, and so will many other groups in the years to come.

APPENDIX I

KUWAITI TWITTER DEBATES

In the following, I will present a short overview of Twitter debates in Kuwait that I have identified within the time frame of this study. These are political debates, covering issues of concern for the opposition, although pro-government Twitter users also participated. These are not *all* political debates in which the opposition engaged on Twitter during the time, and they have not been analysed systematically, as discussed in Chapter 3. Moreover, I only became aware of these debates in 2012 and, consequently, many discussions may have taken place prior to this. The intention here is to demonstrate the extent of and the participation in Twitter debates in Kuwait, the subjects covered by these debates, including the issue of a constitutional emirate long before it was endorsed by oppositional politicians, and to show that online political debates and the Kuwaiti online political public extends beyond the activities of the groups studied.

The debates were organised through hashtags, as is the list which follows. Data from Topsy concerning participation in each debate is stored by the author, as is the complete content of most of the debates, though not all. The figures given below are based on the numbers provided by Topsy concerning each hashtag, which is presented as '[number] tweets', seemingly the number of tweets published using each particular hashtag. Unfortunately, as stated above, Topsy no longer exists. All the material and figures taken from Topsy, however, have been downloaded and are stored by the author. The site provided the following explanation regarding how the numbers referred to here were generated:

> On every search result page Topsy provides you with the count on the left which is the number of search results for that period. It is a count of tweets, uniqued by links or retweets: i.e. multiple retweets are only counted once; multiple tweets for a single url are only counted once.
>
> As twitter is growing, and our counts are cumulative, the number of tweets for a topic can be higher if you check it on any given day compared to the previous day, especially if you're looking at the number over the past month.[1]

The debates are presented chronologically below. For each discussion, the time, hashtag used and number of tweets given by Topsy is provided, as well as a short description of the topic under discussion, if this is not clear from the hashtag.

26–28 April 2012: #ليش_منتخبة (Why elected): debate concerning why Kuwait was in need of an 'elected government'. Modest activity, covered about 1,300 tweets. It was also covered by the online newspaper *alaan.cc*.

24 August 2012: #لماذا_الارادة (Why al-Irada [square]): discussion on why one should take part in a demonstration against the proposed changes to the electoral law that took place on 27 August. Modest activity: about 1,000 tweets.

25–28 August 2012: Competing hashtags employed by those intending to participate on the 27th, and those who do not. Those not participating use the hashtag #لن_أخرج_للارادة (I will not go to al-Irada), while their opponents use #سأخرج_للارادة (I will go to al-Irada) and #أعتصر_ساحة_الارادة (I will attend al-Irada). Those who are not participating generated by far the most activity, about 10,000 tweets, as opposed to 5,000 and 350, respectively, for the two other hashtags.

25 September 2012: #حكم_المحكمة_الدستورية (The verdict of the constitutional court): in reference to the verdict given by the constitutional court on the same day, regarding whether or not the 2006 changes to the electoral law were in line with the constitution. Moderate activity: covering about 1,300 tweets in less than 24 hours.

1–16 October 2012: #انتخابات_بلا_عبث (Elections without interference): runs over several days; in all, generating about 1,700 tweets. The slogan used in the hashtag was painted on walls and bridges in several locations in Kuwait during the same period, in connection with the royal decree changing the electoral law anticipated on 20 October.

15 October 2012: #كافي_عبثا (Enough interference): the name of a demonstration held the same day in protest against regime interference in the elections, in which Musallam al-Barrak gave his famous/infamous speech, generating about 2,500 tweets in one day.

15–16 October 2012: #لن_نسمح_لك (We will not allow you): discussion on the speech given by al-Barrak, generating no less than 6,000 tweets in one day.

18 October 2012: #استدعاء_813_مغرد (The summoning of 813 tweeple): on the persecution of tweeple, covering about 6,200 tweets in one day.

23–24 October 2012: #مقاطعة_تشيليز and #مقاطعة_شيليز (Boycott Chili's): started to initiate a boycott of the restaurant Chili's, which, according to protesters, falsely accused them of causing damage to their facilities in connection with the first 'Dignity of a Nation' protest on 21 October. Moderate activity, generating about 1,500 tweets altogether.

25 October 2012: In response to the hashtag #سأقاطع (I will boycott), the hashtag #سأشارك (I will participate) was launched for those supporting the government and intending to participate in the upcoming elections. Hardly a success at this point, the discussion generated about 160 tweets, but was nevertheless given attention by the newspaper *al-Waṭan*.

29 October 2012: #تعلمت_من_الربيع_العربي (I learned from the Arab spring): generated a lot of attention, although it is difficult to determine the extent to which the discussion is exclusive to Kuwait. It generated about 4,000 tweets in one day.

6 November 2012: #مسيرة_كرامة_خليج (The dignity of the Gulf march): discussion on the prospect of a joint protest in the GCC countries on

11 November, and not all the participants were Kuwaitis. In all, it encompassed about 2,350 tweets.

12 November 2012: #كلنا_حاكم_المطيري (We are all Hakim al-Mutayri): campaign in defence of Hakim al-Mutayri following his arrest due to ten-year-old statements. It generated about 3,000 tweets in one day, but not all in his support.

17–21 November 2012: Sustained activity using the hashtag #الحرية_للمغردين (Freedom for the tweeple): in all, numbering about 1,580 tweets. It was started due to the arrest of several prominent activists, including a member of the royal family.

25–26 November 2012: Discussion/competition between #سجل_المقاطعين (Register/declare those boycotting) and #سجل_المشاركين (Register/declare those who will participate) as to whether or not one should participate in the upcoming elections. The hashtag advocating boycott generated far more activity than its opponent, about 4,300 and 500 tweets, respectively. As we have seen, this debate was also moved offline.

28 November 2012: The one-year anniversary of the resignation of Prime Minister Nasir al-Muhammad marked on Twitter using the hashtag #ذكرى_رحيل_ناصر (Anniversary of Nasir's removal) generating about 500 tweets.

2 December 2012: Following the election, the hashtag #المقاطعة_نجحت (The boycott succeeded) was launched to claim success for the boycott-campaign, generating over 3,000 tweets within 24 hours.

4 December 2012: #مواد_الدستور_الجديد (The articles of the new constitution): debate on possible articles for a new constitution, as demanded by the opposition. Not a great success in terms of participation, generating 800 tweets over a few days.

5 December 2012: #كفالات_الشباب (The bail money for the youth) campaign to gather financial support to pay bail for activists arrested during protests. Generated about 600 tweets and, as we have seen, succeeded in raising money for the cause.

19–20 December 2012: #مسيرة_تويترية (Twitter march): held in connection with offline demonstrations in protest against the recent election. Some participants refer to the Jeddah conference held during the Iraqi occupation, in which the royal family promised to reintroduce democracy in exchange for political support, signalling how critical the situation was seen to be by many in the opposition. Moderate activity: generating about 1,000 tweets within two days.

20 December 2012: #ضرب_بنات_الكويت (The striking of/attacking Kuwait's women): launched to draw attention to alleged abuses committed by the police while dispersing protests, including using violence against female participants. It generated about 500 tweets in one day.

3 January 2013: #اقتراحات_كرامة_وطن5 (Suggestions for Karamat Watan 5): launched by the 'Dignity of a Nation' campaign to gather suggestions for their fifth protest. Not particularly successful, generating only 200 tweets.

3 January 2013: #قانون_الغمز_واللمز: discussion concerning a law proposed by the government which was seen as authoritarian by the opposition. It generated about 600 tweets.

6 January 2013: #أنا_كويتي_وما_أنكسر (I am Kuwaiti and not defeated): launched as a response to alleged police brutality during the fifth 'Dignity of a Nation' protest. It generated about 2,400 tweets over two days. During the same period, the hashtag #الربيع_الكويتي (The Kuwaiti spring) was also used, although to a lesser extent.

8 January 2013: The hashtag #insulttheemir was launched, corresponding to the Kuwaiti emir's visit to the UK, in protest against the arrest of prominent activists, often on the accusation of having insulted the emir. It generated about 600 tweets.

14 January 2013: Bloggers and tweeple called for the unification of the opposition using the hashtag #ائتلاف_المعارضة (the oppositional alliance). The hashtag was revived at the beginning of March, when such an alliance was declared. In all, the hashtag generated about 6,000 tweets.

18 January 2013: #تصريح_فريحة_الاحمد (The statement of Fariha al-Ahmad): launched to discuss, and predominantly denounce, the statements given by the sister of the emir, as referred to in chapter 7. It generated about 3,600 tweets in one day.

Finally, the hashtag #ساحة_الارادة (al-Irada square) was often used before large demonstrations and cannot be tied to any one protest in particular. To give an example, it was used in the run-up to the protests on 27 August 2012 and 15 October 2012, generating 4,400 and 11,000 tweets, respectively.

APPENDIX II

CODING CATEGORIES

This appendix provides a short description of each category and sub-category employed in the coding of the material, along with an example of each of the sub-categories.

Mobilisation

The category covers mobilisation in a broad sense, including mobilising participants for online and offline events, mobilising followers online and mobilising material support and resources. It also includes encouragement, seen as a feature employed by the groups to increase and/or maintain participation. Finally, tweets that were part of online events were also included in this category.

Offline event: Invitation/ information	Tweets containing invitations or information about particular events	we are organizing an Open Microphone event next Sunday 9 December at 6:30pm: different forms of violence [link] join us (Nazra, 7 December 2012)
Offline event: 'Please come'	Tweets encouraging people to take part in particular events	join this global outcry next tuesday 6pm against sexual terrorism practices in #Egypt [link] #endSH #GlobalProtestFeb12 (HarassMap, 6 February 2013)

Online event: Invitation/ information	Tweets containing invitations or information about particular events	Your turn – how would you imagine Egypt without sexual harassment? Post/ tweet/blog and we'll repost/ RT. Use the hashtag #OpAntiSH (HarassMap, 23 January 2013)
Online event: 'Please come'	Tweets encouraging people to take part in particular events	Join a 48hr tweeting/ blogging shout out against Sexual Harassment [link]: #endSH v/ @harassmap & @OpAntiSH (retweeted by HarassMap, 23 January 2013)
Encouragement in general	Tweets providing general encouragement to participants, followers and volunteers	Thanks to all our volunteers, Tahrir Bodyguards & Anti SH group for the great effort & courage in defending our right to safe protesting (OpAntiSH, 8 July 2013)
Part of online event	Tweets that are part of an online event	Because this is a male dominanted society that teaches males that nothing – including women – is off limits because they are Men #بيتحرش_ليه (HarassMap, 16 March 2013)
Linking/ spreading own sites	Tweets mobilising followers/advertising sites or accounts on social media	Follow us on Facebook too: facebook.com/Tahrir. Bodyguards #endSH #Sexualharassment #Egypt (19 March 2013)
Asking for material support	Tweets seeking to mobilise material resources from followers and others	This is a personal initiative so no funds available and we need a tent to act as operations & supplies center - anyone willing 2share tent? (TBG, 28 November 2012)

Discussion

This category covers discussion in various forms. As I have noted in the text, there is little discussion in the form described by Habermas; rather, the protagonists seek to convince others of their views. Thus, agitation and statements are included in this category. Moreover, it covers features that did spark some debate, such as polls and questions. It also covers news about the groups and their work. Finally, it covers tweets that are direct responses to other users, as well as the use of popular hashtags, which, as I have argued, is an important feature in terms of taking part in discussions and conversations (and reaching a broader audience) on Twitter, although it is no guarantee that the tweet in question will be read or generate a response.

Polls	Polls posed by the groups to their followers (and others)	هل تؤيد إستخدام الفتاة للعنف كرد على التحرش الجنسي الذي تعرضت له ؟ Do you support women using violence as a response to sexual harassment that they are subjected to? [link to poll on Facebook] ([group], 14 January 2013)
Questions for discussion	Questions for discussion posed by the groups	Send us ideas on how to deal with groups/mob harassers who harass in numbers, and beat anyone who try to help. #endSH #tahrir (HarassMap, 6 June 2012)
Agitation	Agitation, argumentation, views expressed and so on, given by the groups	STRESSING: Any assaulted woman is the victim of a criminal act – regardless of what she was wearing, where she was, and what she was doing (OpAntiSH, 30 November 2012)
Statements	Statements given by the groups	بيان السور الخامس حول جلسة 8 فبراير [link] #soor5

		Statement from Al-Sur al-Khamis on the session [of the Parliament] on February 8 (al-Sur al-Khamis, 1 February 2011)
Other posts that generate discussion	Other tweets that generate discussion. Following a first reading of parts of the material, this seemed to be a relevant category. However, after some revision of the categories, this category was never used	
Taking part in a discussion	Tweets that are part of a particular discussion or that employ popular hashtags used in the context in question	603 million #women live in countries where domestic violence is not yet considered a crime. #stoptheviolence #VAW (TBG, 13 April 2013)
Responding/ communicating with others	Direct responses or communication with other users online	@[other user] what happened in maadi? (TBG, 6 June 2013)
News	News disseminated on the groups and their work	Tahrir Bodyguard announces the creation of Dignity without Borders (DWB) as a separate and independent group #endSH #DWB (TBG, 31 July 2013)

Media

This category covers content related to the traditional media. Three of the sub-categories cover the groups' dissemination of media attention on themselves, other groups and the issue. The remaining three cover press releases, direct communication with the media and responses to others' statements/appearances in the media.

On themselves	Tweets referring to/ linking to media attention on the group in question	#FF & Much respect to @OpAntiSH @Tahrir Bodyguard for amazing work. check out segment on @DrBassemYoussef show [link] (retweet by TBG, 16 March 2013)
On other groups	Tweets referring to/ linking to media attention on other groups	#شفت_تخرش Harassmap, an online resource for Egyptian women to self-report instances of abuse by text, email,... [link] (ISH, 4 July 2013)
On the issue	Tweets referring to/ linking to media attention on the issue	Unreported World examines the increase in sexual assaults and harassment in Egypt. The programme reveals claims... [link to continuation on Facebook] (Imprint, 8 December 2012)
Press releases	Press releases given by the groups (termed as such, and not as statements as covered under 'discussion')	press release: 'sexual harassment and violence against women and girl during the... [link] (ISH, 2 July 2013)
Communication with media/ journalists	Direct communication or inquiries to the media	Kuwaitis call for #March_ of_Dignity on Sunday 21-10-2012 @ap @reuters @afpfr @BBCWorld @TWCable_NYC @cnn [link] (Karamat Watan, 20 October 2012)
Response to others	Response to media statements or appearances given by others	Follow us & check our timeline for news of #Egypt's Upper House (#Shura Council) disgraceful statements on mob sexual attacks #VAW #EgyWomen (OpAntiSH, 11 February 2013)

Documentation

This category covers the groups' documentation of their work and their issues of concern in many various forms, and their dissemination of this documentation. It also covers tweets in which the groups ask for information or help in providing such documentation, live reports from events, as well as warnings and calls for help published during events, which usually also contained a description of the situation at the given point, and which therefore are included in this category.

Pictures/text/ video from event	Pictures, text and video that document the work of the groups and their events	صورة | د. فيصل المسلم متحدثا من ندوة #حدم Picture: D. Faysal al-Muslim speaking at the seminar of Hadam (Hadam, 26 November 2012)
Testimonies	Testimonies provided by the groups documenting the issue at hand	Testimony from a Survival of Gang Rape on Tahrir Square Vicinity [link] (Nazra, 26 January 2013)
Reports	Reports documenting the issue at hand for a group	Sexual Assault and Rape in Tahrir Square and its Vicinity: A Compendium of Sources 2011 – 2013 [link] (Nazra, 20 May 2013)
Pictures/ videos/text on the issue	Pictures, videos and text that document the issue at hand for a group	Very proud of our supporter & friend @[user] for his new video campaign against sexual harassment in #Egypt. [link] (TBG, 28 March 2013)
Live reporting from event	Live reports from events	فتح البوابة للجمهورلحضور الجلسة #soor5 The doors are opened for the crowd to be present during the session (al-Sur al-Khamis, 28 December 2010)

Warning, call for help, communicating	Warnings or calls for help published during offline events	26 cases of mob sexual assault in #Tahrir tonight. We are doing everything we can but the area is not safe at all (OpAntiSH, 1 July 2013)
Asking for information, etc.	Tweets asking followers, volunteers and others to provide information/testimonies to be used in documentation	IMP to ALL @OpAntiSH volunteers & all witnesses, plz take time to write testimonies & send them to [e-mail] #endSH (OpAntiSH, 29 January 2013)

Information

This category covers information provided by the groups other than that given with regard to specific events or volunteering. This included some published papers and reports, as well as guides on, for instance, how to talk to female protesters who had been attacked.

Papers, etc.	Papers and reports containing information and instructions different from those documenting the issue referred to above	Recommendations to Integrate #Gender Issues and Perspective within Transitional Justice Mechanisms in #Egypt [link] (Nazra, 30 July 2013)
Guides, instructions	Practical guides and instructions provided by the groups	We're operating in #Tahrir today, plz report any cases of mob sexual assault to our hotlines [phone numbers] #endSH #OpAntish (OpAntiSH, 20 July 2013)

Recruitment

This category covers the groups' efforts at recruitment, both in the form of asking people to volunteer and the practical information published in this regard.

Appeals to volunteers	Tweets that ask people to volunteer with a group	@Imprint_Mov is recruiting new volunteers... join us in our journey towards change #endsh #endvaw [link] (retweet by Imprint, 6 April 2013)
Practical information on volunteering (forms, applications)	Practical information concerning how one can volunteer with a group	forms submission phase has ended, thanks to all of the people that applied or even encouraged and wished us [link] (Imprint, 11 April 2013)

Other groups

This category covers direct communication between the groups online, reposting of other groups' content and tweets concerning or articulating cooperation with other groups.

Reposting/ linking to others' content	Tweets that link to content provided by other groups, or reposts of content or links to content given by other groups	Today @NazraEgypt is holding a workshop on psych assistance & support in dealing w survivors of sexual assualt. [link] #endSH (HarassMap, 31 January 2013)
Communicating with others	Direct communication with other groups	@[user] @OpAntiSH Thank you & reciprocated. We are all working together & it keeps us focused & strong to #EndSH #Tahrir (TBG, 3 July 2013)
Cooperating with others	Tweets that display or refer to cooperation with other groups	Join @harassmap @EIPR @UprisingOfWomen @fouadawatch @BaheyaYa Masr under @Opantish tweeting/blogging days [link] #endSH #Egypt (OpAntiSH, 22 January 2013)

Other

This category simply covers the very few tweets that did not fit into any of the other categories and which were not directly related to the work of the groups.

Other	Tweets that do not fit into the other categories	A very warm Merry Christmas to our #Coptic brothers and sisters celebrating today. We pray for peace and prosperity for all! #CopticChristmas (TBG, 7 January 2013)

Tweets

This category simply distinguishes between tweets written by the groups themselves and retweets published by the groups.

Own tweet	Tweets written by the groups themselves	Brutal Sexual Assaults in Vicinity of Tahrir Square & an Unprecedentedly Shameful Reaction from Egyptian Authorities {link} (Nazra, 3 July 2013)
Retweet	Tweets written by others and retweeted by the groups	As soon as the revolutionary fervour was over in #Egypt,same #gender roles were reinstated. Old practices proved to be very hard to change (retweet by TBG, 11 May 2013)

APPENDIX III

TIMELINE OF THE EGYPTIAN CASE

In the following, I will provide a timeline of the Egyptian case, including the main events that took place during the time frame set for this investigation. However, this does not include *all* events that took place, in the sense that not all offline activities of each group are included, but rather the most important and visible ones. Moreover, some events that took place before the time frame will be included, to make it easier to grasp the development of the issue and the groups working on it, within the Egyptian context.

25 May 2005: On what came to be known as Black Wednesday, the attack on female demonstrators protesting against the referendum on the constitution took place. The Association of Egyptian Mothers called for a day of mourning as a response to the attacks, asking all women to wear black on 1 June.

October 2005: The ECWR launches its campaign 'Making Our Streets Safer . . . for Everyone'.

24/25 October 2006: The 'Id al-Fitr scandal – mob sexual harassment of women in downtown Cairo.

9 November 2006: Demonstration is held in front of the journalists' syndicate in protest against the mass sexual harassment in downtown Cairo.

2007: Nazra is founded.

October 2008: Legal precedent is set as the first case of sexual harassment is taken to court in Egypt. The defendant was sentenced to three years in prison and a fine of $970.[1]

16 December 2010: HarassMap launches its website, receiving international media attention even before the site is up and running.[2]

25 December 2010: HarassMap holds its first community outreach day, discussing the issue of sexual harassment with the inhabitants of the neighbourhood they visited.

21 January 2011: HarassMap's planned 'cycling march against harassment' is cancelled due to unforeseen circumstances.[3]

25 January 2011: Egypt's police day and the beginning of the 2011 revolution.

11 February 2011: President Husni Mubarak steps down. CBS reporter Lara Logan is assaulted by a mob and raped in Tahrir Square.

March 2011: The ruling SCAF regime conducts so-called virginity tests on female detainees.

8 March 2011: 'The million-woman march' in Tahrir on International Women's Day. The demand is for equal opportunities, regardless of class, gender or religion. Organised by a number of activists, with various groups taking part, including HarassMap.[4] However, only a few hundred protesters turned out, and they were met by opponents shouting against them.[5] There were also reports of 'thugs' harassing women.[6]

20 March 2011: 'First Annual Anti-Street Harassment Day' organised internationally by the American NGO Stop Street Harassment. HarassMap joins online, and through a community outreach day in Cairo.

20 June 2011: 'A day of blogging and tweeting against sexual harassment and gendered violence', organised by activists, including a HarassMap team member and a well-known leftist activist.[7] HarassMap also joined and compiled all blog posts, totalling more than 150. The official hashtag used was #endSH, which, according to *Egypt Independent*, generated more than 12,000 tweets.[8] Al-Jazeera also had a live segment on the campaign on their programme *The Stream*. It was followed the next day by a meeting held by Nazra and Harassmap, to further discuss the issue offline.

27 August 2011: Meeting held in Zamalek between various activists and groups to plan campaign during ʿId al-Fitr from 31 August until 2 September. It is agreed that a campaign should be launched asking people to take pictures and video of harassment and harassers, so that this could be published online. People are also asked to tweet and blog about the issue. In addition, HarassMap volunteers would distribute flyers on the issue.[9]

November 2011: Muhammad Mahmud clashes, in which assaults on female protesters are reported.

17 December 2011: The 'blue bra girl' incident, referred to as '*sitt al-banāt*' (a reference to the beloved singer Umm Kulthum) in Arabic, in which Central security forces personnel attacked a female protester. The incident sparked outrage and a new million-woman march was held. The SCAF expressed their 'great regret' to the women of Egypt in light of what had happened.[10]

25 January 2012: First anniversary of the revolution, with attacks on female protesters reported during demonstrations in Tahrir Square.

2 June 2012: Female protesters are attacked and assaulted and in one case raped in a demonstration protesting against the sentencing of former president Husni Mubarak.

8 June 2012: Demonstration against the attacks on female protesters that took place six days earlier. This demonstration was also attacked and female protesters were assaulted.

13 June 2012: A further day of blogging and tweeting against harassment, as a follow-up to the previous year's campaign. Does not seem to have been equally successful.

22 June 2012: First event to safeguard female protesters in Tahrir, called 'Securing the Square'.

24 June 2012: Muhammad Mursi is declared the winner of Egypt's presidential elections.

1 July 2012: Imprint movement is founded, among other things as a reaction to the attacks which happened at the beginning of June.

August 2012: Imprint movement starts its patrols on the metro, with the aim of keeping men out of the cars reserved for women. The campaign is undertaken in cooperation with the Metro Company, a private security firm, as well as the police. The campaign is timed to coincide with the celebration of ʿId al-Fitr.[11] Imprint holds metro campaigns regularly throughout the autumn of 2012. HarassMap encourages volunteers to distribute flyers during the holidays.[12] *Egypt Independent* reports many cases of harassment during the holidays.[13]

21 August 2012: The group Didd al-Taharrush (Anti-Harassment) is formed.

September 2012: A 16-year-old girl is allegedly killed by her harasser after she spits in his face.[14]

20 October 2012: I Saw Harassment is founded.

22 October 2012: Before the holidays, the cabinet announces plans to combat sexual harassment. These plans include introducing new laws, as well as monitoring downtown Cairo through surveillance cameras.[15] However, as far as I have been able to document, these plans were never implemented.

25 October 2012: The eve of ʿId al-Adha 2012. During the holidays, 735 cases of sexual harassment are reported to the police, prompting the president to acknowledge the problem and the need to fight it.[16] I Saw Harassment launched a campaign to monitor and intervene in situations in downtown Cairo, operating a hot line from their situation room. The campaign gained wide media attention. The Imprint movement, together with Anti-Harassment, launched their own campaign to keep the Tala'at Harb square in downtown Cairo a harassment-free zone, which also gained wide media attention.

November and December 2012: Massive demonstrations in Cairo, marking the first anniversary of the Muhammad Mahmud clashes, and then against the president's controversial constitutional declaration. During the demonstrations, numerous female protesters are attacked and assaulted and, in some cases, raped. This provokes a massive response from activists.

12 November 2012: A man is sentenced to two years in prison and a $330 fine on charges of sexual harassment, in a case brought by the El-Nadeem Center.[17]

25 November 2012: The group Intifadat al-Mar'a fi al-'Alim al-'Arabi (the Uprising of Women in the Arab World) launches the campaign 'Tell Your Story', in which women are encouraged to tell their stories of sexual harassment and inequality, which will then be published online. The campaign lasts for two weeks and is spread actively online by many of the groups studied here.

27 November 2012: Tahrir Bodyguard is launched.

30 November 2012: OpAntiSH is launched.

24–25 January 2013: 'Two days of blogging and tweeting for the sake of Dignity 23rd and 24th of January' organised by OpAntiSH. A number of groups are listed as participants, including Nazra, HarassMap, I Saw Harassment and Anti-Harassment.[18] The official hashtag used is #EndSH, but many start using #مصر_من_غير_تحرش (Egypt Without Harassment) as well, which is soon acknowledged by the organisers. Limited participation, Topsy lists 1,250 tweets about #endSH and 706 about #مصر_من_غير_تحرش over the seven days prior to 26 January.

25 January 2013: The second anniversary of the revolution, marked by large protests in Tahrir Square. OpAntiSH and I Saw Harassment documented 24 cases of assaults on female protesters, some including rape and two including the use of bladed weapons.

February 2013: Tahrir Bodyguard starts to offer free self-defence classes for women.

6 February 2013: Demonstration under the heading 'The Street Is Ours – No to Harassment and Sexual Assault', organised by I Saw Harassment but joined by a number of groups, including Nazra, OpAntiSH and EIPR. The demonstration is also supported by a number of political parties.[19] According to the BBC, 'hundreds' of protesters took part.[20]

11 February 2013: The infamous debate in the upper house of Egypt's Parliament on the issue of sexual harassment, in which several MPs blame women themselves for the problem. Naturally, this sparks outrage among activist groups and individuals.

12 February 2013: The 'Global Protest Against Sexual Terrorism Practiced on Egyptian Female Protestors', organised by the Uprising of Women in the Arab World. A number of groups take part, including HarassMap, OpAntiSH, I Saw Harassment and Anti-Harassment.[21] Protests took place in more than 20 locations worldwide and, not surprisingly, demonstrators in Cairo voiced their opposition to the upper house of Parliament as well.[22]

8 March 2013: International Women's Day march under the title 'Women with the Revolution', supported by a number of groups.[23]

15 March 2013: New online event, with the title 'Let's reply to the excuses! 48 hours of blogging and tweeting against sexual harassment and its excuses 15th to 17th of March 2013'. Organised by HarassMap, in cooperation with the Uprising of Women in the Arab World, Anti-Harassment and OpAntiSH. The hashtag used is #بيتحرش_ليه, which generated 764 tweets between 15 and 19 March, according to Topsy.

15 March 2013: The popular TV show *Al-Barnamig* airs an episode on the subject of sexual harassment, featuring representatives of OpAntiSH and Tahrir Bodyguard. During the show, mentions of @opantish increase sixfold, according to Topsy on 16 March 2013. The groups both report a tremendous interest in volunteering.

30 June 2013: Demonstrations against President Mursi organised by the Tamarrud (Rebellion) initiative begin in Cairo, after the group claims to have gathered 22 million signatures demanding his resignation. During these demonstrations, Nazra documents 101 cases of assault (and, in some cases, rape) on female protesters.

3 July 2013: The Egyptian army, under the leadership of General al-Sisi, removes the elected president from power, suspends the constitution and installs a new government as a transitional regime.

31 July 2013: Tahrir Bodyguard launches the new group – Dignity Without Borders (DWB).

APPENDIX IV

TIMELINE OF THE KUWAITI CASE

As with the Egyptian case, the timeline does not contain *all* events related to the groups studied, but is rather intended to highlight those deemed most important and to provide an easily accessible overview of the development of the campaign.

January 2006: The so-called succession crisis, continuation of the separation between crown prince and prime minister; Nasir al-Muhammad forms his first government.

April–17 July 2006: The Orange Movement's campaign, resulting in five electoral districts. New elections return a parliamentary majority in favour of the proposed reform and al-Muhammad forms his second government.

17 May 2008: Elections for the National Assembly, al-Muhammad forms his fifth government.

16 May 2009: Elections for the National Assembly, al-Muhammad forms his seventh government.

27/28/29 October 2009: The 'Irhal, nastahiqq al-afdal' (We Deserve Better) campaign launched on several blogs.

16 November 2009: First demonstration of the abovementioned campaign.

22 November 2009: Muhammad al-Jasim arrested.

1 December 2009: Blogs shut down for 24 hours in protest of the lack of freedom of expression.

16 December 2009: Vote of no confidence in the prime minister following an interpellation; 35 votes against, 13 in favour of the PM.

11 May 2010: Muhammad al-Jasim is arrested again.

18 May 2010: Demonstration in support of al-Jasim held by the 'We Deserve Better' campaign; he is released on 28 June.

30 June 2010: Khaled Alfadala sentenced to three months in prison, the campaign 'Kulluna Khaled Alfadala' is launched on Twitter, Facebook, YouTube, the campaign site and various blogs. Released on 12 July.

22 August 2010: The campaign 'Iradat al-Shaʿb' (The will of the people) launched on Facebook demanding, among other things, revisions of the constitution and an elected PM.

1 December 2010: The campaign 'Illa al-Dustur' is launched.

8 December 2010: Security services attack the second meeting of Illa al-Dustur at a *dīwāniyya*, injuring several participants and arresting a famous scholar.

25 December 2010: Al-Sur al-Khamis is founded, calling for a demonstration on 28 December to coincide with the interpellation against the PM under the slogan 'Cooperation is Neglect'.

5 January 2011: Vote of no confidence against the PM; 25 in favour of renewing confidence, 22 against.

28 February 2011: The movement Kafi is founded.

6 March 2011: Hamlat Nurid is formed.

7 March 2011: Shabab al-Hurriyya is formed.

8 March 2011: Demonstration against the PM held by several youth movements.

27 May 2011: The 'Friday of Wrath' demonstration against the PM, who responds by claiming that the protesters do not represent the will of the people.

3 June 2011: New demonstration against the PM, entitled 'Friday of Answer', in reference to the PM's statements given above; 1,500 people attend.

12 June 2011: Shabab al-Taghyir wa-l-Tatwir is founded.

25 June 2011: Al-ʿAdala al-Dusturiyya is founded.

30 August 2011: The campaign site 25millionkd.com is launched, as new evidence of corruption on the part of the PM and pro-government MPs surfaces.

10 September 2011: The September 16 coalition is announced, demanding a constitutional emirate.

16 September 2011: Demonstration held by the September 16 coalition, with about 300 protesters taking part.

Throughout the autumn of 2011: Demonstrations against the PM held almost weekly.

19 October 2011: Up to 12,000 take part in a protest against the PM, held by several youth movements.

15 November 2011: Interpellation against the PM; the opposition holds the majority needed to remove him from his post through a vote of no confidence.

16 November 2011: Demonstration against what are perceived to be the PM's attempts to sidestep the vote of no confidence, ending with several protesters entering the Parliament shouting *'al-sha'b yurīd isqāṭ al-ra'īs'* (The people want the downfall of the President here [referring to the Prime Minister]).

28 November 2011: Al-Muhammad hands in his resignation, ending his ninth and last government.

1 December 2011: Former defence minister Jabir al-Mubarak is announced as the new PM. The following day, Parliament is dissolved and new elections called.

2 February 2012: Election, in which the opposition wins 35 of 50 seats in Parliament.

28 February 2012: Hadam is formed, with Kafi and Al-'Adala al-Dusturiyya joining. Somewhat unclear whether or not Shabab al-Taghyir wa-l-Tatwir takes part.

28 March 2012: The PM is questioned in an open session, for the first time in Kuwaiti history.

26 April 2012: Large debate on Twitter using the hashtag #ليش_منتخبة (Why elected [government]); many other Twitter debates follow.

18 June 2012: The emir suspends Parliament for one month.

20 June 2012: The constitutional court declares the dissolution of the 2009 Parliament unconstitutional and thus reinstates it and makes the 2012 Parliament redundant.

26 June 2012: Demonstration against the verdict of the constitutional court, with up to 5,000 protesters taking part.

15 July 2012: Statement by the 'majority bloc' demanding a constitutional emirate divides the opposition.

15 August 2012: The new cabinet asks the constitutional court to review the 2006 changes to the electoral law.

27 August 2012: As many as 2,000 protesters take part in a demonstration against any changes to the electoral law and in favour of a constitutional emirate. Several demonstrations are held in the weeks that follow.

13 September 2012: A new initiative, called 'Hiwarat al-Taghyir' (Dialogues for Change), is launched, holding discussions on 'Sahat al-Irada' twice a week. On 9 October, it launches its own application for Android and iOS.

25 September 2012: The constitutional court declares the 2006 reform to be constitutional.

7 October 2012: The emir dissolves the 2009 Parliament.

15 October 2012: Demonstration under the slogan *'Kāfī ʿAbathan'* (Enough Interference), drawing up to 5,000 protesters. Al-Barrak gives his famous *'lan nasmaḥu laka'* (We will not allow you [referring to the Emir]) speech, for which he is later prosecuted. The police attack the demonstration, injuring and arresting several, including the son of former speaker of Parliament, Ahmad al-Saʿdun.

19 October 2012: The opposition states that it will boycott the upcoming elections if any changes are made to the electoral law.

20 October 2012: The cabinet approves an emergency decree released by the emir, reducing the number of votes each person has from four to one.

21 October 2012: The first Karamt Watan demonstration, which draws by far the largest crowd in Kuwaiti history, with up to 150,000 people taking part. The police attack the demonstration, injuring several and arresting a number of prominent activists, including Khaled Alfadala. Throughout the autumn, several demonstrations are held in support of detained activists.

4 November 2012: The second Karamt Watan demonstration, with the location changed at the last minute in order to avoid the police, who nevertheless attack and disperse the march. Up to 8,000 taking part; several people are injured or arrested. Serious efforts are made by the regime to identify those behind the marches.

5 November 2012: The popular committee for boycott of the elections is launched.

11 November 2012: Demonstration under the slogan 'Iradat al-Umma', on the 50th anniversary of the Kuwaiti constitution. Many of the up to 50,000 participants are reported to be wearing orange.

30 November 2012: The third Karamat Watan demonstration, with up to 7,500 protesters taking part. The demonstration is allowed to proceed peacefully.

1 December 2012: The election is held, with the opposition boycotting. According to their estimate, turnout was at 28 per cent, whereas official sources claim 43 per cent. Naturally, the new assembly is pro-government.

8 December 2012: The fourth Karamat Watan march attracts as many as 4,500 participants. The demonstration is allowed to proceed peacefully.

December 2012: Several smaller demonstrations against the election are held in the outlying tribal districts.

6 January 2013: The fifth Karamat Watan march, with no more than 400 protesters taking part. Again, the venue is changed at the last minute due to heavy police presence, but security forces nonetheless attack the march, injuring and arresting several demonstrators. Before the march, the organisers ask people to present their suggestions as to how it should be held using the hashtag #اقتراحات_كرامة_وطن5 (suggestions for Karamat Watan 5), though participation is limited.

13 January 2013: The sixth Karamat Watan march is held outside the city centre, with up to 1,000 participants; they are allowed to proceed with the demonstration.

22 January 2013: The seventh Karamat Watan march is held outside the city centre, with few participants. Some demonstrators reportedly throw fireworks at the police, who respond with tear gas.

3 March 2013: The opposition alliance is launched, with Hadam and other youth movements taking part.

NOTES

A Note on Transliteration and Translation

1. This guide is available at: http://ijmes.chass.ncsu.edu/IJMES_Translation_and_Transliteration_Guide.htm. See also the *IJMES* transliteration chart: http://ijmes.chass.ncsu.edu/IJMES_Translation_and_Transliteration_Guide.htm. Accessed: 20 November 2015.
2. The Oxford Dictionaries are used to establish whether or not a word can be said to have been incorporated into English.

Chapter 1 Introduction

1. Text on T-shirt sold at Cairo's Khan el-Khalili market following the 2011 ousting of President Mubarak.
2. See, for instance, *Time* magazine, 24 January 2011, available at http://content.time.com/time/world/article/0,8599,2044142,00.html (accessed 5 April 2016).
3. It might be problematic to apply the term 'revolution' to the events in Egypt in January and February 2011, as it seems more and more unlikely that a regime change actually took place. I do, however, use the term here for the simple reason that these events are usually referred to as 'the Egyptian Revolution of 2011'. Those events and their effects are not, in themselves, the subject of this investigation and my use of the term is not intended to imply any judgement regarding their nature.
4. 'Google+ and how it could help with political activism online', on http://www.tarekshalaby.com, 30 July 2011, available at http://tarekshalaby.com/2011/07/google-and-how-it-could-help-with-political-activism-online/ (accessed 5 April 2016).
5. The number of people killed during the revolution has been contested and is hard to establish definitively. This number is based on an article in *Egypt*

Independent, 4 April 2011, '840 killed in Egypt's revolution, health ministry official says', available at http://www.egyptindependent.com/news/840-killed-egypts-revolution-health-ministry-official-says (accessed 5 April 2016).

6. Twitter, 'About, company', available at https://about.twitter.com/company (accessed 5 April 2016).
7. Facebook, 'Company info', available at http://newsroom.fb.com/company-info/ (accessed 5 April 2016).
8. YouTube, 'Statistikk', available at https://www.youtube.com/yt/press/no/statistics.html (accessed 5 April 2016).
9. All figures are from the sources given above.
10. All numbers pertaining to rates of internet penetration should be used with caution, as this is difficult to assess accurately. Nevertheless, the figure provides an illustration of the current situation. The figure is retrieved from Internet World Statistics, 'Internet Usage Statistics, the Internet Big Picture, World Internet Users and Population Stats', available at http://www.internetworldstats.com/stats.htm (last accessed 5 April 2016).
11. Shani Orgad, 'How can researchers make sense of the issues involved in collecting and interpreting online and offline data', in A. N. Markham and N. K. Baym (eds), *Internet Inquiry Conversations About Method* (Thousand Oaks, 2008), p. 37.
12. Mark Lynch, 'After Egypt: The limits and promise of online challenges to the authoritarian Arab state', *Perspectives on Politics* 9/02 (2011), p. 303.
13. Anette N. Markham and Nancy K. Baym (eds), *Internet Inquiry: Conversations About Method* (Thousand Oaks, 2008).
14. Deborah L. Wheeler, *The Internet in the Middle East – Global Expectations and Local Imaginations in Kuwait* (New York, 2006), p. 49.
15. Ibid.
16. Ibid., pp. 131–62.
17. Albrecht Hofheinz, 'The internet in the Arab world: Playground for political liberalization', *International Politics and Society* 3 (2005), p. 90.
18. Pew, *Social Networking Popular Across the Globe* (2012), available at http://www.pewglobal.org/2012/12/12/social-networking-popular-across-globe/?beta=true&utm_expid=53098246-2.Lly4CFSVQG2lphsg-KopIg.1&utm_referrer=https%3A%2F%2Fwww.google.no%2F (accessed 5 April 2016).
19. Ibid.
20. Mohamed Zayani, *Networked Publics and Digital Contention – The Politics of Everyday Life in Tunisia* (New York, 2015).
21. Peter Dahlgren and Tobias Olsson, 'From public sphere to civic culture: Young citizens' internet use', in R. Butsch (ed.), *Media and Public Spheres* (New York, 2007).
22. Ibid., p. 204.
23. Bruce Etling, John Kelly, Robert Faris and John Palfrey, 'Mapping the Arabic Blogosphere: Politics and Dissent Online', *New Media & Society* 12/8 (2010), pp. 1225–43.

24. Ibid., p. 1231.
25. Ibid., p. 1240.
26. Ibid., p. 1232.
27. C. Radsch, 'Core to commonplace: The evolution of Egypt's blogosphere', *Arab Media & Society* 6 (2008), available at http://www.arabmediasociety.com/UserFiles/AMS6%20Courtney%20Radsch.pdf (accessed 5 April 2016).
28. Ibid.
29. See: Rasha A. Abdulla, 'The revolution will be tweeted', *Cairo Review of Global Affairs* 3 (2011), pp. 41–9; Rania Al Malky, 'Blogging for reform: The case of Egypt' *Arab Media & Society* 1 (2007); Tom Isherwood, 'A new direction or more of the same? Political blogging in Egypt', *Arab Media & Society* 6 (2008), pp. 1–17; Johanne Kuebler, 'Overcoming the digital divide: The internet and political mobilization in Egypt and Tunisia', *CyberOrient* 5/1 (2011), available at http://www.cyberorient.net/article.do?articleId=6212 (accessed 4 April 2016); Merlyna Lim, 'Clicks, cabs, and coffee houses: Social media and oppositional movements in Egypt, 2004–2011', *Journal of Communication* 62/2 (2012), pp. 231–48.
30. Aziz Douai, 'Offline politics in the Arab blogosphere: Trends and prospects in Morocco', in A. Russell and N. Echchaibi (eds), *International Blogging: Identity, Politics, and Networked Publics* (New York, 2009), p. 133.
31. Tim Eaton, 'Internet activism and the Egyptian uprisings: Transforming online dissent into the offline world', *Westminister Papers in Communication and Culture* 9/2 (2013), p. 6.
32. Armando Salvatore, 'Before (and after) the "Arab spring": From connectedness to mobilization in the public sphere', *Oriente Moderno* 91/1 (2011), pp. 8–11.
33. Philip N. Howard and Muzammil M. Hussain, *Democracy's Fourth Wave?: Digital Media and the Arab Spring* (Oxford, 2013), p. 118.
34. Halim Rane and Sumra Salem, 'Social media, social movements and the diffusion of ideas in the Arab uprisings', *Journal of International Communication* 18/1 (2012), pp. 97–111.
35. Nahed Eltantawy and Julie B. Wiest, 'Social media in the Egyptian revolution: Reconsidering resource mobilization theory', *International Journal of Communication* 5 (2011), pp. 1207–24.
36. Sahar Khamis and Katherine Vaughn, 'Cyberactivism in the Egyptian revolution: How civic engagement and citizen journalism tilted the balance', *Arab Media and Society* 13/3 (2011), pp. 1–2.
37. Ibid., pp. 2, 25.
38. Zeynep Tufekci and Christopher Wilson, 'Social media and the decision to participate in political protest: Observations from Tahrir Square', *Journal of Communication* 62/2 (2012), pp. 363–79.
39. Etling et al., 'Mapping the Arabic Blogosphere'; Hofheinz, 'The Internet in the Arab world'.
40. Christopher Wilson and Alexandra Dunn, 'Digital media in the Egyptian revolution: Descriptive analysis from the Tahrir data set', *International Journal of Communication* 5 (2011), pp. 1248–72.

41. Ibid., pp. 1269–70.
42. Ibid.
43. David Faris, *Dissent and Revolution in a Digital Age: Social Media, Blogging and Activism in Egypt* (New York, 2013).
44. Eaton, 'Internet activism and the Egyptian uprisings', p. 5.
45. 'We are all Khalid Said' is a Facebook group started to commemorate a young Egyptian killed by the Alexandrian police, which is seen as perhaps the most important site in terms of mobilisation for the 25 January 2011 protests. The site exists in an Arabic and an English version, with the former being by far the most popular site in terms of followers.
46. Eaton, 'Internet activism and the Egyptian uprisings', p. 20.
47. Mohamed Ben Moussa, 'From Arab street to social movements: Re-theorizing collective action and the role of social media in the Arab Spring', *Westminister Papers in Communication and Culture* 9/2 (2013), pp. 47–71.
48. Rane and Salem, 'Social media, social movements'.
49. Eltantawy and Wiest, 'Social media in the Egyptian revolution'.
50. Dahlgren and Olsson, 'From public sphere to civic culture'; Dale F. Eickelman and Jon W. Anderson, 'Redefining Muslim publics', in D. F. Eickelman and J. W. Anderson (eds), *New Media in the Muslim World: The Emerging Public Sphere* (Bloomington, 2003); Jon Nordenson, *We Want Five! – Kuwait, the Internet, and the Public Sphere* (Saarbrücken, 2010); Carlos Ruiz, David Domingo, Josep Luis Mico, Javier Diaz-Noci, Pere Masip and Koldo Meso, 'Public Sphere 2.0? The democratic qualities of citizen debates in online newspapers', *The International Journal of Press/Politics* 16/4 (2011), pp. 463–87.
51. Yochai Benkler, *The Wealth of Networks: How Social Production Transforms Markets and Freedom* (New Haven and London, 2006); Peter Dahlgren, *Television and the Public Sphere: Citizenship, Democracy and the Media* (London, 1995); Jodi Dean, 'Why the net is not a public sphere', *Constellations* 10/1 (2003), pp. 95–112; Hallvard Moe, 'Everyone a pamphleteer? Reconsidering comparisons of mediated public participation in the print age and the digital era', *Media, Culture & Society* 32/4 (2010), pp. 691–700.
52. Richard Butsch, 'Introduction: How are media public spheres', in R. Butsch (ed.), *Media and Public Spheres* (New York, 2007), p. 3.
53. Zizi Papacharissi, 'The Virtual Sphere 2.0: The internet, the public sphere, and beyond', in A. P. N. H. Chadwick (ed.), *Routledge Handbook of Internet Politics*, Kindle edn (London and New York, 2009), p. 243.
54. Albrecht Hofheinz, 'Nextopia? Beyond Revolution 2.0', *International Journal of Communication* 5 (2011), p. 1422.
55. Lynch, 'After Egypt', p. 307.
56. Ibid.
57. Paolo Gerbaudo, 'The "kill switch" as "suicide switch": Mobilizing side effects of Mubarak's communication blackout', *Westminister Papers in Communication and Culture* 9/2 (2013), p. 30.

58. Ben Moussa, 'From Arab street to social movements', p. 62.
59. Nick Couldry, Sonia Livingstone and Tim Markham, 'Connection or disconnection? Tracking the mediated public sphere in everyday life', in R. Butsh (ed.), *Media and Public Spheres* (New York, 2007), p. 28.
60. Al Malky, 'Blogging for reform'; Rabab El-Mahdi, 'Enough! Egypt's quest for democracy', *Comparative Political Studies* 42/8 (2009), pp. 1011–39; Faris, *Dissent and revolution*; Isherwood, 'A new direction or more of the same?'; Lim, 'Clicks, cabs, and coffee houses'.
61. Eaton, 'Internet activism and the Egyptian uprisings'; Eltantawy and Wiest, 'Social media in the Egyptian revolution'; Gerbaudo, 'The "kill switch"'; Naila Hamdy and Ehab H. Gomaa, 'Framing the Egyptian uprising in Arabic language newspapers and social media', *Journal of Communication* 62/2 (2012), pp. 195–211; Khamis and Vaughn, 'Cyberactivism in the Egyptian revolution'; Tufekci and Wilson, 'Social media and the decision to participate'; Wilson and Dunn, 'Digital media in the Egyptian revolution'.
62. Robert E. Stake, 'Qualitative case studies', in N. K. Denzin and Y. S. Lincoln (eds), *The Sage Handbook of Qualitative Research*, 3rd edn (London and California, 2005), p. 444.
63. Zayani, *Networked Publics*, p. 7.
64. Stake, 'Qualitative case studies', p. 451.
65. J. John Gerring, 'Case selection for case-study analysis: Qualitative and quantitative techniques', in J. M. Box-Steffensmeier, H. E. Brady and D. Collier (eds), *Oxford Handbook of Political Methodology* (Oxford, 2008), p. 645.
66. This is a truth with some modifications. Online content can always be copied by others, downloaded, published on other platforms, and so on. You can delete something from your own site, but that doesn't mean that it is removed from the internet. However, it could also mean just that, especially if it is something that few people take an interest in. Thus, even though it is difficult to delete something completely, the problem is very relevant in studies like this one.
67. Mark Lynch, 'Blogging the new Arab public', *Arab Media & Society* 1/1 (2007), available at http://www.arabmediasociety.com/?article=10 (accessed 4 April 2016).
68. Eaton, 'Internet activism and the Egyptian uprisings', p. 20.
69. Taylor Boas and Shanthi Kalathil, *Open Networks, Closed Regimes: The Impact of the Internet on Authoritarian Rule* (Washington, DC, 2003), p. 2.
70. Zayani, *Networked Publics*, p. 4.
71. United Nations Entity for Gender Equality and the Empowerment of Women (UN Women), The National Council for Women (NCW), *Study on Ways and Methods to Eliminate Sexual Harassment in Egypt* (2013), available at http://web.law.columbia.edu/sites/default/files/microsites/gender-sexuality/un_womensexual-harassment-study-egypt-final-en.pdf (accessed 5 April 2016), p. 6.
72. Ibid.

73. *BBC*, 3 September 2012, 'Egypt's sexual harassment of women "epidemic"', available at http://www.bbc.com/news/world-middle-east-19440656 (accessed 5 April 2016).
74. See, for instance, *MadaMasr*, 7 July 2014, 'Sexual assault and the state: A history of violence', available at http://www.madamasr.com/sections/politics/sexual-assault-and-state-history-violence (accessed 5 April 2016).
75. This point was reiterated in all the interviews conducted in Cairo.
76. *Egypt Independent*, 11 February 2013, 'Shura Council committee says female protesters should take responsibility, if harassed', available at http://www.egyptindependent.com/news/shura-council-committee-says-female-protesters-should-take-responsibility-if-harassed (accessed 5 April 2016).
77. Paul Salem, 'Kuwait: Politics in a participatory emirate', in M. Ottaway and J. Choucair-Vizoso (eds), *Beyond the Facade – Political Reform in the Arab World* (Washington, DC, 2008), p. 211.
78. Nordenson, *We Want Five*.
79. Kjetil Selvik, Jon Nordenson and Tewodros A. Kebede, 'Print media liberalization and electoral coverage bias in Kuwait', *The Middle East Journal* 69/2 (2015), pp. 255–76.
80. Mary Ann Tétreault, *Stories of Democracy: Politics and Society in Contemporary Kuwait* (New York, 2000), p. 60.
81. Michael Herb, 'A nation of bureaucrats: Political participation and economic diversification in Kuwait and the United Arab Emirates', *International Journal of Middle East Studies* 41/03 (2009), p. 380.
82. Ibid.
83. Nordenson, *We Want Five*.
84. *BBC*, 28 November 2011, 'Kuwait's prime minister resigns after protests', available at http://www.bbc.com/news/world-middle-east-15931526 (accessed 5 April 2016).
85. Mary Ann Tétreault, 'Looking for revolution in Kuwait', *Middle East Report Online* (2012), available at http://www.merip.org/mero/mero110112 (accessed 5 April 2016).
86. Stake, 'Qualitative case studies'; Alexander L. George and Andrew Bennett, *Case Studies and Theory Development in the Social Sciences* (Cambridge and London, 2005).

Chapter 2 How Should We Understand Online Activism?

1. Donatella Della Porta and Mario Diani, *Social Movements: An Introduction* (Malden and Oxford, 2006), p. 5.
2. Ibid., pp. 5–19.
3. Mohamed Ben Moussa, 'From Arab street to social movements: Re-theorizing collective action and the role of social media in the Arab Spring', *Westminister Papers in Communication and Culture* 9/2 (2013), pp. 47–71.

4. Ibid., p. 48.
5. Ibid., p. 51.
6. See, for instance: Aziz Douai, 'Offline politics in the Arab blogosphere: Trends and prospects in Morocco', in A. Russell and N. Echchaibi (eds), *International Blogging: Identity, Politics, and Networked Publics* (New York, 2009); Dina Matar, 'Heya TV: A feminist counterpublic for Arab women?', *Comparative Studies of South Asia, Africa and the Middle East* 27/3 (2007), pp. 513–24; Jon Nordenson, *We Want Five! – Kuwait, the Internet, and the Public Sphere* (Saarbrücken, 2010).
7. Samuel P. Huntington, 'Will more countries become democratic?', *Political Science Quarterly* 99/2 (1984), pp. 193–218; Samuel P. Huntington, 'Democracy's third wave', *Journal of Democracy* 2/2 (1991), pp. 12–34.
8. Dale F. Eickelman and Jon W. Anderson, 'Redefining Muslim publics', in D. F. Eickelman and J. W. Anderson (eds), *New Media in the Muslim world: The Emerging Public Sphere* (Bloomington, 2003); Eugenia Siapera, 'Theorizing the Muslim blogosphere: Blogs, rationality, publicness, and individuality', in A. Russell and N. Echchaibi (eds), *International Blogging: Identity, politics, and Networked Publics* (New York, 2009).
9. Della Porta and Diani, *Social Movements*, p. 228.
10. Ibid., p. 232.
11. Ibid., pp. 234–9.
12. Ibid.
13. Paolo Gerbaudo, 'The "kill switch" as "suicide switch": Mobilizing side effects of Mubarak's communication blackout', *Westminister Papers in Communication and Culture* 9/2 (2013), pp. 25–47.
14. Ibid.
15. Michael Warner, 'Publics and counterpublics', *Public Culture* 14/1 (2002), p. 89.
16. Nahed Eltantawy and Julie B. Wiest, 'Social media in the Egyptian revolution: Reconsidering resource mobilization theory', *International Journal of Communication* 5 (2011), pp. 1207–24.
17. Halim Rane and Sumra Salem, 'Social media, social movements and the diffusion of ideas in the Arab uprisings', *Journal of International Communication* 18/1 (2012), pp. 97–111.
18. Naila Hamdy and Ehab H. Gomaa, 'Framing the Egyptian uprising in Arabic language newspapers and social media', *Journal of Communication* 62/2 (2012), pp. 195–211.
19. Jürgen Habermas, Sara Lennox and Frank Lennox, 'The public sphere: An encyclopedia article (1964)', *New German Critique* 3 (1974), p. 49.
20. Jürgen Habermas, *The structural Transformation of the Public Sphere: An Inquiry into a Category of Bourgeois Society*, 12th edn (Cambridge, 1989).
21. Tim O'Reilly, 'What is Web 2.0: Design patterns and business models for the next generation of software', *Communications & Strategies* 1 (2007), pp. 17–37.
22. Ibid.
23. Lev Manovich, 'The practice of everyday (media) life: From mass consumption to mass cultural production?', *Critical Inquiry* 35/2 (2009), p. 320.

24. Max Horkheimer and Theodor W. Adorno, *Kulturindustri: opplysning som massebedrag*, A. Sundland, transl. 2nd edn (Oslo, 1991), pp. 7, 58.
25. Habermas, *The Structural Transformation*; Horkheimer and Adorno, *Kulturindustri*.
26. Peter Dahlgren, 'The internet, public spheres, and political communication: Dispersion and deliberation', *Political Communication* 22/2 (2005), pp. 147–62; Eickelman and Anderson, 'Redefining Muslim publics'; Bruce Etling, John Kelly, Robert Faris and John Palfrey, 'Mapping the Arabic Blogosphere: Politics and Dissent Online', *New Media & Society* 12/8 (2010), pp. 1225–43.
27. Aaron Barlow, *Blogging America: The New Public Sphere* (Westport, CT, London, 2008).
28. Hoda Elsadda, 'Arab women bloggers: The emergence of literary counter-publics', *Middle East Journal of Culture and Communication* 3/3 (2010), pp. 312–32; Nordenson, *We Want Five.*
29. The figure is retrieved from International Telecommunications Union (ITU), the United Nations specialised agency for information and communication technologies. See 'ICTs, the 2013 ICT Facts and Figures', available at http://www.itu.int/en/ITU-D/Statistics/Documents/facts/ICTFactsFigures2013-e.pdf (accessed 6 April 2016).
30. Data from UN Data, 'Adult literacy rate', available at http://data.un.org/Data.aspx?d=SOWC&f=inID%3A74 (accessed 6 April 2016).
31. Yochai Benkler, *The Wealth of Networks: How Social Production Transforms Markets and Freedom* (New Haven and London, 2006), p. 10.
32. O'Reilly, 'What is Web 2.0', pp. 26–7.
33. *Associated Press*, 5 January 2014, 'Selling social media clicks becomes big business', available on *Yahoo News*: http://news.yahoo.com/selling-social-media-clicks-becomes-big-business-151602524.html (accessed 6 April 2016).
34. See, for instance, *NRK*, 1 September 2013, 'Forbrukerombudet lei av Facebook-reklame', available at http://www.nrk.no/kultur/ombudet-lei-av-facebook-reklame-1.11205070 (accessed 6 April 2016).
35. For instance, some of the most popular users on Twitter include Miley Cyrus, Justin Bieber and Britney Spears – all famous and popular artists. However, it should be noted that these are all artists known for publishing controversial statements and provocative pictures, so the content they provide cannot be discarded from the equation.
36. See, for instance, recent cases from Kuwait, such as *rt.com*, 11 June 2013, 'Kuwaiti teacher given 11-year sentence for Twitter criticism of government', available at http://rt.com/news/kuwait-twitter-teacher-arrest-499/ (accessed 6 April 2016).
37. *The Atlantic*, 24 January 2011, 'The inside story of how Facebook responded to Tunisian hacks', available at http://www.theatlantic.com/technology/archive/2011/01/the-inside-story-of-how-facebook-responded-to-tunisian-hacks/70044/?single_page=true (accessed 6 April 2016).

38. *USA Today*, 30 March 2011, 'Facebook shuts fan page for inciting "violence against Jews"', available at http://usatoday30.usatoday.com/news/religion/2011-03-30-facebook_Jewish_Israel_30_ST_N.htm (accessed 6 April 2016).
39. Benkler, *The Wealth of Networks*, p. 17.
40. Nancy Fraser, 'Rethinking the public sphere: A contribution to the critique of actually existing democracy', in C. Calhoun (ed.), *Habermas and the Public Sphere* (Cambridge and London, 1992), pp. 117–18.
41. Ibid., pp. 122–3.
42. Ibid., p. 123.
43. Warner, 'Publics and counterpublics', p. 88.
44. Ernesto Laclau and Chantal Mouffe, *Hegemony and Socialist Strategy: Towards a Radical Democratic Politics*, 2nd edn (London and Brooklyn, 2001), p. 185.
45. Dahlgren, 'The internet, public spheres, and political communication', p. 148.
46. Geoff Eley, 'Nations, publics, and political cultures: Placing Habermas in the nineteenth century', in C. Calhoun (ed.), *Habermas and the Public Sphere* (Cambridge and London, 1992), p. 306.
47. Dahlgren, 'The internet, public spheres, and political communication', p. 157.
48. Jürgen Habermas, 'Further reflections on the public sphere', in C. Calhoun (ed.), *Habermas and the Public Sphere* (Cambridge and London, 1992), pp. 425–6.
49. Jürgen Habermas, 'Political communication in media society: Does democracy still enjoy an epistemic dimension? The impact of normative theory on empirical research', *Communication Theory* 16/4 (2006), p. 423.
50. Ibid., pp. 420–2.
51. Ibid., p. 420.
52. Ilan Kapoor, 'Deliberative democracy or agonistic pluralism? The relevance of the Habermas–Mouffe debate for third world politics', *Alternatives* 27/4 (2002), pp. 459–87.
53. Siapera, 'Theorizing the Muslim blogosphere', p. 42.
54. Chantal Mouffe, 'Space, hegemony and radical critique', *Spatial Politics: Essays for Doreen Massey* (2013), p. 27.
55. Ibid., p. 26.
56. John S. Dryzek and Simon Niemeyer, 'Reconciling pluralism and consensus as political ideals', *American Journal of Political Science* 50/3 (2006), p. 637.
57. Chantal Mouffe, 'Deliberative democracy or agonistic pluralism?', *Social Research* 66/3 (1999), p. 748.
58. Ibid., p. 751.
59. Chantal Mouffe, 'Which public sphere for a democratic society?', *Theoria: A Journal of Social and Political Theory* 99 (2002), p. 57.
60. Ibid., p. 56.
61. Ibid., p. 62.
62. Ibid., p. 61.
63. Mouffe, 'Deliberative democracy or agonistic pluralism?', p. 756.
64. Mouffe, 'Which public sphere', p. 59.

65. Kapoor, 'Deliberative democracy or agonistic pluralism', p. 461.
66. The word Shi'a is spelled according to standard English practice rather than in accordance with the IJMES system otherwise used in this book.
67. Peter Dahlgren and Tobias Olsson, 'From public sphere to civic culture: Young citizens' internet use', in R. Butsch (ed.), *Media and Public Spheres* (New York, 2007).
68. Eickelman and Anderson, 'Redefining Muslim publics'; Matar, 'Heya TV'.
69. Peter Ives, *Language and Hegemony in Gramsci* (London, 2004), pp. 78–9.
70. Lila Abu-Lughod, 'Dialects of women's empowerment: The international circuitry of the Arab Human Development Report 2005', *International Journal of Middle East Studies* 41/01 (2009), p. 91.
71. Siapera, 'Theorizing the Muslim blogosphere', p. 32.
72. Kenneth A. Bollen, 'Political democracy: Conceptual and measurement traps', *Studies in Comparative International Development* 25/1 (1990), pp. 13–14.
73. Armando Salvatore, 'Before (and after) the "Arab spring": From connectedness to mobilization in the public sphere', *Oriente Moderno* 91/1 (2011), pp. 5–12.
74. As quoted by Jurkiewicz in *Being a Blogger in Beirut – Production Practices and Modes of Publicness*, which in turn refers to Haugbølle and Salvatore's "call for a panel on the World Congress of Middle Eastern Studies 2010", which I have not been able to obtain.
75. Sarah Jurkiewicz, 'Being a Blogger in Beirut – Production Practices and Modes of Publicness' (PhD dissertation, Oslo, 2012), p. 291.

Chapter 3 How Should We Study Online Activism?

1. Gail Ramsay, 'What kind of Arabic and why? Language in Egyptian blogs', *Orientalia Suecana* 61 (Supplement) (2013), p. 50.
2. As all the Egyptian groups frequently employ their English names, and also write extensively in English, I will use the English names throughout the text. An exception is made for Nazra, which provides no English translation of its name.
3. The name of this group and that of Youth of Change and Development both contain the Arabic genitive construction *iḍāfa*. This is usually rendered in English using 'of', as in Youth *of* Freedom. However, translating the name as 'Youth for Freedom' would also be possible, and perhaps more intuitively comprehensible in English. I have nevertheless chosen to use 'of', as this is in line with the most common practice.
4. None of the Kuwaiti groups used English translations of their names, so I will use the transliterated version of their Arabic names throughout the text.
5. Jon Nordenson, *We Want Five! – Kuwait, the Internet, and the Public Sphere* (Saarbrücken, 2010).
6. As stated in Chapter 1, the time frame for the Egyptian case stretches from 1 June 2012 to 1 August 2013. The time frame for the Kuwaiti case stretches from 27 October 2009 to 3 March 2013. The reasons behind the differences in the time frames were discussed in Chapter 1.

7. With regard to Harakat Shabab al-Hurriyya, one download of its Twitter profile turned out to be corrupted. By the time I discovered this, the group had changed its profile and deleted the old one. Thus, the time period between the last working sample and the new one was no longer accessible, resulting in the loss of about 800 tweets out of a total of nearly 2,000 for the period covered in my study. The same problem occurred with Hadam, which deleted its old account following a heated interpersonal conflict within the movement. In this case, the result was 400 tweets missing from a total of nearly 900 tweets.
8. I am forever grateful to my colleague, Albrecht Hofheinz, for facilitating this cooperation, and no less to Morten Erlandsen for developing the tools in question, as well as his endless patience and continued support in using them.
9. The material was not gathered until April and May 2014, and the high level of activity of some of the groups meant that, by this time, they had published more than 3,200 tweets since the beginning of the time frames set for the investigation. In practice, this meant that I only had complete Twitter samples for all groups from January 2013, as detailed in the section entitled 'Analysis'. This also meant that comments, retweets, and so on, might have been made following the time frames set for the investigation. While unfortunate, it is likely that the number of people commenting on two- or three-year-old posts is limited.
10. The samples are still in my keeping.
11. Ideally, I would also have interviewed others outside the groups on the impact of online and offline activism, the issue itself and other matters. However, I found that this would have been too extensive, and chose to focus on the main material at hand; namely, the online work of the groups. In addition, I make extensive use of secondary sources, such as newspapers and TV clips, which may help to provide such an 'outside' perspective.
12. The sample for this group does not exist, due to a mistake that I made. As the group is still very active on Twitter, it has not been possible to retrieve the sample at a later time, again due to the 3,200-tweet limit. This is, of course, problematic as I had problems with the other sample of the group as well. Still, I believe the group should be included in the study, because it provides additional information on the Kuwaiti opposition youth groups, and it was part of the same general campaign as the other groups studied. However, the reader should bear these reservations in mind when reading the analysis and the findings presented.
13. See for instance Janet B. Johnson and H. T. Reynolds, *Political Science Research Methods* (Washington, DC, 2005); Steven Stemler, 'An overview of content analysis', *Practical Assessment, Research & Evaluation* 7/17 (2001), pp. 1–10, available at http://www.researchgate.net/profile/Steven_Stemler/publication/269037805_An_overview_of_content_analysis/links/547e0aba0cf2de80e7cc402a.pdf (accessed 5 April 2016).
14. Florian Kohlbacher, 'The use of qualitative content analysis in case study research', *Forum Qualitative Sozialforschung/Forum: Qualitative Social Research*

7/1 (2006), available at http://www.qualitative-research.net/index.php/fqs/article/viewArticle/75 (accessed 4 April 2016), p. 24.

15. Eisa Al Nashmi, Johanna Cleary, Juan-Carlos Molleda and Melinda McAdams, 'Internet political discussions in the Arab world: A look at online forums from Kuwait, Saudi Arabia, Egypt and Jordan', *International Communication Gazette* 72/8 (2010), p. 725.
16. Naila Hamdy and Ehab H. Gomaa, 'Framing the Egyptian uprising in Arabic language newspapers and social media', *Journal of Communication* 62/2 (2012), p. 198.
17. An additional problem in this regard lies in the importance of contextualisation for my analysis, which means that any additional coders would have to be familiar with my cases, further complicating the issue.
18. Wilfried Bos and Christian Tarnai, 'Content analysis in empirical social research', *International Journal of Educational Research* 31 (1999), p. 666.
19. Stemler, 'An overview of content analysis', p. 7.
20. A detailed description of each category with examples is given in Appendix 1 "Coding categories".
21. Robert E. Stake, 'Qualitative case studies', in N. K. Denzin and Y. S. Lincoln (eds), *The Sage Handbook of Qualitative Research*, 3rd edn (London and California, 2005), p. 454.
22. Alexander L. George and Andrew Bennett, *Case Studies and Theory Development in the Social Sciences* (Cambridge and London, 2005), p. 207.
23. George and Bennett, *Case Studies and Theory Development*, p. 151.
24. This figure is based on values from Internet World Stats (http://www.internetworldstats.com/) as figures for each country are not available from ITU. While this site is also widely used, the numbers differ slightly from ITU's, again illustrating the difficulty in accurately assessing internet access around the world.
25. One can argue that the name of the group in Arabic should be spelled 'Kullina Khalid Saʿid', as this would be in line with the pronunciation in Egyptian Arabic, as opposed to Modern Standard Arabic (MSA). However, as the name of the group, when written in Arabic, does not reveal whether it is intended to be read in Egyptian Arabic or MSA, I have written it in MSA in the text, while providing the Egyptian pronunciation here.
26. Wael Ghonim, *Revolution 2.0: The Power of the People is Greater than the People in Power: A Memoir* (London, 2012).
27. All data according to Twitter's 'Year in Review 2011', available at https://yearinreview.twitter.com/en/hottopics.html (accessed 6 April 2016).
28. Tim Eaton, 'Internet activism and the Egyptian uprisings: Transforming online dissent into the offline world', *Westminister Papers in Communication and Culture* 9/2 (2013), p. 15.
29. Peter Dahlgren, 'The internet, public spheres, and political communication: Dispersion and deliberation', *Political Communication* 22/2 (2005), p. 150.

Chapter 4 The Egyptian Case: The Context, the Issue, and My Findings

1. The episode is still available on YouTube: https://www.youtube.com/watch?v=oE1msB3Hu7g (accessed 6 April 2016).
2. Eberhard Kienle, *A Grand Delusion: Democracy and Economic Reform in Egypt* (London and New York, 2001).
3. Mustafa K. Al-Sayyid, 'A Civil Society in Egypt?', *The Middle East Journal* 47/2 (1993), pp. 228–42.
4. Maye Kassem, *Egyptian Politics: The Dynamics of Authoritarian Rule* (London and Boulder, 2004), p. 54.
5. Al-Sayyid, 'A civil society in Egypt?'; Eberhard Kienle, 'More than a response to Islamism: The political deliberalization of Egypt in the 1990s', *The Middle East Journal* 52/2 (1998), pp. 219–35.
6. Vickie Langohr, 'Too much civil society, too little politics: Egypt and liberalizing Arab regimes', *Comparative Politics* 36/2 (2004), p. 182.
7. Al-Sayyid, 'A civil society in Egypt?', p. 237.
8. Kassem, *Egyptian Politics*, p. 89.
9. Kienle, 'More than a response to Islamism'; Langohr, 'Too much civil society'.
10. Kienle, 'More than a response to Islamism', p. 229; Langohr, 'Too much civil society', p. 187.
11. *Al-Arabiya*, 31 May 2012, 'Army lifts three decades-old state of emergency in Egypt', available at http://english.alarabiya.net/articles/2012/05/31/217701.html (accessed 6 April 2016).
12. Al-Sayyid, 'A civil society in Egypt?', p. 235.
13. Kassem, *Egyptian politics*, p. 37.
14. Joakim Parslow, 'Egypts kamp om loven', *Babylon nordisk tidsskrift for midtøstenstudier* 11/1 (2013), p. 8.
15. The term *balṭagī* is listed by Hinds and Badawi as meaning 'thug, bully' (Martin Hinds and El-Said Badawi (eds), *A Dictionary of Egyptian Arabic* (Beirut, 1986)). In everyday usage today, it usually denotes thugs and criminals, sometimes referring to individuals hired by the regime to do its dirty work. Thus, when one refers to *balṭagiyya* or *balṭagiyyat an-niẓām* in a political, and especially an activist, context, it is understood to mean bullies used by the regime.
16. Kienle, 'More than a response to Islamism', p. 224.
17. Kassem, *Egyptian Politics*; Eberhard Kienle, *A Grand Delusion: Democracy and Economic Reform in Egypt* (London and New York, 2001).
18. Rex Brynen, Pete W. Moore, Bassel F. Salloukh and Marie-Jöelle Zahar, *Beyond the Arab Spring: Authoritarianism & Democratization in the Arab World* (Boulder and London, 2012), p. 4.
19. Al-Sayyid, 'A civil society in Egypt?'; Jason Brownlee, 'The decline of pluralism in Mubarak's Egypt', *Journal of Democracy* 13/4 (2002), pp. 6–14; Langohr, 'Too much civil society'.
20. Rabab El-Mahdi, 'Enough! Egypt's quest for democracy', *Comparative Political Studies* 42/8 (2009), p. 1013.

21. Al-Sayyid, 'A civil society in Egypt?', p. 241.
22. Kienle, 'More than a response to Islamism', p. 231.
23. Mustafa K. Al-Sayyid, 'What went wrong with Mubarak's regime?', in D. Tschirgi, W. Kazziha, and S. F. Mcmahon (eds), *Egypt's Tahrir Revolution* (Boulder and London, 2013); Walid Kazziha, 'Egypt under Mubarak: A Family Affair', in D. Tschirgi, W. Kazziha and S. F. Mcmahon (eds), *Egypt's Tahrir Revolution* (Boulder and London, 2013); Courtny Radsch, 'Blogosphere and social media', in Ellen Laipson (ed.), *Seismic Shift: Understanding Change in the Middle East* (Washington, 2011), available at http://papers.ssrn.com/sol3/papers.cfm?abstract_id=2336076 (accessed 5 April 2016).
24. To be precise, the issue at hand was the replacement of Law 32 with Law 153 and, later, Law 84. See: El-Mahdi, 'Enough! Egypt's quest for democracy', p. 1020.
25. Langohr, 'Too much civil society', p. 195.
26. Jean-Pierre Filiu, *The Arab Revolution: Ten Lessons from the Democratic Uprising* (London, 2011), pp. 34, 124.
27. Al Jazeera was first launched in 1996.
28. *Al-Ahram Weekly*, 23–29 June 2005, 'A chronology of dissent'. This article is no longer accessible online, but has been downloaded and saved by the author (last accessed on 26 May 2014).
29. El-Mahdi, 'Enough! Egypt's quest for democracy', p. 1023.
30. *Al-Ahram Weekly*, 23–29 June 2005, 'A chronology of dissent'.
31. Paul Schemm, 'Egypt struggles to control anti-war protests', *Middle East Research and Information Project* (2003), available at http://www.merip.org/mero/mero033103 (accessed 5 April 2016).
32. *Al-Ahram Weekly*, 23–29 June 2005, 'A chronology of dissent'.
33. Yoram Meital, 'The struggle over political order in Egypt: The 2005 elections', *The Middle East Journal* 60/2 (2006), p. 267.
34. Merlyna Lim, 'Clicks, cabs, and coffee houses: Social media and oppositional movements in Egypt, 2004–2011', *Journal of Communication* 62/2 (2012), p. 236.
35. Meital, 'The struggle over political order in Egypt', pp. 267–8.
36. El-Mahdi, 'Enough! Egypt's quest for democracy'; Nadia Ramsis Farah, 'The political economy of Egypt's revolution', in D. Tschirgi, W. Kazziha, and S. F. McMahon (eds), *Egypt's Tahrir Revolution* (Boulder and London, 2013); Kazziha, 'Egypt under Mubarak'.
37. El-Mahdi, 'Enough! Egypt's quest for democracy', p. 1021.
38. Ibid., pp. 1018, 1022.
39. Courtney Radsch, 'Core to commonplace: The evolution of Egypt's blogosphere', *Arab Media & Society* 6 (2008), available at http://www.arabmediasociety.com/UserFiles/AMS6%20Courtney%20Radsch.pdf (accessed 5 April 2016), p. 2.
40. El-Mahdi, 'Enough! Egypt's quest for democracy', p. 1027.

41. In fact, the demonstrations against the US attack on Iraq were the largest demonstrations in Egypt since the Bread Riot of 1977 (El-Mahdi, 'Enough! Egypt's quest for democracy', p. 1025).
42. *New York Times*, 27 February 2005, 'Mubarak pushes Egypt to allow freer elections', available at http://www.nytimes.com/2005/02/27/international/middleeast/27egypt.html?th&_r=0 (accessed 6 April 2016).
43. El-Mahdi, 'Enough! Egypt's quest for democracy'; Meital, 'The struggle over political order in Egypt'.
44. There are, naturally, no official government sources admitting responsibility for the attack. However, both the use of thugs and the attacks on women were known regime tactics. Moreover, all concerned NGOs and groups placed responsibility for the attack on the government. Following the revolution of 2011, these claims have also been published in Egyptian media. See, for instance, the *Egypt Independent*, 25 May 2013, 'This Day in History, 25 May 2005: Mubarak thugs sexually assault journalist Nawal Ali', available at http://www.egyptindependent.com/news/day-history-25-may-2005-mubarak-thugs-sexually-assault-journalist-nawal-ali (accessed 6 April 2016).
45. Meital, 'The struggle over political order in Egypt', pp. 268–9.
46. Rasha A. Abdulla, 'The revolution will be tweeted', *Cairo Review of Global Affairs* 3 (2011), pp. 41–9; Rania Al Malky, 'Blogging for reform: The case of Egypt' *Arab Media & Society* 1 (2007); Tom Isherwood, 'A new direction or more of the same? Political blogging in Egypt', *Arab Media & Society* 6 (2008), pp. 1–17; Lim, 'Clicks, cabs, and coffee houses'; Radsch, 'Core to commonplace'.
47. Isherwood, 'A new direction or more of the same?', p. 4.
48. Radsch, 'Core to commonplace', p. 2.
49. Rasha A. Abdulla, *The Internet in the Arab World: Egypt and Beyond* (New York, 2007); Deborah L. Wheeler, 'Egypt: Building an information society for international development', *Review of African Political Economy* 30/98 (2003), pp. 627–42.
50. The ITU statistics, 'Percentage of individuals using the internet', available at http://www.itu.int/en/ITU-D/Statistics/Pages/stat/default.aspx (accessed 6 April 2016).
51. Lim, 'Clicks, cabs, and coffee houses', p. 237.
52. Ibid. As an interesting case in point, the website of Kifaya, harakamasria.org, was run the activist later to become the popular blogger MaLcoLM X (Isherwood, 'A new direction or more of the same?', p. 4).
53. Lim, 'Clicks, cabs, and coffee houses', p. 236.
54. Ibid.
55. Isherwood, 'A new direction or more of the same?', p. 5.
56. The term 'citizen journalism' is not clearly defined and, as such, might be problematic. Here, however, as it is not the main topic of these investigations, I use it to refer to the dissemination of news and information outside of the

conventional media. For more on the term itself see, for instance, Luke Goode, 'Social news, citizen journalism and democracy', *New Media & Society* 11/8 (2009), pp. 1287–305.

57. Human Rights Watch, 13 January 2007, 'Egypt: Bus driver raped by police faces new risk of torture', available at http://www.hrw.org/news/2007/01/12/egypt-bus-driver-raped-police-faces-new-risk-torture (accessed 6 April 2016).
58. Ibid.
59. Isherwood, 'A new direction or more of the same?', p. 1.
60. Ibid.
61. Abdulla, 'The revolution will be tweeted', p. 43.
62. Al Malky, 'Blogging for reform', p. 2.
63. Ibid., pp. 1–3.
64. David Faris, *Dissent and Revolution in a Digital Age: Social Media, Blogging and Activism in Egypt* (New York, 2013), p. 65.
65. Al Malky, 'Blogging for reform'; Radsch, 'Core to commonplace'.
66. Faris, *Dissent and Revolution*; Mark Lynch, 'Blogging the new Arab public', *Arab Media & Society* 1/1 (2007), available at http://www.arabmediasociety.com/?article=10 (accessed 4 April 2016).
67. Lim, 'Clicks, cabs, and coffee houses', p. 232.
68. Joel Beinin, 'The rise of Egypt's workers' *Carnegie Endowment for International Peace* (2012), available at http://carnegieendowment.org/2012/06/28/rise-of-egypt-s-workers (accessed April 4 2016), p. 1.
69. Ibid., p. 3.
70. Kristian Takvam Kindt, *Unintentional Democrats – Independent Unions in Post-Mubarak Egypt* (Master's) (Oslo, 2013), p. 10.
71. Farah, 'The political economy of Egypt's revolution', p. 54.
72. Youth make up about one-third of the Egyptian population, and youth unemployment stood at 26.3 per cent in 2010, reaching 53.2 per cent among those with secondary education and 39.7 per cent among those with tertiary education. The World Bank, Databank, 'Egypt', available at http://data.worldbank.org/country/egypt-arab-republic (accessed 6 April 2016).
73. Filiu, *The Arab Revolution*; Lim, 'Clicks, cabs, and coffee houses'; Earl Sullivan, 'Youth power and the revolution', in D. Tschirgi, W. Kazziha and S. F. McMahon (eds), *Egypt's Tahrir Revolution* (Boulder and London, 2013).
74. Beinin, 'The Rise of Egypt's Workers', p. 6.
75. Lim, 'Clicks, cabs, and coffee houses', p. 239.
76. Isherwood, 'A new direction or more of the same?'; Mark Lynch, 'Young brothers in cyberspace', *Middle East Report* 37/245 (2007), available at http://www.merip.org/mer/mer245/young-brothers-cyberspace&gt (accessed 4 April 2016).
77. Radsch, 'Core to commonplace'.
78. Ibid.
79. Lynch, 'Young brothers in cyberspace'.
80. Ibid.; Radsch, 'Core to commonplace'.

81. Radsch, 'Core to commonplace', p. 8.
82. Isherwood, 'A new direction or more of the same?', p. 11.
83. Freedom House, 'Egypt', in *Freedom on the Net 2014*, available at https://freedomhouse.org/report/freedom-net/2014/egypt (accessed 6 April 2016).
84. Reporters Without Borders, 2011, 'Egypt', available at http://en.rsf.org/egypt-egypt-11-03-2011,39740.html (accessed 6 April 2016).
85. Lim, 'Clicks, cabs, and coffee houses', p. 241.
86. Wael Ghonim, *Revolution 2.0: The Power of the People is Greater Than the People in Power: A Memoir* (London, 2012), pp. 39–41.
87. Bjørn Olav Utvik, *Islamismen* (Oslo, 2011), pp. 193–4.
88. Kazziha, 'Egypt under Mubarak', p. 34.
89. Ghonim, *Revolution 2.0*, p. 31.
90. The ITU statistics, 'Percentage of individuals using the internet', available at http://www.itu.int/en/ITU-D/Statistics/Pages/stat/default.aspx (accessed 6 April 2016).
91. Ashraf Khalil, *Liberation Square: Inside the Egyptian Revolution and the Rebirth of a Nation* (New York, 2011).
92. See: Brynen et al., *Beyond the Arab Spring*; Filiu, *The Arab Revolution*; Philip N. Howard and Muzammil M. Hussain, *Democracy's Fourth Wave?: Digital Media and the Arab Spring* (Oxford, 2013); Sahar Khamis and Katherine Vaughn, 'Cyberactivism in the Egyptian revolution: How civic engagement and citizen journalism tilted the balance', *Arab Media and Society 13*/3 (2011), pp. 1–37; Dan Tschirgi, Walid Kazziha and Sean F. McMahon (eds), *Egypt's Tahrir Revolution* (Boulder and London, 2013).
93. Abdel-Latif El-Menawy, *Tahrir – The Last 18 Days of Mubarak – An Insider's Account of the Uprising in Egypt* (UK, 2012); Ghonim, *Revolution 2.0*; Khalil, *Liberation Square*; Ahdaf Soueif, *Cairo: Memoir of a City Transformed* (London, 2012).
94. Rasha A. Abdulla, *Mapping Digital Media: Egypt* (2013), available at https://www.opensocietyfoundations.org/sites/default/files/mapping-digital-media-egypt-20130823.pdf (accessed 4 April 2016), p. 2.
95. Paolo Gerbaudo, 'The "kill switch" as "suicide switch": Mobilizing side effects of Mubarak's communication blackout', *Westminister Papers in Communication and Culture* 9/2 (2013), p. 33.
96. Khamis and Vaughn, 'Cyberactivism in the Egyptian revolution'.
97. Nahed Eltantawy and Julie B. Wiest, 'Social media in the Egyptian revolution: Reconsidering resource mobilization theory', *International Journal of Communication* 5 (2011), p. 1218.
98. Lim, 'Clicks, cabs, and coffee houses', p. 244.
99. Faris, *Dissent and Revolution*.
100. Zeynep Tufekci and Christopher Wilson, 'Social media and the decision to participate in political protest: Observations from Tahrir Square', *Journal of Communication* 62/2 (2012), pp. 363–79.

101. Christopher Wilson and Alexandra Dunn, 'Digital media in the Egyptian revolution: Descriptive analysis from the Tahrir data set', *International Journal of Communication* 5 (2011), pp. 1269–70.
102. Internet World Statistics, 'Internet usage statistics for Africa', available at http://www.internetworldstats.com/stats1.htm (accessed 6 April 2016).
103. The ITU statistics, 'Percentage of individuals using the internet', available at http://www.itu.int/en/ITU-D/Statistics/Pages/stat/default.aspx (accessed 6 April 2016).
104. Pew, *Social Networking Popular Across the Globe* (2012), available at http://www.pewglobal.org/2012/12/12/social-networking-popular-across-globe/?beta=true&utm_expid=53098246-2.Lly4CFSVQG2lphsg-KopIg.1&utm_referrer=https%3A%2F%2Fwww.google.no%2F (accessed 5 April 2016), p. 1.
105. Tewodros A. Kedebe, Kristian Takvam Kindt and Jacob Høigilt, *Language Change in Egypt: Social and Cultural Indicators Survey A Tabulation Report* (2013), available at http://www.fafo.no/index.php/nb/zoo-publikasjoner/fafo-rapporter/item/language-change-in-egypt-social-and-cultural-indicators-survey (accessed 4 April 2016), pp. 42–3.
106. Human Rights Watch, 16 January 2012, 'Egypt: Dismantle tools of repression', available at http://www.hrw.org/news/2012/01/16/egypt-dismantle-tools-repression (accessed 6 April 2016).
107. Human Rights Watch, 7 May 2012, 'Egypt: New law keeps military trials of civilians', available at http://www.hrw.org/news/2012/05/07/egypt-new-law-keeps-military-trials-civilians (accessed 6 April 2016).
108. Human Rights Watch, 16 January 2012, 'Egypt: Dismantle tools of repression', available at http://www.hrw.org/news/2012/01/16/egypt-dismantle-tools-repression (accessed 6 April 2016).
109. Freedom House, 'Egypt' in *Freedom in the World 2012*, available at http://freedomhouse.org/report/freedom-world/freedom-world-2012#.U6A3YCgviVo (accessed 6 April 2016).
110. Ibid.
111. Ibid.
112. *Ahram Online*, 27 February 2012, 'Egypt inaugurates toothless upper house', available at http://english.ahram.org.eg/NewsContent/1/0/35506/Egypt/Egypt-inaugurates-toothless-upper-house-.aspx (accessed 6 April 2016).
113. *PBS*, 17 September 2013, 'Timeline: What's happened since Egypt's revolution?', available at http://www.pbs.org/wgbh/pages/frontline/foreign-affairs-defense/egypt-in-crisis/timeline-whats-happened-since-egypts-revolution/ (accessed 6 April 2016).
114. Human Rights Watch, 10 December 2012, 'Egypt: Morsy law invites military trials of civilians', available at http://www.hrw.org/news/2012/12/10/egypt-morsy-law-invites-military-trials-civilians (accessed 6 April 2016).
115. In addition, the decree was accompanied by Law 96, which states that investigation into the killing of protesters should be resumed and establishes a

special court to deal with such events. This court, however, should also deal with certain other offences, such as 'insulting' the authorities. Human Rights Watch, 26 November 2012, 'Egypt: Morsy decree undermines rule of law', available at http://www.hrw.org/news/2012/11/26/egypt-morsy-decree-undermines-rule-law (accessed 6 April 2016).

116. Human Rights Watch, 26 November 2012, 'Egypt: Morsy decree undermines rule of law', available at http://www.hrw.org/news/2012/11/26/egypt-morsy-decree-undermines-rule-law (accessed 6 April 2016).
117. Freedom House, 'Egypt', in *Freedom in the World 2013*, available at https://freedomhouse.org/report/freedom-world/freedom-world-2013#.U6F2HygviVo (accessed 6 April 2016).
118. Reporters Without Borders (RSF), 27 June 2013, 'Mounting freedom of information worries after one year of Morsi', available at http://en.rsf.org/egypt-mounting-freedom-of-information-27-06-2013,44862.html (accessed 6 April 2016).
119. Reporters Without Borders, 12 March 2012, 'Egypt', available at http://en.rsf.org/egypt-egypt-12-03-2012,42049.html (accessed 6 April 2016).
120. Freedom House, 'Egypt', in *Freedom on the Net 2013*, available at https://freedomhouse.org/report/freedom-net/2013/egypt#.VJgk_f8M8KA (accessed 6 April 2016).
121. Human Rights Watch, 30 May 2013, 'Egypt: New draft law an assault on independent groups', available at https://www.hrw.org/news/2013/05/30/egypt-new-draft-law-assault-independent-groups (accessed 6 April 2016).
122. To use the term 'coup' to describe the regime change that occurred during the summer of 2013 has become somewhat controversial. It has been claimed that what took place was, in fact, a second revolution, in which the people were aided by the army. Moreover, critics of the term 'coup' have pointed out that when Mubarak was forced to step down on 11 February 2011, this was also a military coup. However, one fundamental difference is that Mubarak was not elected through free and fair elections. The *Oxford English Dictionary* definition of a coup as 'A sudden, violent and illegal seizure of power from a government' seems to fit the events of 2013 well, although the violence followed in the days, weeks and months afterwards, rather than during the actual removal of the president from power. As for the legality of the move, the constitution valid at the time defines the circumstances for a president's resignation in articles 151–4, and these circumstances were not in place. Hence, while I do not deny the substantial popular backing for the army's move, I will refer to it as a (military) coup.
123. Mike Giglio in *The Daily Beast*, 12 July 2013, 'A Cairo conspiracy', available at http://www.thedailybeast.com/articles/2013/07/12/a-cairo-conspiracy.html (accessed 6 April 2016).
124. Freedom House, 'Egypt', in *Freedom in the World 2014*, available at https://freedomhouse.org/report/freedom-world/2014/egypt-0#.VMfANi6rHSh (accessed 6 April 2016).

125. Alaa al-Aswany, 8 December 2013, 'Egypt's trouble with women', in the *New York Times*, available at http://www.nytimes.com/2013/12/09/opinion/09iht-edalaswany09.html (accessed 6 April 2016).
126. Rantings of a Sandmonkey, 30 October 2006, 'The Eid sexual harassment incident', available at http://www.sandmonkey.org/2006/10/30/the-eid-sexual-harassment-incident/ (accessed 6 April 2016).
127. Malek X, 25 October 2006, 'سعار وسط المدينة الجنسي', no longer available at (last accessed 24 November 2015).
128. See for instance 'Girls in downtown Cairo' published on 7 November 2006, by 'Akhnaton films', available at http://www.youtube.com/watch?v=B2SGam UeMec (accessed 6 April 2016).
129. The blog is found at http://nerro.wordpress.com/. The posts on the demonstration are called 'Let's talk: Let's take an action' (http://nerro.wordpress.com/2006/10/31/lets-talk-lets-take-an-action/#comments) and 'The stand' (http://nerro.wordpress.com/2006/11/01/our-stand/) (accessed 6 April 2016). See also Sharon Otterman, 'Publicizing the private: Egyptian women bloggers speak out', *Arab Media & Society* 1 (2007), available at http://www.arabmediasociety.com/topics/index.php?t_article=28 (accessed 5 April 2016).
130. Nermeena, 20 November 2006, 'IGWS sexual harassment forum', available at http://nerro.wordpress.com/2006/11/20/igws-sexual-harassment-forum/ (accessed 6 April 2016).
131. Nermeena, 22 March 2007, 'ECWR press conference: Making our streets safer for everyone', available at http://nerro.wordpress.com/2007/03/22/ecwr-press-conference-making-our-streets-safer-for-everyone/ (accessed 6 April 2016).
132. ECWR, 6 November 2012, 'Sexual harassment … to where?', available at http://ecwronline.org/?p=1026 (accessed 6 April 2016). However, in a 2008 report published by ECWR, they state that the campaign started in 2004.
133. *Daily News Egypt*, 10 March 2014, 'HarassMap launches new "Don't Be Silent" campaign', available at http://www.dailynewsegypt.com/2014/03/10/harassmap-launches-new-dont-silent-campaign/ (accessed 6 April 2016).
134. Paul Amar, 'Turning the gendered politics of the security state inside out? Charging the police with sexual harassment in Egypt', *International Feminist Journal of Politics* 13/3 (2011), p. 317.
135. See, for instance, The Arabist, 25 June 2008, 'Veil your lollipop', available at http://arabist.net/blog/2008/6/25/veil-your-lollipop.html (accessed 6 April 2016).
136. Rasha Mohammad Hassan, Aliyaa Shoukry and Nehad Abul Komsan, '*Clouds in Egypt's Sky' Sexual Harassment: From Verbal Harassment to Rape* (2008), available at http://egypt.unfpa.org/Images/Publication/2010_03/6eeeb05a-3040-42d2-9e1c-2bd2e1ac8cac.pdf (accessed 4 April 2016), p. 16.
137. United Nations Entity for Gender Equality and the Empowerment of Women (UN Women), The National Council for Women (NCW), *Study on Ways and Methods to Eliminate Sexual Harassment in Egypt* (2013), available at http://web.

law.columbia.edu/sites/default/files/microsites/gender-sexuality/un_womens exual-harassment-study-egypt-final-en.pdf (accessed 5 April 2016).

138. Thomson Reuters Foundation, 12 November 2013, 'POLL – Egypt is worst Arab state for women, Comoros best', available at http://www.trust.org/item/20131108170910-qacvu/?source=spotlight-writaw (accessed 6 April 2016).
139. Etienne G. Krug, Linda L. Dahlberg, James A. Mercy, Anthony B. Zwi and Rafael Lozano (eds), *World Report on Violence and Health* (2002), available at http://www.who.int/violence_injury_prevention/violence/world_report/en/introduction.pdf (accessed 4 April 2016), p. 149.
140. Ibid., pp. 150, 160.
141. Kassem, *Egyptian Politics*, p. 153.
142. Ibid.
143. Ibid., p. 67.
144. Wafaa Osama, 'Targeting women with violence in Egyptian politics', *Babylon nordisk tidsskrift for midtøstenstudier* 3/2 (2005), p. 39.
145. Ibid.
146. See for instance *MadaMasr*, 7 July 2014, 'Sexual assault and the state: A history of violence', available at http://www.madamasr.com/sections/politics/sexual-assault-and-state-history-violence (accessed 6 April 2016).
147. Amar, 'Turning the gendered politics of the security state', p. 309.
148. Osama, 'Targeting women', p. 39.
149. *New York Times*, 10 June 2005, 'Assault on women at protest stirs anger, not fear, in Egypt', available at http://www.nytimes.com/2005/06/10/international/africa/10egypt.html?pagewanted=all&_r = 3& (accessed 6 April 2016).
150. Amnesty International, 6 February 2013, 'Egypt: Gender-based violence against women around Tahrir Square', available at http://www.amnestyusa.org/research/reports/egypt-gender-based-violence-against-women-around-tahrir-square (accessed 6 April 2016).
151. EIPR, 25 May 2005,
استهداف النساء بالاعتداء الجنسي في المظاهرات السلمية جريمة لن يمحوها سوى إقالة وزير الداخلية... خمس منظمات حقوقية تتضامن مع الدعوة إلى يوم الحداد الوطني
available at http://eipr.org/pressrelease/2005/05/26/1169 (accessed 6 April 2016).
152. Amar, 'Turning the gendered politics of the security state', p. 313.
153. Ibid., p. 319.
154. Ibid.
155. *CBS News*, 1 May 2011, 'Lara Logan breaks silence on Cairo assault', available at http://www.cbsnews.com/news/lara-logan-breaks-silence-on-cairo-assault/ (accessed 6 April 2016).
156. Krug et al., *World Report on Violence and Health*, p. 150.
157. Nazra for Feminist Studies, *One Year of Impunity: Violations against Women Human Rights Defenders in Egypt from August to December 2011* (2012), available at http://nazra.org/en/2012/09/%E2%80%9Ci%E2%80%99m-coming-

back-you-i-want-kill-you%E2%80%9D-one-year-impunity (accessed 5 April 2016), p. 7.

158. Most of the information given here concerning recent attacks is taken from reports and briefs compiled by some of the groups studied here. These are also the sources used by Egyptian and international media. How the groups work to compile and disseminate this information will be discussed along with the rest of the findings. Suffice it to say for now, these are not just the only available sources, they are also those trusted by the media.
159. Nazra, *One Year of Impunity*.
160. *CNN*, 22 December 2011, '"Blue bra girl" rallies Egypt's women vs. oppression', available at http://edition.cnn.com/2011/12/22/opinion/coleman-women-egypt-protest/ (accessed 6 April 2016).
161. El-Nadeem Center, Nazra for Feminist Studies, and New Woman Foundation, *Sexual Assault and Rape in Tahrir Square and its Vicinity. A Compendium of Sources 2011–2013* (2013), available at http://nazra.org/en/2013/05/sexual-assault-and-rape-tahrir-square-and-its-vicinity-compendium-sources-2011-2013 (accessed 4 April 2016), pp. 9–10.
162. Many dates and events mentioned in this brief presentation of the campaign studied are referred to later in the discussions. In order to make the material accessible and the narrative easy to follow, I have included a timeline of the campaign in Appendix 2.
163. El-Nadeem et al., *Sexual Assault and Rape in Tahrir Square*, pp. 12–15.
164. The activist has written extensively on the issue on her blog, Zaghaleel: https://zaghaleel.wordpress.com/category/ending-sexual-harassment. The call for demonstration was published on Facebook on 7 June 2012: https://www.facebook.com/events/242430382538659/?ref=4 (accessed 6 April 2016).
165. The event was called 'تأمين الميدان' ('Safeguarding the square'), and was published on Facebook on 5 June 2012: https://www.facebook.com/events/316715905079818/ (accessed 6 April 2016).
166. Interview with representative of Imprint movement. See also the *Guardian*, 5 November 2012, 'How Egyptians are fighting harassment in the streets', available at http://www.theguardian.com/lifeandstyle/2012/nov/05/egyptians-fighting-harassment-streets (accessed 6 April 2016).
167. El-Nadeem et al., *Sexual Assault and Rape in Tahrir Square*, p. 10.
168. Ibid., pp. 16–17.
169. The first metro campaign was announced as a Facebook event, not formally held by Imprint but by individual activists, including one of the founders of Imprint, شباب ضد التحرش - دوريات مترو الانفاق: https://www.facebook.com/events/500615983286391/?ref=22 (accessed 6 April 2016).
170. *Egypt Independent*, 22 August 2012, 'Sexual harassment wave continues for third day'. No longer available online.
171. *USA Today*, 23 October 2012, 'Sexual harassment spikes over Egyptian holiday', available at http://www.usatoday.com/story/news/world/2012/10/30/sexual-harassment-egypt/1669707/ (accessed 6 April 2016).

172. El-Nadeem et al., *Sexual Assault and Rape in Tahrir Square*.
173. *Daily Mail*, 1 December 2012, 'Muslim Brotherhood "paying gangs to go out and rape women and beat men protesting in Egypt" as thousands of demonstrators pour on to the streets', available at http://www.dailymail.co.uk/news/article-2241374/Muslim-Brotherhood-paying-gangs-rape-women-beat-men-protesting-Egypt-thousands-demonstrators-pour-streets.html (accessed 6 April 2016).
174. Channel 4, *Unreported World*, 7 December 2012, 'Egypt: Sex, mobs and revolution', available at http://www.channel4.com/programmes/unreported-world/videos/all/egypt-sex-mobs-and-revolution (accessed 6 April 2016).
175. El-Nadeem et al., *Sexual Assault and Rape in Tahrir Square*, p. 19.
176. See the event page, 'يومين تدوين وزقزقة من أجل الكرامة الإنسانية 23 و 24 يناير.': https://www.facebook.com/events/400348160054591/ (accessed 6 April 2016).
177. Topsy.com listed 1,250 tweets about #endSH and 706 about #مصر_من_غير_تحرش over the past seven days leading up to 26 January 2013. Topsy was a social search and analytics company, which unfortunately is no longer operational. Through their website, topsy.com, statistics on, for instance, the use of particular hashtags could be generated. More information on the site and how it worked is provided in Appendix 4.
178. El-Nadeem et al., *Sexual Assault and Rape in Tahrir Square*, p. 26.
179. Amnesty International, *Egypt: Gender-based Violence Against Women Around Tahrir Square* (2013), available at https://www.amnesty.org/en/documents/MDE12/009/2013/en/ (accessed 4 April 2016), p. 6.
180. Ibid., p. 5.
181. BBC, 6 February 2013, 'Egyptians Protest at Sexual Violence against Women', available at http://www.bbc.com/news/world-middle-east-21356233 (accessed 6 April 2016). See also the event page, 'مسيرة الشارع لنا... لا للتحرش والاعتداء الجنسي': https://www.facebook.com/events/123959144442368/ (accessed 6 April 2016).
182. *New York Times*, 25 March 2013, 'Rise in sexual assaults in Egypt sets off clash over blame', available at http://www.nytimes.com/2013/03/26/world/middleeast/egyptian-women-blamed-for-sexual-assaults.html?hp&_r=2& (accessed 6 April 2016).
183. *Egypt Independent*, 11 February 2013, 'Shura Council Committee says female protesters should take responsibility, if harassed', available at http://www.egyptindependent.com/news/shura-council-committee-says-female-protesters-should-take-responsibility-if-harassed (accessed 6 April 2016).
184. *Daily News Egypt*, 12 February 2013, 'Women take to the streets to protest sexual harassment and assault', available at http://www.dailynewsegypt.com/2013/02/12/women-take-to-the-streets-to-protest-sexual-harassment-and-assault/ (accessed 6 April 2016).
185. According to Topsy, 16 March 2013.
186. Nazra, 3 July 2013, 'Brutal sexual assaults in the vicinity of Tahrir Square and an unprecedentedly shameful reaction from the Egyptian authorities: 101

incidents of sexual assaults during the events of June 30th 2013', joint statement available at http://nazra.org/en/2013/07/brutal-sexual-assaults-vicinity-tahrir-square (accessed 6 April 2016).

187. Human Rights Watch, 3 July 2013, 'Egypt: Epidemic of sexual violence', available at http://www.hrw.org/news/2013/07/03/egypt-epidemic-sexual-vi olence (accessed 6 April 2016).

188. Nazra, 9 June 2014, 'الاعتداءات الجنسية والاغتصاب في ميدان التحرير أثناء دليل علي عدم كفاية التعديلات القانونية الأخيرة للتصدي لتلك الجرائم الاحتفال بحلف يمين الرئيس' available at http://nazra.org/2014/06/%D8%A7%D8%B9%D8%AA%D8%AF%D8%A7%D8%A1%D8%A7%D8%AA-%D8%AC%D9%86%D8%B3%D9%8A%D8%A9-%D9%88%D8%A7%D8%BA%D8%AA%D8%B5%D8%A7%D8%A8-%D9%81%D9%8A-%D9%85%D9%8A%D8%AF%D8%A7%D9%86-%D8%A7%D9%84%D8%AA%D8%AD%D8%B1%D9%8A%D8%B1-%D8%A3%D8%AB%D9%86%D8%A7%D8%A1-%D8%A7%D9%84%D8%A7%D8%AD%D8%AA%D9%81%D8%A7%D9%84-%D8%A8%D8%AD%D9%84%D9%81-%D9%8A%D9%85%D9%8A%D9%86-%D8%A7%D9%84%D8%B1%D8%A6%D9%8A%D8%B3 (accessed 6 April 2016).

189. Nazra, 19 July 2014, 'First verdict in cases of mob-sexual assault and gang rape in Tahrir Square is no end to the story; all previous crimes of sexual violence must be investigated', available at http://nazra.org/en/2014/07/first-verdict-cases-mob-sexual-assault-and-gang-rape-tahrir-square-no-end-story (accessed 6 April 2016).

190. *Al-Ahram*, 12 June 2014, 'السيسي؛ اجراءات حازمة والقانون سينفذ بمنتهى القوة, الرئيس يزور ضحية التحرش ويعتذر لها ولكل سيدة مصرية'

191. *Ahram Online*, 11 June 2014, 'Anti-sexual assault protest held in Egypt's Tahrir Square', available at http://english.ahram.org.eg/NewsContent/1/64/103479/Egypt/Politics-/Antisexual-assault-protest-held-in-Egypts-Tahrir-S.aspx (accessed 6 April 2016).

192. *BBC News*, 5 June 2014, 'Egypt brings in new sexual harassment laws', available at http://www.bbc.com/news/world-middle-east-27726849 (accessed 6 April 2016).

193. Human Rights Watch, 15 June 2014, 'How Egypt can turn the tide on sexual assault', available at http://www.hrw.org/news/2014/06/15/how-egypt-can-turn-tide-sexual-assault (accessed 6 April 2016).

194. A list of the groups, including the addresses of their websites, their accounts on social media and their number of followers is given in the section entitled 'Websites, accounts and pages of the groups studied'.

195. Nazra.org, 'About us': http://nazra.org/en/about-us (accessed 6 April 2016).

196. Imprint, 'About' on Facebook: https://www.facebook.com/Imprint.Movement.eg/info (accessed 6 April 2016).

197. Harassmap.org, 'Who we are': http://harassmap.org/en/who-we-are/ (accessed 6 April 2016).

198. Interview conducted in Cairo, spring 2013.

199. Mosireen, on Twitter (@mosireen), 27 November 2012.
200. *Egypt Independent*, 8 December 2012, 'Hands off: Initiatives grow fighting sexual harassment in Tahrir and elsewhere', available at http://www.egyptindependent.com/news/hands-initiatives-grow-fighting-sexual-harassment-tahrir-and-elsewhere (accessed 6 April 2016).
201. Some of the groups also maintained closed Facebook groups for their members but, as these were not public, they were not included in the material. Similarly, Imprint maintained a closed Google+ account.
202. FrontlineSMS, 'FrontlineSMS overview': http://www.frontlinesms.com/technologies/frontlinesms-overview/ (accessed 6 April 2016).
203. Ushahidi was originally developed as a website to 'map reports of violence in Kenya after the post-election fallout at the beginning of 2008'. Ushahidi, 'Ushahidi's Mission': http://www.ushahidi.com/mission/ (accessed 6 April 2016).
204. NiJeL, 'About NiJeL': http://www.nijel.org/why-nijel/about-nijel/. See also 'Your data, transformed': http://www.nijel.org/why-nijel/transformed/ (both accessed 6 April 2016).
205. These figures are based on the groups' numbers of followers, etc. by the end of the time frame set for this investigation.
206. The group now operates accounts on both Flickr and Google+. However, both these accounts were created after 1 August 2013 – that is, after the end of the time frame set for this investigation – and thus are not included in the material.
207. This account is today named @TahrirBG_DWB. However, it was originally called @TahrirBodyguard, and was started on 27 November 2012. This is the account that was used during the time frame set for this investigation. The group also has a new account, which is the one that is currently called @TahrirBodyguard, created on 1 August 2013, as the old account was taken over by the new group, DWB. The old account, @TahrirBG_DWB, is the one containing all the material referred to in this study.
208. There are, in fact, four addresses that lead to the same site: namely isawharassment.org/, isawharassment.net/, shoftta7rosh.org/ and shoftta7rosh.net/. However, this site was created after the time frame set for this investigation. During the time frame, an older site was used: barlamanalnsaa.com/shoft-ta7rosh. According to Fagan Finder, this site was registered on 13 September 2012 and is on a page containing two other initiatives, Fu'ada Watch and Barlaman al-Nisa' (the Women's Parliament). These initiatives, in turn, stem from the abovementioned group, Appropriate Communication Techniques for Development Center (ACT). The new site contains much more content than the old one, but is not included in the material analysed.
209. The group had a channel on YouTube, launched on 1 June 2013: http://www.youtube.com/channel/UChzlAgVMhCtrQGoUcYoPx7Q/feed. However, by September 2015, this channel appeared to have been discontinued. Nevertheless, the material published within the time frame is, of course, included.

210. Importantly, 'likes' on Facebook in this particular context refers to the number of people who liked their page and subsequently followed the group and received their updates on their timelines. This is not to be confused with the 'likes' given to particular posts referred to below.
211. For the last group, I Saw Harassment, two of the top three aggregate categories were among their top three.
212. For the former, retweets account for between 27.5 per cent and 44 per cent; for the latter, the figure is between 1 per cent and 4 per cent.
213. The tweets of OpAntiSH were, on average, retweeted 11.3 times, HarassMap's and TBG's six times. The corresponding figures for Imprint and ISH are 0.9 and 0.6, respectively.
214. The average number of comments for most groups is between 0.4 and 3. The exception is OpAntiSH, which generated an average of 13.
215. This information concerning popularity of content on Facebook and Twitter is based on the five most retweeted, favourited/liked, shared and commented upon tweets/posts of each group. The figures concerning average retweets, shares, likes and so on, are based on the entire samples.
216. Howard and Hussain, *Democracy's Fourth Wave*, p. 5.
217. The ITU reported the number of mobile phone subscriptions at 105 per 100 inhabitants in 2011, rising to 121 in 2013. ITU, 'Time series by country: Mobile-cellular subscriptions', available at http://www.itu.int/en/ITU-D/Statistics/Pages/stat/default.aspx (accessed 6 April 2016).
218. In 2011, HarassMap won the World Summit Youth Award and in 2012 they won the Deutsche Welle's award for 'best use of technology for social good'. See: the World Summit Youth Award, 2011 winners: http://www.youthaward.org/winners/harassmap. See also: Deutsche Welle, 'The Bobs' 2012 winner: https://thebobs.com/english/category/history/?year=history-2012&content = winner (both accessed 6 April 2016).
219. UN Women, *Study on Ways and Methods to Eliminate Sexual Harassment*.
220. Interview conducted in Cairo, spring 2013.
221. Dubai School of Government, June 2013, *Arab Social Media Report* (5th edition), available at http://www.med-media.eu/wp-content/uploads/2014/07/ASMR_5_Report_Final.pdf (accessed 6 April 2016).
222. I will not include any examples of this practice.
223. One example would be during the 30 June demonstrations, when OpAntiSH took part in heated discussions with the spokesperson as well as those running the official Twitter account of the Muslim Brotherhood, whom they accused of exploiting the issue to their own advantage. However, this was by no means representative of their practice on Twitter.
224. As discussed in Chapter 3, I have removed all user names of individual users, with the exception of a few famous activists and a TV host. The user names of the groups studied have not been removed, as these do not give any information about the individual who has written any particular tweet. A list of all examples given with the original user names is kept by the author.

225. Obviously, this is not a direct translation. Rather, I have used the translation which HarassMap used themselves when writing the statement in both Arabic and English on Facebook on 16 March 2013.
226. This quote was shared by several other groups as well.
227. From 'Position paper on sexual violence against women and the increasing frequency of gang rape in Tahrir Square and its environs', available at http://nazra.org/en/2013/02/position-paper-sexual-violence-against-women-and-increasing-frequency-gang-rape-tahrir (accessed 6 April 2016).
228. Whereas Nazra and Imprint only used hashtags in 25 per cent and 8 per cent of their tweets, respectively, OpAntiSH, for instance, did so in more than half of their tweets.
229. This was done using amara.org, and the subtitles were translated into 22 languages. The video in question, entitled 'This is mob attack', is the video referred to above that gained more than 1.5 million views. The video is available on YouTube: https://www.youtube.com/watch?v=KZyo74ESr2s (accessed 6 April 2016).
230. The initiative was started in May 2013 using indiegogo.com, a site providing a platform for such fundraising.
231. According to the group itself, the drastic increase in their number of followers initially led to Twitter suspending their account on several occasions. The group at one point even created a back-up account, @TahrirBGBackUp.
232. See, for instance, 27 November 2012.
233. Interviews conducted in Cairo, spring 2013.
234. *Egypt Independent*, 22 June 2011, 'The sexual harassment file: Harassment debate lights up blogosphere', available at http://www.egyptindependent.com/news/sexual-harassment-file-harassment-debate-lights-blogosphere (accessed 6 April 2016).
235. For those not familiar with the song, it was released in 1982 and used in the movie *Rocky III*, and has become synonymous with the movie franchise.
236. The article is, understandably, no longer available online. The title in the original Arabic reads as follows: 'شفت تحرش تنفي وقوع أي حالات بالميدان'.
237. See, for instance, *Al-Masri al-Yawm*, 21 October 2012, 'مبادرة «شفت تحرش» للإبلاغ عن مضايقات النساء في العيد' available at http://www.almasryalyoum.com/news/details/226497 (accessed 6 April 2016).
238. Interview conducted in Cairo, spring 2013.
239. When the group organised patrols during the Shamm al-Nasim holiday in May 2013, it published links to no fewer than 12 newspaper articles on their work, all very similar and seemingly based on the same press release (also published by the group).
240. One interesting example occurred on 25 May 2013; that is, on the eighth anniversary of 'Black Wednesday'. Several groups, including EIPR and OpAntiSH, held an event to commemorate what had happened. *Ahram Online* covered the event, writing on the issue of harassment and how the old

regime had employed such tactics against the opposition. *Ahram Online*, 25 May 2013, 'Activists commemorate eighth anniversary of "Black Wednesday"', available at http://english.ahram.org.eg/News/72300.aspx (accessed 6 April 2016).

241. *Egypt Independent*, 4 December 2012, 'Anti-sexual harassment campaigns to increase presence in Tahrir', available at http://www.egyptindependent.com/news/anti-sexual-harassment-campaigns-increase-presence-tahrir (accessed 6 April 2016).
242. See, for instance, *NBC News*, 5 December 2012, '"Men don't have to worry about being caught": Sex mobs target Egypt's women', available at http://worldnews.nbcnews.com/_news/2012/12/05/15675200-men-dont-have-to-worry-about-being-caught-sex-mobs-target-egypts-women (accessed 6 April 2016).
243. Examples of such articles are: *Guardian*, 28 January 2013, 'Tahrir Square sexual assaults reported during anniversary clashes' (http://www.theguardian.com/world/2013/jan/27/tahrir-square-sexual-assaults-reported); *Daily News Egypt*, 27 January 2013, '19 sexual harassment cases in Tahrir, Sky News reporter assaulted in Alexandria' (http://www.dailynewsegypt.com/2013/01/27/19-sexual-harassment-cases-in-tahrir-sky-news-reporter-assaulted-in-alexandria/); *Bloomberg.com*, 28 January 2013, 'Assaults on Egyptian women peak in protest, group says' (http://www.bloomberg.com/news/articles/2013-01-28/assaults-on-egyptian-women-peak-in-protest-group-says) (all accessed 6 April 2016).
244. *Ahram Online*, 1 February 2013, 'UN deplores Tahrir Square rapes, demands action', available at http://english.ahram.org.eg/News/63798.aspx (accessed 6 April 2016).
245. This is evident from, among other things, the coverage given to I Saw Harassment, as relayed on their Facebook page.
246. To give just one example, on 8 April 2013, *Al-Watan* newspaper online published an article announcing that Imprint was now accepting new applications for membership on their Facebook site, available at http://www.elwatannews.com/news/details/159888 (accessed 6 April 2016).
247. See, for instance, *Ahram Online*, 12 November 2012, 'Egyptian man jailed for 2 years for sexual harassment', available at http://english.ahram.org.eg/NewsContent/1/64/57916/Egypt/Politics-/Egyptian-man-jailed-for–years-for-sexual-harassme.aspx (accessed 6 April 2016).
248. 26 June 2014, 'منظمات حقوقية تنتقد كشف بيانات الناجيات من الاعتداء الجنسي بـ«التحرير' available at http://m.almasryalyoum.com/news/details/471395 (accessed 6 April 2016).
249. 1 July 2013, `شفت تحرش تناشد المنظمات الحقوقية بتوثيق شهادات الناجيات من التحرش لتقديم الرئيس لمحاكمة دولية' available at http://www.elwatannews.com/news/details/214686 (accessed 6 April 2016).

250. September 21, 2014, ‘حواء بعد 100 يوم من حكم السيسي’, available at http://www.youm7.com/story/2014/9/21/%D8%AD%D9%88%D8%A7%D8%A1-%D8%A8%D8%B9%D8%AF-100-%D9%8A%D9%88%D9%85-%D9%85%D9%86-%D8%AD%D9%83%D9%85-%D8%A7%D9%84%D8%B3%D9%8A%D8%B3%D9%89%D8%B2%D9%8A%D8%A7%D8%B1%D8%A9-%D8%A7%D9%84%D8%B1%D8%A6%D9%8A%D8%B3-%D9%84%D9%86%D8%A7%D8%AC%D9%8A%D8%A7%D8%AA-%D8%AD%D9%81%D9%84-%D8%A7%D9%84%D8%AA%D9%86%D8%B5/1873519#.VwasRDaLRhE (accessed 6 April 2016).
251. 4 October 2014, ‘شفت تحرش :مستمرون فى مناهضة العنف الجنسى’, available at http://www.gomhuriaonline.com/main.asp?v_article_id=196622 (accessed 6 April 2016).
252. 10 June 2014, ‘ناجيات من التحرش "لا عاهرات ولا خاضعات"’, available at http://www.bbc.co.uk/arabic/middleeast/2014/06/140610_harassment_egypt_story (accessed 6 April 2016).
253. 6 October 2014, ‘معاكسات لفظية وحالات تعدّ أفسدت فرحة العيد في مصر’, available at http://www.alraimedia.com/Articles.aspx?id=533509 (accessed 6 April 2016).
254. 6 July 2013, ‘Sexual harassment taints Egypt’s euphoria’, available at http://www.aljazeera.com/indepth/features/2013/07/20137617131125427.html (accessed 6 April 2016).
255. 2 June 2013, ‘Women in Egypt suffer more sexual violence under Islamist rule’, available at http://english.alarabiya.net/en/perspective/features/2013/06/02/Women-in-Egypt-suffer-more-sexual-violence-under-Islamist-rule-.html (accessed 6 April 2016).
256. 13 June 2013, ‘Doubts remain in Egypt despite Sisi’s action against sexual harassment’, available at http://www.theguardian.com/world/2014/jun/13/doubts-remain-in-egypt-despite-sisis-action-against-sexual-harassment (accessed 6 April 2016).
257. 14 June 2013, ‘Egypt sends 13 to trial for Tahrir Square sexual violence’, available at http://www.haaretz.com/news/middle-east/1.598712 (accessed 6 April 2016).
258. See, for instance, Amnesty International, 6 February 2013, ‘Egypt: Impunity fuels sexual violence’, available at http://www.amnestyusa.org/news/news-item/egypt-impunity-fuels-sexual-violence (accessed 6 April 2016).
259. Interview conducted in Cairo, spring 2013.
260. Nancy Fraser, ‘Rethinking the public sphere: A contribution to the critique of actually existing democracy’, in C. Calhoun (ed.), *Habermas and the Public Sphere* (Cambridge and London, 1992).
261. *MadaMasr*, 26 July 2015, ‘Five takes on female cops fighting harassment on Cairo’s streets’, available at http://www.madamasr.com/sections/politics/five-takes-female-cops-fighting-harassment-cairos-streets (accessed 6 April 2016).
262. Amar, ‘Turning the gendered politics of the security state’.

Chapter 5 The Kuwaiti Case: The Context, the Issue, and My Findings

1. *Alqabas.com*, 16 October 2012, 'خطاب بلا سقف.... واحتكاك مع رجال الأمن' No longer available online. However, the organizers themselves put the number at 20,000, according to a report by alziadiq8.com: http://alziadiq8.com/3663.html (accessed 6 April 2016).
2. The speech in its entirety, as well as an shorter, edited version, is available on YouTube. Full version: https://www.youtube.com/watch?v=n7nnFUOEmBY; short version: https://www.youtube.com/watch?v=5rpa1eiW0Y0 (accessed 6 April 2016).
3. *Al-Watan*, 16 October 2012, p. 1.
4. *Reuters*, 22 February 2015, 'Kuwait court hands down two years jail sentence for insulting emir', available at http://www.reuters.com/article/2015/02/22/us-kuwait-court-idUSKBN0LQ09N20150222 (accessed 6 April 2016).
5. Jill Crystal, *Oil and Politics in the Gulf: Rulers and Merchants in Kuwait and Qatar* (Cambridge, 1995); Michael Herb, *All in the Family: Absolutism, Revolution, and Democracy in Middle Eastern Monarchies* (New York, 1999); Paul Salem, 'Kuwait: Politics in a participatory emirate', in M. Ottaway and J. Choucair-Vizoso (eds), *Beyond the Facade – Political Reform in the Arab World* (Washington, DC, 2008).
6. Crystal, *Oil and Politics in the Gulf*, p. 20.
7. Herb, *All in the Family*, p. 69.
8. Salem, 'Kuwait: Politics in a participatory emirate', p. 213.
9. Crystal, *Oil and Politics in the Gulf*, pp. 24–5.
10. Kjetil Selvik, 'Golfmonarkiene – mer variasjon enn olje kan forklare', *Babylon nordisk tidsskrift for midtøstenstudier* 8/2 (2010), pp. 8–20; Mary Ann Tétreault, *Stories of Democracy: Politics and Society in Contemporary Kuwait* (New York, 2000).
11. Tétreault, *Stories of Democracy*, p. 45.
12. Crystal, *Oil and Politics in the Gulf*, p. 42.
13. However, this does not mean that it always has been respected, as will be discussed later.
14. Crystal, *Oil and Politics in the Gulf*, pp. 45–7.
15. Salem, 'Kuwait: Politics in a participatory emirate', p. 213.
16. Jill Crystal, 'Coalitions in oil monarchies: Kuwait and Qatar', *Comparative Politics* 21/4 (1989), p. 433.
17. Salem, 'Kuwait: Politics in a participatory emirate'.
18. Shafeeq Ghabra, 'Voluntary associations in Kuwait: The foundation of a new system?', *The Middle East Journal* 45/3 (1991), p. 201. Among those elected was Ahmad al-Khatib, the leader of the pan-Arab nationalist movement, who remains a dominant figure in Kuwaiti politics to this day, even participating in events held by the current opposition movement.
19. Ghanim Alnajjar, 'The challenges facing Kuwaiti democracy', *The Middle East Journal* 54/2 (2000), p. 244.

20. Herb, *All in the Family*, p. 161.
21. 'Kuwait Constitution' on *Diwan of His Highness the Prime Minister*, available at https://www.pm.gov.kw/kuwait-constitution.aspx (accessed 6 April 2016).
22. Salem, 'Kuwait: Politics in a participatory emirate', p. 214.
23. Alnajjar, 'The challenges facing Kuwaiti democracy', p. 245.
24. Crystal, *Oil and Politics in the Gulf*, p. 88.
25. Ibid., p. 89. However, not all Bedouins who were given citizenship were given the right to vote, and not all Bedouins living in Kuwait were given citizenship (see Shafeeq Ghabra, 'Kuwait and the dynamics of socio-economic change', *The Middle East Journal* 51/3 (1997), pp. 358–72). This, in turn, gave rise to the issue of the *bidūn*s, that is, inhabitants with no social or political rights – an issue that would subsequently prove highly problematic for the government.
26. Herb, *All in the Family*, p. 164.
27. Crystal, *Oil and Politics in the Gulf*; Herb, *All in the Family.*
28. Should he fail to do so, it would be as though the dissolved Parliament had never been dissolved and it would regain all its powers.
29. Ghabra, 'Voluntary associations in Kuwait'; Herb, *All in the Family.*
30. Crystal, *Oil and Politics in the Gulf*; Herb, *All in the Family.*
31. Ibid.
32. Herb, *All in the Family*, p. 162.
33. Crystal, *Oil and Politics in the Gulf*, p. 104.
34. Ghabra, 'Voluntary associations in Kuwait', p. 211.
35. Ibid.; Deborah L. Wheeler, *The Internet in the Middle East: Global Expectations and Local Imaginations in Kuwait* (New York, 2006).
36. Wheeler, *The Internet in the Middle East*, p. 69.
37. Alnajjar, 'The challenges facing Kuwaiti democracy', p. 257.
38. According to a 2014 study by James Redman, the *dīwāniyāt* are subject to some government control, and are also quite intertwined with the Kuwaiti state, as one of their practical functions is to provide access to people with bureaucratic and political influence (James C. A. Redman, 'The Diwaniyya: Guestroom Sociability and Bureaucratic Brokerage in Kuwait' (PhD Dissertaion, Utah, 2014)).
39. Ghabra, 'Voluntary associations in Kuwait'; Tétreault, *Stories of Democracy.*
40. Herb, *All in the Family*, p. 165.
41. Ibid., p. 167.
42. Ibid., p. 166.
43. Shafeeq Ghabra 'Kuwait and the dynamics of socio-economic change', *The Middle East Journal* 51/3 (1997), p. 370.
44. Salem, 'Kuwait: Politics in a participatory emirate', p. 217.
45. Tétreault, *Stories of Democracy*, p. 58.
46. When it comes to the prime minister, it is stressed in the constitution that he does not have any particular portfolio and thus cannot be questioned in the same manner. However, the Parliament can, in essence, vote on whether or not it is able to cooperate with the PM, which in the end can produce the same

result as when confidence is withdrawn from any other minister. The text of the constitution is available from the Kuwait Government Online site: http://www.e.gov.kw/sites/kgoArabic/Forms/DastoorKuwaity.pdf (accessed 6 April 2016).

47. This number is based on the number of *istijwābāt* presented by members of Parliament, not all of which are necessarily discussed. The constitution stipulates that eight days shall pass after it is put forth before Parliament shall discuss it. This frequently does not happen, either because it is withdrawn or, more often, because the possibility of losing the vote of confidence which such a discussion might entail often has led the government to resign, or the emir to dissolve Parliament, as we shall see.
48. As of 29 July 2014. See 'Interpellations in the history of Kuwaiti Parliamentary life', retrieved from the official site of the Kuwaiti Parliament: http://search.kna.kw/web/Retrieval/GeneralSearch.aspx?tid=9 (accessed 6 April 2016).
49. Michael Herb, 'A nation of bureaucrats: Political participation and economic diversification in Kuwait and the United Arab Emirates', *International Journal of Middle East Studies* 41/03 (2009), p. 380.
50. Mary Ann Tétreault, 'Kuwait's Annus Mirabilis', *Middle East Report Online* 7 (2006), available at http://www.merip.org/mero/mero090706 (accessed 5 April 2016).
51. See, for instance, the editorial of *Al-Qabas* on 3 June 2011.
52. The name of the group in Modern Standard Arabic should, of course, be Nabghīhā Khamsa. However, in Kuwaiti dialect, the ghayn is omitted in this particular verb.
53. A. Ali Dashti, 'The effect of Kuwaiti online readers' comments on sectarian and tribal issues: A case study of the online newspaper *Alaan*', *Journal of Mass Communication & Journalism* 3 (2013), available at http://www.omicsgroup.org/journals/the-effect-of-kuwaiti-online-readers-comments-on-sectarian-and-tribal-issues-a-case-study-of-the-online-newspaper-alaan-2165-7912.1000148.php?aid=11626 (accessed 4 April 2016); Jon Nordenson, *We Want Five! – Kuwait, the Internet, and the Public Sphere* (Saarbrücken, 2010).
54. Nordenson, *We Want Five.*
55. Bjørn Olav Utvik and Jon Nordenson, *Minor Majorities* (2011), paper presented at the Annual Meeting of the Middle East Studies Association, Washington, DC, USA.
56. Herb, 'A nation of bureaucrats', p. 380.
57. Farah Al-Nakib, 'Revisiting ḥaḍar and badū in Kuwait: Citizenship, housing, and the construction of a dichotomy', *International Journal of Middle East Studies* 46/01 (2014), pp. 5–30.
58. Ibid., p. 24.
59. Ibid.
60. Mary Ann Tétreault, 'Patterns of culture and democratization in Kuwait', *Studies in Comparative International Development* 30/2 (1995), pp. 26–45.

61. Ibid., p. 36.
62. Ibid.
63. Ibid., p. 39.
64. *BBC News*, 18 May 2009, 'Q&A: Kuwaiti elections', available at http://news.bbc.co.uk/2/hi/middle_east/8048684.stm (accessed 6 April 2016). Although these figures are a few years old, there is every reason to believe that the underrepresentation of the tribal districts is even more pronounced today, due to higher birth rates.
65. The International Telecommunications Union, statistics, 'Percentage of individuals using the internet', available at http://www.itu.int/en/ITU-D/Statistics/Pages/stat/default.aspx (accessed 6 April 2016).
66. As pointed out in the previous chapter, there is a difference between internet access and internet use, and it is unclear why the sources cited above refer to 'usage' and not 'access'. Unfortunately, statistics on internet use similar to those presented for Egypt in Chapter 4 are not available for Kuwait.
67. The World Bank, Data, 'GDP per capita', available at http://data.worldbank.org/indicator/NY.GDP.PCAP.CD (accessed 6 April 2016).
68. The World Bank, Data, 'Literacy rate, adult total (% of people aged 15 and above)', available at http://data.worldbank.org/indicator/SE.ADT.LITR.ZS (accessed 6 April 2016).
69. Mark Lynch, 'Blogging the new Arab public', *Arab Media & Society* 1/1 (2007), available at http://www.arabmediasociety.com/?article=10 (accessed 4 April 2016).
70. Nordenson, *We Want Five*, p. 42.
71. Ibid.
72. Ghabra, 'Voluntary associations in Kuwait'; Wheeler, *The Internet in the Middle East*.
73. Nordenson, *We Want Five*, p. 42.
74. Ghabra, 'Voluntary associations in Kuwait', p. 206.
75. Kristen Diwan, 'Kuwait's Impatient Youth Movement', in *Foreign Policy*, 29 June 2011, available at http://foreignpolicy.com/2011/06/29/kuwaits-impatient-youth-movement/ (accessed 6 April 2016).
76. Redman, *The Diwaniyya*, p. 95.
77. Mary Ann Tétreault, 'Civil society in Kuwait: Protected spaces and women's rights', *The Middle East Journal* 47/2 (1993), pp. 275–91.
78. Several examples of such open invitations will be provided in the description of the campaign studied, and this was also the case with the so-called Monday *dīwāniyyāt*.
79. Nordenson, *We Want Five*, p. 40.
80. Delia Mocanu, Andrea Baronchelli, Nicola Perra, Bruno Gonçalves, Qian Zhang and Alessandro Vespignani, 'The Twitter of Babel: Mapping world languages through microblogging platforms', *PloS one* 8/4 (2013), e61981, available at http://dx.doi.org/10.1371/journal.pone.0061981 (accessed 4 April 2016).

81. *Al-Arabiya English*, 25 June 2013, 'Tweet politics: Kuwait election hopefuls embrace social media', available at http://english.alarabiya.net/en/media/2013/06/25/Kuwait-parliament-candidates-campaign-using-social-media.html (accessed 6 April 2016).
82. This was a debate on whether or not to boycott the elections of 2 December 2012. The two hashtags used were #سجل_المشاركين and #سجل_المقاطعين.
83. See, for instance, *al-Jazeera*, 8 January 2013, 'Kuwaiti jailed for insulting emir on Twitter', available at http://www.aljazeera.com/news/middleeast/2013/01/2013189218755379.html. See also *al-Arabiya*, 29 September 2014, 'Kuwait revokes citizenship of opposition figure, 17 others', available at http://english.alarabiya.net/en/News/middle-east/2014/09/29/Kuwait-revokes-citizenship-of-opposition-figure-17-others-.html (both accessed 6 April 2016).
84. Tétreault, 'Patterns of culture and democratization in Kuwait', p. 33.
85. Ibid., p. 35.
86. Kjetil Selvik, Jon Nordenson and Tewodros A. Kebede, 'Print media liberalization and electoral coverage bias in Kuwait', *The Middle East Journal* 69/2 (2015), pp. 255–76.
87. Ibid., p. 256.
88. The online newspaper *Alaan.cc*, along with the online newspaper *sabr.cc*, are two Kuwaiti outlets that were clearly sympathetic to the opposition and, in sharp contrast to other media outlets in the country, were trusted by the opposition. As of September 2015, *Alaan.cc* was ranked the 58th most popular website in Kuwait, above, for instance, perhaps the most established of all Kuwaiti newspapers, *Al-Qabas*, according to alexa.com. Since then, however, its popularity has declined. *Sabr.cc* has not been equally popular. I have not succeeded in establishing who owns these two newspapers. However, in a 2013 article on comments in Kuwaiti online newspapers, Dashti refers to Mr Saad Bin Taflah Al-Ajmi, clearly a member of one of Kuwait's largest tribes, as the 'publisher of alaan' in 2008 (Dashti, 'The effect of Kuwaiti online readers').
89. Mary Ann Tétreault and Mohammed Al-Ghanim, 'The day after "victory": Kuwait's 2009 election and the contentious present', *Middle East Report Online* 8 (2009), available at http://www.merip.org/mero/mero070809 (accessed 5 April 2016).
90. Recognising that there are many details and many events and dates to keep track of, a short chronological timeline of this period is included in Appendix 3, to be used as a reference when needed.
91. See Michael Herb's *Kuwait Politics Database*, '2007 طلب طرح الثقة باحمد العبدالله', available at http://www2.gsu.edu/~polmfh/database/positions26.htm (accessed 6 April 2016).
92. See Michael Herb's *Kuwait Politics Database*, '2008 طرح الثقة بنورية الصبيح', available at http://www2.gsu.edu/~polmfh/database/positions38.htm (accessed 6 April 2016).
93. All figures on voting with regard to votes of no confidence are obtained from the website of the Kuwaiti Parliament, 'الاستجوابات في تاريخ الحياة النيابية الكويتية',

available at http://www.kna.kw/clt-html5/run.asp?id=1971 (accessed 6 April 2016).

94. Altariq2009.com, 'إلى المدونات الكويتية مع التحية.'. The blog appears to no longer be available at (last accessed 1 December 2015).
95. The number of blogs involved increased in the following days, reaching 23 on 3 November. This was confirmed on Altariq2009.com, 'جريدة الدار تهاجم تحركنا لرحيل الرئيس'. The blog appears to no longer be available at (last accessed 1 December 2015).
96. The page is found at: https://www.facebook.com/groups/165931078628/ (accessed 6 April 2016).
97. The blog is found at: http://ourroleq8.blogspot.no/ (accessed 6 April 2016).
98. These included Faysal al-Muslim, Walid al-Tabataba'i and Jama'an al-Harbash.
99. This was stated, for instance, on the blog Altariq2009.com on 5 October and 18 October 2009 (last accessed 1 December 2015).
100. Website of the Kuwaiti Parliament, 'الاستجوابات في تاريخ الحياة النيابية الكويتية' available at http://www.kna.kw/clt-html5/run.asp?id=1971 (accessed 6 April 2016).
101. Doron Shultziner and Mary Ann Tétreault, 'Representation and democratic progress in Kuwait', *Representation* 48/3 (2012), p. 287.
102. Ibid.
103. ارادة الشعب on Facebook, 22 August 2010: https://www.facebook.com/eradat.shaab (accessed 6 April 2016). Veterans of the OM were involved also in this initiative.
104. *Alaan.cc*, 22 August 2010, 'من أبرزها: الحكومة المنتخبة وصيانة الحريات', available at http://www.alaan.cc/pagedetails.asp?nid=57706&cid = 30&msg = 1 (accessed 6 April 2016).
105. Human Rights Watch, 23 November 2009, 'Kuwait: Free jailed activist', available at http://www.hrw.org/en/news/2009/11/23/kuwait-free-jailed-activist (accessed 6 April 2016).
106. See, for instance, the blog صندوق حمد 30 November 2009, '4x4', available at http://www.ma6goog.com/2009/12/4-x-4.html (accessed 6 April 2016).
107. See, for instance, the blog صندوق حمد 30 November 2009, 'نأسف: المدونة مغلقة', available at http://sandoog.blogspot.no/2009/11/blog-post_30.html (accessed 6 April 2016).
108. Human Rights Watch, 29 June 2010, 'Kuwait: Political writer released on bail', available at http://www.hrw.org/news/2010/06/29/kuwait-political-writer-released-bail (accessed 6 April 2016).
109. Campaign site: http://www.kalfadala.com/ (no longer functioning) Twitter: @kalfadala Facebook: https://www.facebook.com/kalfadala YouTube: http://www.youtube.com/user/kalfadala
110. Interestingly, this was only days after the soon-to-be-famous 'Kulluna Khalid Sa'id' was created, which, according to its 'About' page, was started on 10 June 2010: https://www.facebook.com/ElShaheeed?fref=ts (accessed 6 April 2016).

111. Amnesty International, *Annual Report 2011*, 'Kuwait', available at http://files.amnesty.org/air11/air_2011_full_en.pdf (accessed 6 April 2016).
112. *Alaan.cc*, 1 December 2010, 'في بيان مشترك لـ23 نائبا', available at http://www.alaan.cc/pagedetails.asp?nid=63555&cid = 30 (accessed 6 April 2016).
113. *The National*, 10 December 2010, 'Kuwaitis angry over police action against rally', available at http://www.thenational.ae/news/world/middle-east/kuwaitis-angry-over-police-action-against-rally (accessed 6 April 2016).
114. Kristin Diwan, 'Kuwait: Too much politics, or not enough?' in *Foreign Policy*, 11 January 2011, available at http://foreignpolicy.com/2011/01/10/kuwait-too-much-politics-or-not-enough/ (accessed 6 April 2016).
115. Alziadiq8, 8 December 2010. 'ندوة "إلا الدستور" الثانية في ديوان د. جمعان الحربش بعد محاولات رفع حصانة المسلم', available at http://alziadiq8.com/112.html (accessed 6 April 2016).
116. *BBC News*, 9 December 2010, 'Kuwait rally: PM Sheikh Nasser faces quiz over clash', available at http://www.bbc.co.uk/news/world-middle-east-11961692 (accessed 6 April 2016).
117. Kristin Diwan, 'Kuwait: Too much politics, or not enough?' in *Foreign Policy*, 11 January 2011, available at http://foreignpolicy.com/2011/01/10/kuwait-too-much-politics-or-not-enough/ (accessed 6 April 2016).
118. In the founding declaration of the movement Kafi, published on the group's blog, the group refers explicitly to the events of 8 December 2010.
119. The forum had the address www.mutirkw.com, but it no longer seems to be operational. The post was published on 27 December 2010.
120. Kristen Diwan, 'Kuwait's impatient youth movement', in *Foreign Policy*, 29 June 2011, available at http://foreignpolicy.com/2011/06/29/kuwaits-impatient-youth-movement/ (accessed 6 April 2016).
121. *Alaan.cc*, 6 March 2011, 'انطلاق حملة نريد', no longer available online.
122. *Al-Watan*, 9 March 2011, pp. 1, 65.
123. These included the aforementioned veteran and member of the constitution writing committee, Ahmad al-Khatib.
124. A total of 18 MPs voted against the PM, while 25 voted to renew confidence.
125. Kristian Coates Ulrichsen, 'Politics and opposition in Kuwait: Continuity and change', *Journal of Arabian Studies* 4/2 (2014), p. 220.
126. Mary Ann Tétreault, 'Looking for revolution in Kuwait', *Middle East Report Online* (2012), available at http://www.merip.org/mero/mero110112 (accessed 5 April 2016).
127. Coates Ulrichsen, 'Politics and opposition in Kuwait', p. 221.
128. *Al-Watan*, 4 June 2011, p. 11.
129. The channel is still operational (as of 9 April 2016), and is found here: http://www.youtube.com/user/otabhq8.
130. Tétreault, 'Looking for revolution in Kuwait'.
131. *Alaan.cc*, 10 September 2011, 'امارة دستورية وحكومة منتخبة', available at http://www.alaan.cc/pagedetails.asp?nid=82340&cid=30 (accessed 9 April 2016).

132. *Al-Rai*, 11 September 2011, 'شباب 16 سبتمبر يريدون... إمارة دستورية', available at http://www.alraimedia.com/Articles.aspx?id=282679 (accessed 9 April 2016). It should be noted, however, that there is some confusion as to whether or not al-Sur al-Khamis saw itself as part of the coalition. Members of the group did take part in the demonstration, and they did release a declaration with the same demands as the other groups. However, at one point they argued that they were not in the coalition, as such.
133. *Al-Watan*, 17 September 2011, p. 8.
134. *Kuwait Times Online*, 3 November 2011, 'Oppn has 26 MPs: Barrak youth activist detained over offensive tweets', no longer accessible online.
135. *Kuwait Times Online*, 20 October 2011, 'MPs, activists call on emir to sack PM, Govt', no longer available online.
136. Kristin Diwan, 'Kuwait's constitutional showdown', in *Foreign Policy*, 17 November 2011, available at http://foreignpolicy.com/2011/11/17/kuwaits-constitutional-showdown/ (accessed 9 April 2016).
137. Michael Herb, *Kuwait Politics Database*, '2012'الاغلبية البرلمانية', available at http://www2.gsu.edu/~polmfh/database/positions51.htm (accessed 9 April 2016).
138. Coates Ulrichsen, 'Politics and opposition in Kuwait', p. 224.
139. See, for instance, Shabab al-Taghyir wa-l-Tatwir on Twitter, 26 February 2012.
140. *Al-Qabas*, 29 February 2012, p. 9.
141. These were published on the website of the group: 'النظام الاساسي'. However, the site appears to no longer be available at (last accessed 1 December 2015).
142. Kwtfuture.com, a Kuwaiti discussion forum, 2 April 2012, 'تأسيس الحركة الديمقراطية المدنية واقرار السياسات والمبادئ العامة', no longer available online.
143. *Sabr.cc*, 28 February 2012, "المؤتمر الشبابي يؤسس "الحركة الديمقراطية المدنية", available at http://www.sabr.cc/inner.aspx?id=24324 (accessed 9 April 2016).
144. See, for instance, the blogger صندوق حمد 29 February 2012, 'الحركة الديمقراطية المدنية... الاسلامية', available at http://sandoog.blogspot.no/2012/02/blog-post_29.html (accessed 9 April 2016).
145. A list of the relevant Twitter debates identified by the author, along with statistics on participation, is provided in Appendix 4.
146. *Al-Arabiyya*, 3 September 2012, 'المعارضة تتسلح بـ"تويتر" لمواجهة الحكومة بالكويت', available at http://www.alarabiya.net/articles/2012/09/03/235804.html (accessed 9 April 2016).
147. The interpellation was presented by Muhammad al-Juwayhil, a politician infamous for his hatred of the tribal population.
148. Tétreault, 'Looking for revolution in Kuwait'.
149. Ibid.
150. *Al-Watan*, 27 June 2012, p. 1.
151. See *Arab Times Kuwait*, 13 July 2012, 'Bloc in people's government call signing set for Monday', no longer available online. See also *Al-Watan Online*, 16 July 2012, '15 ضد 19 ..الأغلبية', available at http://alwatan.kuwait.tt/articledetails.aspx?id=208615 (accessed 9 April 2016).

152. See *Alaan.cc*, 17 July 2012, 'تحديث1 'حدم' تقدم ورقة الإصلاح السياسي', available at http://www.alaan.cc/pagedetails.asp?nid=113666&cid=30 (accessed 9 April 2016).
153. Meaning 'approach'; the name is meant to refer to the need for a 'new approach' on the part of the regime.
154. *Al-Watan Online*, 28 August 2012, 'الارادة..رفض متجدد لتعديل الدوائر ', available at http://alwatan.kuwait.tt/articledetails.aspx?id=216814 (accessed 9 April 2016).
155. Tétreault, 'Looking for revolution in Kuwait'.
156. Ibid.
157. *Al-Watan*, 22 October 2012, pp. 1, 12.
158. The group was mainly active on Twitter, with the profile @kwboycott.
159. *Arab Times Online*, 25 October 2012, 'US affirms right of peaceful assembly', no longer available online.
160. *Bloomberg.com*, 9 November 2012, 'Kuwait arrests two royals over pro-opposition tweets, AFP says', available at http://www.bloomberg.com/news/articles/2012-11-09/kuwait-arrests-two-royals-over-pro-opposition-tweets-afp-says (accessed 9 April 2016).
161. See, for instance, فريج سعود 16 December 2012, '.بيان المدونين', available at http://freejsaud.blogspot.no/2012/12/blog-post.html (accessed 9 April 2016).
162. *Kuwait Times Online*, 16 December 2012, '491 trialed for riots', no longer available online.
163. *Guardian*, 2 December 2012, 'Kuwait election turnout shrinks after opposition boycott', available at http://www.theguardian.com/world/2012/dec/02/kuwait-election-turnout-opposition-boycott (accessed 9 April 2016).
164. Turnout in 2009 was about 60 per cent, then described as low (Mary Ann Tétreault and Mohammed Al-Ghanim, 'The day after "victory": Kuwait's 2009 election and the contentious present', *Middle East Report Online* 8 (2009), available at http://www.merip.org/mero/mero070809 (accessed 5 April 2016)).
165. *Al-Watan*, 9 December 2012, p. 62.
166. *Arab Times Online*, 16 December 2012, '"Security, stability of Kuwait at risk" – "Foreign hands at work"', no longer available online.
167. See, for instance, *rt.com*, 6 January 2013, 'Kuwait anti-government rally dispersed with tear gas, stun grenades', available at https://www.rt.com/news/kuwait-protest-dispersed-gas-grenades-473/ (accessed 9 April 2016).
168. *Gulfnews.com*, 2 January 2013, 'Kuwait opposition divided over new rally', available at http://gulfnews.com/news/gulf/kuwait/kuwait-opposition-divided-over-new-rally-1.1126639 (accessed 9 April 2016).
169. See, for instance, the blog شقران 14 January 2013: http://shagranq8.blogspot.no/2013/01/blog-post_14.html. See also alziadiq8, 14 January 2013, 'بيان 2013-1-14 | (ائتلاف المعارضة) بيان ودعوة عاجلة لتشكيل', available at http://alziadiq8.com/10025.html (both accessed 9 April 2016).
170. *Al-Qabas Online*, 4 March 2013, 'تشكيل الائتلاف المعارض ومكتبه السياسي: حكومة منتخبة.. وحل مجلس الصوت الواحد',

available at http://www.alqabas-kw.com/Articles.aspx?ArticleID=861139&CatID=488 (accessed 9 April 2016).

171. *New York Times*, 30 September 2014, 'Kuwait, fighting dissent from within, revokes citizenship', available at http://www.nytimes.com/2014/10/01/world/middleeast/kuwait-fighting-dissent-from-within-uses-citizenship-as-a-weapon-.html (accessed 9 April 2016).
172. See *gulfnews.com*, 18 May 2015, 'Kuwait's highest court upholds two-year jail for Al Barrak', available at http://gulfnews.com/news/gulf/kuwait/kuwait-s-highest-court-upholds-two-year-jail-for-al-barrak-1.1513094 (accessed 9 April 2016).
173. See, for instance, *al-Jazeera*, 7 July 2014, 'Kuwaiti police fire tear gas at protesters', available at http://www.aljazeera.com/news/middleeast/2014/07/kuwaiti-police-fire-tear-gas-at-protesters-20147623952933363.html (accessed 9 April 2016).
174. See, for instance, Human Rights Watch, 29 March 2015, 'Kuwait: Opposition protest broken up', available at https://www.hrw.org/news/2015/03/29/kuwait-opposition-protest-broken (accessed 9 April 2016).
175. A list of the groups included, the addresses of their websites, their accounts on social media, and their number of followers is given in the section entitled 'Websites, accounts and pages of the groups studied'.
176. The channel is called 'otabhq8', and provides the following description of itself: 'الموقع الرسمي قبيلة عتيبه في دولة الكويت' (The official site [for the] Utayb tribe in the state of Kuwait). As stated above, it is still operational: http://www.youtube.com/user/otabhq8. The video in question is entitled 'بيان تجمع العدالة الدستوريه': http://www.youtube.com/watch?v=264nj13dfBw (accessed 9 April 2016).
177. *Sabr.cc*, 30 September 2012, 'آخر كلام .. "حدم" استبعدت سكرتيرها العام طارق المطيري وحسابها لم يخترق', available at http://www.sabr.cc/inner.aspx?id=42381 (accessed 9 April 2016). Also reiterated on the Twitter account on 3 October 2012.
178. *Al-Rai Online*, 4 October 2012, 'حركة "حدم" تفصل 6 من أعضائها وتحيل 5 آخرين على التحقيق', available at http://www.alraimedia.com/Articles.aspx?id=361389 (accessed 9 April 2016).
179. Importantly, 'likes' on Facebook in this particular context refers to those people who liked their page, and subsequently followed the group and received their updates on their timelines. This is not to be confused with the 'likes' given to particular posts, as referred to below.
180. One might ask why one should include in a study of internet usage among activists a group that published no more than 23 tweets and gained no more than 44 followers. However, this group was part of the same, larger movement that was starting at the end of 2010, and that movement used online platforms to a large extent. They held the same views and took part in the same demonstrations. Moreover, they took part in the September 16 coalition and they later joined Hadam. For these reasons, their markedly different internet usage should only make the group more interesting.

181. When the account was created on 12 June 2011, the name used was @youthchangeQ8, which was later changed to @mohafedheen.
182. This is not the original account of the group, which was @CivilDemocratic. Following the abovementioned split within the group over who actually represented it, the new Twitter account was established. The two accounts existed simultaneously for a few hours, before the old one was discontinued. The new account was established on 14 October 2012.
183. The figures presented are the numbers of followers for each group on the different platforms by the time the time frame set for this investigation ended, although there are a couple of exceptions. All details concerning the groups' online presence are given in the list of references.
184. The old account published a total of 484 tweets, had 1,360 followers and followed no one by the time it was closed on 14/15 October 2012.
185. Karamat Watan is not included in the figure as its extremely high number of followers would render the figure incomprehensible.
186. This figure is based on the total number of tweets I have registered from both the accounts used by the group.
187. A poster for the debate was published on the group's Twitter feed on 20 November 2012. The debate was naturally referred to in several other tweets as well. Interestingly, those representing the boycott side were two veterans of the Orange Movement.
188. Deborah L. Wheeler, 'The Internet and public culture in Kuwait', *International Communication Gazette* 63/2–3 (2001), p. 134.
189. 'Google+ and how it could help with political activism online', on http://www.tarekshalaby.com, 30 July 2011.
190. MySpace is a social networking site introduced in 2003, which suffered seriously from the competition provided by Facebook.
191. See, for instance, Mel Campbell's 'Should we mourn the end of blogs?,' *Guardian*, 17 July 2014: http://www.theguardian.com/commentisfree/2014/jul/17/should-we-mourn-the-end-of-blogs (accessed 9 April 2016).
192. A complete list of the hashtags used, when they were used and how many were involved is provided in Appendix 4. As with any numbers concerning internet usage, these figures should be read with some caution, and they are probably too low to reflect all the activity in question. Importantly, the number of tweets written using a particular hashtag does not tell the whole story of any such debate in terms of content and participants; a few users may have written most of the tweets, or some may have used the hashtag without getting involved in the debate.
193. Another good example of directly addressing blogger colleagues was the post 'أربع مدونات زميلة وندوة', published on 18 October 2009. It appears to no longer be available at (last accessed 1 December 2015).
194. Interviews conducted in Kuwait, autumn 2012.
195. Ibid.

196. As of September 2015, the site was the 63rd most visited in Kuwait, according to Alexa.com. Since then, however, the site's popularity has declined, and it is the 168th most visited, as of April 2016.
197. See, for instance, *Alaan.cc* on 26 April 2012, concerning the debate using the hashtag #ليش_منتخبة: http://www.alaan.cc/pagedetails.asp?nid=105610&cid=30 (accessed 9 April 2016).
198. *KUNA*, 14 July 2013, 'Social media gaining more leverage in Kuwait, needs optimization – experts', available at http://www.kuna.net.kw/ArticleDetails.aspx?id=2322334&language = en (accessed 9 April 2016).
199. See, for instance, *KUNA*, 8 January 2012, 'Number of Facebook users in Kuwait mounts', available at http://www.kuna.net.kw/ArticleDetails.aspx?id=2213298&Language = en. See also Internet World Stats, 'Middle East': http://www.internetworldstats.com/middle.htm (accessed 9 April 2016).
200. *Arab Social Media Report*, 'Twitter in the Arab region', available at http://www.arabsocialmediareport.com/Twitter/LineChart.aspx (accessed 9 April 2016).
201. Mocanu et al., 'The Twitter of Babel'.
202. The final word in the message, '*shabīḥ*', is a reference to Syrian President Bashar al-Asad. It is also a reference to the paramilitary group of thugs allied to his regime known as '*shabīḥa*'.
203. Mark Lynch, 'Young brothers in cyberspace', *Middle East Report* 37/245 (2007), available at http://www.merip.org/mer/mer245/young-brothers-cyberspace&gt (accessed 4 April 2016); Courtney Radsch, 'Core to commonplace: The evolution of Egypt's blogosphere', *Arab Media & Society*, 6 (2008), available at http://www.arabmediasociety.com/UserFiles/AMS6%20Courtney%20Radsch.pdf (accessed 5 April 2016).
204. These two hashtags were also used before the 19 October 2011 demonstration.
205. The hashtag #انتخابات_بلا_عبث generated some 1,700 tweets in early October 2012.
206. See, for instance, *al-Watan*, 11 November 2012, 'السعدون في تجمع الإرادة: التراجع عن الصوت الواحد لوقف الحراك', available at http://alwatan.kuwait.tt/articledetails.aspx?id=232859 (accessed 9 April 2016). See also *al-Qabas*, 11 November 2012, 'مقاطعة الانتخابات.. والحراك مستمر لوقف العبث بالدستور', available at http://www.alqabas-kw.com/ArticlePrint.aspx?id=834006&mode = print (accessed 9 April 2016).
207. On Twitter, every user will see all the tweets of those they follow in real time on their feed. Alternatively, they may follow a particular hashtag, which Kuwaitis participating in debates most probably did. Then, all tweets using this hashtag appear in real time on the user's feed. However, as some of these debates generated up to 10,000 tweets, it is implausible that any given user could have read them all.
208. As stated by Twitter; 'Top Tweets are Tweets that lots of people are interacting with and sharing via Retweets, replies, and more", Twitter, 'FAQs about top search results': https://support.twitter.com/articles/131209 (accessed 9 April 2016).

209. Selvik et al., 'Print media liberalization', p. 256.
210. The live coverage was particularly dominant in *Alaan.cc*, which provided such updates from more or less all demonstrations. See, for instance, *Alaan.cc* on 27 August 2012: http://www.alaan.cc/pagedetails.asp?nid=117927&cid = 30 (accessed 9 April 2016).
211. Available at http://www.alaan.cc/pagedetails.asp?nid=125631&cid = 30#.VwkZJTaLRhE (accessed 9 April 2016).
212. Nordenson, *We Want Five.*

Chapter 6 Comparing the Cases

1. Kristian Coates Ulrichsen, 'Politics and opposition in Kuwait: Continuity and change', *Journal of Arabian Studies* 4/2 (2014), p. 215.
2. Clearly, the Kuwaiti groups faced severe difficulties due to the actions of the regime, but these do not seem to have been based on formal requirements. That being said, the regime did change the formal requirements regarding public demonstrations towards the end of the time frame studied.
3. Elections for the lower house of Parliament, which held legislative powers, were held from late November 2011 until January 2012.However, the elected assembly was dissolved by the Supreme Council of the Armed Forces (SCAF) following a Supreme Court ruling in June 2012. Legislative powers were given to the upper house of Parliament, intended as a consultative body, in December 2012. Turnout in the elections for the upper house was at 7 per cent. See: *Reuters*, 2 June 2013, 'Egypt parliament ruled illegal, but to stay on', available at http://www.reuters.com/article/2013/06/02/us-egypt-parliament-idUSBRE95104J20130602#uxQlEKr8wU0x7dFi.97 (accessed 9 April 2016).
4. The United Nations, *Human Development Index 2015*, 'Table 1: Human development index and its components', available at http://hdr.undp.org/en/content/table-1-human-development-index-and-its-components (accessed 9 April 2016).
5. The International Monetary Fund, 'World Economic Outlook Database', available at http://www.imf.org/external/pubs/ft/weo/2014/02/weodata/index.aspx (accessed 9 April 2016).
6. See, for instance, 'Egypt' and 'Kuwait' on Internetworldstats.com. Again, these numbers should not be read without reservations, and there are several complicating factors, including foreigners living in both countries, whether or not one counts citizens or inhabitants in Kuwait and the wide distribution of internet cafes and pirate connections in Egypt. Yet, even so, the picture is quite clear.
7. David Faris, *Dissent and Revolution in a Digital Age: Social Media, Blogging and Activism in Egypt* (New York, 2013).
8. Tim Eaton, 'Internet activism and the Egyptian uprisings: Transforming online dissent into the offline world', *Westminister Papers in Communication and Culture* 9/2 (2013), p. 13.

9. However, HarassMap did operate one until the launch of their website, before the beginning of the time frame set for my investigation.
10. Teresa Pepe, 'Fictionalized Identities in the Egyptian Blogosphere' (PhD Dissertaion, Oslo, 2014).
11. It should be noted here that the two groups in Kuwait that spent by far the most time responding with their followers were Shabab al-Hurriyya and Shabab al-Taghyir wa-l-Tatwir, the two Islamist groups. However, these responses were part of political debates, rather than of the nature described above.
12. Faris, *Dissent and Revolution*, pp. 8–9.
13. For a short description, as well as the videos produced by the group, see their YouTube page: http://www.youtube.com/user/Mosireen (accessed 9 April 2016).
14. Nancy K. Baym and Danah Boyd, 'Socially mediated publicness: An introduction', *Journal of Broadcasting & Electronic Media*, 56/3 (2012), p. 328.

Chapter 7 Assessing the Campaigns

1. Peter Dahlgren, 'The internet, public spheres, and political communication: Dispersion and deliberation', *Political Communication* 22/2 (2005), pp. 147–62.
2. Interview conducted in Cairo, spring 2013.
3. Ibid. For the Tunisian initiative, see their Facebook page: https://www.facebook.com/ShoftTa7rosh.Tunisia?fref=ts (accessed 10 April 2016).
4. It should be pointed out here that the time frame of the Kuwaiti case is longer than that of the Egyptian case, and therefore this outcome might have been expected. However, the Egyptian groups were still active as of late March 2016, although this situation may change due to severe and increasingly enforced restrictions on the part of the authorities.
5. For footage from the march, see AlZiadiQ8, ‘مسيرة كرامة وطن ″8 تحت شعار (الشعب يريد تطهير القضاء) وهجوم القوات الخاصة عليها 6-7-2014“ صور + فيديو:’ available at http://alziadiq8.com/82723.html (accessed 10 April 2016).
6. This is quite clear from their online activities, but was also confirmed during interviews.
7. It should be noted that this was not the first time that the technology behind the website was used, but it was the first time it was appropriated for this particular purpose. This has since been copied in other countries; see, for instance, the *Huffington Post*, 11 February 2013, 'Could mobile technology combat sexual harassment?', available at http://www.huffingtonpost.ca/hina-p-ansari/harassmap-egypt_b_2654388.html (accessed 10 April 2016).
8. More information on this group is available on their Facebook site: https://www.facebook.com/intifadat.almar2a/info/?tab=page_info (accessed 10 April

2016). The group has held several online events, but was also central in the 12 February 2013 international demonstration against harassment and assault.

9. Interview with opposition activist, Kjetil Selvik, Chr. Michelsen Institute.
10. These were presented on the group's website, www.cdmkw.com, which no longer appears to be acceessible (last accessed 1 December 2015).
11. From the online discussion forum kwtfuture.com, 2 April 2012, on the first elected board of the group. Available at http://www.kwtfuture.com/vb/t26554.html. The site was last accessed on 20 November 2014, but now appears to no longer be available.
12. Interview with opposition activist, Kjetil Selvik, Chr. Michelsen Institute.
13. Interview conducted in Cairo, spring 2013.
14. *Ahram Online*, 8 September 2012, 'Fighting the good fight against sexual harassment: New, effective initiatives', available at http://english.ahram.org.eg/NewsContentPrint/1/0/52259/Egypt/0/Fighting-the-good-fight-against-sexual-harassment-.aspx (accessed 10 April 2016).
15. *Ahram Online*, 2 October 2013, 'Policewomen patrol women's carriages on Cairo's packed Metro', available at http://english.ahram.org.eg/News/83027.aspx (accessed 10 April 2016).
16. For instance, party volunteers took part in the 6 February 2013 demonstration 'The Street Is Ours – No to Harassment and Sexual Assault'. See the event page, 'مسيرة الشارع لنا ... لا للتحرش والاعتداء الجنسي', available at https://www.facebook.com/events/123959144442368/ (accessed 10 April 2016).
17. See, for instance, *Egypt Independent*, 6 February 2014, 'Women march against sexual harassment', available at http://www.egyptindependent.com/news/women-march-against-sexual-harassment (accessed 10 April 2016).
18. See, for instance, *MadaMasr*, 28 June 2014, 'Government vs. sexual violence', available at http://www.madamasr.com/sections/politics/government-vs-sexual-violence (accessed 10 April 2016).
19. *Daily News Egypt*, 6 June 2014, 'Anti-harassment group praises new harassment law', available at http://www.dailynewsegypt.com/2014/06/06/anti-harassment-group-praises-new-harassment-law/ (accessed 10 April 2016).
20. *Ahram Online*, 18 June 2014, 'New police department for crimes of violence against women', available at http://english.ahram.org.eg/NewsContent/1/0/104090/Egypt/0/New-police-department-for-crimes-of-violence-again.aspx (accessed 10 April 2016).
21. *MadaMasr*, 28 June 2014, 'Government vs. sexual violence'.
22. Ibid.
23. *Reuters*, 9 December 2013, 'Kuwaiti court acquits 70 accused over 2011 storming of parliament', available at http://www.reuters.com/article/2013/12/09/us-kuwait-politics-court-idUSBRE9B80F720131209 (accessed 10 April 2016).
24. Interview conducted in Kuwait, autumn 2012.

25. Mary Ann Tétreault, 'Looking for revolution in Kuwait', *Middle East Report Online* (2012), available at http://www.merip.org/mero/mero110112 (accessed 5 April 2016).
26. This was a clear reference to the battle of al-Jahra', as referred to in Chapter 5.
27. Interview with opposition activist, Kjetil Selvik, Chr. Michelsen Institute.
28. Deborah L. Wheeler, *The Internet in the Middle East: Global Expectations and Local Imaginations in Kuwait* (New York, 2006), p. 133.
29. This phrase refers to al-Barrak's thinly veiled threat to the emir himself, stating that the people would not allow him to lead Kuwait into autocracy. Addressing the emir directly in such a manner was unprecedented in Kuwaiti politics.
30. According to the rate given by Den Norske Bank on 10 April 2016. Their currency converter is available at https://www.dnb.no/bedrift/markets/valuta-renter/kalkulator/valutakalkulator.html.
31. See, for instance, *Al-Arabiya News*, 19 March 2014, 'Viral video of harassed blonde Egypt woman sparks backlash', available at http://english.alarabiya.net/en/variety/2014/03/19/-Viral-video-of-harassed-blonde-Egypt-women-sparks-backlash.html (accessed 10 April 2016).
32. Interview conducted in Cairo, spring 2013.
33. There were, however, numerous demonstrations in support of the ousted president. These were outlawed and routinely met with violence by the police. The groups studied here did not take part in these.
34. *BBC News*, 26 July 2013, 'Q&A: Kuwait parliamentary election', available at http://www.bbc.com/news/world-middle-east-23449066 (accessed 10 April 2016).
35. *Al-Arabiya News*, 28 July 2013, 'Kuwait liberals make slight gains in parliamentary election results', available at http://english.alarabiya.net/en/News/middle-east/2013/07/28/Kuwait-liberals-make-slight-gains-in-parliamentary-polls.html (accessed 10 April 2016). For more on the composition of the new Parliament, see Michael Herb's *Kuwait Politics Database*, 'مجلس الأمة 2013', available at http://www2.gsu.edu/~polmfh/database/maj201307.htm (accessed 10 April 2016).
36. Christopher Davidson, *After the Sheikhs: The Coming Collapse of the Gulf Monarchies* (London, 2012).
37. Interview conducted in Cairo, spring 2013.
38. David Faris, *Dissent and Revolution in a Digital Age: Social Media, Blogging and Activism in Egypt* (New York, 2013), p. 65.
39. *Ahram Online*, 5 November 2014, 'UN review points at Egypt's NGO and protest laws', available at http://english.ahram.org.eg/NewsContent/1/64/114821/Egypt/Politics-/UN-review-points-at-Egypts-NGO-and-protest-laws.aspx (accessed 10 April 2016).
40. Interview conducted in Cairo, spring 2013.

41. Jean-Pierre Filiu, *The Arab Revolution: Ten Lessons from the Democratic Uprising* (London, 2011), pp. 31–42.
42. Shafeeq Ghabra, 'Voluntary associations in Kuwait: The foundation of a new system?', *The Middle East Journal* 45/3 (1991), p. 206.
43. Shafeeq Ghabra 'Kuwait and the dynamics of socio-economic change', *The Middle East Journal* 51/3 (1997), p. 361.
44. Interview with opposition activist, Kjetil Selvik, Chr. Michelsen Institute.
45. Farah Al-Nakib, 'Revisiting ḥaḍar and badū in Kuwait: Citizenship, housing, and the construction of a dichotomy', *International Journal of Middle East Studies* 46/01 (2014), pp. 5–30.
46. Interview conducted in Cairo, spring 2013.
47. This was confirmed in all interviews conducted in Cairo.
48. 'About us' on nazra.org: http://nazra.org/en/about-us (accessed 10 April 2016).
49. *MadaMasr*, 23 September 2014, 'President amends law to include life sentence for receiving funds, arms', available at http://www.madamasr.com/news/presi dent-amends-law-include-life-sentence-receiving-funds-arms (accessed 10 April 2016).
50. *MadaMasr*, 5 April 2015, 'Ministry to investigate NGO over awareness programs for same sex partners', available at http://www.madamasr.com/news/ ministry-investigate-ngo-over-awareness-programs-same-sex-partners (accessed 10 April 2016).
51. As described above, TBG also launched a new organisation in August 2013, DWB, which was meant to provide a more comprehensive approach to the issues at hand. This organisation, however, has been largely inactive online since early 2015. However, its accounts are still operational, so the group seems to be dormant rather than closed.
52. See for instance *Ahram Online*, 18 July 2015, 'Egyptian police arrest 29 men for sexual harassment during Eid: MOI', available at http://english.ahram.org.eg/ NewsContent/1/64/135659/Egypt/Politics-/Egyptian-police-arrest–men-for-sexual-harassment-.aspx (accessed 10 April 2016).

Chapter 8 Understanding Online Activism

1. Nancy K. Baym and Danah Boyd, 'Socially mediated publicness: An introduction', *Journal of Broadcasting & Electronic Media*, 56/3 (2012), p. 320.
2. Nancy Fraser, 'Rethinking the public sphere: A contribution to the critique of actually existing democracy', in C. Calhoun (ed.), *Habermas and the Public Sphere* (Cambridge and London, 1992).
3. United Nations Entity for Gender Equality and the Empowerment of Women (UN Women), The National Council for Women (NCW), *Study on Ways and Methods to Eliminate Sexual Harassment in Egypt* (2013), available at http://web. law.columbia.edu/sites/default/files/microsites/gender-sexuality/un_womens exual-harassment-study-egypt-final-en.pdf (accessed 5 April 2016).

4. David Faris, *Dissent and Revolution in a Digital Age: Social Media, Blogging and Activism in Egypt* (New York, 2013), p. 122.
5. Farah Al-Nakib, 'Revisiting ḥaḍar and badū in Kuwait: Citizenship, housing, and the construction of a dichotomy', *International Journal of Middle East Studies* 46/01 (2014), pp. 5–30; Shafeeq Ghabra, 'Kuwait and the dynamics of socio-economic change', *The Middle East Journal* 51/3 (1997), pp. 358–72.
6. Peter Dahlgren, 'The internet, public spheres, and political communication: Dispersion and deliberation', *Political Communication* 22/2 (2005), pp. 147–62; Geoff Eley, 'Nations, publics, and political cultures: Placing Habermas in the nineteenth century', in C. Calhoun (ed.), *Habermas and the Public Sphere* (Cambridge and London, 1992); Fraser, 'Rethinking the Public Sphere'; Dina Matar, 'Heya TV: A feminist counterpublic for Arab women?', *Comparative Studies of South Asia, Africa and the Middle East* 27/3 (2007), pp. 513–24; Chantal Mouffe, 'Which public sphere for a democratic society?', *Theoria: A Journal of Social and Political Theory* 99 (2002), pp. 55–65; Michael Warner, 'Publics and counterpublics', *Public Culture* 14/1 (2002), pp. 49–90.
7. Warner, 'Publics and counterpublics', p. 88.
8. Matar, 'Heya TV', p. 515.
9. Faris, *Dissent and Revolution*, p. 144.
10. Ibid.
11. Christopher Wilson and Alexandra Dunn, 'Digital media in the Egyptian revolution: Descriptive analysis from the Tahrir data set', *International Journal of Communication* 5 (2011), pp. 1248–72.
12. See Michael Herb's *Kuwait Politics Database*, 'February 2012 elections', available at http://www.kuwaitpolitics.org/voterank17.htm (accessed 11 April 2016).
13. Jürgen Habermas, 'Political communication in media society: Does democracy still enjoy an epistemic dimension? The impact of normative theory on empirical research', *Communication Theory* 16/4 (2006), p. 423.
14. Jürgen Habermas, 'Further reflections on the public sphere', in C. Calhoun (ed.), *Habermas and the Public Sphere* (Cambridge and London, 1992).
15. Chantal Mouffe, 'Space, hegemony and radical critique', *Spatial Politics: Essays for Doreen Massey* (2013), p. 28.
16. Warner, 'Publics and counterpublics', p. 77.
17. Matar, 'Heya TV', p. 520.
18. Clearly, this is dependent on the context, as what might be difficult and embarrassing is relative. If one lives in poverty and all one's friends live in poverty, this would hardly be embarrassing to talk about. However, this only reinforces the point: in that case, it is a common, public problem, not something private.
19. *MadaMasr*, 28 October 2015, 'Wave of anger against TV anchor for airing photos of assault victim', available at http://www.madamasr.com/news/wave-anger-against-tv-anchor-airing-photos-assault-victim (accessed 11 April 2016).

20. Bassem Youssef on Twitter, @DrBassemYoussef, 30 October 2015.
21. *Al-Arabiya English*, 30 October 2015, 'Egypt TV show suspended after sexual harassment victim blamed', available at http://english.alarabiya.net/en/media/television-and-radio/2015/10/30/Egypt-TV-show-suspended-after-sexual-harassment-victim-blamed-.html (accessed 11 April 2016).
22. Peter Dahlgren and Tobias Olsson, 'From public sphere to civic culture: Young citizens' internet use', in R. Butsch (ed.), *Media and Public Spheres* (New York, 2007).

Chapter 9 Online Activism in Egypt and Kuwait: Conclusions

1. Exceptions might be Flickr and Instagram, but these platforms were employed by only a few groups.
2. Max Horkheimer and Theodor W. Adorno, *Kulturindustri: Opplysning som massebedrag*, A. Sundland, trans. 2nd edn (Oslo, 1991).
3. Manar Shorbagy, 'Egyptian women in revolt: Ordinary women, extraordinary roles', in D. Tschirgi, W. Kazziha and S. F. McMahon (eds), *Egypt's Tahrir Revolution* (Boulder and London, 2013).
4. Interview conducted in Kuwait, autumn 2012.
5. David Faris, *Dissent and Revolution in a Digital Age: Social Media, Blogging and Activism in Egypt* (New York, 2013).

Appendix I Kuwaiti Twitter debates

1. Topsy, 'support'. URL: http://about.topsy.com/support/search/. No longer available online.

Appendix III Timeline of the Egyptian case

1. Paul Amar, 'Turning the gendered politics of the security state inside out? Charging the police with sexual harassment in Egypt', *International Feminist Journal of Politics* 13/3 (2011), p. 320.
2. *Christian Science Monitor*, 23 November 2010, 'In Cairo, an effort to put sexual harassment on the map – via Twitter and Text'. Available online: http://www.csmonitor.com/World/Middle-East/2010/1123/In-Cairo-an-effort-to-put-sexual-harassment-on-the-map-via-Twitter-and-text (accessed 4 May 2016).
3. HarassMap blog, 20 January 2011, 'إعتذار: تأجيل مسيرة الدراجات" عايزين شوارع مصر آمان يا شباب.' The article was last accessed on 23 September 2014. In November 2015, HarassMap launched a

new blog, and so the old blog is no longer accessible. However, the content of the old blog is stored by the author.

4. More information on the march is available at the site of the group 'مليونية المرأة': https://www.facebook.com/profile.php?id=100002138404317 (accessed 1 December 2015).
5. *CNN*, 8 March 2011, 'Egypt's million woman march fizzles into shouting matches', available online: http://edition.cnn.com/2011/WORLD/meast/03/08/egypt.women/ (accessed 1 December 2015).
6. *Ahram Online*, 8 March 2011, 'Egyptian million woman march ends with a gunshot', available online: http://english.ahram.org.eg/NewsContent/1/64/7292/Egypt/Politics-/Egyptian-million-woman-march-ends-with-a-gunshot.aspx (accessed 4 May 2016).
7. From the event page on Facebook, 'يوم التدوين والزقزقة ضد التحرش الجنسي والعنف الجندري في مصر.': https://www.facebook.com/events/179745172081220/ (unfortunately, this page is no longer available online, last accessed 24 September 2014).
8. *Egypt Independent*, 22 June 2011, 'The sexual harassment file: Harassment debate lights up blogosphere', available online: http://www.egyptindependent.com/news/sexual-harassment-file-harassment-debate-lights-blogosphere (accessed 4 May 2016).
9. From HarassMap's blog post on the issue, 'عيد مصر أمان في مكان... أيام التوعية والتدوين ضد التحرش الجنسي' (no longer available online).
10. *CNN*, 21 December 2011, 'Women march in Cairo to protest violence; Military promises to listen', available online: http://edition.cnn.com/2011/12/20/world/africa/egypt-unrest/ (accessed 4 May 2016).
11. The first metro campaign was announced as a Facebook event, not formally held by Imprint but by individual activists, including one of the founders of Imprint, 'شباب ضد التحرش - دوريات مترو الانفاق'.
12. HarassMap, Facebook, 15 August 2012.
13. *Egypt Independent*, 22 August 22, 2012, 'Sexual harassment wave continues for third day', available online: http://www.egyptindependent.com/news/sexual-harassment-wave-continues-third-day (accessed 4 May 2016).
14. *Huffington Post UK*, 28 September 2012, 'Egyptian teenager Eman Mostafa who was groped "spat in attacker's face and was gunned down"', available online: http://www.huffingtonpost.co.uk/2012/09/28/egypt-teen-girl-groped-spat-eman-mostafa-killed_n_1923237.html (accessed 4 May 2016).
15. *Ahram Online*, 22 October 2012, 'Egypt's cabinet plans new law to fight sexual harassment', available online: http://english.ahram.org.eg/NewsContent/1/0/56273/Egypt/0/Egypts-cabinet-plans-new-law-to-fight-sexual-harra.aspx (accessed 4 May 2016).
16. *USA Today*, 30 October 2012, 'Sexual harassment spikes over Egyptian holiday', available online: http://www.usatoday.com/story/news/world/2012/10/30/sexual-harassment-egypt/1669707/ (accessed 4 May 2016).

17. *Ahram Online*, 12 November 2012, 'Egyptian man jailed for 2 years for sexual harassment', available online: http://english.ahram.org.eg/NewsContent/1/64/57916/Egypt/Politics-/Egyptian-man-jailed-for–years-for-sexual-harassme.aspx (accessed 4 May 2016).
18. See the event page, 'يومين تدوين وزقزقة من أجل الكرامة الإنسانية 23 و 24 يناير.': https://www.facebook.com/events/400348160054591/ (accessed 4 May 2016).
19. See the event page, 'مسيرة الشارع لنا... لا للتحرش والاعتداء الجنسي,': https://www.facebook.com/events/123959144442368/ (accessed 4 May 2016).
20. *BBC News*, 6 February 2013, 'Egyptians protest at sexual violence against women', available online: http://www.bbc.com/news/world-middle-east-21356233 (accessed 4 May 2016).
21. See the event page, 'Global protest against sexual terrorism practiced on Egyptian female protestors': https://www.facebook.com/events/150788335077948/?ref=22 (accessed 4 May 2016).
22. *Daily News Egypt*, 12 February 2013, 'Women take to the streets to protest sexual harassment and assault', available online: http://www.dailynewsegypt.com/2013/02/12/women-take-to-the-streets-to-protest-sexual-harassment-and-assault/ (accessed 4 May 2016).
23. See event page 'مسيرة 8 مارس 2013 / نساء مع الثورة,': https://www.facebook.com/events/445459645523945/?ref=22. See also the statement from the New Women Foundation: 'بيان مسيرة 8 مارس 2013.': http://nwrcegypt.org/%D8%A8%D9%8A%D8%A7%D9%86-%D9%85%D8%B3%D9%8A%D8%B1%D8%A9-8-%D9%85%D8%A7%D8%B1%D8%B3-2013/ (accessed 4 May 2016).

LIST OF WORKS CITED

Abdulla, R. A., *The Internet in the Arab World: Egypt and Beyond* (New York, 2007).

——— 'The revolution will be tweeted', *Cairo Review of Global Affairs* 3 (2011), pp. 41–9.

——— *Mapping Digital Media: Egypt* (2013), available at https://www.opensocietyfoundations.org/sites/default/files/mapping-digital-media-egypt-20130823.pdf (accessed 4 April 2016).

Abu-Lughod, L., 'Dialects of women's empowerment: The international circuitry of the Arab Human Development Report 2005', *International Journal of Middle East Studies* 41/01 (2009), pp. 83–103.

Al Malky, R., 'Blogging for reform: The case of Egypt', *Arab Media & Society* 1 (2007).

Alnajjar, G., 'The challenges facing Kuwaiti democracy', *The Middle East Journal* 54/2 (2000), pp. 242–58.

Al-Nakib, F., 'Revisiting ḥaḍar and badū in Kuwait: Citizenship, housing, and the construction of a dichotomy', *International Journal of Middle East Studies* 46/1 (2014), pp. 5–30.

Al Nashmi, E., Cleary, J., Molleda, J.-C. and McAdams, M., 'Internet political discussions in the Arab world: A look at online forums from Kuwait, Saudi Arabia, Egypt and Jordan', *International Communication Gazette* 72/8 (2010), pp. 719–38.

Al-Sayyid, M. K., 'A civil society in Egypt?', *The Middle East Journal* 47/2 (1993), pp. 228–42.

——— 'What went wrong with Mubarak's regime?', in D. Tschirgi, W. Kazziha and S. F. Mcmahon (eds), *Egypt's Tahrir Revolution* (Boulder and London, 2013).

Amar, P., 'Turning the gendered politics of the security state inside out? Charging the police with sexual harassment in Egypt', *International Feminist Journal of Politics* 13/3 (2011), pp. 299–328.

Amnesty International, *Egypt: Gender-Based Violence Against Women around Tahrir Square* (2013), available at https://www.amnesty.org/en/documents/MDE12/009/2013/en/ (accessed 4 April 2016).

Barlow, A., *Blogging America: The New Public Sphere* (Westport, Connecticut and London, 2008).

Baym, N. K. and Boyd, D., 'Socially mediated publicness: an introduction', *Journal of Broadcasting & Electronic Media*, 56/3 (2012), pp. 320–9.

Beinin, J., 'The rise of Egypt's workers', *Carnegie Endowment for International Peace* (2012), available at http://carnegieendowment.org/2012/06/28/rise-of-egypt-s-workers (accessed 4 April 2016).

Ben Moussa, M., 'From Arab street to social movements: Re-theorizing collective action and the role of social media in the Arab Spring', *Westminster Papers in Communication and Culture* 9/2 (2013), pp. 47–71.

Benkler, Y., *The Wealth of Networks: How Social Production Transforms Markets and Freedom* (New Haven and London, 2006).

Boas, T. and Kalathil, S., *Open Networks, Closed Regimes: The Impact of the Internet on Authoritarian Rule* (Washington, DC, 2003).

Bollen, K. A., 'Political democracy: Conceptual and measurement traps', *Studies in Comparative International Development* 25/1 (1990), pp. 7–24.

Bos, W. and Tarnai, C., 'Content analysis in empirical social research', *International Journal of Educational Research* 31 (1999), pp. 659–71.

Brownlee, J., 'The decline of pluralism in Mubarak's Egypt', *Journal of Democracy* 13/4 (2002), pp. 6–14.

Brynen, R., Moore, P. W., Salloukh, B. F. and Zahar, M. -J., *Beyond the Arab Spring: Authoritarianism & Democratization in the Arab World* (Boulder and London, 2012).

Butsch, R., 'Introduction: How are media public spheres', in R. Butsch (ed.), *Media and Public Spheres* (New York, 2007).

Coates Ulrichsen, K., 'Politics and opposition in Kuwait: Continuity and change', *Journal of Arabian Studies* 4/2 (2014), pp. 214–30.

Couldry, N., Livingstone, S. and Markham, T., 'Connection or disconnection? Tracking the mediated public sphere in everyday life', in R. Butsh (ed.), *Media and Public Spheres* (New York, 2007).

Crystal, J., 'Coalitions in oil monarchies: Kuwait and Qatar', *Comparative Politics* 21/4 (1989), pp. 427–43.

——— *Oil and Politics in the Gulf: Rulers and Merchants in Kuwait and Qatar* (Cambridge, 1995).

Dahlgren, P., *Television and the Public Sphere: Citizenship, Democracy and the Media* (London, 1995).

——— 'The Internet, public spheres, and political communication: Dispersion and deliberation', *Political Communication* 22/2 (2005), pp. 147–62.

Dahlgren, P. and Olsson, T., 'From public sphere to civic culture: Young citizens' internet use', in R. Butsch (ed.), *Media and Public Spheres* (New York, 2007).

Dashti, A., 'The role of online journalism in political disputes in Kuwait', *Journal of Arab & Muslim Media Research* 2/1–2 (2009), pp. 91–112.

——— 'The effect of Kuwaiti online readers' comments on sectarian and tribal issues: A case study of the online newspaper Alaan', *Journal of Mass Communication & Journalism* 3 (2013), available at http://www.omicsgroup.org/journals/the-effect-of-kuwaiti-online-readers-comments-on-sectarian-and-tribal-issues-a-case-study-of-the-online-newspaper-alaan-2165-7912.1000148.php?aid=11626 (accessed 4 April 2016).

Davidson, C., *After the Sheikhs: The Coming Collapse of the Gulf Monarchies* (London, 2012).

Dean, J., 'Why the net is not a public sphere', *Constellations* 10/1 (2003), pp. 95–112.

Della Porta, D. and Diani, M., *Social Movements: An Introduction* (Malden and Oxford, 2006).

Douai, A., 'Offline politics in the Arab blogosphere: Trends and prospects in Morocco', in A. Russell and N. Echchaibi (eds), *International Blogging: Identity, Politics, and Networked Publics* (New York, 2009).

Dryzek, J. S. and Niemeyer, S., 'Reconciling pluralism and consensus as political ideals', *American Journal of Political Science* 50/3 (2006), pp. 634–49.

Eaton, T., 'Internet activism and the Egyptian uprisings: Transforming online dissent into the offline world', *Westminister Papers in Communication and Culture* 9/2 (2013), pp. 3–25.

Eickelman, D. F. and Anderson, J. W., 'Redefining Muslim publics', in D. F. Eickelman and J. W. Anderson (eds), *New Media in the Muslim World: The Emerging Public Sphere* (Bloomington, 2003).

El-Mahdi, R., 'Enough! Egypt's quest for democracy', *Comparative Political Studies* 42/8 (2009), pp. 1011–39.

El-Menawy, A. L., *Tahrir – The Last 18 Days of Mubarak – An Insider's Account of the Uprising in Egypt* (London, 2012).

El-Nadeem Center, Nazra for Feminist Studies and New Woman Foundation, *Sexual Assault and Rape in Tahrir Square and its Vicinity: A Compendium of Sources 2011–2013* (2013), available at http://nazra.org/en/2013/05/sexual-assault-and-rape-tahrir-square-and-its-vicinity-compendium-sources-2011-2013 (accessed 4 April 2016).

Eley, G., 'Nations, publics, and political cultures: Placing Habermas in the nineteenth century', in C. Calhoun (ed.), *Habermas and the Public Sphere* (Cambridge and London, 1992).

Elsadda, H., 'Arab women bloggers: The emergence of literary counterpublics', *Middle East Journal of Culture and Communication* 3/3 (2010), pp. 312–32.

Eltantawy, N. and Wiest, J. B., 'Social media in the Egyptian revolution: Reconsidering resource mobilization theory', *International Journal of Communication* 5 (2011), pp. 1207–24.

Etling, B., Kelly, J., Faris, R. and Palfrey, J., 'Mapping the Arabic Blogosphere: Politics and Dissent Online', *New Media & Society* 12/8 (2010), pp. 1225–43.

Farah, N. R., 'The political economy of Egypt's revolution', in D. Tschirgi, W. Kazziha and S. F. McMahon (eds), *Egypt's Tahrir Revolution* (Boulder and London, 2013).

Faris, D., *Dissent and Revolution in a Digital Age: Social Media, Blogging and Activism in Egypt* (New York, 2013).

Filiu, J.-P., *The Arab Revolution: Ten Lessons from the Democratic Uprising* (London, 2011).

Fontana, A. and Frey, J. H., 'The interview: From neutral stance to political involvement', in N. K. Denzin and Y. S. Lincoln (eds), *The Sage Handbook of Qualitative Research* (London, 2005).

Fraser, N., 'Rethinking the public sphere: A contribution to the critique of actually existing democracy', in C. Calhoun (ed.), *Habermas and the Public Sphere* (Cambridge and London, 1992).

George, A. L. and Bennett, A., *Case Studies and Theory Development in the Social Sciences* (Cambridge and London, 2005).

Gerbaudo, P., 'The "kill switch" as "suicide switch": Mobilizing side effects of Mubarak's communication blackout', *Westminster Papers in Communication and Culture* 9/2 (2013), pp. 25–47.

Gerring, J., 'Case selection for case-study analysis: Qualitative and quantitative techniques', in J. M. Box-Steffensmeier, H. E. Brady and D. Collier (eds), *Oxford Handbook of Political Methodology* (Oxford, 2008).

Ghabra, S., 'Voluntary associations in Kuwait: The foundation of a new system?', *The Middle East Journal* 45/3 (1991), pp. 199–215.

——— 'Kuwait and the dynamics of socio-economic change', *The Middle East Journal* 51/3 (1997), pp. 358–72.

Ghonim, W., *Revolution 2.0: The Power of the People is Greater than the People in Power: A Memoir* (London, 2012).

Goode, L., 'Social news, citizen journalism and democracy', *New Media & Society* 11/8 (2009), pp. 1287–305.

Habermas, J., *The Structural Transformation of the Public Sphere: An Inquiry into a Category of Bourgeois Society*, 12th edn (Cambridge, 1989).

——— 'Further reflections on the public sphere', in C. Calhoun (ed.), *Habermas and the Public Sphere* (Cambridge and London, 1992).

——— 'Political communication in media society: Does democracy still enjoy an epistemic dimension? The impact of normative theory on empirical research', *Communication Theory* 16/4 (2006), pp. 411–26.

Habermas, J., Lennox, S. and Lennox, F., 'The public sphere: An encyclopedia article (1964)', *New German Critique* 3 (1974), pp. 49–55.

Hamdy, N. and Gomaa, E. H., 'Framing the Egyptian uprising in Arabic language newspapers and social media', *Journal of Communication* 62/2 (2012), pp. 195–211.

Hassan, R. M., Shoukry, A. and Komsan, N. A., *'Clouds in Egypt's Sky' Sexual Harassment: From Verbal Harassment to Rape* (2008), available at http://egypt.unfpa.org/Images/Publication/2010_03/6eeeb05a-3040-42d2-9e1c-2bd2e1ac8cac.pdf (accessed 4 April 2016).

Herb, M., *All in the Family: Absolutism, Revolution, and Democracy in Middle Eastern Monarchies* (New York, 1999).

——— 'A nation of bureaucrats: Political participation and economic diversification in Kuwait and the United Arab Emirates', *International Journal of Middle East Studies* 41/03 (2009), pp. 375–95.

Hinds, M. and Badawi, E.-S. (eds), *A Dictionary of Egyptian Arabic* (Beirut, 1986).

Hofheinz, A., 'The internet in the Arab world: Playground for political liberalization', *International Politics and Society* 3 (2005), pp. 75–96.

——— 'Nextopia? Beyond Revolution 2.0', *International Journal of Communication* 5 (2011), pp. 1417–34.

Horkheimer, M. and Adorno, T. W., *Kulturindustri: Opplysning som massebedrag*, A. Sundland, trans. 2nd edn (Oslo, 1991).

Howard, P. N. and Hussain, M. M., *Democracy's Fourth Wave?: Digital Media and the Arab Spring* (Oxford, 2013).

Huntington, S. P., 'Will more countries become democratic?', *Political Science Quarterly* 99/2 (1984), pp. 193–218.

——— 'Democracy's third wave', *Journal of Democracy* 2/2 (1991), pp. 12–34.

Isherwood, T., 'A new direction or more of the same? Political blogging in Egypt', *Arab Media & Society* 6 (2008), pp. 1–17.

Ives, P., *Language and Hegemony in Gramsci* (London, 2004).

Johnson, J. B. and Reynolds, H. T., *Political Science Research Methods* (Washington, 2005).

Jurkiewicz, S., 'Being a Blogger in Beirut – Production Practices and Modes of Publicness' (PhD Dissertaion, Oslo, 2012).

Kapoor, I., 'Deliberative democracy or agonistic pluralism? The relevance of the Habermas–Mouffe debate for third world politics', *Alternatives* 27/4 (2002), pp. 459–87.

Kassem, M., *Egyptian Politics: The Dynamics of Authoritarian Rule* (London and Boulder, 2004).

Kazziha, W., 'Egypt under Mubarak: A family affair', in D. Tschirgi, W. Kazziha and S. F. Mcmahon (eds), *Egypt's Tahrir Revolution* (Boulder and London, 2013).

Kedebe, T. A., Kindt, K. T. and Høigilt, J., *Language Change in Egypt: Social and Cultural Indicators Survey – A Tabulation Report* (2013), available at http://www.fafo.no/index.php/nb/zoo-publikasjoner/fafo-rapporter/item/language-change-in-egypt-social-and-cultural-indicators-survey (accessed 4 April 2016).

Khalil, A., *Liberation Square: Inside the Egyptian Revolution and the Rebirth of a Nation* (New York, 2011).

Khamis, S. and Vaughn, K., 'Cyberactivism in the Egyptian revolution: How civic engagement and citizen journalism tilted the balance', *Arab Media and Society* 13/3 (2011), pp. 1–37.

Kienle, E., 'More than a response to Islamism: The political deliberalization of Egypt in the 1990s', *The Middle East Journal* 52/2 (1998), pp. 219–35.

——— *A Grand Delusion: Democracy and Economic Reform in Egypt* (London and New York, 2001).

Kohlbacher, F., 'The use of qualitative content analysis in case study research', *Forum Qualitative Sozialforschung/Forum: Qualitative Social Research* 7/1 (2006), available at http://www.qualitative-research.net/index.php/fqs/article/viewArticle/75 (accessed 4 April 2016).

Krug, E. G., Dahlberg, L. L., Mercy, J. A., Zwi, A. B. and Lozano, R. (eds), *World Report on Violence and Health* (2002), available at http://www.who.int/violence_injury_prevention/violence/world_report/en/introduction.pdf (accessed April 4 2016).

Kuebler, J., 'Overcoming the digital divide: The internet and political mobilization in Egypt and Tunisia', *CyberOrient* 5/1 (2011), available at http://www.cyberorient.net/article.do?articleId=6212 (accessed 4 April 2016).

Laclau, E. and Mouffe, C., *Hegemony and Socialist Strategy: Towards a Radical Democratic Politics,* 2nd edn (London and Brooklyn, 2001).

Langohr, V., 'Too much civil society, too little politics: Egypt and liberalizing Arab regimes', *Comparative Politics* 36/2 (2004), pp. 181–204.

Lim, M., 'Clicks, cabs, and coffee houses: Social media and oppositional movements in Egypt, 2004–2011', *Journal of Communication* 62/2 (2012), pp. 231–48.

Lynch, M., 'Blogging the new Arab public', *Arab Media & Society* 1/1 (2007), available at http://www.arabmediasociety.com/?article=10 (accessed 4 April 2016).

——— 'Young brothers in cyberspace', *Middle East Report* 37/245 (2007), available at http://www.merip.org/mer/mer245/young-brothers-cyberspace&gt (accessed 4 April 2016).

——— 'After Egypt: The limits and promise of online challenges to the authoritarian Arab state', *Perspectives on Politics* 9/02 (2011), pp. 301–10.

Manovich, L., 'The practice of everyday (media) life: From mass consumption to mass cultural production?', *Critical Inquiry* 35/2 (2009), pp. 319–31.

Markham, A. N. and Baym, N. K. (eds), *Internet Inquiry: Conversations About Method* (Thousand Oaks, 2008).

Matar, D., 'Heya TV: A feminist counterpublic for Arab women?', *Comparative Studies of South Asia, Africa and the Middle East* 27/3 (2007), pp. 513–24.

Meital, Y., 'The struggle over political order in Egypt: The 2005 elections', *The Middle East Journal* 60/2 (2006), pp. 257–79.

Mocanu, D., Baronchelli, A., Perra, N., Gonçalves, B., Zhang, Q. and Vespignani, A., 'The Twitter of Babel: Mapping world languages through microblogging platforms', *PloS one* 8/4 (2013), e61981, available at http://dx.doi.org/10.1371/journal.pone.0061981 (accessed April 4 2016).

Moe, H., 'Everyone a pamphleteer? Reconsidering comparisons of mediated public participation in the print age and the digital era', *Media, Culture & Society* 32/4 (2010), pp. 691–700.

Mouffe, C., 'Deliberative democracy or agonistic pluralism?', *Social Research* 66/3 (1999), pp. 745–58.

——— 'Which public sphere for a democratic society?', *Theoria: A Journal of Social and Political Theory* 99 (2002), pp. 55–65.

——— 'Space, Hegemony and Radical Critique', *Spatial Politics: Essays for Doreen Massey* (2013), pp. 19–31.

Nazra for Feminist Studies, *One Year of Impunity Violations against Women Human Rights Defenders in Egypt from August to December 2011* (2012), available at http://nazra.org/en/2012/09/%E2%80%9Ci%E2%80%99m-coming-back-you-i-want-kill-you%E2%80%9D-one-year-impunity (accessed 5 April 2016).

Nordenson, J., *We Want Five! – Kuwait, the Internet, and the Public Sphere* (Saarbrücken, 2010).

O'Reilly, T., 'What is Web 2.0: Design patterns and business models for the next generation of software', *Communications & Strategies* 1 (2007), pp. 17–37.

Orgad, S., 'How can researchers make sense of the issues involved in collecting and interpreting online and offline data', in A. N. Markham and N. K. Baym (eds), *Internet Inquiry Conversations About Method* (Thousand Oaks, 2008).

Osama, W., 'Targeting women with violence in Egyptian Politics', *Babylon nordisk tidsskrift for midtøstenstudier* 3/2 (2005), pp. 32–9.

Otterman, S., 'Publicizing the private: Egyptian women bloggers speak out', *Arab Media & Society* 1 (2007), available at http://www.arabmediasociety.com/topics/index.php?t_article=28 (accessed 5 April 2016).

Papacharissi, Z., 'The Virtual Sphere 2.0: The internet, the public sphere, and beyond', in A. P. N. H. Chadwick (ed.), *Routledge Handbook of Internet Politics*, Kindle edn (London and New York, 2009).

Parslow, J., 'Egypts kamp om loven', *Babylon nordisk tidsskrift for midtøstenstudier* 11/1 (2013), pp. 8–18.

Pepe, T., 'Fictionalized Identities in the Egyptian Blogosphere' (PhD Dissertation, Oslo, 2014).

Pew, *Social Networking Popular Across the Globe* (2012), available at http://www.pewglobal.org/2012/12/12/social-networking-popular-across-globe/?beta=true&utm_expid=53098246-2.Lly4CFSVQG2lphsg-KopIg.1&utm_referrer=https%3A%2F%2Fwww.google.no%2F (accessed 5 April 2016).

Radsch, C., 'Core to commonplace: The evolution of Egypt's blogosphere', *Arab Media & Society* 6 (2008), available at http://www.arabmediasociety.com/UserFiles/AMS6%20Courtney%20Radsch.pdf (accessed 5 April 2016).

——— 'Blogosphere and social media', in Ellen Laipson (ed.), *Seismic Shift: Understanding Change in the Middle East* (Washington, 2011), available at http://papers.ssrn.com/sol3/papers.cfm?abstract_id=2336076 (accessed 5 April 2016).

Ramsay, G., 'What kind of Arabic and why? Language in Egyptian blogs', *Orientalia Suecana* 61 (Supplement) (2013), pp. 49–87.

Rane, H. and Salem, S., 'Social media, social movements and the diffusion of ideas in the Arab uprisings', *Journal of International Communication* 18/1 (2012), pp. 97–111.

Redman, J. C. A., 'The Diwaniyya: Guestroom Sociability and Bureaucratic Brokerage in Kuwait' (PhD Dissertation, Utah, 2014).

Ruiz, C., Domingo, D., Mico, J. L., Diaz-Noci, J., Masip, P. and Meso, K., 'Public Sphere 2.0? The Democratic Qualities of Citizen Debates in Online Newspapers', *The International Journal of Press/Politics* 16/4 (2011), pp. 463–87.

Salem, P., 'Kuwait: Politics in a Participatory Emirate', in M. Ottaway and J. Choucair-Vizoso (eds), *Beyond the Facade – Political Reform in the Arab World* (Washington, DC, 2008).

Salvatore, A., 'Before (and after) the "Arab spring": From connectedness to mobilization in the public sphere', *Oriente Moderno* 91/1 (2011), pp. 5–12.

Schemm, P., 'Egypt struggles to control anti-war protests', *Middle East Research and Information Project* (2003), available at http://www.merip.org/mero/mero033103 (accessed 5 April 2016).

Selvik, K., 'Golfmonarkiene – mer variasjon enn olje kan forklare', *Babylon nordisk tidsskrift for midtøstenstudier* 8/2 (2010), pp. 8–20.

Selvik, K., Nordenson, J. and Kebede, T. A., 'Print media liberalization and electoral coverage bias in Kuwait', *The Middle East Journal* 69/2 (2015), pp. 255–76.

Shorbagy, M., 'Egyptian women in revolt: Ordinary women, extraordinary roles', in D. Tschirgi, W. Kazziha and S. F. McMahon (eds), *Egypt's Tahrir Revolution* (Boulder and London, 2013).

Shultziner, D. and Tétreault, M. A., 'Representation and democratic progress in Kuwait', *Representation* 48/3 (2012), pp. 281–93.

Siapera, E., 'Theorizing the Muslim blogosphere: Blogs, rationality, publicness, and individuality', in A. Russell and N. Echchaibi (eds), *International Blogging: Identity, Politics, and Networked Publics* (New York, 2009).

Soueif, A., *Cairo: Memoir of a City Transformed* (London, 2012).

Stake, R. E., 'Qualitative case studies', in N. K. Denzin and Y. S. Lincoln (eds), *The Sage Handbook of Qualitative Research*, 3rd edn (London and California, 2005).

Stemler, S., 'An overview of content analysis', *Practical Assessment, Research & Evaluation* 7/17 (2001), pp. 1–10, available at http://www.researchgate.net/profile/Steven_Stemler/publication/269037805_An_overview_of_content_analysis/links/547e0aba0cf2de80e7cc402a.pdf (accessed 5 April 2016).

Sullivan, E., 'Youth power and the revolution', in D. Tschirgi, W. Kazziha and S. F. McMahon (eds), *Egypt's Tahrir Revolution* (Boulder and London, 2013).

Takvam Kindt, K., 'Unintentional Democrats: Independent Unions in Post-Mubarak Egypt' (Master's thesis, Oslo, 2013).

Tétreault, M. A., 'Civil society in Kuwait: Protected spaces and women's rights', *The Middle East Journal* 47/2 (1993), pp. 275–91.

——— 'Patterns of culture and democratization in Kuwait', *Studies in Comparative International Development* 30/2 (1995), pp. 26–45.

——— *Stories of Democracy: Politics and Society in Contemporary Kuwait* (New York, 2000).

——— 'Kuwait's Annus Mirabilis', *Middle East Report Online* 7 (2006), available at http://www.merip.org/mero/mero090706 (accessed 5 April 2016).

——— 'Looking for revolution in Kuwait', *Middle East Report Online* (2012), available at http://www.merip.org/mero/mero110112 (accessed 5 April 2016).

Tétreault, M. A. and Al-Ghanim, M., 'The day after "victory": Kuwait's 2009 election and the contentious present', *Middle East Report Online* 8 (2009), available at http://www.merip.org/mero/mero070809 (accessed 5 April 2016).

Tschirgi, D., Kazziha, W. and McMahon, S. F. (eds), *Egypt's Tahrir Revolution* (Boulder and London, 2013).

Tufekci, Z. and Wilson, C., 'Social media and the decision to participate in political protest: Observations from Tahrir Square', *Journal of Communication* 62/2 (2012), pp. 363–79.

United Nations Entity for Gender Equality and the Empowerment of Women (UN Women), The National Council for Women (NCW), *Study on Ways and Methods to Eliminate Sexual Harassment in Egypt* (2013), available at http://web.law.columbia.edu/sites/default/files/microsites/gender-sexuality/un_womensexual-harassment-study-egypt-final-en.pdf (accessed 5 April 2016).

Utvik, B. O., *Islamismen* (Oslo, 2011).

Utvik, B. O. and Nordenson, J., *Minor Majorities* (2011), paper presented at the The Annual Meeting of the Middle East Studies Association, Washington, DC, USA.

Warner, M., 'Publics and counterpublics', *Public Culture* 14/1 (2002), pp. 49–90.

Wheeler, D. L., 'The internet and public culture in Kuwait', *International Communication Gazette* 63/2–3 (2001), pp. 187–201.

——— 'Egypt: Building an information society for international development', *Review of African Political Economy* 30/98 (2003), pp. 627–42.

——— *The Internet in the Middle East – Global Expectations and Local Imaginations in Kuwait* (New York, 2006).

Wilson, C. and Dunn, A., 'Digital media in the Egyptian revolution: Descriptive analysis from the Tahrir data set', *International Journal of Communication* 5 (2011), pp. 1248–72.

Zayani, M., *Networked Publics and Digital Contention – The Politics of Everyday Life in Tunisia* (New York, 2015).

NEWSPAPERS, TV STATIONS AND OTHER NEWS OUTLETS CITED

English Language News Outlets

Ahram Online, http://english.ahram.org.eg/
Al-Ahram Weekly, http://weekly.ahram.org.eg/
Al-Arabiya News, http://english.alarabiya.net/
Arab Times Kuwait Online, http://www.arabtimesonline.com/
The Associated Press, http://ap.org/
The Atlantic, http://www.theatlantic.com/
BBC, http://www.bbc.com/
Bloomberg, http://www.bloomberg.com/
The Cairo Post, http://thecairopost.com/
The Cairo Review of Global Affairs, No 3, fall 2011. See also: http://thecairoreview.com
CBS News, http://www.cbsnews.com/
Channel 4, UK, http://www.channel4.com/
The Christian Science Monitor, http://www.csmonitor.com/
CNN, http://cnn.com
Daily Mail, http://www.dailymail.co.uk/home/index.html
Daily News Egypt, http://www.dailynewsegypt.com/
Egypt Independent, http://www.egyptindependent.com/
Foreign Policy, http://foreignpolicy.com/
Guardian, http://www.theguardian.com/uk
Gulfnews.com, http://gulfnews.com/
Haaretz, http://www.haaretz.com/
Huffington Post, UK, http://www.huffingtonpost.co.uk/
Al-Jazeera English, http://www.aljazeera.com/
Kuwait News Agency, http://www.kuna.net.kw/Default.aspx?language=en
Kuwait Times, http://news.kuwaittimes.net/
The National, http://www.thenational.ae/

NBC News, http://www.nbcnews.com/
New York Times, http://www.nytimes.com
Public Broadcasting Service, http://www.pbs.org/
Russia Today, http://rt.com/
Time Magazine, http://time.com/
USA Today, http://www.usatoday.com/

Arabic Language News Outlets

الأهرام اليومي, *al-Ahram al-Yawmi*, http://www.ahram.org.eg/
الآن, *al-An*, http://www.alaan.cc/
الجمهورية, *al-Gumhuriyya*, http://www.gomhuriaonline.com/main.asp
الرأي, *al-Ra'y*, http://www.alraimedia.com/
سبر, *Sabr*, http://www.sabr.cc/
BBC عربي, *BBC Arabic*, http://www.bbc.co.uk/arabic
العربية, *al-'Arabiyya*, http://www.alarabiya.net/
القبس, *al-Qabas*, http://www.alqabas.com.kw/
المصري اليوم, *al-Masri al-Yawm*, http://www.almasryalyoum.com/
الوطن, *al-Watan*, http://www.elwatannews.com/
الوطن (الكويت), *al-Watan*, http://alwatan.kuwait.tt/
اليوم السابع, *al-Yawm al-Sabi'*, http://www.youm7.com/

Other News Outlets

Aftenposten, http://www.aftenposten.no/
Norsk Rikskringkasting (NRK), http://www.nrk.no/

BLOGS, WEBSITES AND ORGANISATIONS CITED

Blogs

The Arabist, http://arabist.net/
Baheyya, http://baheyya.blogspot.no/
Kuwait Gate, http://kuwaitgate.blogspot.no/
MaLek X, http://malek-x.net/ (no longer available online)
Nermeena, http://nerro.wordpress.com/
Rantings of a Sandmonkey, http://www.sandmonkey.org/
Tarek Shalaby, http://tarekshalaby.com/
Zaghaleel, http://zaghaleel.wordpress.com/

ارحل نستحق الأفضل, Irhal nastahiqq al-afdal, http://ourroleq8.blogspot.no/
الزيادي, al-Ziyadi, http://alziadiq8.com/
شقران, Shagran, http://shagranq8.blogspot.no/
صندوق حمد, Sandug Hamad, http://sandoog.blogspot.no/
طاخ طيخ (ma6goog), Takh tikh, http://www.ma6goog.com/
الطارق, al-Tariq, http://www.altariq2009.com/
فريج سعود, Firij Su'ud, http://freejsaud.blogspot.no/?view=timeslide

Websites

Alexa, http://www.alexa.com/
Den Norske Bank, https://www.dnb.no/
Facebook, https://www.facebook.com/
Internet World Stats, http://www.internetworldstats.com/
Topsy, http://topsy.com/ (which, unfortunately, no longer exists, as detailed in Appendix 4)
Twitter, https://twitter.com/
Wordpress, https://wordpress.com/
YouTube, https://www.youtube.com/

منتديات مستقبل الكويت, muntadayat mustagbal al-Kuwayt, http://www.kwtfuture.com/vb/forum.php (no longer available online)

Organisations

Amnesty International, http://www.amnesty.org/
Deutsche Welle, The Bobs, http://thebobs.com/english/
The Egyptian Center for Women's Rights, http://ecwronline.org/
The Egyptian Initiative for Personal Rights, المبادرة المصرية للحقوق الشخصية, http://eipr.org/
Freedom House, https://freedomhouse.org/
Frontline SMS, http://www.frontlinesms.com/
Human Rights Watch, http://www.hrw.org/
The International Monetary Fund, World Economic Outlook Reports, http://www.imf.org/external/ns/cs.aspx?id=29
International Telecommunications Union (ITU), http://www.itu.int/en/Pages/default.aspx
NiJeL, http://www.nijel.org/
Reporters Without Borders, http://en.rsf.org/
Thomson Reuters Foundation, http://www.trust.org/
UNdata (of the The United Nations Statistics Division (UNSD)), http://data.un.org/
United Nations Development Programme, Human Development Reports, http://hdr.undp.org/en/data
Ushahidi, http://www.ushahidi.com/
The World Bank, databank, http://databank.worldbank.org/data/home.aspx
The World Summit Youth Award, http://www.youthaward.org/

Academic and Official Websites

Arab Social Media Report, http://www.arabsocialmediareport.com/home/index.aspx?&PriMenuID=1&mnu=Pri
Al-Diwan Al-Amiri, State of Kuwait, http://www.da.gov.kw/eng/index.php
Diwan of His Highness the Prime Minister, Kuwait, http://www.pm.gov.kw/home.aspx
Economic and Social Data Service, ESDS Qualidata, now part of UK Data Service, http://ukdataservice.ac.uk/
Kuwait National Assembly, http://www.kna.kw/clt/index.asp
Kuwait Politics Database, http://www2.gsu.edu/~polmfh/database/database.htm

INTERVIEWS CONDUCTED

The research questions guiding this study are rather open-ended, and this had to be reflected in my interviews. Accordingly, these were conducted using the flexible approach often referred to as *semi-structured interviews*. Each interview was preceded by a detailed reading of a group's online activities, which naturally triggered some questions about specific events. The goal was to allow the interviewees to speak freely about their work, thereby pointing out what they themselves saw as important – which I might have missed or ignored – while also getting their views on specific questions prepared beforehand.

It is, of course, crucial to make sure that no interviewees are put in harm's way. All interviewees were presented with a description of this project, as well as information about how I would make use of the information they disclosed. I asked each informant whether or not he or she wished to be named. While all responded affirmatively to this, the ever-changing political situation in both countries should also inform my choices. With regard to the Egyptian case, an unprecedented crackdown on political activism has taken place in the country since the 2013 military coup, and literally thousands of activists are now detained. The same considerations come into play for Kuwait. Several activists have been arrested and sentenced for what they have written online, including one person who received a ten-year sentence for insulting the Emir and calling for the overthrow of the regime. The Kuwaiti state has also intensified its efforts to monitor the online environment, and the new 'cybercrimes law' that took effect in January 2016 has further restricted freedom of expression online, in particular criticism of the government. I do not name the interviewees from Kuwait, nor from Egypt. This should not be taken as an indication of the content of the interviews, but purely as a reflection of the current political situation in the countries studied. As the interviews are not my main source of material, I seldom quote directly from them, but rather use them as supplementary information. The interviews conducted were as follows:

Egypt

Between 25 January and 24 May 2013, interviews were conducted in Cairo with leading representatives of all the groups studied. The interviews were held either in public places, such as cafés, in the offices of the group interviewed or via Skype. Each interview typically lasted between one and two hours. Some of those interviewed were later contacted by phone or email to clarify certain points and details.

Kuwait

Between 22 October and 2 November 2012, interviews were conducted with two central opposition activists/bloggers and one scholar, also active on the political scene. Two of the interviews lasted about two hours, one conducted at a café and the other at an office. The third interview was conducted over the course of several meetings, in all lasting several hours. One of these activists also provided additional information through several emails.

An interview was also conducted with a central opposition activist/blogger via email, but this interview was not completed and not all of my questions were answered.

In addition, Kjetil Selvik of the Christian Michelsen Institute in Bergen kindly gave me access to his notes from an interview that he conducted with a central opposition activist and allowed me to use the information conveyed, for which I am extremely grateful.

For any further details, please contact the author. All details on all the interviews conducted are kept by the author.

WEBSITES, ACCOUNTS AND PAGES OF THE GROUPS STUDIED

These are the sites of the groups used in this study. Some of the groups have created new sites following the end of the time frame set for this study and these are not included.

Egypt

خريطة التحرش الجنسي (HarassMap)

Website: http://harassmap.org/ar/
Twitter: @harassmap
Facebook: https://www.facebook.com/HarassMapEgypt
YouTube: https://www.youtube.com/user/HarassMapEgypt

نظرة للدراسات النسوية (Nazra for Feminist Studies)

Website: http://nazra.org/
Twitter: @NazraEgypt
Facebook: https://www.facebook.com/Nazra.for.Feminist.Studies
YouTube: http://www.youtube.com/user/nazraegypt
Flickr: https://www.flickr.com/photos/nazraegypt

شفت تحرش (Transl.: I Saw Harassment)

Website: http://barlamanalnsaa.com/shoft-ta7rosh
http://www.isawharassment.org/ar/ (established after the time frame of this study)
Twitter: @ShoftTa7rosh
Facebook: https://www.facebook.com/Shoft.Ta7rosh
YouTube: http://www.youtube.com/channel/UChzlAgVMhCtrQGoUcYoPx7Q/feed (this channel is no longer operational, but is still linked to on the new website)

حركة بصمة (Imprint movement)

Twitter: @Imprint_Mov
Facebook: https://www.facebook.com/Imprint.Movement.eg
YouTube: https://www.youtube.com/user/ImprintMovement

حماية التحرير (Tahrir Bodyguard)

Twitter: @TahrirBodyguard (since 1 August 2013: @TahrirBG_DWB)
Facebook: https://www.facebook.com/Tahrir.Bodyguards
YouTube: https://www.youtube.com/channel/UCl5sdV3hpzz0Lay6HwjP-OQ/feed

قوة ضد التحرش/الإعتداء الجنسي الجماعي (Op Anti-Sexual Harassment/Assault [sic]) (OpAntiSH)

Twitter: @OpAntiSH
Facebook: https://www.facebook.com/opantish
YouTube: http://www.youtube.com/user/OpAntiSH

Kuwait

السور الخامس (Transl.: The Fifth Fence [a reference to Kuwait City's old city wall])

Website: http://www.soor5.com/
Twitter: @soor_5
Yfrog: yfrog.com/user/soor_5 (this is no longer accessible online)

كافي (Transl.: Enough)

Blog: http://kafiq8.blogspot.no/
Twitter: @Kafi_Q8
Facebook: https://www.facebook.com/KafiQ8
YouTube: https://www.youtube.com/user/KafiQ8/

حركة شباب الحرية (Transl.: Youth of Freedom Movement)

Twitter: @shbabq8

شباب التغيير والتطوير (Transl.: Youth of Change and Development)

Twitter: @mohafedheen (previously: @youthchangeQ8)
Facebook: facebook.com/pages/168440033219001/شباب-التغيير-والتطوير-الكويت

العدالة الدستورية (Transl.: Constitutional Justice)

Twitter: @aladalh2011

الحركة الديمقراطية المدنية (حدم) (Transl.: The Civil Democratic Movement)

Website: http://www.cdmkw.com/
Twitter: @CDMkuwait (previously: @CivilDemocratic)
YouTube: https://www.youtube.com/user/CDMQ8
Instagram: http://instagram.com/cdmkuwait

كرامة وطن (Transl.: Dignity of a Nation)

Blog: http://karametwatan.wordpress.com/
Twitter: @KarametWatan

مقاطعون (Transl.: (We are) Boycotting/Boycotters)

Blog: http://kwboycott.wordpress.com/
Twitter: @kwboycott

INDEX

www.ingramcontent.com/pod-product-compliance
Ingram Content Group UK Ltd.
Pitfield, Milton Keynes, MK11 3LW, UK
UKHW020204290926
15470UKWH00001B/6

9 781784 537784